Introduction to econometrics

SECOND EDITION

Christopher Dougherty

London School of Economics

OXFORD
UNIVERSITY PRESS

OXFORD
UNIVERSITY PRESS

Great Clarendon Street, Oxford OX2 6DP
Oxford University Press is a department of the University of Oxford.
It furthers the University's objective of excellence in research, scholarship,
and education by publishing worldwide in

Oxford New York

Auckland Cape Town Dar es Salaam Hong Kong Karachi
Kuala Lumpur Madrid Melbourne Mexico City Nairobi
New Delhi Shanghai Taipei Toronto

With offices in

Argentina Austria Brazil Chile Czech Republic France Greece
Guatemala Hungary Italy Japan South Korea Poland Portugal
Singapore Switzerland Thailand Turkey Ukraine Vietnam

Oxford is a registered trade mark of Oxford University Press
in the UK and in certain other countries

Published in the United States
by Oxford University Press Inc., New York

A catalogue record for this book is available from the British Library

Library of Congress Cataloging in Publication Data
(Data available)

ISBN - 13: 978-0-19-877643-7
ISBN - 10: 0-19-877643-8

7 9 10 8

Typeset by Newgen Imaging Systems (P) Ltd, Chennai, India
Printed in Great Britain
on acid-free paper by
Antony Rowe Ltd., Chippenham, Wiltshire

Preface

This is a textbook for a year-long undergraduate course in econometrics. It continues to fill a need, unmet by current texts, that has been generated by the changing profile of the typical econometrics student. Econometric courses often used to be optional for economics majors, but now they are increasingly compulsory. Several factors are responsible. Perhaps the most important is the growing recognition that some understanding of empirical research techniques is not just a desirable but an essential part of the basic training of an economist, and that courses limited to applied statistics are inadequate for this purpose. No doubt this has been reinforced by the fact that graduate level courses in econometrics have become much more ambitious, with the consequence that a lack of exposure to econometrics at an undergraduate level is now a handicap in gaining admission to the leading graduate schools. There are also supply side factors. The wave that has lifted econometrics to prominence in economics teaching comes on the heels of another that did the same for mathematics and statistics. Without this prior improvement in quantitative training, the shift of econometrics to the core of the economics curriculum would not have been possible. The shift has also been facilitated by the increasing abundance of well-qualified teachers in econometrics.

As a consequence of this development, students in econometrics courses are more varied in their capabilities than ever before. No longer are they a self-selected minority of mathematical high-fliers. The typical student now is a regular economics major who has taken basic, but not advanced, courses in calculus and statistics. The democratization of econometrics has created a need for a broader range of textbooks than before, particularly for the newcomers. The mathematical high-fliers have for many years been served by a number of accomplished texts. The newcomers have been less well served. This new edition continues to be chiefly addressed to them.

Objectives of the text

The aim of the text is to provide a framework for a year's instruction with the depth and breadth of coverage that would enable the student to continue with the subject at the graduate level. A primary concern has been to keep the mathematical demands on the reader to a minimum. For nearly everyone, there is a limit to that rate at which formal mathematical analysis can be digested. If this limit is exceeded, the reader spends most of his or her energy grappling with the technicalities instead of the substance, fatigue sets in, comprehension suffers, and a journey of discovery becomes a chore or even worse.

Fortunately, the mathematical burden can be greatly lightened by expressing regression coefficients in terms of sample covariances and variances. For instructors and their most gifted students the package of mathematical analysis may be irrelevant, but that is certainly not the case for the audience to which this text is addressed, many of whom will have emerged from their previous quantitative courses a little unsteady on their feet. The convention adopted here makes it possible to dispense with the dreaded Σ-notation, a millstone for many students. When I made this change some years ago in the course I teach, I found it led to a dramatic improvement in comprehension, especially in the discussion of the properties of regression estimators.

A second concern has been to eliminate the noneconometric stumbling blocks that can hold back the development of the understanding of econometrics. Many of the difficulties that arise in an introductory course are not technical in nature (and many technical items, for instance the use of dummy variables, seem to present no trouble at all). For example, many students have difficulty in expressing regression results verbally in terms comprehensible to the nonspecialist. And if the regression is double-logarithmic, the weirdest gobbledygook is likely to emerge, even if it has been demonstrated mathematically beforehand that a slope coefficient can be interpreted as an elasticity. The reason, no doubt, is that when taught about elasticities in a basic mathematics course, students are so preoccupied with the mathematical properties that they never have the time to become fluent with their practical meaning. For them the elasticity has remained an imprecisely understood mathematical artefact. The text contains a number of digressions in boxes to deal with problems such as these.

There are also some digressions when discussing examples of applications to economics. It is easy for the Friedman permanent income hypothesis (macroeconomic theory course) and the Friedman permanent income hypothesis (econometrics course) to remain distinct and unrelated topics. Since it is not realistic to expect college-level theory courses to become involved with econometrics, the onus of forging the link inevitably lies with econometricians.

Changes to this edition

Restructuring of the book

The requirements of the classical linear regression model may be approximated in the analysis of cross-section data, but this is certainly not true for time series data. It therefore seems sensible to restrict the basic exposition of the model and its problems to cross-section data and to leave a discussion of its application to time-series data until this has been completed. This is how the text now stands, with Chapters 1–11 covering the former and Chapters 12–14 the latter.

New topics

The text now covers a number of new topics that are mostly more ambitious technically than the rest of the material, the motivation for including them being their increasingly common use in everyday applied journal articles and work-shops. The main ones are binary choice models (logit, probit, tobit, and sample selection bias), maximum likelihood estimation, the Durbin-Wu-Hausman test, and, at an introductory level, time-series topics such as nonstationary processes, unit root tests, cointegration, and error-correction models.

Addition of new data sets

The Demand Functions data set that provided the backbone suite of practical exercises in the first edition has been retained and updated but, since the data are time series, its use is now restricted to the last three chapters. For the main part of the text its place has been taken by the Educational Attainment and Earnings Functions data set, with the Consumer Expenditure Survey data set, also cross-section data, being provided for use with the on-line *Student Guide*. These data sets, together with some further minor data sets, are described in Appendix B and they can be downloaded with manuals from the website. They will be updated periodically.

New companion website for lecturers and students

http://www.oup.com/uk/best.textbooks/economics/dougherty2e/

Visit the companion website for this text where you will find additional resources for lecturers and students. These include

- PowerPoint slideshows that offer a graphical treatment of most of the topics in the text. Narrative boxes provide an explanation of the slides.
- Links to data sets and manuals.
- Instructor's Manuals for the text and data sets, detailing the exercises and their solutions.
- A student's area that provides answers to the starred exercises in the text and offers additional exercises, mostly based on the Consumer Expenditure Survey data set, again with answers.

It is hoped that the provision of these materials will not only be helpful for the study of econometrics but also make it more enjoyable.

Christopher Dougherty
January 2002

Contents

6 Dummy variables

7 Specification of regression variables: a preliminary skirmish

8 Heteroscedasticity

9 Stochastic regressors and measurement errors

Review:
Random variables and
sampling theory

In the discussion of estimation techniques in this text, much attention is given to the following properties of estimators: unbiasedness, consistency, and efficiency. It is essential that you have a secure understanding of these concepts, and the text assumes that you have taken an introductory statistics course that has treated them in some depth. This chapter offers a brief review.

Discrete random variables

Your intuitive notion of probability is almost certainly perfectly adequate for the purposes of this text, and so we shall skip the traditional section on pure probability theory, fascinating subject though it may be. Many people have direct experience of probability through games of chance and gambling, and their interest in what they are doing results in an amazingly high level of technical competence, usually with no formal training.

We shall begin straight-away with discrete random variables. A random variable is any variable whose value cannot be predicted exactly. A *discrete* random variable is one that has a specific set of possible values. An example is the total score when two dice are thrown. An example of a random variable that is not discrete is the temperature in a room. It can take any one of a continuous range of values and is an example of a *continuous* random variable. We shall come to these later in this review.

Continuing with the example of the two dice, suppose that one of them is green and the other red. When they are thrown, there are 36 possible experimental *outcomes*, since the green one can be any of the numbers from 1 to 6 and the red one likewise. The random variable defined as their sum, which we will denote X, can take only one of 11 *values*—the numbers from 2 to 12. The relationship between the experimental outcomes and the values of this random variable is illustrated in Figure R.1.

Assuming that the dice are fair, we can use Figure R.1 to work out the probability of the occurrence of each value of X. Since there are 36 different combinations of the dice, each outcome has probability 1/36. {Green = 1, red = 1} is the only combination that gives a total of 2, so the probability of $X = 2$ is 1/36. To

red green	1	2	3	4	5	6
1	2	3	4	5	6	7
2	3	4	5	6	7	8
3	4	5	6	7	8	9
4	5	6	7	8	9	10
5	6	7	8	9	10	11
6	7	8	9	10	11	12

Figure R.1 Outcomes in the example with two dice

Table R.1

Value of X	2	3	4	5	6	7	8	9	10	11	12
Frequency	1	2	3	4	5	6	5	4	3	2	1
Probability	1/36	2/36	3/36	4/36	5/36	6/36	5/36	4/36	3/36	2/36	1/36

obtain $X = 7$, we would need {green $= 1$, red $= 6$} or {green $= 2$, red $= 5$} or {green $= 3$, red $= 4$} or {green $= 4$, red $= 3$} or {green $= 5$, red $= 2$} or {green $= 6$, red $= 1$}. In this case six of the possible outcomes would do, so the probability of throwing 7 is 6/36. All the probabilities are given in Table R.1. If you add all the probabilities together, you get exactly 1. This is because it is 100 percent certain that the value must be one of the numbers from 2 to 12.

The set of all possible values of a random variable is described as the *population* from which it is drawn. In this case, the population is the set of numbers from 2 to 12.

Exercises

R.1 A random variable X is defined to be the difference between the higher value and the lower value when two dice are thrown. If they have the same value, X is defined to be 0. Find the probability distribution for X.

R.2* A random variable X is defined to be the larger of the two values when two dice are thrown, or the value if the values are the same. Find the probability distribution for X. [*Note*: Answers to exercises marked with an asterisk are provided in the *Student Guide*.]

Expected values of discrete random variables

The expected value of a discrete random variable is the weighted average of all its possible values, taking the probability of each outcome as its weight. You calculate it by multiplying each possible value of the random variable by its probability and adding. In mathematical terms, if the random variable is denoted X, its expected value is denoted $E(X)$.

Let us suppose that X can take n particular values $x_1, x_2, \ldots, x_n$ and that the probability of x_i is p_i. Then

$$E(X) = x_1 p_1 + \cdots + x_n p_n = \sum_{i=1}^{n} x_i p_i. \tag{R.1}$$

(Appendix R.1 provides an explanation of Σ notation for those who would like to review its use.)

In the case of the two dice, the values x_1 to x_n were the numbers 2 to 12: $x_1 = 2$, $x_2 = 3, \ldots, x_{11} = 12$, and $p_1 = 1/36$, $p_2 = 2/36, \ldots, p_{11} = 1/36$. The easiest and neatest way to calculate an expected value is to use a spreadsheet. The left half of Table R.2 shows the working in abstract. The right half shows the working for the present example. As you can see from the table, the expected value is equal to 7.

Table R.2 Expected value of X, example with two dice

X	p	Xp	X	p	Xp
x_1	p_1	$x_1 p_1$	2	1/36	2/36
x_2	p_2	$x_2 p_2$	3	2/36	6/36
x_3	p_3	$x_3 p_3$	4	3/36	12/36
...	...	...	5	4/36	20/36
...	...	...	6	5/36	30/36
...	...	...	7	6/36	42/36
...	...	...	8	5/36	40/36
...	...	...	9	4/36	36/36
...	...	...	10	3/36	30/36
...	...	...	11	2/36	22/36
x_n	p_n	$x_n p_n$	12	1/36	12/36
Total		$E(X) = \sum_{i=1}^{n} x_i p_i$			252/36=7

Before going any further, let us consider an even simpler example of a random variable, the number obtained when you throw just one die. (*Pedantic note*: This is the singular of the word whose plural is dice. Two dice, one die. Like two mice, one mie.) (Well, two mice, one mouse. Like two hice, one house. Peculiar language, English.)

There are six possible outcomes: $x_1 = 1, x_2 = 2, x_3 = 3, x_4 = 4, x_5 = 5, x_6 = 6$. Each has probability 1/6. Using these data to compute the expected value, you find that it is equal to 3.5. Thus in this case the expected value of the random variable is a number you could not obtain at all.

The expected value of a random variable is frequently described as its population mean. In the case of a random variable X, the population mean is often denoted by μ_X, or just μ, if there is no ambiguity.

Exercises

R.3   Find the expected value of X in Exercise R.1.
R.4* Find the expected value of X in Exercise R.2.

Expected values of functions of discrete random variables

Let $g(X)$ be any function of X. Then $E[g(X)]$, the expected value of $g(X)$, is given by

$$E[g(X)] = g(x_1)p_1 + \cdots + g(x_n)p_n = \sum_{i=1}^{n} g(x_i)p_i, \qquad (R.2)$$

where the summation is taken over all possible values of X.

The left half of Table R.3 illustrates the calculation of the expected value of a function of X. Suppose that X can take the n different values x_1 to x_n, with associated probabilities p_1 to p_n. In the first column, you write down all the values that X can take. In the second, you write down the corresponding probabilities. In the third, you calculate the value of the function for the corresponding value of X. In the fourth, you multiply columns 2 and 3. The answer is given by the total of column 4.

The right half of Table R.3 shows the calculation of the expected value of X^2 for the example with two dice. You might be tempted to think that this is equal to μ^2, but this is not correct. $E(X^2)$ is 54.83. The expected value of X was shown in Table R.2 to be equal to 7. Thus it is not true that $E(X^2)$ is equal to μ^2, which means that you have to be careful to distinguish between $E(X^2)$ and $[E(X)]^2$ (the latter being $E(X)$ multiplied by $E(X)$, that is, μ^2).

Table R.3 Expected value of $g(X)$, example with two dice

Expected value of $g(X)$				Expected value of X^2			
X	p	$g(X)$	$g(X)p$	X	p	X^2	$X^2 p$
x_1	p_1	$g(x_1)$	$g(x_1)p_1$	2	1/36	4	0.11
x_2	p_2	$g(x_2)$	$g(x_2)p_2$	3	2/36	9	0.50
x_3	p_3	$g(x_3)$	$g(x_3)p_3$	4	3/36	16	1.33
...	...	...	...	5	4/36	25	2.78
...	...	...	...	6	5/36	36	5.00
...	...	...	...	7	6/36	49	8.17
...	...	...	...	8	5/36	64	8.89
...	...	...	...	9	4/36	81	9.00
...	...	...	...	10	3/36	100	8.33
...	...	...	...	11	2/36	121	6.72
x_n	p_n	$g(x_n)$	$g(x_n)p_n$	12	1/36	144	4.00
Total			$E[g(X)] = \sum_{i=1}^{n} g(x_i)p_i$				54.83

Exercises

R.5 If X is a random variable with mean μ, and λ is a constant, prove that the expected value of λX is $\lambda \mu$.

R.6 Calculate $E(X^2)$ for X defined in Exercise R.1.

R.7* Calculate $E(X^2)$ for X defined in Exercise R.2.

Expected value rules

There are three rules that we are going to use over and over again. They are virtually self-evident, and they are equally valid for discrete and continuous random variables.

Rule 1   The expected value of the sum of several variables is equal to the sum of their expected values. For example, if you have three random variables X, Y, and Z,

$$E(X + Y + Z) = E(X) + E(Y) + E(Z). \qquad (R.3)$$

Rule 2   If you multiply a random variable by a constant, you multiply its expected value by the same constant. If X is a random variable and b is a constant,

$$E(bX) = bE(X). \tag{R.4}$$

Rule 3   The expected value of a constant is that constant. For example, if b is a constant,

$$E(b) = b. \tag{R.5}$$

Rule 2 has already been proved as Exercise R.5. Rule 3 is trivial in that it follows from the definition of a constant. Although the proof of Rule 1 is quite easy, we will omit it here.

Putting the three rules together, you can simplify more complicated expressions. For example, suppose you wish to calculate $E(Y)$, where

$$Y = b_1 + b_2 X. \tag{R.6}$$

and b_1 and b_2 are constants. Then,

$$\begin{aligned} E(Y) &= E(b_1 + b_2 X) \\ &= E(b_1) + E(b_2 X) \quad \text{using Rule 1} \\ &= b_1 + b_2 E(X) \qquad \text{using Rules 2 and 3.} \end{aligned} \tag{R.7}$$

Therefore, instead of calculating $E(Y)$ directly, you could calculate $E(X)$ and obtain $E(Y)$ from equation (R.7).

Exercise

R.8   Let X be the total when two dice are thrown. Calculate the possible values of Y, where Y is given by

$$Y = 2X + 3.$$

and hence calculate $E(Y)$. Show that this is equal to $2E(X) + 3$.

Independence of random variables

Two random variables X and Y are said to be independent if $E[g(X)h(Y)]$ is equal to $E[g(X)]E[h(Y)]$ for any functions $g(X)$ and $h(Y)$. Independence implies, as an important special case, that $E(XY)$ is equal to $E(X)E(Y)$.

Population variance of a discrete random variable

In this text there is only one function of X in which we shall take much interest, and that is its population variance, a useful measure of the dispersion of its probability distribution. It is defined as the expected value of the square of the

Table R.4 Population variance of X, example with two dice

X	p	$X - \mu$	$(X - \mu)^2$	$(X - \mu)^2 p$
2	1/36	−5	25	0.69
3	2/36	−4	16	0.89
4	3/36	−3	9	0.75
5	4/36	−2	4	0.44
6	5/36	−1	1	0.14
7	6/36	0	0	0.00
8	5/36	1	1	0.14
9	4/36	2	4	0.44
10	3/36	3	9	0.75
11	2/36	4	16	0.89
12	1/36	5	25	0.69
Total				5.83

difference between X and its mean, that is, of $(X-\mu)^2$, where μ is the population mean. It is usually denoted σ_X^2, with the subscript being dropped when it is obvious that it is referring to a particular variable.

$$\sigma_X^2 = E[(X - \mu)^2]$$

$$= (x_1 - \mu)^2 p_1 + \cdots + (x_n - \mu)^2 p_n = \sum_{i=1}^{n} (x_i - \mu)^2 p_i. \qquad (R.8)$$

From σ_X^2 one obtains σ_X, the population standard deviation, an equally popular measure of the dispersion of the probability distribution; the standard deviation of a random variable is the square root of its variance.

We will illustrate the calculation of population variance with the example of the two dice. Since $\mu = E(X) = 7, (X - \mu)^2$ is $(X - 7)^2$ in this case. We shall calculate the expected value of $(X - 7)^2$ using Table R.3 as a pattern. An extra column, $(X - \mu)$, has been introduced as a step in the calculation of $(X - \mu)^2$. By summing the last column in Table R.4, one finds that σ_X^2 is equal to 5.83. Hence σ_X, the standard deviation, is equal to $\sqrt{5.83}$, which is 2.41.

One particular use of the expected value rules that is quite important is to show that the population variance of a random variable can be written

$$\sigma_X^2 = E(X^2) - \mu^2, \qquad (R.9)$$

an expression that is sometimes more convenient than the original definition. The proof is a good example of the use of the expected value rules. From its definition,

$$
\begin{aligned}
\sigma_X^2 &= E[(X - \mu)^2] \\
&= E(X^2 - 2\mu X + \mu^2) \\
&= E(X^2) + E(-2\mu X) + E(\mu^2) \\
&= E(X^2) - 2\mu E(X) + \mu^2 \\
&= E(X^2) - 2\mu^2 + \mu^2 \\
&= E(X^2) - \mu^2.
\end{aligned}
\tag{R.10}
$$

Thus, if you wish to calculate the population variance of X, you can calculate the expected value of X^2 and subtract μ^2.

Exercise

R.9   Calculate the population variance and the standard deviation of X as defined in Exercise R.1, using the definition given by equation (R.8).

R.10* Calculate the population variance and the standard deviation of X as defined in Exercise R.2, using the definition given by equation (R.8).

R.11 Using equation (R.9), find the variance of the random variable X defined in Exercise R.1 and show that the answer is the same as that obtained in Exercise R.9. (*Note*: You have already calculated μ in Exercise R.3 and $E(X^2)$ in Exercise R.6.)

R.12* Using equation (R.9), find the variance of the random variable X defined in Exercise R.2 and show that the answer is the same as that obtained in Exercise R.10. (*Note*: You have already calculated μ in Exercise R.4 and $E(X^2)$ in Exercise R.7.)

Probability density

Discrete random variables are very easy to handle in that, by definition, they can take only a finite set of values. Each of these values has a 'packet' of probability associated with it, and, if you know the size of these packets, you can calculate the population mean and variance with no trouble. The sum of the probabilities is equal to 1. This is illustrated in Figure R.2 for the example with two dice. X can take values from 2 to 12 and the associated probabilities are as shown.

Unfortunately, the analysis in this text usually deals with continuous random variables, which can take an infinite number of values. The discussion will be illustrated with the example of the temperature in a room. For the sake of argument, we will assume that this varies within the limits of 55 to 75 °F, and initially we will suppose that it is equally likely to be anywhere within this range.

packets of
probability

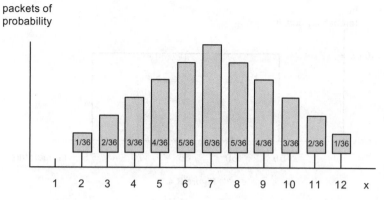

Figure R.2 Discrete probabilities (example with two dice)

Since there are an infinite number of different values that the temperature can take, it is useless trying to divide the probability into little packets and we have to adopt a different approach. Instead, we talk about the probability of the random variable lying within a given interval, and we represent the probability graphically as an area within the interval. For example, in the present case, the probability of X lying in the interval 59 to 60 is 0.05 since this range is one twentieth of the complete range 55 to 75. Figure R.3 shows the rectangle depicting the probability of X lying in this interval. Since its area is 0.05 and its base is one, its height must be 0.05. The same is true for all the other one-degree intervals in the range that X can take.

Having found the height at all points in the range, we can answer such questions as 'What is the probability that the temperature lies between 65 and 70 °F?'. The answer is given by the area in the interval 65 to 70, represented by the shaded area in Figure R.4. The base of the shaded area is 5, and its height is 0.05, so the area is 0.25. The probability is a quarter, which is obvious anyway in that 65 to 70 °F is a quarter of the whole range.

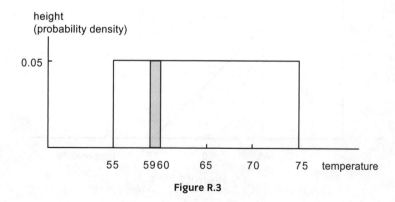

Figure R.3

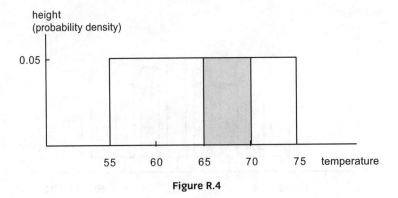

Figure R.4

The height at any point is formally described as the probability density at that point, and, if it can be written as a function of the random variable, it is known as the 'probability density function'. In this case it is given by $f(x)$, where X is the temperature and

$$f(x) = 0.05 \quad \text{for } 55 \leq x \leq 75$$
$$f(x) = 0 \qquad \text{for } x < 55 \text{ or } x > 75.$$

(R.11)

The foregoing example was particularly simple to handle because the probability density function was constant over the range of possible values of X. Next we will consider an example in which the function is not constant, because not all temperatures are equally likely. We will suppose that the central heating and air conditioning have been fixed so that the temperature never falls below $65\,°\text{F}$, and that on hot days the temperature will exceed this, with a maximum of $75\,°\text{F}$ as before. We will suppose that the probability is greatest at $65\,°\text{F}$ and that it decreases evenly to 0 at $75\,°\text{F}$, as shown in Figure R.5.

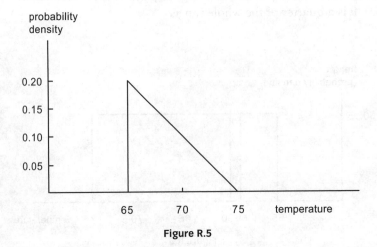

Figure R.5

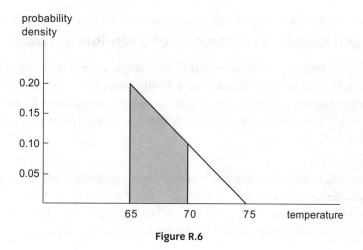

Figure R.6

The total area within the range, as always, is equal to 1, because the total probability is equal to 1. The area of the triangle is $1/2 \times$ base $\times$ height, so one has

$$1/2 \times 10 \times \text{height} = 1 \qquad\qquad \text{(R.12)}$$

and the height at $65\,°F$ is equal to 0.20.

Suppose again that we want to know the probability of the temperature lying between 65 and $70\,°F$. It is given by the shaded area in Figure R.6, and with a little geometry you should be able to verify that it is equal to 0.75. If you prefer to talk in terms of percentages, this means that there is a 75 percent chance that the temperature will lie between 65 and $70\,°F$, and only a 25 percent chance that it will lie between 70 and $75\,°F$.

In this case the probability density function is given by $f(x)$, where

$$f(x) = 1.5 - 0.02x \quad \text{for } 65 \leq x \leq 75$$
$$f(x) = 0 \qquad\qquad \text{for } x < 65 \text{ or } x > 75. \qquad \text{(R.13)}$$

(You can verify that $f(x)$ gives 0.20 at $65\,°F$ and 0 at $75\,°F$.)

Now for some good news and some bad news. First, the bad news. If you want to calculate probabilities for more complicated, curved functions, simple geometry will not do. In general you have to use integral calculus or refer to specialized tables, if they exist. Integral calculus is also used in the definitions of the expected value and variance of a continuous random variable.

Now for the good news. First, specialized probability tables do exist for all the functions that are going to interest us in practice. Second, expected values and variances have much the same meaning for continuous random variables that they have for discrete ones (formal definitions will be found in Appendix R.2), and the expected value rules work in exactly the same way.

Fixed and random components of a random variable

Instead of regarding a random variable as a single entity, it is often possible and convenient to break it down into a fixed component and a pure random component, the fixed component always being the population mean. If X is a random variable and μ its population mean, one may make the following decomposition:

$$X = \mu + u, \tag{R.14}$$

where u is what will be called the pure random component (in the context of regression analysis, it is usually described as the disturbance term).

You could of course look at it the other way and say that the random component, u, is defined to be the difference between X and μ:

$$u = X - \mu. \tag{R.15}$$

It follows from its definition that the expected value of u is 0. From equation (R.15),

$$E(u_i) = E(x_i - \mu) = E(x_i) + E(-\mu) = \mu - \mu = 0. \tag{R.16}$$

Since all the variation in X is due to u, it is not surprising that the population variance of X is equal to the population variance of u. This is easy to prove. By definition,

$$\sigma_X^2 = E[(X - \mu)^2] = E(u^2) \tag{R.17}$$

and

$$\sigma_u^2 = E[(u - \text{mean of } u)^2]$$
$$= E[(u - 0^2] = E(u^2). \tag{R.18}$$

Hence σ^2 can equivalently be defined to be the variance of X or u.

To summarize, if X is a random variable defined by (R.14), where μ is a fixed number and u is a random component, with mean 0 and population variance σ^2, then X has population mean μ and population variance σ^2.

Estimators

So far we have assumed that we have exact information about the random variable under discussion, in particular that we know the probability distribution, in the case of a discrete random variable, or the probability density function, in the case of a continuous variable. With this information it is possible to work out the population mean and variance and any other population characteristics in which we might be interested.

Table R.5

Population characteristic		Estimator
Mean	μ	$\bar{X} = \dfrac{1}{n} \displaystyle\sum_{i=1}^{n} x_i$
Population variance	σ^2	$s^2 = \dfrac{1}{n-1} \displaystyle\sum_{i=1}^{n} (x_i - \bar{X})^2$

Now, in practice, except for artificially simple random variables such as the numbers on thrown dice, you do not know the exact probability distribution or density function. It follows that you do not know the population mean or variance. However, you would like to obtain an estimate of them or some other population characteristic.

The procedure is always the same. You take a sample of n observations and derive an estimate of the population characteristic using some appropriate formula. You should be careful to make the important distinction that the formula is technically known as an *estimator*; the number that is calculated from the sample using it is known as the *estimate*. The estimator is a general rule or formula, whereas the estimate is a specific number that will vary from sample to sample.

Table R.5 gives the usual estimators for the two most important population characteristics. The sample mean, $\bar{X}$, is the usual estimator of the population mean, and the formula for s^2 given in Table R.5 is the usual estimator of the population variance.

Note that these are the *usual* estimators of the population mean and variance; they are not the only ones. You are probably so accustomed to using the sample mean as an estimator of μ that you are not aware of any alternatives. Of course, not all the estimators you can think of are equally good. The reason that we do in fact use $\bar{X}$ is that it is the best according to two very important criteria, unbiasedness and efficiency. These criteria will be discussed later.

Estimators are random variables

An estimator is a special case of a random variable. This is because it is a combination of the values of X in a sample, and, since X is a random variable, a combination of a set of its values must also be a random variable. For instance, take $\bar{X}$, the estimator of the mean:

$$\bar{X} = \frac{1}{n}(x_1 + x_2 + \cdots + x_n) = \frac{1}{n} \sum_{i=1}^{n} x_i. \qquad \text{(R.19)}$$

We have just seen that the value of X in observation i may be decomposed into two parts: the fixed part, μ, and the pure random component, u_i:

$$x_i = \mu + u_i. \tag{R.20}$$

Hence

$$\bar{X} = \frac{1}{n}(\mu + \mu + \cdots + \mu) + \frac{1}{n}(u_1 + u_2 + \cdots + u_n)$$

$$= \frac{1}{n}(n\mu) + \bar{u} = \mu + \bar{u}, \tag{R.21}$$

where $\bar{u}$ is the average of u_i in the sample.

From this you can see that $\bar{X}$, like X, has both a fixed component and a pure random component. Its fixed component is μ, the population mean of X, and its pure random component is $\bar{u}$, the average of the pure random components in the sample.

The probability density functions of both X and $\bar{X}$ have been drawn in the same diagram in Figure R.7. By way of illustration, X is assumed to have a normal distribution. You will see that the distributions of both X and $\bar{X}$ are centered over μ, the population mean. The difference between them is that the distribution for $\bar{X}$ is narrower and taller. $\bar{X}$ is likely to be closer to μ than a single observation on X, because its random component $\bar{u}$ is an average of the pure random components $u_1, u_2, \ldots, u_n$ in the sample, and these are likely to cancel each other out to some extent when the average is taken. Consequently the population variance of $\bar{u}$ is only a fraction of the population variance of u. It will be shown in Section 1.7 that, if the population variance of u is σ^2, then the population variance of $\bar{u}$ is σ^2/n.

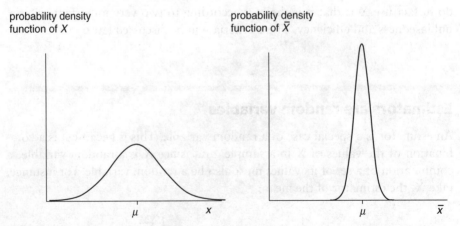

probability density
function of X

probability density
function of $\bar{X}$

Figure R.7 Comparison of the probability density functions of a single observation and the mean of a sample

s^2, the unbiased estimator of the population variance of X, is also a random variable. Subtracting (R.21) from (R.20),

$$x_i - \bar{X} = u_i - \bar{u}. \tag{R.22}$$

Hence

$$s^2 = \frac{1}{n-1} \sum_{i=1}^{n} [(x_i - \bar{X})^2] = \frac{1}{n-1} \sum_{i=1}^{n} [(u_i - \bar{u})^2]. \tag{R.23}$$

Thus s^2 depends on (and only on) the pure random components of the observations on X in the sample. Since these change from sample to sample, the value of the estimator s^2 will change from sample to sample.

Unbiasedness

Since estimators are random variables, it follows that only by coincidence will an estimate be exactly equal to the population characteristic. Generally there will be some degree of error, which will be small or large, positive or negative, according to the pure random components of the values of X in the sample.

Although this must be accepted, it is nevertheless desirable that the estimator should be accurate on average in the long run, to put it intuitively. To put it technically, we should like the expected value of the estimator to be equal to the population characteristic. If this is true, the estimator is said to be *unbiased*. If it is not, the estimator is said to be *biased*, and the difference between its expected value and the population characteristic is described as the *bias*.

Let us start with the sample mean. Is this an unbiased estimator of the population mean? Is $E(\bar{X})$ equal to μ? Yes, it is, and it follows immediately from (R.21).

$\bar{X}$ has two components, μ and $\bar{u}$. $\bar{u}$ is the average of the pure random components of the values of X in the sample, and since the expected value of the pure random component in any observation is 0, the expected value of $\bar{u}$ is 0. Hence

$$E(\bar{X}) = E(\mu + \bar{u}) = E(\mu) + E(\bar{u}) = \mu + 0 = \mu. \tag{R.24}$$

However, this is not the only unbiased estimator of μ that we could construct. To keep the analysis simple, suppose that we have a sample of just two observations, x_1 and x_2. Any weighted average of the observations x_1 and x_2 will be an unbiased estimator, provided that the weights add up to 1. To see this, suppose we construct a generalized estimator:

$$Z = \lambda_1 x_1 + \lambda_2 x_2. \tag{R.25}$$

The expected value of Z is given by

$$E(Z) = E(\lambda_1 x_1 + \lambda_2 x_2) = E(\lambda_1 x_1) + E(\lambda_2 x_2)$$
$$= \lambda_1 E(x_1) + \lambda_2 E(x_2) = \lambda_1 \mu + \lambda_2 \mu$$
$$= (\lambda_1 + \lambda_2)\mu. \tag{R.26}$$

If λ_1 and λ_2 add up to 1, we have $E(Z) = \mu$, and Z is an unbiased estimator of μ.

Thus, in principle, we have an infinite number of unbiased estimators. How do we choose among them? Why do we always in fact use the sample average, with $\lambda_1 = \lambda_2 = 0.5$? Perhaps you think that it would be unfair to give the observations different weights, or that asymmetry should be avoided on principle. However, we are not concerned with fairness, or with symmetry for its own sake. We will find in the next section that there is a more compelling reason.

So far we have been discussing only estimators of the population mean. It was asserted that s^2, as defined in Table R.5, is an estimator of the population variance, σ^2. One may show that the expected value of s^2 is σ^2, and hence that it is an unbiased estimator of the population variance, provided that the observations in the sample are generated independently of each other. The proof, though not mathematically difficult, is laborious, and it has been consigned to Appendix R.3 at the end of this review.

Efficiency

Unbiasedness is one desirable feature of an estimator, but it is not the only one. Another important consideration is its reliability. It is all very well for an estimator to be accurate on average in the long run, but, as Keynes once said, in the long run we are all dead. We want the estimator to have as high a probability as possible of giving a close estimate of the population characteristic, which means that we want its probability density function to be as concentrated as possible around the true value. One way of summarizing this is to say that we want its population variance to be as small as possible.

Suppose that we have two estimators of the population mean, that they are calculated using the same information, that they are both unbiased, and that their probability density functions are as shown in Figure R.8. Since the probability density function for estimator B is more highly concentrated than that for estimator A, it is more likely to give an accurate estimate. It is therefore said to be more *efficient*, to use the technical term.

Note carefully that the definition says 'more likely'. Even though estimator B is more efficient, that does not mean that it will always give the more accurate estimate. Some times it will have a bad day, and estimator A will have a good day, and A will be closer to the truth. But the probability of A being more accurate than B will be less than 50 percent.

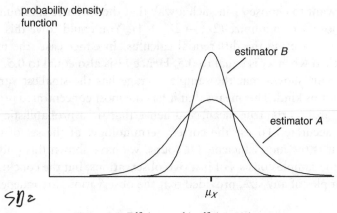

Figure R.8 Efficient and inefficient estimators

It is rather like the issue of whether you should fasten your seat belt when driving a vehicle. A large number of surveys in different countries have shown that you are much less likely to be killed or seriously injured in a road accident if you wear a seat belt, but there are always the odd occasions when individuals not wearing belts have miraculously escaped when they could have been killed, had they been strapped in. The surveys do not deny this. They simply conclude that the odds are on the side of belting up. Similarly, the odds are on the side of the efficient estimator. (*Gruesome comment*: In countries where wearing seat belts has been made compulsory, there has been a fall in the supply of organs from crash victims for transplants.)

We have said that we want the variance of an estimator to be as small as possible, and that the efficient estimator is the one with the smallest variance. We shall now investigate the variance of the generalized estimator of the population mean and show that it is minimized when the two observations are given equal weight.

Provided that x_1 and x_2 are independent observations, the population variance of the generalized estimator is given by

$$\sigma_Z^2 = \text{population variance of } (\lambda_1 x_1 + \lambda_2 x_2)$$
$$= \sigma_{\lambda_1 x_1}^2 + \sigma_{\lambda_2 x_2}^2 + 2\sigma_{\lambda_1 x_1, \lambda_2 x_2}$$
$$= \lambda_1^2 \sigma_{x_1}^2 + \lambda_2^2 \sigma_{x_2}^2 + 2\lambda_1 \lambda_2 \sigma_{x_1 x_2}$$
$$= (\lambda_1^2 + \lambda_2^2)\sigma^2 \quad \text{if } x_1 \text{ and } x_2 \text{ are independent.} \tag{R.27}$$

(We are anticipating the variance rules discussed in Chapter 1. $\sigma_{x_1 x_2}$, the population covariance of x_1 and x_2, is 0 if x_1 and x_2 are generated independently.)

Now, we have already seen that λ_1 and λ_2 must add up to 1 if the estimator is to be unbiased. Hence for unbiased estimators λ_2 equals $(1 - \lambda_1)$ and

$$\lambda_1^2 + \lambda_2^2 = \lambda_1^2 + (1 - \lambda_1)^2 = 2\lambda_1^2 - 2\lambda_1 + 1. \tag{R.28}$$

Since we want to choose λ_1 in such a way that the variance is minimized, we want to choose it to minimize $(2\lambda_1^2 - 2\lambda_1 + 1)$. You could solve this problem graphically or by using the differential calculus. In either case, the minimum value is reached when λ_1 is equal to 0.5. Hence λ_2 is also equal to 0.5.

We have thus shown that the sample average has the smallest variance of estimators of this kind. This means that it has the most concentrated probability distribution around the true mean, and hence that (in a probabilistic sense) it is the most accurate. To use the correct terminology, of the set of unbiased estimators, it is the most efficient. Of course we have shown this only for the case where the sample consists of just two observations, but the conclusions are valid for samples of any size, provided that the observations are independent of one another.

Two final points. First, efficiency is a *comparative* concept. You should use the term only when comparing alternative estimators. You should not use it to summarize changes in the variance of a single estimator. In particular, as we shall see in the next section, the variance of an estimator generally decreases as the sample size increases, but it would be wrong to say that the estimator is becoming more efficient. You must reserve the term for comparisons of *different* estimators. Second, you can compare the efficiency of alternative estimators only if they are using the same information, for example, the same set of observations on a number of random variables. If the estimators use different information, one may well have a smaller variance, but it would not be correct to describe it as being more efficient.

Exercise

R.13   For the special case $\sigma^2 = 1$ and a sample of two observations, calculate the variance of the generalized estimator of the population mean using equation (28) with values of λ_1 from 0 to 1 at steps of 0.1, and plot it in a diagram. Is it important that the weights λ_1 and λ_2 should be exactly equal?

R.14   Show that, when you have n observations, the condition that the generalized estimator $(\lambda_1 x_1 + \cdots + \lambda_n x_n)$ should be an unbiased estimator of μ is $\lambda_1 + \cdots + \lambda_n = 1$.

Conflicts between unbiasedness and minimum variance

We have seen in this review that it is desirable that an estimator be unbiased and that it have the smallest possible variance. These are two quite different criteria and occasionally they conflict with each other. It sometimes happens that one can construct two estimators of a population characteristic, one of which is unbiased (A in Figure R.9), the other being biased but having smaller variance (B).

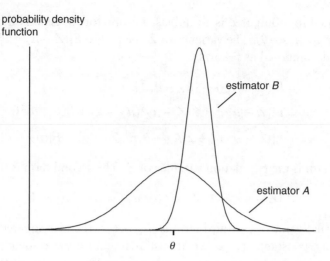

Figure R.9 Which estimator is to be preferred? *A* is unbiased but *B* has smaller variance

A will be better in the sense that it is unbiased, but *B* is better in the sense that its estimates are always close to the true value. How do you choose between them?

It will depend on the circumstances. If you are not bothered by errors, provided that in the long run they cancel out, you should probably choose *A*. On the other hand, if you can tolerate small errors, but not large ones, you should choose *B*.

Technically speaking, it depends on your loss function, the cost to you of an error as a function of its size. It is usual to choose the estimator that yields the smallest expected loss, which is found by weighting the loss function by the probability density function. (If you are risk-averse, you may wish to take the variance of the loss into account as well.)

A common example of a loss function, illustrated by the quadratic curve in Figure R.10, is the square of the error. The expected value of this, known as the mean square error (MSE), has the simple decomposition:

$$\text{MSE of estimator} = \text{Variance of estimator} + \text{Bias}^2. \qquad (R.29)$$

To show this, suppose that you are using an estimator Z to estimate an unknown population parameter θ. Let the expected value of Z be μ_Z. This

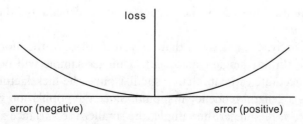

Figure R.10 Loss function

will be equal to θ only if Z is an unbiased estimator. In general there will be a bias, given by $(\mu_Z - \theta)$. The variance of Z is equal to $E[(Z - \mu_Z)^2]$. The MSE of Z can be decomposed as follows:

$$E[(Z - \theta)^2] = E[(\{Z - \mu_Z\} + \{\mu_Z - \theta\})^2]$$
$$= E[(Z - \mu_Z)^2 + 2(Z - \mu_Z)(\mu_Z - \theta) + (\mu_Z - \theta)^2]$$
$$= E[(Z - \mu_Z)^2] + 2(\mu_Z - \theta)E(Z - \mu_Z) + E[(\mu_Z - \theta)^2]. \quad \text{(R.30)}$$

The first term is the population variance of Z. The second term is 0 because

$$E(Z - \mu_Z) = E(Z) + E(-\mu_Z) = \mu_Z - \mu_Z = 0. \quad \text{(R.31)}$$

The expected value of the third term is $(\mu_Z - \theta)^2$, the bias squared, since both μ_Z and θ are constants. Hence we have shown that the mean square error of the estimator is equal to the sum of its population variance and the square of its bias.

In Figure R.9, estimator A has no bias component, but it has a much larger variance component than B and therefore could be inferior by this criterion.

The MSE is often used to generalize the concept of efficiency to cover comparisons of biased as well as unbiased estimators. However, in this text, comparisons of efficiency will mostly be confined to unbiased estimators.

Exercise

R.15 Give examples of applications where you might (1) prefer an estimator of type A, (2) prefer one of type B, in Figure R.9.

R.16 Draw a loss function for getting to an airport later (or earlier) than the official check-in time.

R.17 If you have two estimators of an unknown population parameter, is the one with the smaller variance necessarily more efficient?

The effect of increasing the sample size on the accuracy of an estimate

We shall continue to assume that we are investigating a random variable X with unknown mean μ and population variance σ^2, and that we are using $\bar{X}$ to estimate μ. How does the accuracy of $\bar{X}$ depend on the number of observations, n?

Not surprisingly, the answer is that, as you increase n, the more accurate $\bar{X}$ is likely to be. In any single experiment, a bigger sample will not necessarily yield a more accurate estimate than a smaller one—the luck factor is always at work—but as a general tendency it should. Since the population variance of $\bar{X}$ is given by σ^2/n, the bigger the sample, the smaller the variance and hence the more tightly compressed is the probability density function of $\bar{X}$.

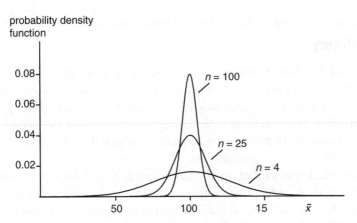

Figure R.11 Effect of increasing the sample size on the distribution of $\bar{X}$

This is illustrated in Figure R.11. We are assuming that X is normally distributed and that it has mean 100 and standard deviation 50. If the sample size is 4, the standard deviation of $\bar{X}, \sigma/\sqrt{n}$, is equal to $50/\sqrt{4} = 25$. If the sample size is 25, the standard deviation is 10. If it is 100, the standard deviation is 5. Figure R.11 shows the corresponding probability density functions. That for $n = 100$ is taller than the others in the vicinity of μ, showing that the probability of it giving an accurate estimate is higher. It is lower elsewhere.

The larger the sample size, the narrower and taller will be the probability density function of $\bar{X}$. If n becomes really large, the probability density function will be indistinguishable from a vertical line located at $\bar{X} = \mu$. For such a sample the random component of $\bar{X}$ becomes very small indeed, and so $\bar{X}$ is bound to be very close to μ. This follows from the fact that the standard deviation of $\bar{X}, \sigma/\sqrt{n}$, becomes very small as n becomes large.

In the limit, as n tends to infinity, $\sigma/\sqrt{n}$ tends to 0 and $\bar{X}$ tends to μ exactly. This may be written mathematically

$$\lim_{n \to \infty} \bar{X} = \mu \qquad (\text{R.32})$$

An equivalent and more common way of expressing it is to use the term *plim*, where plim means 'probability limit' and emphasizes that the limit is being reached in a probabilistic sense:

$$\text{plim } \bar{X} = \mu \qquad (\text{R.33})$$

when, for any arbitrarily small numbers ε and δ, the probability of $\bar{X}$ being more than ε different from μ is less than δ, provided that the sample is large enough.

Exercise

R.18* In general, the variance of the distribution of an estimator decreases when the sample size is increased. Is it correct to describe the estimator as becoming more efficient?

Consistency

In general, if the plim of an estimator is equal to the true value of the population characteristic, it is said to be *consistent*. To put it another way, a consistent estimator is one that is bound to give an accurate estimate of the population characteristic if the sample is large enough, regardless of the actual observations in the sample. In most of the contexts considered in this text, an unbiased estimator will also be a consistent one.

It sometimes happens that an estimator that is biased for small samples may be consistent (it is even possible for an estimator that does not have a finite expected value for small samples to be consistent). Figure R.12 illustrates how the probability distribution might look for different sample sizes. The distribution is said to be asymptotically (meaning, in large samples) unbiased because it becomes centered on the true value as the sample size becomes large. It is said to be consistent because it finally collapses to a single point, the true value.

An estimator is described as *inconsistent* either if its distribution fails to collapse as the sample size becomes large or if the distribution collapses at a point other than the true value.

As we shall see later in this text, estimators of the type shown in Figure R.12 are quite important in regression analysis. Sometimes it is impossible to find an estimator that is unbiased for small samples. If you can find one that is at least consistent, that may be better than having no estimator at all, especially if you are able to assess the direction of the bias in small samples. However, it should

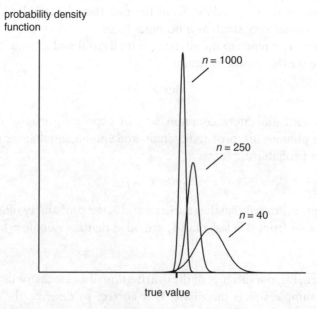

Figure R.12 Estimator that is consistent despite being biased in finite samples

be borne in mind that a consistent estimator could in principle perform worse (for example, have a larger mean square error) than an inconsistent one in small samples, so you must be on your guard. In the same way that you might prefer a biased estimator to an unbiased one if its variance is smaller, you might prefer a consistent, but biased, estimator to an unbiased one if its variance is smaller, and an inconsistent one to either if its variance is smaller still.

Two useful rules

Sometimes one has an estimator calculated as the ratio of two quantities that have random components, for example

$$Z = X/Y, \tag{R.34}$$

where X and Y are quantities that have been calculated from a sample. Usually it is difficult to analyze the expected value of Z. In general it is *not* equal to $E(X)$ divided by $E(Y)$. If there is any finite probability that Y may be equal to 0, the expected valueof Z will not even be defined. However, if X and Y tend to finite quantities plim X and plim Y in large samples, and plim Y is not equal to 0, the limiting value of Z is given by

$$\text{plim } Z = \frac{\text{plim } X}{\text{plim } Y}. \tag{R.35}$$

Hence, even if we are not in a position to say anything definite about the small sample properties of Z, we may be able to tell whether it is consistent.

For example, suppose that the population means of two random variables X and Y are μ_X and μ_Y, respectively, and that both are subject to random influences, so that

$$X = \mu_X + u_X \tag{R.36}$$

$$Y = \mu_Y + u_Y, \tag{R.37}$$

where u_X and u_Y are random components with 0 means. If we are trying to estimate the ratio μ_X/μ_Y from sample data, the estimator $Z = \bar{X}/\bar{Y}$ will be consistent, for

$$\text{plim } Z = \frac{\text{plim } \bar{X}}{\text{plim } \bar{Y}} = \frac{\mu_X}{\mu_Y} \tag{R.38}$$

and we are able to say that Z will be an accurate estimator for large samples, even though we may not be able to say anything about $E(Z)$ for small samples.

There is a counterpart rule for the product of two random variables. Suppose

$$Z = XY. \tag{R.39}$$

Except in the special case where X and Y are distributed independently, it is not true that $E(Z)$ is equal to the product of $E(X)$ and $E(Y)$. However, even if X and Y are not distributed independently, it is true that

$$\text{plim } Z = \text{plim } X \times \text{plim } Y, \tag{R.40}$$

provided that plim X and plim Y exist.

Exercise

R.19 Is unbiasedness either a necessary or a sufficient condition for consistency?

R.20 A random variable X can take the values 1 and 2 with equal probability. For n equal to 2, demonstrate that $E(\bar{Y})$ is not equal to $1/E(\bar{X})$.

R.21* Repeat Exercise 20 supposing that X takes the values 0 and 1 with equal probability.

Appendix R.1

Σ notation: A review

Σ notation provides a quick way of writing the sum of a series of similar terms. Anyone reading this text ought to be familiar with it, but here is a brief review for those who need a reminder.

We will begin with an example. Suppose that the output of a sawmill, measured in tons, in month i is q_i, with q_1 being the gross output in January, q_2 being the gross output in February, etc. Let output for the year be denoted Z. Then

$$Z = q_1 + q_2 + q_3 + q_4 + q_5 + q_6 + q_7 + q_8 + q_9 + q_{10} + q_{11} + q_{12}.$$

In words, one might summarize this by saying that Z is the sum of the q_i, beginning with q_1 and ending with q_{12}. Obviously there is no need to write down all 12 terms when defining Z. Sometimes you will see it simplified to

$$Z = q_1 + \cdots + q_{12},$$

it being understood that the missing terms are included in the summation.

Σ notation allows you to write down this summary in a tidy symbolic form:

$$Z = \sum_{i=1}^{12} q_i.$$

The expression to the right of the Σ sign tells us what kind of term is going to be summed, in this case, terms of type q_i. Underneath the Σ sign is written the subscript that is going to alter in the summation, in this case i, and its starting point, in this case 1. Hence we know that the first term will be q_1. The $=$ sign reinforces the fact that i should be set equal to 1 for the first term.

Above the Σ sign is written the last value of i, in this case 12, so we know that the last term is q_{12}. It is automatically understood that all the terms between q_1 and q_{12} will also be included in the summation, and so we have effectively rewritten the second definition of Z.

Suppose that the average price per ton of the output of the mill in month i is p_i. The value of output in month i will be $p_i q_i$, and the total value during the year will be V, where V is given by

$$V = p_1 q_1 + \cdots + p_{12} q_{12}.$$

We are now summing terms of type $p_i q_i$ with the subscript i running from 1 to 12, and using Σ notation this may be written as

$$V = \sum_{i=1}^{12} p_i q_i.$$

If c_i is the total cost of operating the mill in month i, profit in month i will be $(p_i q_i - c_i)$, and hence the total profit over the year, P, will be given by

$$P = (p_1 q_1 - c_1) + \cdots + (p_{12} q_{12} - c_{12}),$$

which may be summarized as

$$P = \sum_{i=1}^{12} (p_i q_i - c_i).$$

Note that the profit expression could also have been written as total revenue minus total costs:

$$P = (p_1 q_1 + \cdots + p_{12} q_{12}) - (c_1 + \cdots + c_{12}),$$

and this can be summarized in Σ notation as

$$P = \sum_{i=1}^{12} p_i q_i - \sum_{i=1}^{12} c_i.$$

If the price of output is constant during the year at level p, the expression for the value of annual output can be simplified:

$$V = pq_1 + \cdots + pq_{12} = p(q_1 + \cdots + q_{12})$$

$$= p \sum_{i=1}^{12} q_i.$$

Hence

$$\sum_{i=1}^{12} pq_i = p \sum_{i=1}^{12} q_i.$$

If the output in each month is constant at level q, the expression for annual output can also be simplified:

$$Z = q_1 + \cdots + q_{12} = q + \cdots + q = 12q.$$

Hence, in this case,

$$\sum_{i=1}^{12} q_i = 12q.$$

We have illustrated three rules, which can be stated formally:

Σ *Rule* 1   (illustrated by the decomposition of profit into total revenue minus total cost)

$$\sum_{i=1}^{n} (x_i + y_i) = \sum_{i=1}^{n} x_i + \sum_{i=1}^{n} y_i.$$

Σ *Rule* 2   (illustrated by the expression for V when the price was constant)

$$\sum_{i=1}^{n} ax_i = a \sum_{i=1}^{n} x_i \quad \text{(if } a \text{ is a constant).}$$

Σ *Rule* 3   (illustrated by the expression for Z when quantity was constant)

$$\sum_{i=1}^{n} a = na \quad \text{(if } a \text{ is a constant).}$$

Often it is obvious from the context what are the initial and final values of the summation. In such cases $\sum_{i=1}^{n} x_i$ is often simplified to $\sum x_i$. Furthermore, it is often equally obvious what subscript is being changed, and the expression is simplified to just $\sum x$.

Appendix R.2

Expected value and variance of a continuous random variable

The definition of the expected value of a continuous random variable is very similar to that for a discrete random variable:

$$E(X) = \int xf(x)\,dx,$$

where $f(x)$ is the probability density function of X, with the integration being performed over the interval for which $f(x)$ is defined.

In both cases the different possible values of X are weighted by the probability attached to them. In the case of the discrete random variable, the summation is done on a packet-by-packet basis over all the possible values of X. In the continuous case, it is of course done on a continuous basis, integrating replacing summation, and the probability density function $f(x)$ replacing the packets of probability p_i. However, the principle is the same.

In the section on discrete random variables, it was shown how to calculate the expected value of a function of $X, g(X)$. You make a list of all the different values that $g(X)$ can take, weight each of them by the corresponding probability, and sum.

Discrete	Continuous
$E(X) = \sum_{i=1}^{n} x_i p_i$	$E(X) = \int xf(x)dx$
(Summation over all possible values)	(Integration over the range for which $f(x)$ is defined)

The process is exactly the same for a continuous random variable, except that it is done on a continuous basis, which means summation by integration instead of Σ summation. In the case of the discrete random variable, $E[g(X)]$ is equal to $\sum_{i=1}^{n} g(x_i)p_i$ with the summation taken over all possible values of X. In the continuous case, it is defined by

$$E[g(X)] = \int g(x)f(x)\,dx,$$

with the integration taken over the whole range for which $f(x)$ is defined.

As in the case of discrete random variables, there is only one function in which we have an interest, the population variance, defined as the expected value of $(X - \mu^2)$, where $\mu = E(X)$ is the population mean. To calculate the variance, you have to sum $(X - \mu)^2$, weighted by the appropriate probability, over all the possible values of X. In the case of a continuous random variable, this means that you have to evaluate

$$\sigma_X^2 = E[(X - \mu)^2] = \int (x - \mu)^2 f(x)\, dx.$$

It is instructive to compare this with equation (R.8), the parallel expression for a discrete random variable:

$$\sigma_X^2 = E[(X - \mu)^2] = \sum_{i=1}^{n} (x_i - \mu)^2 p_i.$$

As before, when you have evaluated the population variance, you can calculate the population standard deviation, σ, by taking its square root.

Appendix R.3

Proof that s^2 is an unbiased estimator of the population variance

It was asserted in Table R.5 that an unbiased estimator of σ^2 is given by s^2, where

$$s^2 = \frac{1}{n - 1} \sum_{i=1}^{n} (x_i - \bar{X})^2.$$

We will begin the proof by rewriting $(x_i - \bar{X})^2$ in a more complicated, but helpful, way:

$$(x_i - \bar{X})^2 = [(x_i - \mu) - (\bar{X} - \mu)]^2 \quad \text{(the } \mu \text{ terms cancel if you expand)}$$
$$= (x_i - \mu)^2 - 2(x_i - \mu)(\bar{X} - \mu) + (\bar{X} - \mu)^2.$$

Hence

$$\sum_{i=1}^{n} (x_i - \bar{X})^2 = \sum_{i=1}^{n} (x_i - \mu)^2 - 2(\bar{X} - \mu) \sum_{i=1}^{n} (x_i - \mu) + n(\bar{X} - \mu)^2.$$

The first term is the sum of the first terms of the previous equation using Σ notation. Similarly the second term is the sum of the second terms of the previous equation using Σ notation and the fact that $(\bar{X} - \mu)$ is a common factor. When we come to sum the third terms of the previous equation they are all equal to $(\bar{X} - \mu)^2$, so their sum is simply $n(\bar{X} - \mu)^2$, with no need for Σ notation.

The second component may be rewritten $-2n(\bar{X} - \mu)^2$ since

$$\sum_{i=1}^{n}(x_i - \mu) = \sum_{i=1}^{n}x_i - n\mu = n\bar{X} - n\mu = n(\bar{X} - \mu),$$

and we have

$$\sum_{i=1}^{n}(x_i - \bar{X})^2 = \sum_{i=1}^{n}(x_i - \mu)^2 - 2n(\bar{X} - \mu)^2 + n(\bar{X} - \mu)^2$$

$$= \sum_{i=1}^{n}(x_i - \mu)^2 - n(\bar{X} - \mu)^2.$$

Applying expectations to this equation, we have

$$E\left[\sum_{i=1}^{n}(x_i - \bar{X})^2\right] = E\left[\sum_{i=1}^{n}(x_i - \mu)^2\right] - nE[(\bar{X} - \mu)^2]$$

$$= E[(x_1 - \mu)^2] + \cdots + E[(x_n - \mu)^2] - nE[(\bar{X} - \mu)^2]$$

$$= n\sigma^2 - n\sigma_{\bar{X}}^2$$

$$= n\sigma^2 - n(\sigma^2/n) = (n-1)\sigma^2.$$

using the fact that the population variance of $\bar{X}$ is equal to σ^2/n. This is proved in Section 1.7. Hence

$$E(s^2) = E\left[\frac{1}{n-1}\sum_{i=1}^{n}(x_i - \bar{X})^2\right] = \frac{1}{n-1}E\left[\sum_{i=1}^{n}(x_i - \bar{X})^2\right]$$

$$= \frac{1}{n-1}(n-1)\sigma^2 = \sigma^2.$$

Thus s^2 is an unbiased estimator of σ^2.

1 Covariance, variance, and correlation

This chapter introduces covariance and correlation, two concepts that will prepare the way for the treatment of regression analysis to come. A second and equally important objective is to show how to manipulate expressions involving sample variance and covariance. Several detailed examples are provided to give you practice. They are used very extensively in future chapters and it is vital that they become second nature to you. They simplify the mathematics and make the analysis much easier to follow.

1.1 Sample covariance

Sample covariance is a measure of association between two variables. The concept will be illustrated with a simple example. Table 1.1 shows years of schooling, S, and hourly earnings in 1994, in dollars, Y, for a subset of twenty respondents from the United States National Longitudinal Survey of Youth, the data set that is used for many of the practical illustrations and exercises in this text. S is the

Table 1.1

Observation	S	Y	Observation	S	Y
1	15	17.24	11	17	15.38
2	16	15.00	12	12	12.70
3	8	14.91	13	12	26.00
4	6	4.50	14	9	7.50
5	15	18.00	15	15	5.00
6	12	6.29	16	12	21.63
7	12	19.23	17	16	12.10
8	18	18.69	18	12	5.55
9	12	7.21	19	12	7.50
10	20	42.06	20	14	8.00

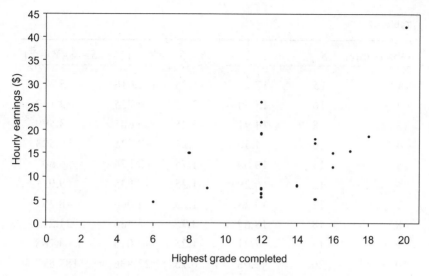

Figure 1.1 Hourly earnings and schooling, 20 NLSY respondents

highest grade completed, in the case of those who did not go on to college, and 12 plus the number of years of college completed, for those who did. Figure 1.1 shows the data plotted as a scatter diagram. You can see that there is a weak positive association between the two variables.

The sample covariance, $\text{Cov}(X, Y)$, is a statistic that enables you to summarize this association with a single number. In general, given n observations on two variables X and Y, the sample covariance between X and Y is given by

$$\text{Cov}(X, Y) = \frac{1}{n}[(X_1 - \bar{X})(Y_1 - \bar{Y}) + \cdots + (X_n - \bar{X})(Y_n - \bar{Y})]$$

$$= \frac{1}{n}\sum_{i=1}^{n}(X_i - \bar{X})(Y_i - \bar{Y}), \tag{1.1}$$

where, as usual, a bar over the symbol for a variable denotes its sample mean.

Note: In Section 1.4 we will also define the population covariance. To distinguish between the two, we will use $\text{Cov}(X, Y)$ to refer to the sample covariance and σ_{XY} to refer to the population covariance between X and Y. This convention is parallel to the one we will use for variance: $\text{Var}(X)$ referring to the sample variance, and σ_X^2 referring to the population variance.

Further note: Some texts define sample covariance, and sample variance, dividing by $n - 1$ instead of n, for reasons that will be explained in Section 1.5.

The calculation of the sample covariance for S and Y is shown in Table 1.2. We start by calculating the sample means for schooling and earnings, which we will denote $\bar{S}$ and $\bar{Y}$. $\bar{S}$ is 13.250 and $\bar{Y}$ is 14.2245. We then calculate the deviations of S and Y from these means for each individual in the sample (fourth and fifth columns of the table). Next we calculate the product of the deviations for

Table 1.2

Observation	S	Y	$(S - \bar{S})$	$(Y - \bar{Y})$	$(S - \bar{S})(Y - \bar{Y})$
1	15	17.24	1.75	3.016	5.277
2	16	15.00	2.75	0.775	2.133
3	8	14.91	−5.25	0.685	−3.599
4	6	4.50	−7.25	−9.725	70.503
5	15	18.00	1.75	3.776	6.607
6	12	6.29	−1.25	−7.935	9.918
7	12	19.23	−1.25	5.006	−6.257
8	18	18.69	4.75	4.466	21.211
9	12	7.21	−1.25	−7.015	8.768
10	20	42.06	6.75	27.836	187.890
11	17	15.38	3.75	1.156	4.333
12	12	12.70	−1.25	−1.525	1.906
13	12	26.00	−1.25	11.776	−14.719
14	9	7.50	−4.25	−6.725	28.579
15	15	5.00	1.75	−9.225	−16.143
16	12	21.63	−1.25	7.406	−9.257
17	16	12.10	2.75	−2.125	−5.842
18	12	5.55	−1.25	−8.675	10.843
19	12	7.50	−1.25	−6.725	8.406
20	14	8.00	0.75	−6.225	−4.668
Total	265	284.49			305.888
Average	13.250	14.2245			15.294

each individual (sixth column). Finally we calculate the mean of these products, 15.294, and this is the sample covariance.

You will note that in this case the covariance is positive. This is as you would expect. A positive association, as in this example, will be summarized by a positive sample covariance, and a negative association by a negative one.

It is worthwhile investigating the reason for this. Figure 1.2 is the same as Figure 1.1, but the scatter of observations has been quartered by vertical and horizontal lines drawn through the points $\bar{S}$ and $\bar{Y}$, respectively. The intersection of these lines is therefore the point $(\bar{S}, \bar{Y})$, the point giving mean schooling and mean hourly earnings for the sample. To use a physical analogy, this is the center of gravity of the points representing the observations.

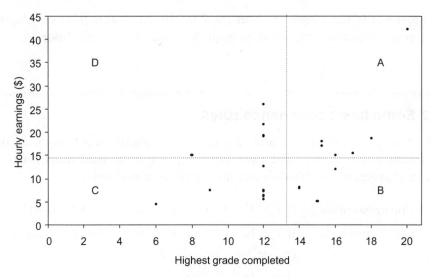

Figure 1.2 Highest grade completed

Any point lying in quadrant A is for an individual with above-average school-ing and above-average earnings. For such an observation, both $(S-\bar{S})$ and $(Y-\bar{Y})$ are positive, and $(S-\bar{S})(Y-\bar{Y})$ must therefore be positive, so the observation makes a positive contribution to the covariance expression. *Example*: Indivi-dual 10, who majored in biology in college and then went to medical school, has twenty years of schooling and her earnings are the equivalent of $42.06 per hour. $(S-\bar{S})$ is 6.75, $(Y-\bar{Y})$ is 27.84, and the product is 187.89.

Next consider quadrant B. Here the individuals have above-average school-ing but below-average earnings. $(S-\bar{S})$ is positive, but $(Y-\bar{Y})$ is negative, so $(S-\bar{S})(Y-\bar{Y})$ is negative and the contribution to the covariance is negative. *Example:* Individual 20 completed two years of four-year college majoring in media studies, but then dropped out, and earns only $8.00 per hour working in the office of an automobile repair shop.

In quadrant C, both schooling and earnings are below average, so $(S-\bar{S})$ and $(Y-\bar{Y})$ are both negative, and $(S-\bar{S})(Y-\bar{Y})$ is positive. *Example:* Individual 4, who was born in Mexico and had only six years of schooling, is a manual worker in a market garden and has very low earnings.

Finally, individuals in quadrant D have above-average earnings despite hav-ing below-average schooling, so $(S-\bar{S})$ is negative, $(Y-\bar{Y})$ is positive, and $(S-\bar{S})(Y-\bar{Y})$ makes a negative contribution to the covariance. *Example:* Indi-vidual 3 has slightly above-average earnings as a construction laborer, despite only completing elementary school.

Since the sample covariance is the average value of $(S-\bar{S})(Y-\bar{Y})$ for the 20 observations, it will be positive if positive contributions from quadrants A and C dominate and negative if the negative ones from quadrants B and D dominate.

In other words, the sample covariance will be positive if, as in this example, the scatter is upward-sloping, and negative if the scatter is downward-sloping.

1.2 Some basic covariance rules

There are some rules that follow in a perfectly straightforward way from the definition of covariance, and since they are going to be used many times in future chapters it is worthwhile establishing them immediately:

Covariance Rule 1 If $Y = V + W, \text{Cov}(X, Y) = \text{Cov}(X, V) + \text{Cov}(X, W)$.

Covariance Rule 2 If $Y = bZ$, where b is a constant and Z is a variable,
$$\text{Cov}(X, Y) = b\text{Cov}(X, Z).$$

Covariance Rule 3 If $Y = b$, where b is a constant, $\text{Cov}(X, Y) = 0$.

Proof of covariance rule 1

Since $Y = V + W, Y_i = V_i + W_i$ and $\bar{Y} = \bar{V} + \bar{W}$. Hence

$$\text{Cov}(X, Y) = \frac{1}{n}\sum_{i=1}^{n}(X_i - \bar{X})(Y_i - \bar{Y})$$

$$= \frac{1}{n}\sum_{i=1}^{n}(X_i - \bar{X})([V_i + W_i] - [\bar{V} + \bar{W}])$$

$$= \frac{1}{n}\sum_{i=1}^{n}(X_i - \bar{X})([V_i - \bar{V}] + [W_i - \bar{W}])$$

$$= \frac{1}{n}\sum_{i=1}^{n}(X_i - \bar{X})(V_i - \bar{V}) + \frac{1}{n}\sum_{i=1}^{n}(X_i - \bar{X})(W_i - \bar{W})$$

$$= \text{Cov}(X, Y) + \text{Cov}(X, W). \tag{1.2}$$

Proof of covariance rule 2

If $Y = bZ, Y_i = bZ_i$ and $\bar{Y} = b\bar{Z}$. Hence

$$\text{Cov}(X, Y) = \frac{1}{n}\sum_{i=1}^{n}(X_i - \bar{X})(Y_i - \bar{Y}) = \frac{1}{n}\sum_{i=1}^{n}(X_i - \bar{X})(bZ_i - b\bar{Z})$$

$$= \frac{b}{n}\sum_{i=1}^{n}(X_i - \bar{X})(Z_i - \bar{Z}) = b\,\text{Cov}(X, Z). \tag{1.3}$$

Proof of covariance rule 3

This is trivial. If $Y = b$, $\bar{Y} = b$ and $Y_i - \bar{Y} = 0$ for all observations. Hence

$$\text{Cov}(X, Y) = \frac{1}{n} \sum_{i=1}^{n} (X_i - \bar{X})(Y_i - \bar{Y}) = \frac{1}{n} \sum_{i=1}^{n} (X_i - \bar{X})(b - b)$$

$$= \frac{1}{n} \sum_{i=1}^{n} (X_i - \bar{X})(0) = 0. \tag{1.4}$$

Further developments

With these basic rules, you can simplify much more complicated covariance expressions. For example, if a variable Y is equal to the sum of three variables U, V, and W,

$$\text{Cov}(X, Y) = \text{Cov}(X, [U + V + W]) = \text{Cov}(X, U) + \text{Cov}(X, [V + W]), \tag{1.5}$$

using Rule 1 and breaking up Y into two parts, U and $V + W$. Hence

$$\text{Cov}(X, Y) = \text{Cov}(X, U) + \text{Cov}(X, V) + \text{Cov}(X, W), \tag{1.6}$$

using Rule 1 again.

Another example: If $Y = b_1 + b_2 Z$, where b_1 and b_2 are constants and Z is a variable,

$$\begin{aligned}
\text{Cov}(X, Y) &= \text{Cov}(X, [b_1 + b_2 Z]) \\
&= \text{Cov}(X, b_1) + \text{Cov}(X, b_2 Z) && \text{using Rule 1.} \\
&= 0 + \text{Cov}(X, b_2 Z) && \text{using Rule 3.} \\
&= b_2 \text{Cov}(X, Z) && \text{using Rule 2.} \tag{1.7}
\end{aligned}$$

1.3 Alternative expression for sample covariance

The sample covariance between X and Y has been defined as

$$\text{Cov}(X, Y) = \frac{1}{n} \sum_{i=1}^{n} (X_i - \bar{X})(Y_i - \bar{Y}). \tag{1.8}$$

An alternative, and equivalent, expression is

$$\text{Cov}(X, Y) = \left[\frac{1}{n} \sum_{i=1}^{n} X_i Y_i \right] - \bar{X}\bar{Y}. \tag{1.9}$$

You may find this to be more convenient if you are unfortunate enough to have to calculate a covariance by hand. In practice you will normally perform calculations of this kind using a statistical package on a computer.

It is easy to prove that the two expressions are equivalent.

$$\text{Cov}(X, Y) = \frac{1}{n} \sum_{i=1}^{n} (X_i - \bar{X})(Y_i - \bar{Y})$$

$$= \frac{1}{n} \sum_{i=1}^{n} (X_i Y_i - X_i \bar{Y} - \bar{X} Y_i + \bar{X} \bar{Y})$$

$$= \frac{1}{n} (X_1 Y_1 - X_1 \bar{Y} - \bar{X} Y_1 + \bar{X} \bar{Y}$$

$$+ \ldots$$

$$+ X_n Y_n - X_n \bar{Y} - \bar{X} Y_n + \bar{X} \bar{Y}). \tag{1.10}$$

Adding each column, and using the fact that $\sum_{i=1}^{n} X_i = n\bar{X}$ and $\sum_{i=1}^{n} Y_i = n\bar{Y}$,

$$\text{Cov}(X, Y) = \frac{1}{n} \left[\sum_{i=1}^{n} X_i Y_i - \bar{Y} \sum_{i=1}^{n} X_i - \bar{X} \sum_{i=1}^{n} Y_i + n\bar{X}\bar{Y} \right]$$

$$= \frac{1}{n} \left[\sum_{i=1}^{n} X_i Y_i - n\bar{X}\bar{Y} - n\bar{X}\bar{Y} + n\bar{X}\bar{Y} \right]$$

$$= \frac{1}{n} \left[\sum_{i=1}^{n} X_i Y_i - n\bar{X}\bar{Y} \right]$$

$$= \frac{1}{n} \left[\sum_{i=1}^{n} X_i Y_i \right] - \bar{X}\bar{Y}. \tag{1.11}$$

Exercises

1.1   In a large bureaucracy the annual salary of each individual, Y, is determined by the formula

$$Y = 10,000 + 500S + 200T,$$

where S is the number of years of schooling of the individual and T is the length of time, in years, of employment. X is the individual's age. Calculate $\text{Cov}(X, Y), \text{Cov}(X, S)$, and $\text{Cov}(X, T)$ for the sample of five individuals shown in the table and verify that

$$\text{Cov}(X, Y) = 500\, \text{Cov}(X, S) + 200\, \text{Cov}(X, T).$$

Explain analytically why this should be the case.

Individual	Age (years)	Years of schooling	Length of service	Salary
1	18	11	1	15,700
2	29	14	6	18,200
3	33	12	8	17,600
4	35	16	10	20,000
5	45	12	5	17,000

1.2* In a certain country the tax paid by a firm, T, is determined by the rule

$$T = -1.2 + 0.2P - 0.1I,$$

where P is profits and I is investment, the third term being the effect of an investment incentive. S is sales. All variables are measured in \$ million at annual rates. Calculate $\text{Cov}(S, T)$, $\text{Cov}(S, P)$, and $\text{Cov}(S, I)$ for the sample of four firms shown in the table and verify that

$$\text{Cov}(S, T) = 0.2 \, \text{Cov}(S, P) - 0.1 \, \text{Cov}(S, I).$$

Explain analytically why this should be the case.

Firm	Sales	Profits	Investment	Tax
1	100	20	10	1.8
2	50	9	4	0.2
3	80	12	4	0.8
4	70	15	6	1.2

1.4 Population covariance

If X and Y are random variables, the expected value of the product of their deviations from their means is defined to be the population covariance, σ_{XY}:

$$\sigma_{XY} = E[(X - \mu_X)(Y - \mu_Y)], \tag{1.12}$$

where μ_X and μ_Y are the population means of X and Y, respectively.

As you would expect, if the population covariance is unknown, the sample covariance will provide an estimate of it, given a sample of observations.

However, the estimate will be biased downwards, for

$$E[\text{Cov}(X, Y)] = \frac{n-1}{n}\sigma_{XY}. \tag{1.13}$$

The reason is that the sample deviations are measured from the sample means of X and Y and tend to underestimate the deviations from the true means. Obviously we can construct an unbiased estimator by multiplying the sample estimate by $n/(n-1)$. A proof of (1.13) will not be given here, but you could construct one yourself using Appendix R.3 as a guide (first read Section 1.5). The rules for population covariance are exactly the same as those for sample covariance, but the proofs will be omitted because they require integral calculus.

If X and Y are independent, their population covariance is 0, since then

$$E[(X - \mu_X)(Y - \mu_Y)] = E(X - \mu_X)E(Y - \mu_Y)$$
$$= 0 \times 0. \tag{1.14}$$

by virtue of the independence property noted in the Review and the fact that $E(X)$ and $E(Y)$ are equal to μ_X and μ_Y, respectively.

1.5 Sample variance

In the Review the term *variance* was used to refer to the *population* variance. For purposes that will become apparent in the discussion of regression analysis, it will be useful to introduce, with three warnings, the notion of sample variance. For a sample of n observations, $X_1, \ldots, X_n$, the sample variance will be defined as the average squared deviation in the sample:

$$\text{Var}(X) = \frac{1}{n}\sum_{i=1}^{n}(X_i - \bar{X})^2. \tag{1.15}$$

The three warnings are:

1. The sample variance, thus defined, is a biased estimator of the population variance. Appendix R.3 demonstrates that s^2, defined as

$$s^2 = \frac{1}{n-1}\sum_{i=1}^{n}(X_i - \bar{X})^2$$

is an unbiased estimator of σ^2. It follows that the expected value of $\text{Var}(X)$ is $[(n-1)/n]\sigma^2$ and that it is therefore biased downwards. Note that as n becomes large, $(n-1)/n$ tends to 1, so the bias becomes progressively attenuated. It can easily be shown that plim $\text{Var}(X)$ is equal to σ^2 and hence that it is an example of a consistent estimator that is biased for small samples.

2. Because s^2 is unbiased, some texts prefer to define it as the sample variance and either avoid referring to Var(X) at all or find some other name for it. Unfortunately, there is no generally agreed convention on this point. In each text, you must check the definition.

3. Because there is no agreed convention, there is no agreed notation, and a great many symbols have been pressed into service. In this text the population variance of a variable X is denoted σ_X^2. If there is no ambiguity concerning the variable in question, the subscript may be dropped. The sample variance will always be denoted Var(X).

Why does the sample variance underestimate the population variance? The reason is that it is calculated as the average squared deviation from the sample mean rather than the true mean. Because the sample mean is automatically in the center of the sample, the deviations from it tend to be smaller than those from the population mean.

1.6 Variance rules

There are some straightforward and very useful rules for variances, which are counterparts of those for covariance discussed in Section 1.2. They apply equally to sample variance and population variance:

Variance Rule 1   If $Y = V + W$, Var(Y) = Var(V) + Var(W)
$$+ 2\operatorname{Cov}(V, W).$$

Variance Rule 2   If $Y = bZ$, where b is a constant, Var(Y) = b^2 Var(Z).

Variance Rule 3   If $Y = b$, where b is a constant, Var(Y) = 0.

Variance Rule 4   If $Y = V + b$, where b is a constant, Var(Y) = Var(V).

First, note that the variance of a variable X can be thought of as the covariance of X with itself:

$$\operatorname{Var}(X) = \frac{1}{n}\sum_{i=1}^{n}(X_i - \bar{X})^2 = \frac{1}{n}\sum_{i=1}^{n}(X_i - \bar{X})(X_i - \bar{X}) = \operatorname{Cov}(X, X). \quad (1.16)$$

In view of this equivalence, we can make use of the covariance rules to establish the variance rules. We are also able to obtain an alternative form for Var(X), making use of (1.9), the alternative form for sample covariance:

$$\operatorname{Var}(X) = \left[\frac{1}{n}\sum_{i=1}^{n}X_i^2\right] - \bar{X}^2. \quad (1.17)$$

Proof of variance rule 1

If $Y = V + W$,

$$\text{Var}(Y) = \text{Cov}(Y, Y) = \text{Cov}(Y, [V + W]) = \text{Cov}(Y, V) + \text{Cov}(Y, W)$$

using Covariance Rule 1

$$= \text{Cov}([V + W], V) + \text{Cov}([V + W], W)$$

$$= \text{Cov}(V, V) + \text{Cov}(W, V) + \text{Cov}(V, W) + \text{Cov}(W, W)$$

using Covariance Rule 1 again

$$= \text{Var}(V) + \text{Var}(W) + 2\text{Cov}(V, W). \tag{1.18}$$

Proof of variance rule 2

If $Y = bZ$, where b is a constant, using Covariance Rule 2 twice,

$$\text{Var}(Y) = \text{Cov}(Y, Y) = \text{Cov}(bZ, Y) = b\,\text{Cov}(Z, Y)$$

$$= b\,\text{Cov}(Z, bZ) = b^2\,\text{Cov}(Z, Z) = b^2\,\text{Var}(Z). \tag{1.19}$$

Proof of variance rule 3

If $Y = b$, where b is a constant, using Covariance Rule 3,

$$\text{Var}(Y) = \text{Cov}(b, b) = 0. \tag{1.20}$$

This is trivial. If Y is a constant, its average value is the same constant and $(Y - \bar{Y})$ is 0 for all observations. Hence $\text{Var}(Y)$ is 0.

Proof of variance rule 4

If $Y = V + b$, where V is a variable and b is a constant, using Variance Rule 1,

$$\text{Var}(Y) = \text{Var}(V + b) = \text{Var}(V) + \text{Var}(b) + 2\text{Cov}(V, b)$$

$$= \text{Var}(V), \tag{1.21}$$

using Variance Rule 3 and Covariance Rule 3. Population variance obeys the same rules, but again the proofs are omitted because they require integral calculus.

Exercises

1.3   Using the data in Exercise 1.1, calculate $\text{Var}(Y)$, $\text{Var}(S)$, $\text{Var}(T)$, and $\text{Cov}(S, T)$ and verify that

$$\text{Var}(Y) = 250{,}000\,\text{Var}(S) + 40{,}000\,\text{Var}(T) + 200{,}000\,\text{Cov}(S, T),$$

explaining analytically why this should be the case.

1.4* Using the data in Exercise 1.2, calculate $\text{Var}(T)$, $\text{Var}(P)$, $\text{Var}(I)$ and $\text{Cov}(P,I)$, and verify that

$$\text{Var}(T) = 0.04\,\text{Var}(P) + 0.01\,\text{Var}(I) - 0.04\,\text{Cov}(P,I),$$

explaining analytically why this should be the case.

1.7 **Population variance of the sample mean**

If two variables X and Y are independent (and hence their population covariance σ_{XY} is 0), the population variance of their sum is equal to the sum of their population variances:

$$\sigma_{X+Y}^2 = \sigma_X^2 + \sigma_Y^2 + 2\sigma_{XY}$$
$$= \sigma_X^2 + \sigma_Y^2. \tag{1.22}$$

This result can be extended to obtain the general rule that the population variance of the sum of any number of mutually independent variables is equal to the sum of their variances, and one is able to show that, if a random variable X has variance σ^2, the population variance of the sample mean, $\bar{X}$, will be equal to σ^2/n, where n is the number of observations in the sample, provided that the observations are generated independently.

$$\sigma_{\bar{X}}^2 = \text{population variance of } \frac{1}{n}(X_1 + \cdots + X_n)$$

$$= \frac{1}{n^2}\sigma_{(X_1+\cdots+X_n)}^2$$

$$= \frac{1}{n^2}[\sigma_{X_1}^2 + \cdots + \sigma_{X_n}^2]$$

$$= \frac{1}{n^2}[\sigma^2 + \cdots + \sigma^2]$$

$$= \frac{1}{n^2}[n\sigma^2] = \frac{\sigma^2}{n}. \tag{1.23}$$

As we have seen in the Review, the sample mean is the most efficient unbiased estimator of the population mean provided that the observations are independently drawn from the same distribution.

1.8 **The correlation coefficient**

In this chapter a lot of attention has been given to covariance. This is because it is very convenient mathematically, not because it is a particularly good measure of association. We shall discuss its deficiencies in this respect in Section 1.9. A much more satisfactory measure is its near-relative, the correlation coefficient.

Like variance and covariance, the correlation coefficient comes in two forms, population and sample. The population correlation coefficient is traditionally denoted ρ, the Greek letter that is the equivalent of 'r', and pronounced 'row', as in row a boat. For variables X and Y it is defined by

$$\rho_{XY} = \frac{\sigma_{XY}}{\sqrt{\sigma_X^2 \sigma_Y^2}}. \tag{1.24}$$

If X and Y are independent, ρ_{XY} will be equal to 0 because the population covariance will be 0. If there is a positive association between them, σ_{XY}, and hence ρ_{XY}, will be positive. If there is an exact positive linear relationship, ρ_{XY} will assume its maximum value of 1. Similarly, if there is a negative relationship, ρ_{XY} will be negative, with minimum value of -1.

The sample correlation coefficient, r_{XY}, is defined by replacing the population covariance and variances in (1.24) by their unbiased estimators. We have seen that these may be obtained by multiplying the sample variances and covariances by $n/(n-1)$. Hence

$$r_{XY} = \frac{\dfrac{n}{n-1}\text{Cov}(X, Y)}{\sqrt{\dfrac{n}{n-1}\text{Var}(X)\dfrac{n}{n-1}\text{Var}(Y)}}. \tag{1.25}$$

The factors $n/(n-1)$ cancel, so we can conveniently define the sample correlation by

$$r_{XY} = \frac{\text{Cov}(X, Y)}{\sqrt{\text{Var}(X)\text{Var}(Y)}}. \tag{1.26}$$

Like ρ, r has maximum value 1, which is attained when there is a perfect positive association between the sample values of X and Y (when you plot the scatter diagram, the points lie exactly on an upward-sloping straight line). Similarly, it has minimum value -1, attained when there is a perfect negative association (the points lying exactly on a downward-sloping straight line). A value of 0 indicates that there is no association between the observations on X and Y in the sample. Of course the fact that $r = 0$ does not necessarily imply that $\rho = 0$ or vice versa.

Illustration

We will use the education and earnings example in Section 1.1 to illustrate the calculation of the sample correlation coefficient. The data are given in Table 1.1 and they are plotted in Figure 1.1. We have already calculated $\text{Cov}(S, Y)$ in

Table 1.3

Observation	S	Y	$(S - \bar{S})$	$(Y - \bar{Y})$	$(S - \bar{S})^2$	$(Y - \bar{Y})^2$	$(S - \bar{S}) \times (Y - \bar{Y})$
1	15	17.24	1.75	3.016	3.063	9.093	5.277
2	16	15.00	2.75	0.775	7.563	0.601	2.133
3	8	14.91	−5.25	0.685	27.563	0.470	−3.599
4	6	4.50	−7.25	−9.725	52.563	94.566	70.503
5	15	18.00	1.75	3.776	3.063	14.254	6.607
6	12	6.29	−1.25	−7.935	1.563	62.956	9.918
7	12	19.23	−1.25	5.006	1.563	25.055	−6.257
8	18	18.69	4.75	4.466	22.563	19.941	21.211
9	12	7.21	−1.25	−7.015	1.563	49.203	8.768
10	20	42.06	6.75	27.836	45.563	774.815	187.890
11	17	15.38	3.75	1.156	14.063	1.335	4.333
12	12	12.70	−1.25	−1.525	1.563	2.324	1.906
13	12	26.00	−1.25	11.776	1.563	138.662	−14.719
14	9	7.50	−4.25	−6.725	18.063	45.219	28.579
15	15	5.00	1.75	−9.225	3.063	85.091	−16.143
16	12	21.63	−1.25	7.406	1.563	54.841	−9.257
17	16	12.10	2.75	−2.125	7.563	4.514	−5.842
18	12	5.55	−1.25	−8.675	1.563	75.247	10.843
19	12	7.50	−1.25	−6.725	1.563	45.219	8.406
20	14	8.00	0.75	−6.225	0.563	38.744	−4.668
Total	265	284.49			217.750	1,542.150	305.888
Average	13.250	14.2245			10.888	77.108	15.294

Table 1.2, equal to 15.294, so we now need only Var(S) and Var(Y), calculated in Table 1.3.

From the sixth and seventh columns of Table 1.3, you can see that Var(S) is 10.888 and Var(Y) is 77.108. Hence

$$r_{SY} = \frac{15.924}{\sqrt{10.888 \times 77.108}} = \frac{15.924}{28.975} = 0.55. \tag{1.27}$$

Exercises

1.5 In the years following World War II, the economic growth of those countries that had suffered the greatest destruction, Germany and Japan, was more rapid than that of most other industrialized countries. Various hypotheses were offered to explain this. Nicholas Kaldor, a Hungarian economist, argued that the countries that had suffered the worst devastation had had to invest comprehensively with new plant and equipment. Because they were using up-to-date technology, their marginal costs were lower than those of their competitors in export markets, and they gained market share. Because they gained market share, they needed to increase their productive capacity and this meant additional investment, further lowering their marginal costs and increasing their market share. Meanwhile those countries that had suffered least, such as the US and the UK, had less need to re-invest. As a consequence the same process worked in the opposite direction. Their marginal costs were relatively high, so they lost market share and had less need to increase capacity. As evidence for this hypothesis, Kaldor showed that there was a high correlation between the output growth rate, x, and the productivity growth rate, p, in the manufacturing sectors in the twelve countries listed in the table.

Annual growth rates (%)

	Employment	Productivity
Austria	2.0	4.2
Belgium	1.5	3.9
Canada	2.3	1.3
Denmark	2.5	3.2
France	1.9	3.8
Italy	4.4	4.2
Japan	5.8	7.8
Netherlands	1.9	4.1
Norway	0.5	4.4
West Germany	2.7	4.5
UK	0.6	2.8
USA	0.8	2.6

Source: Nicholas Kaldor, *Causes of the Slow Rate of Economic Growth of the United Kingdom* (Cambridge University Press, 1966)

When a critic pointed out that it was inevitable that x and p would be highly correlated, irrespective of the validity of this hypothesis, Kaldor proposed a variation on his hypothesis. Economic growth was initially high in all countries for a few years after the war, but in some, particularly the US and the UK, it was soon checked by a shortage of labor, and a negative cycle took hold. In others, like Germany and Japan, where agriculture still accounted for a large share of employment, the manufacturing sector could continue to grow by attracting workers from the agricultural sector, and they would then have an advantage. A positive correlation between the growth rate of employment, e, and that of productivity would be evidence in favor of his hypothesis.

The table reproduces his data set, which relates to the period 1953–4 to 1963–4 (annual exponential growth rates). Plot a scatter diagram and calculate the sample correlation coefficient for e and p. [If you are not able to use a spreadsheet application for this purpose, you are strongly advised to use equations (1.9) and (1.17) for the sample covariance and variance and to keep a copy of your calculation, as this will save you time with another exercise in Chapter 2.] Comment on your findings.

1.6 Suppose that the observations on two variables X and Y lie on a straight line

$$Y = b_1 + b_2 X.$$

Demonstrate that $\text{Cov}(X, Y) = b_2 \text{Var}(X)$ and that $\text{Var}(Y) = b_2^2 \text{Var}(X)$, and hence that the sample correlation coefficient is equal to 1 if the slope of the line is positive, -1 if it is negative.

1.7* Suppose that a variable Y is defined by the exact linear relationship

$$Y = b_1 + b_2 X$$

and suppose that a sample of observations has been obtained for X, Y, and a third variable, Z. Show that the sample correlation coefficient for Y and Z must be the same as that for X and Z, if b_2 is positive.

1.9 Why covariance is not a good measure of association

The correlation coefficient is a much better measure of association than the covariance, the main reason being that the covariance depends on the units in which the variables X and Y happen to be measured, whereas the correlation coefficient does not. This will be demonstrated for the sample concepts; the proof for the population concepts will be left as an exercise.

Returning to the schooling and earnings example, we will investigate what happens when hourly earnings are measured in cents rather than dollars. The covariance will be affected, but the correlation coefficient will not.

We will denote the revised earnings data by Y'. The data for S and Y' are shown in Table 1.4. Of course the data for Y' are just the data for Y in Table 1.2, multiplied by 100. As a consequence, the average value of Y' in the sample is 100 times as large as the average value of Y. When we come to calculate the

Table 1.4

Observation	S	Y'	$(S - \bar{S})$	$(Y' - \bar{Y}')$	$(S - \bar{S}^2)$	$(Y' - \bar{Y}')^2$	$(S - \bar{S}) \times (Y' - \bar{Y}')$
1	15	1724	1.75	301.6	3.063	90930	527.7
2	16	1500	2.75	77.5	7.563	6010	213.3
3	8	1491	−5.25	68.5	27.563	4700	−359.9
4	6	450	−7.25	−972.5	52.563	945660	7050.3
5	15	1800	1.75	377.6	3.063	142540	660.7
6	12	629	−1.25	−793.5	1.563	629560	991.8
7	12	1923	−1.25	500.6	1.563	250550	−625.7
8	18	1869	4.75	446.6	22.563	199410	2121.1
9	12	721	−1.25	−701.5	1.563	492030	876.8
10	20	4206	6.75	2783.6	45.563	7748150	18789.0
11	17	1538	3.75	115.6	14.063	13350	433.3
12	12	1270	−1.25	−152.5	1.563	23240	190.6
13	12	2600	−1.25	1177.6	1.563	1386620	−1471.9
14	9	750	−4.25	−672.5	18.063	452190	2857.9
15	15	500	1.75	−922.5	3.063	850910	−1614.3
16	12	2163	−1.25	740.6	1.563	548410	−925.7
17	16	1210	2.75	−212.5	7.563	45140	−584.2
18	12	555	−1.25	−867.5	1.563	752470	1084.3
19	12	750	−1.25	−672.5	1.563	452190	840.6
20	14	800	0.75	−622.5	0.563	387440	−466.8
Total	265	28449			217.750	15421500	30588.8
Average	13.25	1422.45			10.888	771080	1529.4

earnings deviations $(Y' - \bar{Y}')$, these are 100 times those in Table 1.2 because $(Y' - \bar{Y}') = (100Y - 100\bar{Y}) = 100(Y - \bar{Y})$. Hence the products $(S - \bar{S})(Y' - \bar{Y}')$ are 100 times those in Table 1.2 and the sample covariance, 1529.4, is 100 times that obtained when hourly earnings were measured in dollars. However, the correlation coefficient is unaffected. The correlation coefficient for S and Y' is

$$r_{SY'} = \frac{\text{Cov}(S, Y')}{\sqrt{\text{Var}(S)\text{Var}(Y')}} = \frac{1529.4}{\sqrt{10.888 \times 771080}} = 0.55. \qquad (1.28)$$

The numerator (the top half of the fraction) has been multiplied by 100, but so has the denominator (the bottom half), since $\text{Var}(Y')$ is $100^2\text{Var}(Y)$. (Remember that, when you multiply a variable by a constant, you multiply its variance by the constant squared.) The denominator is multiplied by 100, rather than 100^2, because $Var(Y')$ is under a square root.

Exercise

1.8 Demonstrate that, in general, the sample correlation coefficient is not affected by a change in the unit of measurement of one of the variables.

2 Simple regression analysis

This chapter shows how a hypothetical linear relationship between two variables can be quantified using appropriate data. The principle of least squares regression analysis is explained, and expressions for the coefficients are derived.

Most students taking an introductory econometrics course will already have taken a basic calculus course and should have no trouble following the derivations of the regression coefficients. Those who have not should skip Section 2.3 and the proof in Section 2.5. They will then have to take the expressions on trust, but they should still be able to understand in general terms how the expressions have been derived.

2.1 The simple linear model

The correlation coefficient may indicate that two variables are associated with one another, but it does not give any idea of the kind of relationship involved. We will now take the investigation a step further in those cases for which we are willing to hypothesize that one variable depends on another.

It must be stated immediately that one would not expect to find an exact relationship between any two economic variables, unless it is true as a matter of definition. In textbook expositions of economic theory, the usual way of dealing with this awkward fact is to write down the relationship as if it were exact and to warn the reader that it is really only an approximation. In statistical analysis, however, one generally acknowledges the fact that the relationship is not exact by explicitly including in it a random factor known as the disturbance term.

We shall start with the simplest possible model:

$$Y_i = \beta_1 + \beta_2 X_i + u_i. \tag{2.1}$$

Y_i, the value of the dependent variable in observation i, has two components: (1) the nonrandom component $\beta_1 + \beta_2 X_i$, X being described as the explanatory (or independent) variable, and the fixed quantities β_1 and β_2 as the parameters of the equation, and (2) the disturbance term, u_i.

Figure 2.1 illustrates how these two components combine to determine Y. X_1, X_2, X_3, and X_4 are four hypothetical values of the explanatory variable. If the

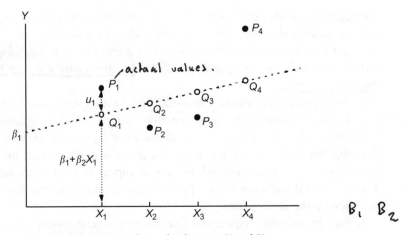

Figure 2.1 True relationship between Y and X

relationship between Y and X were exact, the corresponding values of Y would be represented by the points $Q_1 - Q_4$ on the line. The disturbance term causes the actual values of Y to be different. In the diagram, the disturbance term has been assumed to be positive in the first and fourth observations and negative in the other two, with the result that, if one plots the actual values of Y against the values of X, one obtains the points $P_1 - P_4$.

It must be emphasized that in practice the P points are all one can see of Figure 2.1. The actual values of β_1 and β_2, and hence the location of the Q points, are unknown, as are the values of the disturbance term in the observations. The task of regression analysis is to obtain estimates of β_1 and β_2, and hence an estimate of the location of the line, given the P points.

Why does the disturbance term exist? There are several reasons.

1. *Omission of explanatory variables:* The relationship between Y and X is almost certain to be a simplification. In reality there will be other factors affecting Y that have been left out of (2.1), and their influence will cause the points to lie off the line. It often happens that there are variables that you would like to include in the regression equation but cannot because you are unable to measure them. For example, later on in this chapter we will fit an earnings function relating hourly earnings to years of schooling. We know very well that schooling is not the only determinant of earnings and eventually we will improve the model by including other variables, such as years of work experience. However, even the best-specified earnings function accounts for at most half of the variation in earnings. Many other factors affect the chances of obtaining a good job, like the unmeasurable attributes of an individual, and even pure luck in the sense of the individual finding a job which is a good match for his or her attributes. All of these other factors contribute to the disturbance term.

2. *Aggregation of variables:* In many cases the relationship is an attempt to summarize in aggregate a number of microeconomic relationships. For example,

the aggregate consumption function is an attempt to summarize a set of individual expenditure decisions. Since the individual relationships are likely to have different parameters, any attempt to relate aggregate expenditure to aggregate income can only be an approximation. The discrepancy is attributed to the disturbance term.

3. *Model misspecification:* The model may be misspecified in terms of its structure. Just to give one of the many possible examples, if the relationship refers to time-series data, the value of Y may depend not on the actual value of X but on the value that had been anticipated in the previous period. If the anticipated and actual values are closely related, there will appear to be a relationship between Y and X, but it will only be an approximation, and again the disturbance term will pick up the discrepancy.

4. *Functional misspecification:* The functional relationship between Y and X may be misspecified mathematically. For example, the true relationship may be nonlinear instead of linear. We will consider the fitting of nonlinear relationships in Chapter 5. Obviously, one should try to avoid this problem by using an appropriate mathematical specification, but even the most sophisticated specification is likely to be only an approximation, and the discrepancy contributes to the disturbance term.

5. *Measurement error:* If the measurement of one or more of the variables in the relationship is subject to error, the observed values will not appear to conform to an exact relationship, and the discrepancy contributes to the disturbance term.

The disturbance term is the collective outcome of all these factors. Obviously, if you were concerned only with measuring the effect of X on Y, it would be much more convenient if the disturbance term did not exist. Were it not for its presence, the P points in Figure 2.1 would coincide with the Q points, you would know that every change in Y from observation to observation was due to a change in X, and you would be able to calculate β_1 and β_2 exactly. However, in fact, part of each change in Y is due to a change in u, and this makes life more difficult. For this reason, u is sometimes described as noise.

2.2 Least squares regression

Suppose that you are given the four observations on X and Y represented in Figure 2.1 and you are asked to obtain estimates of the values of β_1 and β_2 in equation (2.1). As a rough approximation, you could do this by plotting the four P points and drawing a line to fit them as best you can. This has been done in Figure 2.2. The intersection of the line with the Y-axis provides an estimate of the intercept β_1, which will be denoted b_1, and the slope provides an estimate of the slope coefficient β_2, which will be denoted b_2. The fitted line will be written

$$\hat{Y}_i = b_1 + b_2 X_i, \tag{2.2}$$

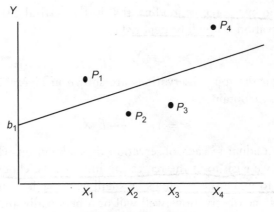

Figure 2.2 Fitted line

the caret mark over Y indicating that it is the fitted value of Y corresponding to X, not the actual value. In Figure 2.3, the fitted points are represented by the points $R_1 - R_4$.

One thing that should be accepted from the beginning is that you can never discover the true values of β_1 and β_2, however much care you take in drawing the line. b_1 and b_2 are only estimates, and they may be good or bad. Once in a while your estimates may be absolutely accurate, but this can only be by coincidence, and even then you will have no way of knowing that you have hit the target exactly.

This remains the case even when you use more sophisticated techniques. Drawing a regression line by eye is all very well, but it leaves a lot to subjective judgment. Furthermore, as will become obvious, it is not even possible when you have a variable Y depending on two or more explanatory variables instead of only one. The question arises, is there a way of calculating good estimates of β_1 and β_2 algebraically?

The first step is to define what is known as a residual for each observation. This is the difference between the actual value of Y in any observation and the

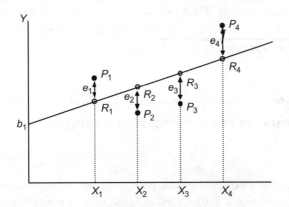

Figure 2.3 Fitted regression line showing residuals

fitted value given by the regression line, that is, the vertical distance between P_i and R_i in observation i. It will be denoted e_i:

$$e_i = Y_i - \hat{Y}_i. \tag{2.3}$$

The residuals for the four observations are shown in Figure 2.3. Substituting (2.2) into (2.3), we obtain

$$e_i = Y_i - b_1 - b_2 X_i \tag{2.4}$$

and hence the residual in each observation depends on our choice of b_1 and b_2. Obviously, we wish to fit the regression line, that is, choose b_1 and b_2, in such a way as to make the residuals as small as possible. Equally obviously, a line that fits some observations well will fit others badly and vice versa. We need to devise a criterion of fit that takes account of the size of all the residuals simultaneously.

There are a number of possible criteria, some of which work better than others. It is useless minimizing the sum of the residuals, for example. The sum will automatically be equal to 0 if you make b_1 equal to $\bar{Y}$ and b_2 equal to 0, obtaining the horizontal line $Y = \bar{Y}$. The positive residuals will then exactly balance the negative ones but, other than this, the line will not fit the observations.

One way of overcoming the problem is to minimize RSS, the sum of the squares of the residuals. For Figure 2.3,

$$RSS = e_1^2 + e_2^2 + e_3^2 + e_4^2. \tag{2.5}$$

The smaller one can make RSS, the better is the fit, according to this criterion. If one could reduce RSS to 0, one would have a perfect fit, for this would imply that all the residuals are equal to 0. The line would go through all the points, but of course in general the disturbance term makes this impossible.

There are other quite reasonable solutions, but the least squares criterion yields estimates of b_1 and b_2 that are unbiased and the most efficient of their type, provided that certain conditions are satisfied. For this reason, the least squares technique is far and away the most popular in uncomplicated applications of regression analysis. The form used here is usually referred to as ordinary least squares and abbreviated OLS. Variants designed to cope with particular problems will be discussed later in the text.

2.3 Least squares regression: two examples

Example 1

First, a very simple example indeed, with only two observations, just to show the mechanics working. Y is observed to be equal to 3 when X is equal to 1; Y is equal to 5 when X is equal to 2, as shown in Figure 2.4.

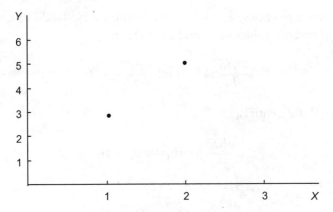

Figure 2.4 Two-observation example

We shall assume that the true model is

$$Y_i = \beta_1 + \beta_2 X_i + u_i \tag{2.6}$$

and we shall estimate the coefficients b_1 and b_2 of the equation

$$\hat{Y}_i = b_1 + b_2 X_i. \tag{2.7}$$

Obviously, when there are only two observations, we can obtain a perfect fit by drawing the regression line through the two points, but we shall pretend that we have not realized this. Instead we shall arrive at this conclusion by using the regression technique.

When X is equal to 1, $\hat{Y}$ is equal to $(b_1 + b_2)$ according to the regression line. When X is equal to 2, $\hat{Y}$ is equal to $(b_1 + 2b_2)$. Therefore, we can set up Table 2.1. So the residual for the first observation, e_1, which is given by $(Y_1 - \hat{Y}_1)$, is equal to $(3 - b_1 - b_2)$, and e_2, given by $(Y_2 - \hat{Y}_2)$, is equal to $(5 - b_1 - 2b_2)$. Hence

$$
\begin{aligned}
RSS &= (3 - b_1 - b_2)^2 + (5 - b_1 - 2b_2)^2 \\
&= 9 + b_1^2 + b_2^2 - 6b_1 - 6b_2 + 2b_1 b_2 \\
&\quad + 25 + b_1^2 + 4b_2^2 - 10b_1 - 20b_2 + 4b_1 b_2 \\
&= 34 + 2b_1^2 + 5b_2^2 - 16b_1 - 26b_2 + 6b_1 b_2.
\end{aligned}
\tag{2.8}
$$

Table 2.1

X	Y	$\hat{Y}$	e
1	3	$b_1 + b_2$	$3 - b_1 - b_2$
2	5	$b_1 + 2b_2$	$5 - b_1 - 2b_2$

Now we want to choose b_1 and b_2 to minimize RSS. To do this, we use the calculus and find the values of b_1 and b_2 that satisfy

$$\frac{\partial RSS}{\partial b_1} = 0 \quad \text{and} \quad \frac{\partial RSS}{\partial b_2} = 0. \tag{2.9}$$

Taking partial differentials,

$$\frac{\partial RSS}{\partial b_1} = 4b_1 + 6b_2 - 16 \tag{2.10}$$

and

$$\frac{\partial RSS}{\partial b_2} = 10b_2 + 6b_1 - 26. \tag{2.11}$$

and so we have

$$2b_1 + 3b_2 - 8 = 0 \tag{2.12}$$

and

$$3b_1 + 5b_2 - 13 = 0. \tag{2.13}$$

Solving these two equations, we obtain $b_1 = 1$ and $b_2 = 2$, and hence the regression equation

$$\hat{Y}_i = 1 + 2X_i. \tag{2.14}$$

Just to check that we have come to the right conclusion, we shall calculate the residuals:

$$e_1 = 3 - b_1 - b_2 = 3 - 1 - 2 = 0. \tag{2.15}$$
$$e_2 = 5 - b_1 - 2b_2 = 5 - 1 - 4 = 0. \tag{2.16}$$

Thus both the residuals are 0, implying that the line passes exactly through both points, which of course we knew from the beginning.

Example 2

We shall take the example in the previous section and add a third observation: Y is equal to 6 when X is equal to 3. The three observations, shown in Figure 2.5, do not lie on a straight line, so it is impossible to obtain a perfect fit. We will use least squares regression analysis to calculate the position of the line.

We start with the standard equation

$$\hat{Y}_i = b_1 + b_2 X_i. \tag{2.17}$$

For values of X equal to 1, 2, and 3, this gives fitted values of Y equal to $(b_1 + b_2)$, $(b_1 + 2b_2)$, and $(b_1 + 3b_2)$, respectively, and one has Table 2.2.

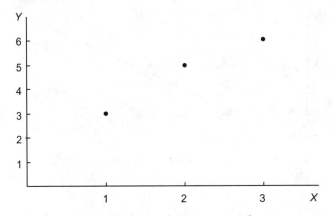

Figure 2.5 Three-observation example

Hence

$$RSS = (3 - b_1 - b_2)^2 + (5 - b_1 - 2b_2)^2 + (6 - b_1 - 3b_2)^2$$
$$= 9 + b_1^2 + b_2^2 - 6b_1 - 6b_2 + 2b_1b_2$$
$$+ 25 + b_1^2 + 4b_2^2 - 10b_1 - 20b_2 + 4b_1b_2$$
$$+ 36 + b_1^2 + 9b_2^2 - 12b_1 - 36b_2 + 6b_1b_2$$
$$= 70 + 3b_1^2 + 14b_2^2 - 28b_1 - 62b_2 + 12b_1b_2. \qquad (2.18)$$

The first-order conditions $\partial RSS / \partial b_1 = 0$ and $\partial RSS / \partial b_2 = 0$ give us

$$6b_1 + 12b_2 - 28 = 0 \qquad (2.19)$$

and

$$12b_1 + 28b_2 - 62 = 0. \qquad (2.20)$$

Solving these two equations, one obtains $b_1 = 1.67$ and $b_2 = 1.50$. The regression equation is therefore

$$\hat{Y}_i = 1.67 + 1.50X_i. \qquad (2.21)$$

The three points and the regression line are shown in Figure 2.6.

Table 2.2

X	Y	$\hat{Y}$	e
1	3	$b_1 + b_2$	$3 - b_1 - b_2$
2	5	$b_1 + 2b_2$	$5 - b_1 - 2b_2$
3	6	$b_1 + 3b_2$	$6 - b_1 - 3b_2$

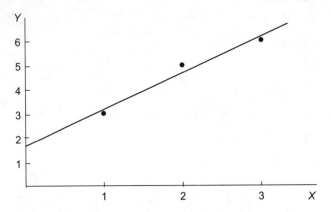

Figure 2.6 Three-observation example with regression line

2.4 Least squares regression with one explanatory variable

We shall now consider the general case where there are n observations on two variables X and Y and, supposing Y to depend on X, we will fit the equation

$$\hat{Y}_i = b_1 + b_2 X_i. \tag{2.22}$$

The fitted value of the dependent variable in observation i, $\hat{Y}_i$, will be $(b_1 + b_2 X_i)$, and the residual e_i will be $(Y_i - b_1 - b_2 X_i)$. We wish to choose b_1 and b_2 so as to minimize the residual sum of the squares, RSS, given by

$$RSS = e_1^2 + \cdots + e_n^2 = \sum_{i=1}^{n} e_i^2. \tag{2.23}$$

We will find that RSS is minimized when

$$b_2 = \frac{\text{Cov}(X, Y)}{\text{Var}(X)} \tag{2.24}$$

and

$$b_1 = \bar{Y} - b_2 \bar{X}. \tag{2.25}$$

The derivation of the expressions for b_1 and b_2 will follow the same procedure as the derivation in the two preceding examples, and you can compare the general version with the examples at each step. We will begin by expressing the square of the residual in observation i in terms of b_1, b_2, and the data on X and Y:

$$e_i^2 = (Y_i - \hat{Y}_i)^2 = (Y_i - b_1 - b_2 X_i)^2$$
$$= Y_i^2 + b_1^2 + b_2^2 X_i^2 - 2b_1 Y_i - 2b_2 X_i Y_i + 2b_1 b_2 X_i. \qquad (2.26)$$

Summing over all the n observations, we can write RSS as

$$RSS = (Y_1 - b_1 - b_2 X_1)^2 + \cdots + (Y_n - b_1 - b_2 X_n)^2$$
$$= Y_1^2 + b_1^2 + b_2^2 X_1^2 - 2b_1 Y_1 - 2b_2 X_1 Y_1 + 2b_1 b_2 X_1$$
$$+ \cdots$$
$$+ Y_n^2 + b_1^2 + b_2^2 X_n^2 - 2b_1 Y_n - 2b_2 X_n Y_n + 2b_1 b_2 X_n$$
$$= \sum_{i=1}^{n} Y_i^2 + nb_1^2 + b_2^2 \sum_{i=1}^{n} X_i^2 - 2b_1 \sum_{i=1}^{n} Y_i - 2b_2 \sum_{i=1}^{n} X_i Y_i + 2b_1 b_2 \sum_{i=1}^{n} X_i. \qquad (2.27)$$

Note that RSS is effectively a quadratic expression in b_1 and b_2, with numerical coefficients determined by the data on X and Y in the sample. We can influence the size of RSS only through our choice of b_1 and b_2. The data on X and Y, which determine the locations of the observations in the scatter diagram, are fixed once we have taken the sample. The equation is the generalized version of equations (2.8) and (2.18) in the two examples.

The first-order conditions for a minimum, $\partial RSS/\partial b_1 = 0$ and $\partial RSS/\partial b_2 = 0$, yield the following equations:

$$2nb_1 - 2 \sum_{i=1}^{n} Y_i + 2b_2 \sum_{i=1}^{n} X_i = 0. \qquad (2.28)$$

$$2b_2 \sum_{i=1}^{n} X_i^2 - 2 \sum_{i=1}^{n} X_i Y_i + 2b_1 \sum_{i=1}^{n} X_i = 0. \qquad (2.29)$$

These equations are known as the normal equations for the regression coefficients and are the generalized versions of (2.12) and (2.13) in the first example, and (2.19) and (2.20) in the second. Equation (2.28) allows us to write b_1 in terms of $\bar{Y}$, $\bar{X}$, and the as yet unknown b_2. Noting that $\bar{X} = \dfrac{1}{n} \sum_{i=1}^{n} X_i$ and $\bar{Y} = \dfrac{1}{n} \sum_{i=1}^{n} Y_i$, (2.28) may be rewritten

$$2nb_1 - 2n\bar{Y} + 2b_2 n\bar{X} = 0 \qquad (2.30)$$

and hence

$$b_1 = \bar{Y} - b_2 \bar{X}. \qquad (2.31)$$

Substituting for b_1 in (2.29), and again noting that $\sum_{i=1}^{n} X_i = n\bar{X}$, we obtain

$$2b_2 \sum_{i=1}^{n} X_i^2 - 2 \sum_{i=1}^{n} X_i Y_i + 2(\bar{Y} - b_2\bar{X})n\bar{X} = 0. \tag{2.32}$$

Separating the terms involving b_2 and not involving b_2 on opposite sides of the equation, we have

$$2b_2 \left[\left(\sum_{i=1}^{n} X_i^2 \right) - n\bar{X}^2 \right] = 2 \sum_{i=1}^{n} X_i Y_i - 2n\bar{X}\bar{Y}. \tag{2.33}$$

Dividing both sides by $2n$,

$$\left[\frac{1}{n} \left(\sum_{i=1}^{n} X_i^2 \right) - \bar{X}^2 \right] b_2 = \frac{1}{n} \left(\sum_{i=1}^{n} X_i Y_i \right) - \bar{X}\bar{Y}. \tag{2.34}$$

Using the alternative expressions for sample variance and covariance, this may be rewritten

$$b_2 \operatorname{Var}(X) = \operatorname{Cov}(X, Y) \tag{2.35}$$

and so

$$b_2 = \frac{\operatorname{Cov}(X, Y)}{\operatorname{Var}(X)}. \tag{2.36}$$

Having found b_2 from (2.36), you find b_1 from (2.31). Those who know about the second order conditions will have no difficulty confirming that we have minimized RSS.

In the second numerical example in Section 2.3, $\operatorname{Cov}(X, Y)$ is equal to 1.000, $\operatorname{Var}(X)$ to 0.667, $\bar{Y}$ to 4.667, $\bar{X}$ to 2.000, so

$$b_2 = 1.000/0.667 = 1.50 \tag{2.37}$$

and

$$b_1 = \bar{Y} - b_2\bar{X} = 4.667 - 1.50 \times 2.000 = 1.667, \tag{2.38}$$

which confirms the original calculation.

Alternative expressions for b_2

From the definitions of $\operatorname{Cov}(X, Y)$ and $\operatorname{Var}(X)$ one can obtain alternative expressions for b_2 in Σ notation:

$$b_2 = \frac{\operatorname{Cov}(X, Y)}{\operatorname{Var}(X)} = \frac{\dfrac{1}{n} \sum_{i=1}^{n} (X_i - \bar{X})(Y_i - \bar{Y})}{\dfrac{1}{n} \sum_{i=1}^{n} (X_i - \bar{X})^2} = \frac{\sum_{i=1}^{n} (X_i - \bar{X})(Y_i - \bar{Y})}{\sum_{i=1}^{n} (X_i - \bar{X})^2}. \tag{2.39}$$

One may obtain further variations using the alternative expressions for $\text{Cov}(X, Y)$ and $\text{Var}(X)$ provided by equations (1.8) and (1.16):

$$b_2 = \frac{\dfrac{1}{n}\displaystyle\sum_{i=1}^{n} X_i Y_i - \bar{X}\bar{Y}}{\dfrac{1}{n}\displaystyle\sum_{i=1}^{n} X_i^2 - \bar{X}^2} = \frac{\displaystyle\sum_{i=1}^{n} X_i Y_i - n\bar{X}\bar{Y}}{\displaystyle\sum_{i=1}^{n} X_i^2 - n\bar{X}^2}. \tag{2.40}$$

2.5 Two decompositions of the dependent variable

In the preceding pages we have encountered two ways of decomposing the value of the dependent variable in a regression model. They are going to be used throughout the text, so it is important that they be understood properly and that they be kept apart conceptually.

The first decomposition relates to the process by which the values of Y are generated:

$$Y_i = \beta_1 + \beta_2 X_i + u_i. \tag{2.41}$$

In observation i, Y_i is generated as the sum of two components, the nonstochastic component, $\beta_1 + \beta_2 X_i$, and the disturbance term u_i. This decomposition is purely theoretical. We will use it in the analysis of the properties of the regression estimators. It is illustrated in Figure 2.7a, where QT is the nonstochastic component of Y and PQ is the disturbance term.

The other decomposition relates to the regression line:

$$\begin{aligned} Y_i &= \hat{Y}_i + e_i \\ &= b_1 + b_2 X_i + e_i. \end{aligned} \tag{2.42}$$

Once we have chosen the values of b_1 and b_2, each value of Y is split into the fitted value, $\hat{Y}_i$, and the residual, e_i. This decomposition is operational, but it

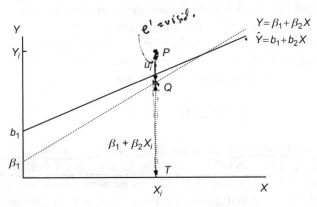

Figure 2.7(a) Decomposition of Y into nonstochastic component and disturbance term

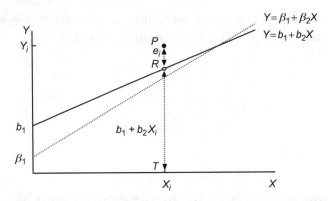

Figure 2.7(b) Decomposition of Y into fitted value and residual

is to some extent arbitrary because it depends on our criterion for determining b_1 and b_2 and it will inevitably be affected by the particular values taken by the disturbance term in the observations in the sample. It is illustrated in Figure 2.7b, where RT is the fitted value and PR is the residual.

non stochastic component.

2.6 Interpretation of a regression equation

There are two stages in the interpretation of a regression equation. The first is to turn the equation into words so that it can be understood by a noneconometrician. The second is to decide whether this literal interpretation should be taken at face value or whether the relationship should be investigated further.

Both stages are important. We will leave the second until later and concentrate for the time being on the first. It will be illustrated with an earnings function, hourly earnings in 1994, *EARNINGS*, measured in dollars, being regressed on schooling, S, measured as highest grade completed, for the 570 respondents in *EAEF* Data Set 21. The Stata output for the regression is shown in Table 2.3. The scatter diagram and regression line are shown in Figure 2.8.

For the time being, ignore everything except the column headed 'coef.' in the bottom half of the table. This gives the estimates of the coefficient of S and the constant, and thus the following fitted equation:

$$\widehat{EARNINGS} = -1.39 + 1.07S \qquad (2.43)$$

Interpreting it literally, the slope coefficient indicates that, as S increases by one unit (of S), *EARNINGS* increases by 1.07 units (of *EARNINGS*). Since S is measured in years, and *EARNINGS* is measured in dollars per hour, the coefficient of S implies that hourly earnings increase by $\$1.07$ for every extra year of schooling.

Table 2.3

```
. reg EARNINGS S

    Source |       SS        df      MS              Number of obs =      570
-----------+-----------------------------           F( 1,   568) =    65.64
     Model | 3977.38016       1  3977.38016          Prob > F      =   0.0000
  Residual | 34419.6569     568  60.5979875          R-squared     =   0.1036
-----------+-----------------------------           Adj R-squared =   0.1020
     Total | 38397.0371     569  67.4816117          Root MSE      =   7.7845


-----------------------------------------------------------------------------
  EARNINGS |     Coef.   Std. Err.      t     P>|t|    [95%  Conf. Interval]
-----------+-----------------------------------------------------------------
         S |  1.073055   .1324501    8.102    0.000    .8129028    1.333206
     _cons | -1.391004   1.820305   -0.764    0.445   -4.966354    2.184347
-----------------------------------------------------------------------------
```

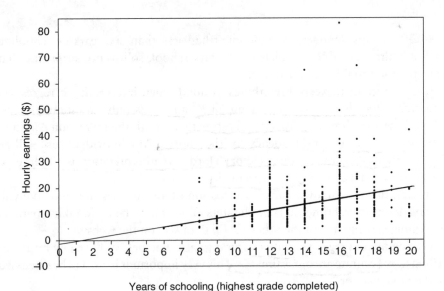

Figure 2.8 A simple earnings function

   What about the constant term? Strictly speaking, it indicates the predicted level of *EARNINGS* when *S* is 0. Sometimes the constant will have a clear meaning, but sometimes not. If the sample values of the explanatory variable are a long way from 0, extrapolating the regression line back to 0 may be dangerous. Even if the regression line gives a good fit for the sample of observations, there is no guarantee that it will continue to do so when extrapolated to the left or to the right.
   In this case a literal interpretation of the constant would lead to the nonsensical conclusion that an individual with no schooling would have hourly earnings of

---

BOX 2.1   Interpretation of a linear regression equation

This is a foolproof way of interpreting the coefficients of a linear regression

$$\hat{Y}_i = b_1 + b_2 X_i$$

when Y and X are variables with straightforward natural units (not logarithms or other functions).

The first step is to say that a one-unit increase in X (measured in units of X) will cause a b_2 unit increase in Y (measured in units of Y). The second step is to check to see what the units of X and Y actually are, and to replace the word 'unit' with the actual unit of measurement. The third step is to see whether the result could be expressed in a better way, without altering its substance.

The constant, b_1, gives the predicted value of Y (in units of Y) for X equal to 0. It may or may not have a plausible meaning, depending on the context.

−$ 1.39. In this data set, no individual had less than six years of schooling and only three failed to complete elementary school, so it is not surprising that extrapolation to 0 leads to trouble.

It is important to keep three things in mind when interpreting a regression equation. First, b_1 is only an estimate of β_1 and b_2 is only an estimate of β_2, so the interpretation is really only an estimate. Second, the regression equation refers only to the general tendency for the sample. Any individual case will be further affected by the random factor. Third, the interpretation is conditional on the equation being correctly specified.

In fact, this is actually a naïve specification of an earnings function. We will reconsider it several times in later chapters. You should be undertaking parallel experiments using one of the other *EAEF* data sets on the website.

Having fitted a regression, it is natural to ask whether we have any means of telling how accurate are our estimates. This very important issue will be discussed in the next chapter.

Exercises

Note: Some of the exercises in this and later chapters require you to fit regressions using one of the *EAEF* data sets on the website (http://econ.lse.ac.uk/ie/). You will need to download the *EAEF* regression exercises manual and one of the twenty data sets.

2.1   The table shows the average rates of growth of GDP, g, and employment, e, for twenty-five OECD countries for the period 1988–97. The regression output shows the result of regressing e on g. Provide an interpretation of the coefficients.

Average rates of employment growth and GDP growth 1988–97

	Employment	GDP		Employment	GDP
Australia	1.68	3.04	Korea	2.57	7.73
Austria	0.65	2.55	Luxembourg	3.02	5.64
Belgium	0.34	2.16	Netherlands	1.88	2.86
Canada	1.17	2.03	New Zealand	0.91	2.01
Denmark	0.02	2.02	Norway	0.36	2.98
Finland	−1.06	1.78	Portugal	0.33	2.79
France	0.28	2.08	Spain	0.89	2.60
Germany	0.08	2.71	Sweden	−0.94	1.17
Greece	0.87	2.08	Switzerland	0.79	1.15
Iceland	−0.13	1.54	Turkey	2.02	4.18
Ireland	2.16	6.40	United Kingdom	0.66	1.97
Italy	−0.30	1.68	United States	1.53	2.46
Japan	1.06	2.81			

```
. reg e g

  Source |       SS       df       MS              Number of obs =      25
---------+------------------------------           F(  1,    23) =   33.22
   Model | 14.2762167     1  14.2762167            Prob > F      =  0.0000
Residual | 9.88359869    23  .429721682            R-squared     =  0.5909
---------+------------------------------           Adj R-squared =  0.5731
   Total | 24.1598154    24  1.00665898            Root MSE      =  .65553


-------------------------------------------------------------------------
       e |    Coef.   Std. Err.      t     P>|t|    [95% Conf. Interval]
---------+---------------------------------------------------------------
       g |  .4846863   .0840907    5.764   0.000    .3107315    .6586411
   _cons | -.5208643   .2707298   -1.924   0.067   -1.080912    .039183
-------------------------------------------------------------------------
```

2.2 Calculate by hand a regression of the data for *p* on the data for *e* in Exercise 1.5, first using all twelve observations, then excluding the observation for Japan, and provide an economic interpretation. (*Note:* You do not need to calculate the regression coefficients from scratch, since you have already performed most of the arithmetical calculations in Exercise 1.5.)

2.3 Fit an educational attainment function using your *EAEF* data set, regressing *S* on *ASVABC* and give an interpretation of the coefficients.

2.4 Fit an earnings function parallel to that discussed in Section 2.6, using your *EAEF* data set, and give an interpretation of the coefficients.

2.5* The output below shows the result of regressing the weight of the respondent in 1985, measured in pounds, on his or her height, measured in inches, using *EAEF* Data Set 21. Provide an interpretation of the coefficients.

```
. reg WEIGHT85 HEIGHT

    Source |       SS       df       MS              Number of obs =     550
-----------+------------------------------           F(  1,   548) =  343.00
     Model |  245463.095     1   245463.095           Prob > F      =  0.0000
  Residual |  392166.897   548   715.633025           R-squared     =  0.3850
-----------+------------------------------           Adj R-squared =  0.3838
     Total |  637629.993   549   1161.43897           Root MSE      =  26.751


-------------------------------------------------------------------------------
 WEIGHT85 |     Coef.   Std. Err.      t     P>|t|    [95% Conf. Interval]
----------+--------------------------------------------------------------------
   HEIGHT |   5.399304   .2915345   18.520   0.000    4.826643    5.971966
    _cons |  -210.1883   19.85925  -10.584   0.000   -249.1979   -171.1788
-------------------------------------------------------------------------------
```

2.6 Two individuals fit earnings functions relating *EARNINGS* to *S* as defined in Section 2.6, using *EAEF* Data Set 21. The first individual does it correctly and obtains the result found in Section 2.6:

$$EAR\widehat{N}INGS = -1.39 + 1.07S.$$

The second individual makes a mistake and regresses *S* on *EARNINGS*, obtaining the following result:

$$\hat{S} = 12.255 + 0.097EARNINGS.$$

From this result the second individual derives

$$EAR\widehat{N}INGS = -126.95 + 10.36S.$$

Explain why this equation is different from that fitted by the first individual.

2.7* Derive, with a proof, the slope coefficients that would have been obtained in Exercise 2.5 if weight and height had been measured in metric units. (*Note:* one pound is 454 grams, and one inch is 2.54 cm.)

2.8* A researcher has data on the aggregate expenditure on services, *Y*, and aggregate disposable personal income, *X*, both measured in $ billion at constant prices, for each of the US states and fits the equation

$$Y_i = \beta_1 + \beta_2 X_i + u_i.$$

The researcher initially fits the equation using OLS regression analysis. However, suspecting that tax evasion causes both *Y* and *X* to be substantially underestimated, the researcher adopts two alternative methods of compensating for the under-reporting:

1. The researcher adds $90 billion to the data for Y in each state and $200 billion to the data for X.

2. The researcher increases the figures for both Y and X in each state by 10 percent.

Evaluate the impact of the adjustments on the regression results.

2.9* A researcher has international cross-section data on aggregate wages, W, aggregate profits, P, and aggregate income, Y, for a sample of n countries. By definition,

$$Y_i = W_i + P_i.$$

The regressions

$$\hat{W}_i = a_1 + a_2 Y_i$$
$$\hat{P}_i = b_1 + b_2 Y_i$$

are fitted using OLS regression analysis. Show that the regression coefficients will automatically satisfy the following equations:

$$a_2 + b_2 = 1.$$
$$a_1 + b_1 = 0.$$

Explain intuitively why this should be so.

2.10* Derive from first principles the least squares estimator of β_2 in the model

$$Y_i = \beta_2 X_i + u_i.$$

2.11 Derive from first principles the least squares estimator of β_1 in the even more primitive model

$$Y_i = \beta_1 + u_i.$$

(In other words, Y consists simply of a constant plus a disturbance term. First define RSS and then differentiate.)

2.7 Goodness of fit: R^2

The aim of regression analysis is to explain the behavior of the dependent variable Y. In any given sample, Y is relatively low in some observations and relatively high in others. We want to know why. The variations in Y in any sample can be summarized by the sample variance, $\text{Var}(Y)$. We should like to be able to account for the size of this variance.

We have seen that we can split the value of Y_i in each observation into two components, $\hat{Y}_i$ and e_i, after running a regression.

$$Y_i = \hat{Y}_i + e_i. \tag{2.44}$$

We can use this to decompose the variance of Y:

$$\text{Var}(Y) = \text{Var}(\hat{Y} + e)$$
$$= \text{Var}(\hat{Y}) + \text{Var}(e) + 2\text{Cov}(\hat{Y}, e). \tag{2.45}$$

Now it so happens the $\text{Cov}(\hat{Y}, e)$ must be equal to 0 (see Box 2.2). Hence we obtain

$$\text{Var}(Y) = \text{Var}(\hat{Y}) + \text{Var}(e). \tag{2.46}$$

This means the we can decompose the variance of Y into two parts, $\text{Var}(\hat{Y})$, the part 'explained' by the regression line, and $\text{Var}(e)$, the 'unexplained' part. (*Note:* The words *explained* and *unexplained* have been put in quotation marks because the explanation may in fact be false. Y might really depend on some other variable Z, and X might be acting as a proxy for Z (more about this later). It would be safer to use the expression *apparently explained* instead of *explained*.)

In view of (2.46), $\text{Var}(\hat{Y})/\text{Var}(Y)$ is the proportion of the variance explained by the regression line. This proportion is known as the coefficient of determination or, more usually, R^2:

$$R^2 = \frac{\text{Var}(\hat{Y})}{\text{Var}(Y)}. \tag{2.47}$$

The maximum value of R^2 is 1. This occurs when the regression line fits the observations exactly, so that $\hat{Y}_i = Y_i$ in all observations and all the residuals are 0. Then $\text{Var}(\hat{Y}) = \text{Var}(Y)$, $\text{Var}(e)$ is 0, and one has a perfect fit. If there is no apparent relationship between the values of Y and X in the sample, R^2 will be close to 0.

Often it is convenient to decompose the variance as 'sums of squares'. From (2.46) one has

$$\frac{1}{n}\sum_{i=1}^{n}(Y_i - \bar{Y})^2 = \frac{1}{n}\sum_{i=1}^{n}(\hat{Y}_i - \bar{\hat{Y}})^2 + \frac{1}{n}\sum_{i=1}^{n}(e_i - \bar{e})^2 \tag{2.48}$$

and so

$$\sum_{i=1}^{n}(Y_i - \bar{Y})^2 = \sum_{i=1}^{n}(\hat{Y}_i - \bar{Y})^2 + \sum_{i=1}^{n}e_i^2 \tag{2.49}$$

multiplying through by n and using $\bar{e} = 0$ and $\bar{\hat{Y}} = \bar{Y}$ (see Box 2.2). Thus

$$TSS = ESS + RSS, \tag{2.50}$$

where TSS, the total sum of squares, is given by the left side of the equation and ESS, the explained sum of squares, and RSS, the residual sum of squares, are the two terms on the right side.

$y\mu$

BOX 2.2   Three useful results relating to OLS regressions

$$(1)\,\bar{e} = 0, (2)\,\bar{\hat{Y}} = \bar{Y}, (3)\,\mathrm{Cov}(\hat{Y}, e) = 0.$$

Proof of (1)

$$e_i = Y_i - \hat{Y}_i = Y_i - b_1 - b_2 X_i$$

So

$$\sum_{i=1}^{n} e_i = \sum_{i=1}^{n} Y_i - nb_1 - b_2 \sum_{i=1}^{n} X_i$$

Dividing by n,

$$\bar{e} = \bar{Y} - b_1 - b_2 \bar{X}$$
$$= \bar{Y} - (\bar{Y} - b_2 \bar{X}) - b_2 \bar{X} = 0$$

Proof of (2)

$$e_i = Y_i - \hat{Y}_i$$

so

$$\sum_{i=1}^{n} e_i = \sum_{i=1}^{n} Y_i - \sum_{i=1}^{n} \hat{Y}_i$$

Dividing by n,

$$\bar{e} = \bar{Y} - \bar{\hat{Y}}$$

But $\bar{e} = 0$, so $\bar{\hat{Y}} = \bar{Y}$.

Proof of (3)

$$\mathrm{Cov}(\hat{Y}, e) = \mathrm{Cov}([b_1 + b_2 X], e) = \mathrm{Cov}(b_1, e) + \mathrm{Cov}(b_2 X, e)$$
$$= b_2 \mathrm{Cov}(X, e) = b_2 \mathrm{Cov}(X, [Y - b_1 - b_2 X])$$
$$= b_2 [\mathrm{Cov}(X, Y) - \mathrm{Cov}(X, b_1) - b_2 \mathrm{Var}(X)]$$
$$= b_2 [\mathrm{Cov}(X, Y) - b_2 \mathrm{Var}(X)]$$
$$= b_2 \left[\mathrm{Cov}(X, Y) - \frac{\mathrm{Cov}(X, Y)}{\mathrm{Var}(X)} \mathrm{Var}(X) \right] = 0$$

Other things being equal, one would like R^2 to be as high as possible. In particular, we would like the coefficients b_1 and b_2 to be chosen in such a way as to maximize R^2. Does this conflict with our criterion that b_1 and b_2 should be chosen to minimize the sum of the squares of the residuals? No, they are easily shown to be equivalent criteria. In view of (2.46) we can rewrite R^2 as

$$R^2 = 1 - \frac{\mathrm{Var}(e)}{\mathrm{Var}(Y)}. \tag{2.51}$$

Thus

$$R^2 = 1 - \frac{\dfrac{1}{n}\displaystyle\sum_{i=1}^{n} e_i^2}{\text{Var}(Y)} = 1 - \frac{\dfrac{1}{n}RSS}{\text{Var}(Y)}. \tag{2.52}$$

and so the values of b_1 and b_2 that minimize the residual sum of squares automatically maximize R^2.

Alternative interpretation of R^2

It should be intuitively obvious that, the better is the fit achieved by the regression equation, the higher should be the correlation coefficient for the actual and predicted values of Y. We will show that R^2 is in fact equal to the square of this correlation coefficient, which we will denote $r_{Y\hat{Y}}$

$$
\begin{aligned}
r_{Y\hat{Y}} &= \frac{\text{Cov}(Y, \hat{Y})}{\sqrt{\text{Var}(Y)\text{Var}(\hat{Y})}} = \frac{\text{Cov}([\hat{Y} + e], \hat{Y})}{\sqrt{\text{Var}(Y)\text{Var}(\hat{Y})}} \\[2ex]
&= \frac{\text{Cov}(\hat{Y}, \hat{Y}) + \text{Cov}(e, \hat{Y})}{\sqrt{\text{Var}(Y)\text{Var}(\hat{Y})}} = \frac{\text{Var}(\hat{Y})}{\sqrt{\text{Var}(Y)\text{Var}(\hat{Y})}} \\[2ex]
&= \frac{\sqrt{\text{Var}(\hat{Y})\text{Var}(\hat{Y})}}{\sqrt{\text{Var}(Y)\text{Var}(\hat{Y})}} = \sqrt{\frac{\text{Var}(\hat{Y})}{\text{Var}(Y)}} = \sqrt{R^2}
\end{aligned} \tag{2.53}
$$

Note that the proof makes use of the fact that $\text{Cov}(e, \hat{Y}) = 0$ (see Box. 2.2).

Example of how R^2 is calculated

R^2 is always calculated by the computer as part of the regression output, so this example is for illustration only. We shall use the primitive three-observation example described in Section 2.3, where the regression line

$$\hat{Y}_i = 1.6667 + 1.5000X_i \tag{2.54}$$

was fitted to the observations on X and Y in Table 2.4. The table also shows $\hat{Y}_i$ and e_i for each observation, calculated from (2.52), and all the other data needed to calculate $\text{Var}(Y)$, $\text{Var}(\hat{Y})$, and $\text{Var}(e)$. (Note that $\bar{e}$ must be 0, so $\text{Var}(e)$ is $\dfrac{1}{n}\displaystyle\sum_{i=1}^{n} e_i^2$.)

From Table 2.4, you can see that $\text{Var}(Y) = 1.5556$, $\text{Var}(\hat{Y}) = 1.5000$, and $\text{Var}(e) = 0.0556$. Note that $\text{Var}(Y) = \text{Var}(\hat{Y}) + \text{Var}(e)$, as it must. From these

Table 2.4

Observation	X	Y	$\hat{Y}$	e	$Y - \bar{Y}$	$\hat{Y} - \bar{\hat{Y}}$	$(Y - \bar{Y})^2$	$(\hat{Y} - \bar{\hat{Y}})^2$	e^2
1	1	3	3.1667	−0.1667	−1.6667	−1.5	2.7778	2.25	0.0278
2	2	5	4.6667	0.3333	0.3333	0.0	0.1111	0.00	0.1111
3	3	6	6.1667	−0.1667	1.3333	1.5	1.7778	2.25	0.0278
Total	6	14	14				4.6667	4.50	0.1667
Average	2	4.6667	4.6667				1.5556	1.50	0.0556

figures, we can calculate R^2 using either (2.47) or (2.51):

$$R^2 = \frac{\text{Var}(\hat{Y})}{\text{Var}(Y)} = \frac{1.5000}{1.5556} = 0.96. \tag{2.55}$$

$$R^2 = 1 - \frac{\text{Var}(e)}{\text{Var}(Y)} = 1 - \frac{0.0556}{1.5556} = 0.96. \tag{2.56}$$

Exercises

2.12 Using the data in Table 2.4, calculate the correlation between Y and $\hat{Y}$ and verify that its square is equal to the value of R^2.

2.13 What was the value of R^2 in the educational attainment regression fitted by you in Exercise 2.3? Comment on it.

2.14 What was the value of R^2 in the earnings function fitted by you in Exercise 2.4? Comment on it.

2.15* The output below shows the result of regressing weight in 1994 on height, using *EAEF* Data Set 21. In 1994 the respondents were aged 29–36. Explain why R^2 is lower than in the regression reported in Exercise 2.5.

```
. reg WEIGHT94 HEIGHT

  Source |       SS       df       MS              Number of obs =     545
---------+------------------------------           F( 1,   543) =  247.48
   Model | 268361.40        1   268361.40          Prob > F      =  0.0000
Residual | 588805.041     543  1084.35551          R-squared     =  0.3131
---------+------------------------------           Adj R-squared =  0.3118
   Total | 857166.44      544  1575.6736           Root MSE      =   32.93


------------------------------------------------------------------------------
WEIGHT94 |     Coef.   Std. Err.      t     P>|t|    [95% Conf. Interval]
---------+--------------------------------------------------------------------
  HEIGHT |  5.659775     .35977    15.732    0.000    4.953064    6.366487
   _cons | -212.8358    24.51422   -8.682    0.000   -260.9901   -164.6815
------------------------------------------------------------------------------
```

3 Properties of the regression coefficients and hypothesis testing

With the aid of regression analysis we can obtain estimates of the parameters of a relationship. However, they are only *estimates*. The next question to ask is, how reliable are they? We shall answer this first in general terms, investigating the conditions for unbiasedness and the factors governing their variance. Building on this, we shall develop a means of testing whether a regression estimate is compatible with a specific prior hypothesis concerning the true value of a parameter, and hence we shall derive a confidence interval for the true value, that is, the set of all hypothetical values not contradicted by the experimental result. We shall also see how to test whether the goodness of fit of a regression equation is better than might be expected on the basis of pure chance.

3.1 The random components of the regression coefficients

A least squares regression coefficient is a special form of random variable whose properties depend on those of the disturbance term in the equation. This will be demonstrated first theoretically and then by means of a controlled experiment. In particular, we will investigate the implications for the regression coefficients of certain assumptions concerning the disturbance term.

Throughout the discussion we shall continue to work with the simple regression model where Y depends on X according to the relationship

$$Y_i = \beta_1 + \beta_2 X_i + u_i, \tag{3.1}$$

and we are fitting the regression equation

$$\hat{Y}_i = b_1 + b_2 X_i \tag{3.2}$$

given a sample of n observations. We shall also continue to assume that X is a nonstochastic exogenous variable; that is, that its value in each observation may be considered to be predetermined by factors unconnected with the present relationship.

First, note that Y_i has two components. It has a nonrandom component $(\beta_1 + \beta_2 X_i)$, which owes nothing to the laws of chance (β_1 and β_2 may be unknown, but nevertheless they are fixed constants), and it has the random component u_i.

This implies that, when we calculate b_2 according to the usual formula

$$b_2 = \frac{\text{Cov}(X, Y)}{\text{Var}(X)} \tag{3.3}$$

b_2 also has a random component. $\text{Cov}(X, Y)$ depends on the values of Y, and the values of Y depend on the values of u. If the values of the disturbance term had been different in the n observations, we would have obtained different values of Y, hence of $\text{Cov}(X, Y)$, and hence of b_2.

We can in theory decompose b_2 into its nonrandom and random components. In view of (3.1),

$$\text{Cov}(X, Y) = \text{Cov}(X, [\beta_1 + \beta_2 X + u])$$
$$= \text{Cov}(X, \beta_1) + \text{Cov}(X, \beta_2 X) + \text{Cov}(X, u) \tag{3.4}$$

using Covariance Rule 1 in Section 1.2. By Covariance Rule 3, $\text{Cov}(X, \beta_1)$ must be equal to 0. By Covariance Rule 2, $\text{Cov}(X, \beta_2 X)$ is equal to $\beta_2 \text{Cov}(X, X)$. $\text{Cov}(X, X)$ is the same as $\text{Var}(X)$. Hence we can write

$$\text{Cov}(X, Y) = \beta_2 \text{Var}(X) + \text{Cov}(X, u) \tag{3.5}$$

and so

$$b_2 = \frac{\text{Cov}(X, Y)}{\text{Var}(X)} = \beta_2 + \frac{\text{Cov}(X, u)}{\text{Var}(X)}. \tag{3.6}$$

Thus we have shown that the regression coefficient b_2 obtained from any sample consists of (1) a fixed component, equal to the true value, β_2, and (2) a random component dependent on $\text{Cov}(X, u)$, which is responsible for its variations around this central tendency. Similarly, one may easily show that b_1 has a fixed component equal to the true value, β_1, plus a random component that depends on the random factor u.

Note that you are not able to make these decompositions in practice because you do not know the true values of β_1 and β_2 or the actual values of u in the sample. We are interested in them because they enable us to say something about the theoretical properties of b_1 and b_2, given certain assumptions.

3.2 A Monte Carlo experiment

Nobody seems to know for certain how the Monte Carlo experiment got its name. Probably it has something to do with the famous casino, as a symbol of the laws of chance.

The basic concept will be explained by means of an analogy. Suppose you have trained a pig to find truffles for you. These fungi grow wild in the ground in France and Italy and are considered to be delicious. They are expensive because they are hard to find, and a good truffle pig is highly valued. The question is, how do you know if your pig is any good at truffle hunting? It may find them from time to time, but for all you know it may miss a lot as well. If you were really interested you could evaluate your pig by taking a piece of land, burying truffles in several places, letting the pig loose, and seeing how many it located. By means of this controlled experiment, you would have a direct measure of its success rate.

What has this got to do with regression analysis? The problem is that we never know the true values of β_1 and β_2 (otherwise, why should we use regression analysis to estimate them?), so we have no means of telling whether the technique is giving us good or bad estimates. A Monte Carlo experiment is an artificial, controlled experiment that allows us to check.

The simplest possible Monte Carlo experiment has three parts. First,

1. you choose the true values of β_1 and β_2,

2. you choose the value of X in each observation, and

3. you use some random number generating process to provide the random factor u in each observation.

Second, you *generate* the value of Y in each observation, using the relationship (3.1) and the values of β_1, β_2, X, and u. Third, using only the values of Y thus generated and the data for X, you use regression analysis to obtain estimates b_1 and b_2. You can then see if b_1 is a good estimator of β_1 and if b_2 is a good estimator of β_2, and this will give you some idea of whether the regression technique is working properly.

In the first two steps you are preparing a challenge for the regression technique. You are in complete control of the model that you are constructing and you *know* the true values of the parameters because you yourself have determined them. In the third step you see whether the regression technique can meet your challenge and provide good estimates of β_1 and β_2 using only the data on Y and X. Note that the inclusion of a stochastic term in the generation of Y is responsible for the element of challenge. If you did not include it, the observations would lie exactly on the straight line (3.1), and it would be a trivial matter to determine the exact values of β_1 and β_2 from the data on Y and X.

Quite arbitrarily, let us put β_1 equal to 2 and β_2 equal to 0.5, so the true relationship is

$$Y_i = 2 + 0.5X_i + u_i. \tag{3.7}$$

To keep things simple, we will assume that we have 20 observations and that the values of X go from 1 to 20. For u, the disturbance term, we will use random numbers drawn from a normally distributed population with 0 mean and unit variance. We will need a set of 20 and will denote them rn_1 to rn_{20}. u_1, the disturbance term in the first observation, is simply equal to rn_1, u_2 to rn_2, etc.

Given the values of X_i and u_i in each observation, it is possible to calculate the value of Y_i using (3.7), and this is done in Table 3.1.

Table 3.1

X	u	Y	X	u	Y
1	−0.59	1.91	11	1.59	9.09
2	−0.24	2.76	12	−0.92	7.08
3	−0.83	2.67	13	−0.71	7.79
4	0.03	4.03	14	−0.25	8.75
5	−0.38	4.12	15	1.69	11.19
6	−2.19	2.81	16	0.15	10.15
7	1.03	6.53	17	0.02	10.52
8	0.24	6.24	18	−0.11	10.89
9	2.53	9.03	19	−0.91	10.59
10	−0.13	6.87	20	1.42	13.42

If you now regress Y on X, you obtain

$$\hat{Y}_i = 1.63 + 0.54X_i. \tag{3.8}$$

In this case b_1 is an underestimate of β_1 (1.63 as opposed to 2.00) and b_2 is a slight overestimate of β_2 (0.54 as opposed to 0.50). The discrepancies are caused by the collective effects of the disturbance terms in the 20 observations.

Of course, one experiment such as this is hardly enough to allow us to evaluate the regression technique. It gave quite good results, but perhaps this was a fluke. To check further, we will repeat the experiment, keeping the *same* true equation (3.7) and the *same* values of X, but using a *new* set of random numbers for the disturbance term drawn from the same distribution (0 mean and unit variance). From these, and the values of X, we generate a new set of values for Y.

To save space, the table giving the new values of u and Y is omitted. The result when the new values of Y are regressed on X is

$$\hat{Y}_i = 2.52 + 0.48X_i. \tag{3.9}$$

This second experiment also turned out quite well. Now b_1 is an overestimate of β_1 and b_2 is a slight underestimate of β_2. Table 3.2 gives the estimates b_1 and b_2 with the experiment repeated 10 times, using a different set of random numbers for the disturbance term in each case.

You can see that, although you sometimes get overestimates and sometimes underestimates, on the whole b_1 and b_2 are clustered around the true values of 2.00 and 0.50, respectively. And there are more good estimates than bad ones. Taking b_2, for example, if you repeated the experiment a very large number of

Table 3.2

Sample	b_1	b_2
1	1.63	0.54
2	2.52	0.48
3	2.13	0.45
4	2.14	0.50
5	1.71	0.56
6	1.81	0.51
7	1.72	0.56
8	3.18	0.41
9	1.26	0.58
10	1.94	0.52

times and constructed a frequency table, you would obtain an approximation to the probability density function shown in Figure 3.1. It is a normal distribution with mean 0.50 and standard deviation 0.0388.

It has been asserted that the discrepancies between the regression coefficients and the true values of the parameters are caused by the disturbance term u. A consequence of this is that the bigger is the random element, the less accurate will be the estimate, in general.

This will be illustrated with a second set of Monte Carlo experiments related to the first. We shall use the same values for β_1 and β_2 as before, and the same values of X, and the same source of random numbers for the disturbance term, but we will now make the disturbance term in each observation, which will be

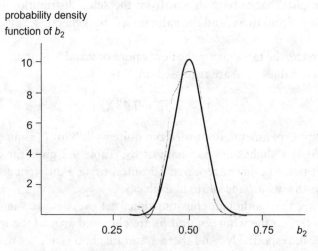

Figure 3.1 Distribution of b_2 in the Monte Carlo experiment

Table 3.3

X	u	Y	X	u	Y
1	−1.18	1.32	11	3.18	10.68
2	−0.48	2.52	12	−1.84	6.16
3	−1.66	1.84	13	−1.42	7.08
4	0.06	3.94	14	−0.50	8.50
5	−0.76	3.74	15	3.38	12.88
6	−4.38	0.62	16	0.30	10.30
7	2.06	7.56	17	0.04	10.54
8	0.48	6.48	18	−0.22	10.78
9	5.06	11.56	19	−1.82	9.68
10	−0.26	6.74	20	2.84	14.84

denoted u', equal to twice the random number drawn: $u'_1 = 2rn_1, u'_2 = 2rn_2$, etc. In fact, we will use exactly the same sample of random numbers as before, but double them. Corresponding to Table 3.1, we now have Table 3.3.

Regressing Y on X, we now obtain the equation

$$\hat{Y}_i = 1.26 + 0.58X_i. \tag{3.10}$$

This is much less accurate than its counterpart, equation (3.8).

Table 3.4 gives the results for all 10 experiments, putting $u' = 2rn$. We will call this set of experiments II and the original set, summarized in Table 3.2, I. Comparing Tables 3.2 and 3.4, you can see that the values of b_1 and b_2 are much

Table 3.4

Sample	b_1	b_2
1	1.26	0.58
2	3.05	0.45
3	2.26	0.39
4	2.28	0.50
5	1.42	0.61
6	1.61	0.52
7	1.44	0.63
8	4.37	0.33
9	0.52	0.65
10	1.88	0.55

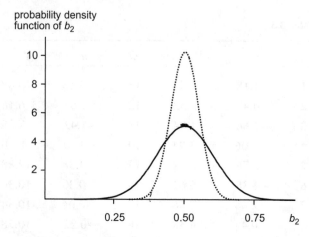

Figure 3.2 Distribution of b_2 when the standard deviation of u is doubled

more erratic in the latter, although there is still no systematic tendency either to underestimate or to overestimate.

Detailed inspection reveals an important feature. In Set I, the value of b_2 in sample 1 was 0.54, an overestimate of 0.04. In Set II, the value of b_2 in sample 1 was 0.58, an overestimate of 0.08. Exactly twice as much as before. The same is true for each of the other nine samples, and also for the regression coefficient b_1 in each sample. Doubling the disturbance term in each observation causes a doubling of the errors in the regression coefficients.

This result follows directly from the decomposition of b_2 given by (3.6). In Set I the error component of b_2 is given by $\mathrm{Cov}(X, u)/\mathrm{Var}(X)$. In Set II it is given by $\mathrm{Cov}(X, u')/\mathrm{Var}(X)$, and

$$\frac{\mathrm{Cov}(X, u')}{\mathrm{Var}(X)} = \frac{\mathrm{Cov}(X, 2u)}{\mathrm{Var}(X)} = 2\frac{\mathrm{Cov}(X, u)}{\mathrm{Var}(X)}. \tag{3.11}$$

The increase in inaccuracy is reflected in the probability density function for b_2 in Set II, shown as the solid curve in Figure 3.2. This is still centered over the true value, 0.50, but, if you compare it with that for Set I, the dotted curve, you will see that it is flatter and wider. Doubling the values of u has caused a doubling of the standard deviation of the distribution.

3.3 Assumptions concerning the disturbance term

It is thus obvious that the properties of the regression coefficients depend criti- cally on the properties of the disturbance term. Indeed the latter has to satisfy four conditions, known as the Gauss–Markov conditions, if ordinary least squares regression analysis is to give the best possible results. If they are not satisfied, the user should be aware of the fact. If remedial action is possible, he or she should be capable of taking it. If it is not possible, he or she should be able to judge how seriously the results may have been affected. We shall list the conditions one by one, explaining briefly why they are important. The last three will be treated in detail in later chapters.

Gauss–Markov condition 1: $E(u_i) = 0$ for all observations

The first condition is that the expected value of the disturbance term in any observation should be 0. Sometimes it will be positive, sometimes negative, but it should not have a systematic tendency in either direction.

Actually, if an intercept is included in the regression equation, it is usually reasonable to assume that this condition is satisfied automatically since the role of the intercept is to pick up any systematic but constant tendency in Y not accounted for by the explanatory variables included in the regression equation.

Gauss–Markov condition 2: Population variance of u_i constant for all observations

The second condition is that the population variance of the disturbance term should be constant for all observations. Sometimes the disturbance term will be greater, sometimes smaller, but there should not be any a priori reason for it to be more erratic in some observations than in others. The constant is usually denoted σ_u^2, often abbreviated to σ^2, and the condition is written

$$\sigma_{u_i}^2 = \sigma_u^2 \text{ for all } i. \tag{3.12}$$

Since $E(u_i)$ is 0, the population variance of u_i is equal to $E(u_i^2)$, so the condition can also be written

$$E(u_i^2) = \sigma_u^2 \text{ for all } i. \tag{3.13}$$

σ_u, of course, is unknown. One of the tasks of regression analysis is to estimate the standard deviation of the disturbance term.

If this condition is not satisfied, the OLS regression coefficients will be inefficient, and you should be able to obtain more reliable results by using a modification of the regression technique. This will be discussed in Chapter 8.

Gauss–Markov condition 3: u_i distributed independently of $u_j(i \neq j)$

This condition states that there should be no systematic association between the values of the disturbance term in any two observations. For example, just because the disturbance term is large and positive in one observation, there should be no tendency for it to be large and positive in the next (or large and negative, for that matter, or small and positive, or small and negative). The values of the disturbance term should be absolutely independent of one another.

The condition implies that $\sigma_{u_i u_j}$, the population covariance between u_i and u_j, is 0, because

$$\sigma_{u_i u_j} = E[(u_i - \mu_u)(u_j - \mu_u)] = E(u_i u_j)$$

$$= E(u_i)E(u_j) = 0. \qquad (3.14)$$

(Note that the population means of u_i and u_j are 0, by virtue of the first Gauss–Markov condition, and that $E(u_i u_j)$ can be decomposed as $E(u_i)E(u_j)$ if u_i and u_j are generated independently—see the Review chapter.)

If this condition is not satisfied, OLS will again give inefficient estimates. Chapter 13 discusses the problems that arise and ways of getting around them.

Gauss–Markov condition 4: *u* distributed independently of the explanatory variables

The final condition comes in two versions, weak and strong. The strong version is that the explanatory variables should be nonstochastic, that is, not have random components. This is actually very unrealistic for economic variables and we will eventually switch to the weak version of the condition, where the explanatory variables are allowed to have random components provided that they are distributed independently of the disturbance term. However, for the time being we will use the strong version because it simplifies the analysis of the properties of the estimators.

It is not easy to think of truly nonstochastic variables, other than time, so the following example is a little artificial. Suppose that we are relating earnings to schooling, S, in terms of highest grade completed. Suppose that we know from the national census that 1 percent of the population have $S = 8$, 3 percent have $S = 9$, 5 percent have $S = 10$, 7 percent have $S = 11$, 43 percent have $S = 12$ (graduation from high school), and so on. Suppose that we have decided to undertake a survey with sample size 1,000 and we want the sample to match the population as far as possible. We might then select what is known as a stratified random sample, designed so that it includes 10 individuals with $S = 8$, 30 individuals with $S = 9$, and so on. The values of S in the sample would then be predetermined and therefore nonstochastic. Schooling and other demographic variables in large surveys drawn in such a way as to be representative of the population as a whole, like the National Longitudinal Survey of Youth, probably approximate this condition quite well.

If this condition is satisfied, it follows that $\sigma_{X_i u_i}$, the population covariance between the explanatory variable and the disturbance term is 0. Since $E(u_i)$ is 0, and the term involving X is nonstochastic,

$$\sigma_{X_i u_i} = E[\{X_i - E(X_i)\}\{u_i - \mu_u\}]$$

$$= (X_i - X_i)E(u_i) = 0. \qquad (3.15)$$

Chapters 9 and 10 discuss two important cases in which this condition is unlikely to be satisfied, and the consequences.

Today:

The normality assumption

In addition to the Gauss–Markov conditions, one usually assumes that the disturbance term is normally distributed. You should know all about the normal distribution from your introductory statistics course. The reason is that if u is normally distributed, so will be the regression coefficients, and this will be useful to us later in the chapter when we come to the business of performing tests of hypotheses and constructing confidence intervals for β_1 and β_2 using the regression results.

The justification for the assumption depends on the Central Limit Theorem. In essence, this states that, if a random variable is the composite result of the effects of a large number of other random variables, it will have an approximately normal distribution even if its components do not, provided that none of them is dominant. The disturbance term u is composed of a number of factors not appearing explicitly in the regression equation so, even if we know nothing about the distribution of these factors (or even their identity), we are entitled to assume that it is normally distributed.

3.4 Unbiasedness of the regression coefficients

From (3.6) we can show that b_2 must be an unbiased estimator of β_2 if the fourth Gauss–Markov condition is satisfied:

$$E(b_2) = E\left[\beta_2 + \frac{\text{Cov}(X,u)}{\text{Var}(X)}\right] = \beta_2 + E\left[\frac{\text{Cov}(X,u)}{\text{Var}(X)}\right] \tag{3.16}$$

since β_2 is a constant. If we adopt the strong version of the fourth Gauss–Markov condition and assume that X is nonrandom, we may also take $\text{Var}(X)$ as a given constant, and so

$$E(b_2) = \beta_2 + \frac{1}{\text{Var}(X)}E[\text{Cov}(X,u)]. \tag{3.17}$$

We will demonstrate that $E[\text{Cov}(X,u)]$ is 0:

$$E[\text{Cov}(X,u)] = E\left[\frac{1}{n}\sum_{i=1}^{n}(X_i-\bar{X})(u_i-\bar{u})\right]$$

$$= \frac{1}{n}(E[X_1-\bar{X})(u_1-\bar{u})] + \cdots + E[(X_n-\bar{X})(u_n-\bar{u})])$$

$$= \frac{1}{n}\sum_{i=1}^{n}E[(X_i-\bar{X})(u_i-\bar{u})]$$

$$= \frac{1}{n}\sum_{i=1}^{n}(X_i-\bar{X})E(u_i-\bar{u}) = 0. \tag{3.18}$$

In the second line, the second expected value rule has been used to bring $(1/n)$ out of the expression as a common factor, and the first rule has been used to break up the expectation of the sum into the sum of the expectations. In the fourth line, the term involving X has been brought out because X is nonstochastic. By virtue of the first Gauss–Markov condition, $E(u_i)$ is 0 , and hence $E(\bar{u})$ is also 0. Therefore $E[\text{Cov}(X, u)]$ is 0 and

$$E(b_2) = \beta_2. \tag{3.19}$$

In other words, b_2 is an unbiased estimator of β_2. We can obtain the same result with the weak version of the fourth Gauss–Markov condition (allowing X to have a random component but assuming that it is distributed independently of u); this is demonstrated in Chapter 9.

Unless the random factor in the n observations happens to cancel out exactly, which can happen only by coincidence, b_2 will be different from β_2 for any given sample, but in view of (3.19) there will be no systematic tendency for it to be either higher or lower. The same is true for the regression coefficient b_1. Using equation (2.31),

$$b_1 = \bar{Y} - b_2\bar{X}. \tag{3.20}$$

Hence

$$E(b_1) = E(\bar{Y}) - \bar{X}E(b_2). \tag{3.21}$$

Since Y_i is determined by

$$Y_i = \beta_1 + \beta_2 X_i + u_i \tag{3.22}$$

we have

$$E(Y_i) = \overline{\beta_1 + \beta_2 X_i} + E(u_i)$$
$$= \beta_1 + \beta_2 X_i \tag{3.23}$$

because $E(u_i)$ is 0 if the first Gauss–Markov condition is satisfied. Hence

$$E(\bar{Y}) = \beta_1 + \beta_2\bar{X}. \tag{3.24}$$

Substituting this into (3.21), and using the result that $E(b_2) = \beta_2$,

$$E(b_1) = (\beta_1 + \beta_2\bar{X}) - \bar{X}\beta_2 = \beta_1. \tag{3.25}$$

Thus b_1 is an unbiased estimator of β_1 provided that Gauss–Markov conditions 1 and 4 are satisfied. Of course in any given sample the random factor will cause b_1 to differ from β_1.

3.5 Precision of the regression coefficients

Now we shall consider $\sigma_{b_1}^2$ and $\sigma_{b_2}^2$, the population variances of b_1 and b_2 about their population means. These are given by the following expressions (proofs for equivalent expressions can be found in Thomas, 1983, Section 8.3.3):

$$\sigma_{b_1}^2 = \frac{\sigma_u^2}{n}\left[1 + \frac{\bar{X}^2}{\text{Var}(X)}\right] \quad \text{and} \quad \sigma_{b_2}^2 = \frac{\sigma_u^2}{n\text{Var}(X)}. \tag{3.26}$$

Equation (3.26) has three obvious implications. First, the variances of both b_1 and b_2 are directly inversely proportional to the number of observations in the sample. This makes good sense. The more information you have, the more accurate your estimates are likely to be.

Second, the variances are proportional to the variance of the disturbance term. The bigger the variance of the random factor in the relationship, the worse the estimates of the parameters are likely to be, other things being equal. This is illustrated graphically in Figures 3.3a and 3.3b. In both diagrams the nonstochastic component of the relationship between Y and X, depicted by the dotted line, is given by

$$Y_i = 3.0 + 0.8X_i. \tag{3.27}$$

There are twenty observations, with the values of X being the integers from 1 to 20. The same random numbers are used to generate the values of the disturbance term, but those in Figure 3.3b have been multiplied by a factor of 5. As a consequence the regression line, depicted by the solid line, is a much poorer approximation to the nonstochastic relationship in Figure 3.3b than in Figure 3.3a.

Third, the variance of the regression coefficients is inversely related to the variance of X. What is the reason for this? Remember that (1) the regression coefficients are calculated on the assumption that the observed variations in Y are due to variations in X, but (2) they are in reality *partly* due to variations in X and *partly* to variations in u. The smaller the variance of X, the greater is likely to be the relative influence of the random factor in determining the variations in Y and the more likely is regression analysis to give inaccurate estimates. This is illustrated by Figures 3.4a and 3.4b. The nonstochastic component of the relationship is given by (3.27), and the disturbance terms are identical. In Figure 3.4a the values of X are the integers from 1 to 20. In Figure 3.4b, the values of X are the numbers 9.1, 9.2, ..., 10.9, 11. In Figure 3.4a, the variance in X is responsible for most of the variance in Y and the relationship between the two variables can be determined relatively accurately. However, in Figure 3.4b, the variance of X is so small that it is overwhelmed by the effect of the variance of u. As a consequence its effect is difficult to pick out and the estimates of the regression coefficients will be relatively inaccurate.

Of course, Figures 3.3 and 3.4 make the same point in different ways. As can be seen from (3.26), it is the *relative* size of σ_u^2 and $\text{Var}(X)$ that is important, rather than the *actual* size of either.

In practice, one cannot calculate the population variances of either b_1 or b_2 because σ_u^2 is unknown. However, we can derive an estimator of σ_u^2 from the residuals. Clearly the scatter of the residuals around the regression line will reflect the unseen scatter of u about the line $Y_i = \beta_1 + \beta_2X_i$, although in general the

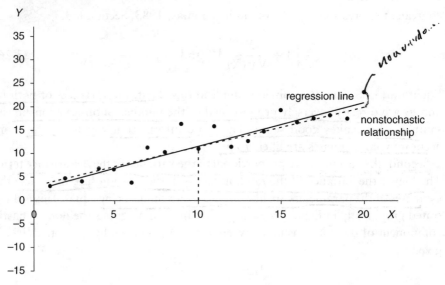

Figure 3.3a Disturbance term with relatively small variance

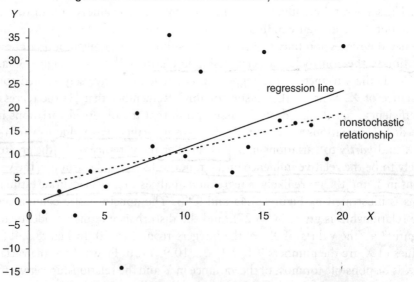

Figure 3.3b Disturbance term with relatively large variance

residual and the value of the disturbance term in any given observation are not equal to one another. Hence the sample variance of the residuals, Var(e), which we can measure, will be a guide to σ_u^2, which we cannot.

Before going any further, ask yourself the following question. Which line is likely to be closer to the points representing the sample of observations on X and Y, the true line $Y_i = \beta_1 + \beta_2 X_i$ or the regression line $\hat{Y}_i = b_1 + b_2 X_i$? The answer is the regression line, because by definition it is drawn in such a way as to minimize the sum of the squares of the distances between it and the observations. Hence the spread of the residuals will tend to be smaller than the spread of the

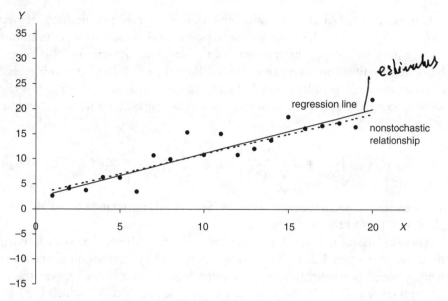

Figure 3.4a *X* with relatively large variance

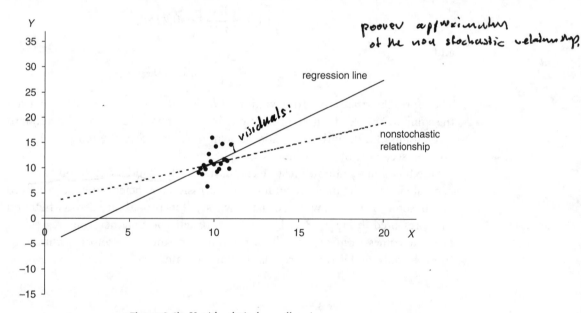

Figure 3.4b *X* with relatively small variance

values of u, and $\text{Var}(e)$ will tend to underestimate σ_u^2. Indeed, it can be shown that the expected value of $\text{Var}(e)$, when there is just one explanatory variable, is $[(n-2)/n]\,\sigma_u^2$. However, it follows that, if one defines s_u^2 by

$$s_u^2 = \frac{n}{n-2}\text{Var}(e),\tag{3.28}$$

s_u^2 will be an unbiased estimator of σ_u^2 (for a proof, see Thomas).

Using (3.26) and (3.28), one can obtain estimates of the population variances of b_1 and b_2 and, by taking square roots, estimates of their standard deviations. Rather than talk about the 'estimate of the standard deviation of the probability density function' of a regression coefficient, which is a bit cumbersome, one uses the term 'standard error' of a regression coefficient, which in this text will frequently be abbreviated to s.e. For simple regression analysis, therefore, one has

$$\text{s.e.}(b_1) = \sqrt{\frac{s_u^2}{n}\left[1 + \frac{\bar{X}^2}{\text{Var}(X)}\right]} \quad \text{and} \quad \text{s.e.}(b_2) = \sqrt{\frac{s_u^2}{n\text{Var}(X)}}. \tag{3.29}$$

The standard errors of the regression coefficients will automatically be calculated for you as part of the computer output.

These relationships will be illustrated with the Monte Carlo experiment described in Section 3.2. In Set I, u was determined by random numbers drawn from a population with 0 mean and unit variance, so $\sigma_u^2 = 1$. X was the set of numbers from 1 to 20, and one can easily calculate $\text{Var}(X)$, which is 33.25. Hence

$$\sigma_{b_1}^2 = \frac{1}{20}\left[1 + \frac{10.5^2}{33.25}\right] = 0.2158, \tag{3.30}$$

and

$$\sigma_{b_2}^2 = \frac{1}{20 \times 33.25} = 0.001504. \tag{3.31}$$

Therefore, the true standard deviation of b_2 is $\sqrt{0.001504} = 0.039$. What did the computer make of it in the 10 samples in Set I? It has to calculate the standard error using (3.29), with the results shown in Table 3.5 in the ten samples. As you can see, most of the estimates are quite good.

One fundamental point must be emphasized. The standard error gives only a general guide to the likely accuracy of a regression coefficient. It enables you to obtain some idea of the width, or narrowness, of its probability density function as represented in Figure 3.1, but it does *not* tell you whether your regression estimate comes from the middle of the function, and is therefore accurate, or from the tails, and is therefore relatively inaccurate.

Table 3.5

Sample	s.e.(b_2)	Sample	s.e.(b_2)
1	0.043	6	0.044
2	0.041	7	0.039
3	0.038	8	0.040
4	0.035	9	0.033
5	0.027	10	0.033

The higher the variance of the disturbance term, the higher the sample variance of the residuals is likely to be, and hence the higher will be the standard errors of the coefficients in the regression equation, reflecting the risk that the coefficients are inaccurate. However, it is only a *risk*. It is possible that in any particular sample the effects of the disturbance term in the different observations will cancel each other out and the regression coefficients will be accurate after all. The trouble is that in general there is no way of telling whether you happen to be in this fortunate position or not.

Exercises

Where performance on a game of skill is measured numerically, the improvement that comes with practice is called a learning curve. This is especially obvious with some arcade-type games. The first time players try a new one, they are likely to score very little. With more attempts, their scores should gradually improve as they become accustomed to the game, although obviously there will

Observation	X	u	Y
1	0	−236	264
2	1	−96	504
3	2	−332	368
4	3	12	812
5	4	−152	748
6	5	−876	124
7	6	412	1,512
8	7	96	1,296
9	8	1,012	2,312
10	9	−52	1,348
11	10	636	2,136
12	11	−368	1,232
13	12	−284	1,416
14	13	−100	1,700
15	14	676	2,576
16	15	60	2,060
17	16	8	2,108
18	17	−44	2,156
19	18	−364	1,936
20	19	568	2,968

be variations caused by the luck factor. Suppose that their scores are determined by the learning curve

$$Y_i = 500 + 100X_i + u_i,$$

where Y is the score, X is the number of times that they have played before, and u is a disturbance term.

The table gives the results of the first twenty games of a new player: X automatically goes from 0 to 19; u was set equal to 400 times the numbers generated by a normally distributed random variable with 0 mean and unit variance; and Y was determined by X and u according to the learning curve.

Regressing Y on X, one obtains the equation (standard errors in parentheses):

$$\hat{Y} = 369 + 116.8X.$$
$$(190) \quad (17.1)$$

3.1 Why is the constant in this equation not equal to 500 and the coefficient of X not equal to 100?

3.2 What is the meaning of the standard errors?

3.3 The experiment is repeated with nine other new players (the disturbance term being generated by 400 times a different set of twenty random numbers in each case), and the regression results for all ten players are shown in the table. Why do the constant, the coefficient of X, and the standard errors vary from sample to sample?

Player	Constant	Standard error of constant	Coefficient of X	Standard error of coefficient of X
1	369	190	116.8	17.1
2	699	184	90.1	16.5
3	531	169	78.5	15.2
4	555	158	99.5	14.2
5	407	120	122.6	10.8
6	427	194	104.3	17.5
7	412	175	123.8	15.8
8	613	192	95.8	17.3
9	234	146	130.1	13.1
10	485	146	109.6	13.1

3.4 The variance of X is equal to 33.25 and the population variance of u is equal to 160,000. Using equation (3.29), show that the standard deviation of the probability density function of the coefficient of X is equal to 15.5. Are the standard errors in the table good estimates of this standard deviation?

3.6 **The Gauss–Markov theorem**

In the Review, we considered estimators of the unknown population mean μ of a random variable X, given a sample of observations. Although we instinctively use the sample mean $\bar{X}$ as our estimator, we saw that it was only one of an infinite number of possible unbiased estimators of μ. The reason that the sample mean is preferred to any other estimator is that, under certain assumptions, it is the most efficient.

Similar considerations apply to regression coefficients. We shall see that the OLS estimators are not the only unbiased estimators of the regression coefficients, but, provided that the Gauss–Markov conditions are satisfied, they are the most efficient. The other side of the coin is that, if the Gauss–Markov conditions are *not* satisfied, it will in general be possible to find estimators that are more efficient than OLS.

We will not attempt a general discussion of these issues here. We will instead give an illustration. We shall assume that we have a relationship given by

$$Y_i = \beta_1 + \beta_2 X_i + u_i,\tag{3.32}$$

and we shall confine our attention to estimators of β_2. Someone who had never heard of regression analysis, on seeing a scatter diagram of a sample of observations, might be tempted to obtain an estimate of the slope merely by joining the first and the last observations, and by dividing the increase in the height by the horizontal distance between them, as in Figure 3.5. The estimator b_2 would then be given by

$$b_2 = \frac{Y_n - Y_1}{X_n - X_1}.\tag{3.33}$$

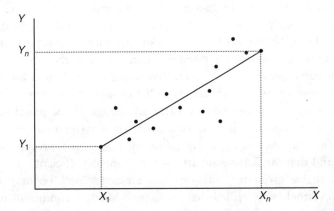

Figure 3.5 Naïve estimation of b_2

What are the properties of this estimator? First, we will investigate whether it is biased or unbiased. Applying (3.32) to the first and last observations, we have

$$Y_1 = \beta_1 + \beta_2 X_1 + u_1 \tag{3.34}$$

and

$$Y_n = \beta_1 + \beta_2 X_n + u_n. \tag{3.35}$$

Hence

$$b_2 = \frac{\beta_2 X_n + u_n - \beta_2 X_1 - u_1}{X_n - X_1}$$

$$= \beta_2 + \frac{u_n - u_1}{X_n - X_1}. \tag{3.36}$$

Thus we have decomposed this naïve estimator into two components, the true value and an error term. This decomposition is parallel to that for the OLS estimator in Section 3.1, but the error term is different. The expected value of the estimator is given by

$$E(b_2) = E(\beta_2) + E\left[\frac{u_n - u_1}{X_n - X_1}\right]$$

$$= \beta_2 + \frac{1}{X_n - X_1} E(u_n - u_1), \tag{3.37}$$

since β_2 is a constant and X_1 and X_n are nonstochastic. If the first Gauss–Markov condition is satisfied,

$$E(u_n - u_1) = E(u_n) - E(u_1) = 0. \tag{3.38}$$

Therefore, despite being naïve, this estimator is unbiased.

This is not by any means the only estimator besides OLS that is unbiased. You could derive one by joining any two arbitrarily selected observations, and in fact the possibilities are infinite if you are willing to consider less naïve procedures.

It is intuitively easy to see that we would not prefer a naïve estimator such as (3.33) to OLS. Unlike OLS, which takes account of every observation, it employs only the first and the last and is wasting most of the information in the sample. The naïve estimator will be sensitive to the value of the disturbance term u in those two observations, whereas the OLS estimator combines all the values of the disturbance term and takes greater advantage of the possibility that to some extent they cancel each other out. More rigorously, it can be shown that the population variance of the naïve estimator is greater than that of the OLS estimator, and that the naïve estimator is therefore less efficient.

With less naïve estimators the superior efficiency of OLS may not be so obvious. Nevertheless, provided that the Gauss–Markov conditions for the disturbance term are satisfied, the OLS regression coefficients will be best linear unbiased estimators (BLUE): unbiased, as has already been demonstrated; linear, because they are linear functions of the values of Y; and best because they are the most efficient of the class of unbiased linear estimators. This is proved by the Gauss–Markov theorem (for a concise treatment not using matrix algebra, see Johnston and Dinardo, 1997).

Exercises

3.5 An investigator correctly believes that the relationship between two variables X and Y is given by

$$Y_i = \beta_1 + \beta_2 X_i + u_i.$$

Given a sample of n observations, the investigator estimates β_2 by calculating it as the average value of Y divided by the average value of X. Discuss the properties of this estimator. What difference would it make if it could be assumed that β_1 is equal to 0?

3.6* An investigator correctly believes that the relationship between two variables X and Y is given by

$$Y_i = \beta_1 + \beta_2 X_i + u_i.$$

Given a sample of observations on Y, X and a third variable Z (which is not a determinant of Y), the investigator estimates β_2 as $\text{Cov}(Y, Z)/\text{Cov}(X, Z)$. Discuss the properties of this estimator. (It can be shown that its population variance is equal to the population variance of the corresponding OLS estimator divided by the square of r_{XZ}, where r_{XZ} is the correlation coefficient for X and Z.)

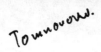
PParsham

3.7 **Testing hypotheses relating to the regression coefficients**

Which comes first, theoretical hypothesizing or empirical research? This is a bit like asking which came first, the chicken or the egg. In practice, theorizing and experimentation feed on each other, and questions of this type cannot be answered. For this reason, we will approach the topic of hypothesis testing from both directions. On the one hand, we may suppose that the theory has come first and that the purpose of the experiment is to evaluate its plausibility. This will lead to the execution of significance tests. Alternatively, we may perform the experiment first and then consider what theoretical hypotheses would be consistent with the results. This will lead to the construction of confidence intervals.

You will already have encountered the logic underlying significance tests and confidence intervals in an introductory statistics course. You will thus be familiar with most of the concepts in the following applications to regression analysis. There is, however, one topic that may be new: the use of one-tailed tests. Such tests are used very frequently in regression analysis. Indeed, they are, or they ought to be, more common than the traditional textbook two-tailed tests. It is therefore important that you understand the rationale for their use, and this involves a sequence of small analytical steps. None of this should present any difficulty, but be warned that, if you attempt to use a short cut or, worse, try to reduce the whole business to the mechanical use of a few formulae, you will be asking for trouble.

important

Formulation of a null hypothesis

We will start by assuming that the theory precedes the experiment and that you have some hypothetical relationship in your mind. For example, you may believe that the percentage rate of price inflation in an economy, p, depends on the percentage rate of wage inflation, w, according to the linear equation

$$p = \beta_1 + \beta_2 w + u, \tag{3.39}$$

where β_1 and β_2 are parameters and u is a disturbance term. You might further hypothesize that, apart from the effects of the disturbance term, price inflation is equal to wage inflation. Under these circumstances you would say that the hypothesis that you are going to test, known as your *null hypothesis* and denoted H_0, is that β_2 is equal to 1. We also define an *alternative hypothesis*, denoted H_1, which represents your conclusion if the experimental test indicates that H_0 is false. In the present case H_1 is simply that β_2 is not equal to 1. The two hypotheses are stated using the notation

$$H_0: \quad \beta_2 = 1$$
$$H_1: \quad \beta_2 \neq 1.$$

In this particular case, if we really believe that price inflation is equal to wage inflation, we are trying to establish the credibility of H_0 by subjecting it to the strictest possible test and hoping that it emerges unscathed. In practice, however, it is more usual to set up a null hypothesis and attack it with the objective of establishing the alternative hypothesis as the correct conclusion. For example, consider the simple earnings function

$$EARNINGS = \beta_1 + \beta_2 S + u, \tag{3.40}$$

where $EARNINGS$ is hourly earnings in dollars and S is years of schooling. On very reasonable theoretical grounds, you expect earnings to be dependent on schooling, but your theory is not strong enough to enable you to specify a particular value for β_2. You can nevertheless establish the dependence of earnings on schooling by the inverse procedure in which you take as your null hypothesis the assertion that earnings does *not* depend on schooling, that is, that β_2 is 0. Your alternative hypothesis is that β_2 is not equal to 0, that is, that schooling *does* affect earnings. If you can reject the null hypothesis, you have established the relationship, at least in general terms. Using the conventional notation, your null and alternative hypotheses are H_0: $\beta_2 = 0$ and H_1: $\beta_2 \neq 0$, respectively.

The following discussion uses the simple regression model

$$Y_i = \beta_1 + \beta_2 X_i + u_i. \tag{3.41}$$

It will be confined to the slope coefficient, β_2, but exactly the same procedures are applied to the constant term, β_1. We will take the general case, where you have defined a null hypothesis that β_2 is equal to some specific value, say β_2^0 and the alternative hypothesis is that β_2 is not equal to this value (H_0: $\beta_2 = \beta_2^0$, H_1: $\beta_2 \neq \beta_2^0$); you may be attempting to attack or defend the null hypothesis as it suits your purpose. We will assume that the four Gauss–Markov conditions are satisfied.

Developing the implications of a hypothesis

If H_0 is correct, values of b_2 obtained using regression analysis in repeated samples will be distributed with mean β_2^0 and variance $\sigma_u^2/[n\,\text{Var}(X)]$ (see 3.26). We will now introduce the assumption that u has a normal distribution. If this is the case, b_2 will also be normally distributed, as shown in Figure 3.6. 'sd' in the figure refers to the standard deviation of b_2, that is $\sqrt{\sigma_u^2/[n\,\text{Var}(X)]}$. In view of the structure of the normal distribution, most values of b_2 will lie within two standard deviations of β_2^0 (if H_0: $\beta_2 = \beta_2^0$ is true).

Initially we will assume that we know the standard deviation of the distribution of b_2. This is a most unreasonable assumption, and we will drop it later. In

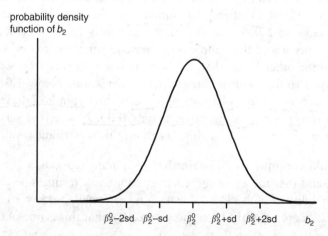

probability density function of b_2

$\beta_2^0-2\text{sd}$ $\beta_2^0-\text{sd}$ β_2^0 $\beta_2^0+\text{sd}$ $\beta_2^0+2\text{sd}$ b_2

Figure 3.6 Structure of the normal distribution of b_2 in terms of standard deviations about the mean

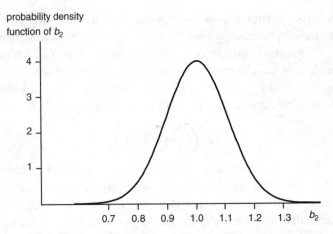

Figure 3.7 Example distribution of b_2 (price inflation/wage inflation model)

practice we have to estimate it, along with β_1 and β_2, but it will simplify the discussion if for the time being we suppose that we know it exactly, and hence are in a position to draw Figure 3.6.

We will illustrate this with the price inflation/wage inflation model (3.39). Suppose that for some reason we know that the standard deviation of b_2 is equal to 0.1. Then, if our null hypothesis H_0: $\beta_2 = 1$ is correct, regression estimates would be distributed as shown in Figure 3.7. You can see that, provided that the null hypothesis is correct, the estimates will generally lie between 0.8 and 1.2.

Compatibility, freakiness, and the significance level

Now we come to the crunch. Suppose that we take an actual sample of observations on average rates of price inflation and wage inflation over the past five years for a sample of countries and estimate β_2 using regression analysis. If the estimate is close to 1.0, we should almost certainly be satisfied with the null hypothesis, since it and the sample result are compatible with one another, but suppose, on the other hand, that the estimate is a long way from 1.0. Suppose that it is equal to 0.7. This is three standard deviations below 1.0. If the null hypothesis is correct, the probability of b_2 being three standard deviations away from the mean, positive or negative, is only 0.0027, which is very low. You could come to either of two conclusions about this worrisome result:

1. You could continue to maintain that your null hypothesis H_0: $\beta_2 = 1$ is correct, and that the experiment has given a freak result. You concede that the probability of such a low value of b_2 is very small, but nevertheless it does occur 0.27 percent of the time and you reckon that this is one of those times.

2. You could conclude that the hypothesis is contradicted by the regression result. You are not convinced by the explanation in (1) because the probability

is so small and you think that a much more likely explanation is that β_2 is not really equal to 1. In other words, you adopt the alternative hypothesis $H_1: \beta_2 \neq 1$ instead.

How do you decide when to choose (1) and when to choose (2)? Obviously, the smaller the probability of obtaining a regression estimate such as the one you have obtained, given your hypothesis, the more likely you are to abandon the hypothesis and choose (2). How small should the probability be before choosing (2)?

There is, and there can be, no definite answer to this question. In most applied work in economics either 5 percent or 1 percent is taken as the critical limit. If 5 percent is taken, the switch to (2) is made when the null hypothesis implies that the probability of obtaining such an extreme value of b_2 is less than 5 percent. The null hypothesis is then said to be rejected at the 5 percent significance level.

This occurs when b_2 is more than 1.96 standard deviations from β_2^0. If you look up the normal distribution table, Table A.1 at the end of the text, you will see that the probability of b_2 being more than 1.96 standard deviations above its mean is 2.5 percent, and similarly the probability of it being more than 1.96 standard deviations below its mean is 2.5 percent. The total probability of it being more than 1.96 standard deviations away is thus 5 percent.

We can summarize this decision rule mathematically by saying that we will reject the null hypothesis if

$$z > 1.96 \quad \text{or} \quad z < -1.96, \tag{3.42}$$

where z is the number of standard deviations between the regression estimate and the hypothetical value of β_2:

$$z = \frac{\text{distance between regression estimate and hypothetical value}}{\text{standard deviation of } b_2} = \frac{b_2 - \beta_2^0}{\text{s.d.}(b_2)}. \tag{3.43}$$

The null hypothesis will not be rejected if

$$-1.96 \leq z \leq 1.96. \tag{3.44}$$

This condition can be expressed in terms of b_2 and β_2^0 by substituting for z from (3.43):

$$-1.96 \leq \frac{b_2 - \beta_2^0}{\text{s.d.}(b_2)} \leq 1.96. \tag{3.45}$$

Multiplying through by the standard deviation of b_2, one obtains

$$-1.96 \, \text{s.d.}(b_2) \leq b_2 - \beta_2^0 \leq 1.96 \, \text{s.d.}(b_2) \tag{3.46}$$

from which one obtains

$$\beta_2^0 - 1.96 \, \text{s.d.}(b_2) \leq b_2 \leq \beta_2^0 + 1.96 \, \text{s.d.}(b_2). \tag{3.47}$$

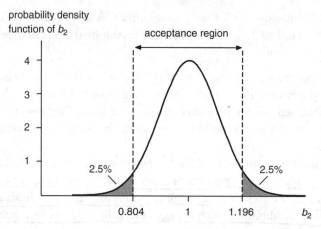

Figure 3.8 Acceptance region for b_2, 5 percent significance level

Equation (3.47) gives the set of values of b_2 which will not lead to the rejection of a specific null hypothesis $\beta_2 = \beta_2^0$. It is known as the *acceptance region* for b_2, at the 5 percent significance level.

In the case of the price inflation/wage inflation example, where s.d.(b_2) is equal to 0.1, you would reject at the 5 percent level if b_2 lies more than 0.196 above or below the hypothetical mean, that is, above 1.196 or below 0.804. The acceptance region is therefore those values of b_2 from 0.804 to 1.196. This is illustrated by the unshaded area in Figure 3.8.

Similarly, the null hypothesis is said to be rejected at the 1 percent significance level if the hypothesis implies that the probability of obtaining such an extreme value of b_2 is less than 1 percent. This occurs when b_2 is more than 2.58 standard deviations above or below the hypothetical value of β_2, that is, when

$$z > 2.58 \quad \text{or} \quad z < -2.58. \tag{3.48}$$

Looking at the normal distribution table again, you will see that the probability of b_2 being more than 2.58 standard deviations above its mean is 0.5 percent, and there is the same probability of it being more than 2.58 standard deviations below it, so the combined probability of such an extreme value is 1 percent. In the case of our example, you would reject the null hypothesis $\beta_2 = 1$ if the regression estimate lay above 1.258 or below 0.742.

You may ask, why do people usually report, or at least consider reporting, the results at both the 5 percent and the 1 percent significance levels? Why not just one? The answer is that they are trying to strike a balance between the risks of making Type I errors and Type II errors. *A Type I error occurs when you reject a true null hypothesis. A Type II error occurs when you do not reject a false one.*

Obviously, the lower your critical probability, the smaller is the risk of a Type I error. If your significance level is 5 percent, you will reject a true hypothesis 5 percent of the time. If it is 1 percent, you will make a Type I error 1 percent

---

BOX 3.1   **Type I and Type II errors in everyday life**

The problem of trying to avoid Type I and Type II errors will already be familiar to everybody. A criminal trial provides a particularly acute example. Taking as the null hypothesis that the defendant is innocent, Type I error occurs when the jury wrongly decides that the defendant is guilty. A Type II error occurs when the jury wrongly acquits the defendant.

---

of the time. Thus the 1 percent significance level is safer in this respect. If you reject the hypothesis at this level, you are almost certainly right to do so. For this reason the 1 percent significance level is described as *higher* than the 5 percent.

At the same time, if the null hypothesis happens to be false, the higher your significance level, the wider is your acceptance region, the greater is your chance of not rejecting it, and so the greater is the risk of a Type II error. Thus you are caught between the devil and the deep blue sea. If you insist on a very high significance level, you incur a relatively high risk of a Type II error if the null hypothesis happens to be false. If you choose a low significance level, you run a relatively high risk of making a Type I error if the null hypothesis happens to be true.

Most people take out an insurance policy and perform the test at both these levels, being prepared to quote the results of each. Actually, it is frequently superfluous to quote both results explicitly. Since b_2 has to be more extreme for the hypothesis to be rejected at the 1 percent level than at the 5 percent level, if you reject at the 1 percent level it automatically follows that you reject at the 5 percent level, and there is no need to say so. Indeed, you look ignorant if you do. And if you do not reject at the 5 percent level, it automatically follows that you will not reject at the 1 percent level, and again you would look ignorant if you said so. The only time when you should quote both results is when you reject the null hypothesis at the 5 percent level but not at the 1 percent level.

What happens if the standard deviation of b_2 is not known

So far we have assumed that the standard deviation of b_2 is known, which is most unlikely in practice. It has to be estimated by the standard error of b_2, given by (3.29). This causes two modifications to the test procedure. First, z is now defined using s.e.(b_2) instead of s.d.(b_2), and it is referred to as the t statistic:

$$t = \frac{b_2 - \beta_2^0}{\text{s.e.}(b_2)}. \tag{3.49}$$

Second, the critical levels of t depend upon what is known as a t distribution instead of a normal distribution. We will not go into the reasons for this, or even describe the t distribution mathematically. Suffice to say that it is a cousin of the normal distribution, its exact shape depending on the number of degrees of freedom in the regression, and that it approximates the normal distribution increasingly closely as the number of degrees of freedom increases. You will certainly have encountered the t distribution in your introductory statistics course. Table A.2 at the end of the text gives the critical values of t cross-classified by significance level and the number of degrees of freedom.

The estimation of each parameter in a regression equation consumes one degree of freedom in the sample. Hence the number of degrees of freedom is equal to the number of observations in the sample minus the number of parameters estimated. The parameters are the constant (assuming that this is specified in the regression model) and the coefficients of the explanatory variables. In the present case of simple regression analysis, only two parameters, β_1 and β_2, are estimated and hence the number of degrees of freedom is $n - 2$. It should be emphasized that a more general expression will be required when we come to multiple regression analysis.

The critical value of t, which we will denote t_{crit}, replaces the number 1.96 in (3.45), so the condition that a regression estimate should not lead to the rejection of a null hypothesis $H_0: \beta_2 = \beta_2^0$ is

$$-t_{\text{crit}} \leq \frac{b_2 - \beta_2^0}{\text{s.e.}(b_2)} \leq t_{\text{crit}}. \tag{3.50}$$

Hence we have the decision rule: reject H_0 if $\left|\frac{b_2 - \beta_2^0}{\text{s.e.}(b_2)}\right| > t_{\text{crit}}$, do not reject if $\left|\frac{b_2 - \beta_2^0}{\text{s.e.}(b_2)}\right| \leq t_{\text{crit}}$, where $\left|\frac{b_2 - \beta_2^0}{\text{s.e.}(b_2)}\right|$ is the absolute value (numerical value, neglecting the sign) of t.

Examples

Table 3.6

```
. reg EARNINGS S
      Source |       SS          df        MS                Number of obs =      570
-------------+------------------------------              F(  1,    568) =    65.64
       Model |  3977.38016       1   3977.38016           Prob > F        =   0.0000
    Residual |  34419.6569     568   60.5979875           R-squared       =   0.1036
-------------+------------------------------              Adj R-squared   =   0.1020
       Total |  38397.0371     569   67.4816117           Root MSE        =   7.7845


    EARNINGS |      Coef.   Std. Err.      t     P>|t|      [95% Conf. Interval]
-------------+----------------------------------------------------------------
           S |   1.073055   .1324501    8.102   0.000      .8129028    1.333206
       _cons |  -1.391004   1.820305   -0.764   0.445     -4.966354    2.184347
```

In Section 2.6 hourly earnings were regressed on years of schooling using data from the United States National Longitudinal Survey of Youth with the output shown in Table 3.6. The first two columns give the names of the variables, here just S and the intercept (Stata denotes this as _cons) and the estimates of their coefficients. The third column gives the corresponding standard errors. Let us suppose that one of the purposes of the regression was to confirm our intuition that earnings are affected by education. Accordingly, we set up the null hypothesis that β_2 is equal to 0 and try to refute it. The corresponding t statistic, using (3.49), is simply the estimate of the coefficient divided by its standard error:

$$t = \frac{b_2 - \beta_2^0}{\text{s.e.}(b_2)} = \frac{b_2 - 0}{\text{s.e.}(b_2)} = \frac{1.0731}{0.1325} = 8.10. \tag{3.51}$$

Since there are 570 observations in the sample and we have estimated two parameters, the number of degrees of freedom is 568. Table A.2 does not give the critical values of t for 568 degrees of freedom, but we know that they must be lower than the corresponding critical values for 500, since the critical value is inversely related to the number of degrees of freedom. The critical value with 500 degrees of freedom at the 5 percent level is 1.965. Hence we can be sure that we would reject H_0 at the 5 percent level with 568 degrees of freedom and we conclude that schooling does affect earnings.

To put this test into words, with 568 degrees of freedom the upper and lower 2.5 percent tails of the t distribution start approximately 1.965 standard deviations above and below its mean of 0. The null hypothesis will not be rejected if the regression coefficient is estimated to lie within 1.965 standard deviations of 0. In this case, however, the discrepancy is equivalent to 8.10 estimated standard deviations and we come to the conclusion that the regression result contradicts the null hypothesis.

Of course, since we are using the 5 percent significance level as the basis for the test, there is in principle a 5 percent risk of a Type I error, if the null hypothesis is true. In this case we could reduce the risk to 1 percent by using the 1 percent significance level instead. The critical value of t at the 1 percent significance level with 500 degrees of freedom is 2.586. Since the t statistic is greater than this, we see that we can easily reject the null hypothesis at this level as well.

Note that when the 5 percent and 1 percent tests lead to the same conclusion, there is no need to report both, and indeed you would look ignorant if you did. Read carefully Box 3.3 on reporting test results.

This procedure of establishing a relationship between a dependent and an explanatory variable by setting up, and then refuting, a null hypothesis that β_2 is equal to 0 is used very frequently indeed. Consequently all serious regression applications automatically print out the t statistic for this special case, that is, the coefficient divided by its standard error. The ratio is often denoted 'the' t statistic. In the regression output, the t statistics for the constant and slope coefficient appear in the middle column.

> ### BOX 3.2   The reject/fail-to-reject terminology
>
> In this section it has been shown that you should reject the null hypothesis if the absolute value of the t statistic is greater than t_{crit}, and that you fail to reject it otherwise. Why 'fail to reject', which is a clumsy expression? Would it not be better just to say that you accept the hypothesis if the absolute value of the t statistic is less than t_{crit}?
>
> The argument against using the term accept is that you might find yourself 'accepting' several mutually exclusive hypotheses at the same time. For instance, in the price inflation/wage inflation example, you would not reject a null hypothesis $H_0: \beta_2 = 0.9$, or a null hypothesis $H_0: \beta_2 = 0.8$. It is logical to say that you would not reject these null hypotheses, as well as the null hypothesis $H_0: \beta_2 = 1$ discussed in the text, but it makes little sense to say that you simultaneously accept all three hypotheses. In the next section you will see that one can define a whole range of hypotheses which would not be rejected by a given experimental result, so it would be incautious to pick out one as being 'accepted'.

However, if the null hypothesis specifies some nonzero value of β_2, the more general expression (3.50) has to be used and the t statistic has to be calculated by hand. For example, consider again the price inflation/wage inflation model (3.39) and suppose that the fitted model is (standard errors in parentheses):

$$\hat{p} = -1.21 + 0.82w.$$
$$(0.05) \quad (0.10) \tag{3.52}$$

If we now investigate the hypothesis that price inflation is equal to wage inflation, our null hypothesis is that the coefficient of w is equal to 1.0. The corresponding t statistic is

$$t = \frac{b_2 - \beta_2^0}{\text{s.e.}(b_2)} = \frac{0.82 - 1.00}{0.10} = -1.80. \tag{3.53}$$

If there are, say, twenty observations in the sample, the number of degrees of freedom is 18 and the critical value of t at the 5 percent significance level is 2.101. The absolute value of our t statistic is less than this, so on this occasion we do not reject the null hypothesis. The estimate 0.82 is below our hypothesized value 1.00, but not so far below as to exclude the possibility that the null hypothesis is correct. One final note on reporting regression results: some writers place the t statistic in parentheses under a coefficient, instead of the standard error. You should be careful to check, and when you are presenting results yourself, you should make it clear which you are giving.

p values

The fifth column of the output in Table 3.6, headed P > |t|, provides an alternative approach to reporting the significance of regression coefficients. The figures

---

BOX 3.3   Reporting the results of *t* tests

Suppose you have a theoretical relationship

$$Y_i = \beta_1 + \beta_2 X_i + u_i$$

and your null and alternative hypotheses are $H_0: \beta_2 = \beta_2^0$, $H_1: \beta_2 \neq \beta_2^0$. Given an experimental estimate b_2 of β_2, the acceptance and rejection regions for the hypothesis for the 5 percent and 1 percent significance levels can be represented in general terms by the left part of Figure 3.9.

The right side of the figure gives the same regions for a specific example, the price inflation/wage inflation model, the null hypothesis being that β_2 is equal to 1. The null hypothesis will not be rejected at the 5 percent level if b_2 lies within 2.101 standard errors of 1, that is, in the range 0.79 to 1.21, and it will not be rejected at the 1 percent level if b_2 lies within 2.878 standard deviations of 1, that is, in the range 0.71 to 1.29.

From Figure 3.9 it can be seen that there are three types of decision zone:

1. where b_2 is so far from the hypothetical β_2 that the null hypothesis is rejected at both the 5 percent and the 1 percent levels,

2. where b_2 is far enough from the hypothetical β_2 for the null hypothesis to be rejected at the 5 percent but not the 1 percent level,

3. where b_2 is close enough to the hypothetical β_2 for the null hypothesis not to be rejected at either level.

From the diagram it can be verified that if the null hypothesis is rejected at the 1 percent level, it is automatically rejected at the 5 percent level. Hence in case (1) it is only necessary to report the rejection of the hypothesis at the 1 percent level. To report that it is rejected also at the 5 percent level is superfluous and suggests that you are not aware of this. It would be a bit like reporting that a certain high-jumper can clear two metres, and then adding that the athlete can also clear one and a half metres.

In case (3), likewise, you only need to make one statement, in this case that the hypothesis is not rejected at the 5 percent level. It automatically follows that it is not rejected at the 1 percent level, and to add a statement to this effect as well would be like saying that the high-jumper cannot clear one and a half metres, and also reporting that the athlete cannot clear two metres either.

Only in case (2) is it necessary (and desirable) to report the results of both tests.

Note that if you find that you can reject the null hypothesis at the 5 percent level, you should not stop there. You have established that the null hypothesis can be rejected at that level, but there remains a 5 percent chance of a Type I error. You should also perform the test at the 1 percent level. If you find that you can reject the null hypothesis at this level, this is the outcome that you should report. The risk of a Type I error is now only 1 percent and your conclusion is much more convincing. This is case (1) above. If you cannot reject at the 1 percent level, you have reached case (2) and you should report the results of both tests.

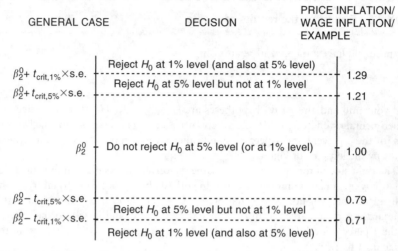

GENERAL CASE	DECISION	PRICE INFLATION/ WAGE INFLATION/ EXAMPLE
$\beta_2^0 + t_{\text{crit},1\%} \times \text{s.e.}$	Reject H_0 at 1% level (and also at 5% level)	1.29
$\beta_2^0 + t_{\text{crit},5\%} \times \text{s.e.}$	Reject H_0 at 5% level but not at 1% level	1.21
β_2^0	Do not reject H_0 at 5% level (or at 1% level)	1.00
$\beta_2^0 - t_{\text{crit},5\%} \times \text{s.e.}$		0.79
$\beta_2^0 - t_{\text{crit},1\%} \times \text{s.e.}$	Reject H_0 at 5% level but not at 1% level	0.71
	Reject H_0 at 1% level (and also at 5% level)	

Figure 3.9 Reporting the results of a t test (no need to report conclusions in parentheses)

in this column give the probability of obtaining the corresponding t statistic as a matter of chance, if the null hypothesis H_0: $\beta_2 = 0$ were true. A p value of less than 0.01 means that the probability is less than 1 percent, which in turn means that the null hypothesis would be rejected at the 1 percent level; a p value between 0.01 and 0.05 means that the null hypothesis would be rejected at the 5 percent, but not the 1 percent level; and a p value of 0.05 or more means that it would not be rejected at the 5 percent level.

The p value approach is more informative than the 5 percent/1 percent approach, in that it gives the exact probability of a Type I error, if the null hypothesis is true. For example, in the earnings function output above, the p value for the intercept is 0.445, meaning that the probability of obtaining a t statistic of 0.764 or greater, in absolute terms, on a pure chance basis is in this case 44.5 percent. Hence the null hypothesis that the intercept is 0 would not be rejected at any sensible significance level. In the case of the slope coefficient, the p value is 0.0000, meaning that the probability of obtaining a t statistic as large as 8.102, or larger, as a matter of chance is less than 0.005 percent. Hence we would reject the null hypothesis that the slope coefficient is 0 at the 1 percent level. Indeed we would reject it at the 0.1 percent level—see below. Choice between the p value approach and the 5 percent/1 percent approach appears to be entirely conventional. The medical literature uses p values, but the economics literature generally uses 5 percent/1 percent.

0.1 percent tests

If the t statistic is very high, you should check whether you can reject the null hypothesis at the 0.1 percent level. If you can, you should always report the result of the 0.1 percent test in preference to that of the 1 percent test because it demonstrates that you are able to reject the null hypothesis with an even smaller risk of a Type I error.

Exercises

3.7   Give more examples of everyday instances in which decisions involving possible Type I and Type II errors may arise.

3.8   Before beginning a certain course, 36 students are given an aptitude test. The scores, and the course results (pass/fail) are given in the table.

Student	Test score	Course result	Student	Test score	Course result	Student	Test score	Course result
1	30	fail	13	26	fail	25	9	fail
2	29	pass	14	43	pass	26	36	pass
3	33	fail	15	43	fail	27	61	pass
4	62	pass	16	68	pass	28	79	fail
5	59	fail	17	63	pass	29	57	fail
6	63	pass	18	42	fail	30	46	pass
7	80	pass	19	51	fail	31	70	fail
8	32	fail	20	45	fail	32	31	pass
9	60	pass	21	22	fail	33	68	pass
10	76	pass	22	30	pass	34	62	pass
11	13	fail	23	40	fail	35	56	pass
12	41	pass	24	26	fail	36	36	pass

Do you think that the aptitude test is useful for selecting students for admission to the course, and if so, how would you determine the pass mark? (Discuss the trade-off between Type I and Type II errors associated with the choice of pass-mark.)

3.9   A researcher hypothesizes that years of schooling, S, may be related to the number of siblings (brothers and sisters), SIBLINGS, according to the relationship

$$S = \beta_1 + \beta_2 SIBLINGS + u.$$

She is prepared to test the null hypothesis $H_0: \beta_2 = 0$ against the alternative hypothesis $H_1: \beta_2 \neq 0$ at the 5 percent and 1 percent levels. She has a sample of sixty observations. What should she report

1. if $b_2 = 0.20$, s.e.$(b_2) = 0.07$?
2. if $b_2 = -0.12$, s.e.$(b_2) = 0.07$?

3. if $b_2 = 0.06$, s.e.$(b_2) = 0.07$?

4. if $b_2 = -0.20$, s.e.$(b_2) = 0.07$?

3.10* A researcher with a sample of 50 individuals with similar education but differing amounts of training hypothesizes that hourly earnings, *EARN-INGS*, may be related to hours of training, *TRAINING*, according to the relationship

$$EARNINGS = \beta_1 + \beta_2 TRAINING + u.$$

He is prepared to test the null hypothesis $H_0: \beta_2 = 0$ against the alternative hypothesis $H_1: \beta_2 \neq 0$ at the 5 percent and 1 percent levels. What should he report

1. if $b_2 = 0.30$, s.e.$(b_2) = 0.12$?

2. if $b_2 = 0.55$, s.e.$(b_2) = 0.12$?

3. if $b_2 = 0.10$, s.e.$(b_2) = 0.12$?

4. if $b_2 = -0.27$, s.e.$(b_2) = 0.12$?

3.11 Perform a *t* test on the slope coefficient and the intercept of the educational attainment function fitted using your *EAEF* data set, and state your conclusions.

3.12 Perform a *t* test on the slope coefficient and the intercept of the earnings function fitted using your *EAEF* data set, and state your conclusions.

3.13* In Exercise 2.1, the growth rate of employment was regressed on the growth rate of GDP for a sample of 25 OECD countries. Perform *t* tests on the slope coefficient and the intercept and state your conclusions.

3.8 Confidence intervals

Thus far we have been assuming that the hypothesis preceded the empirical investigation. This is not necessarily the case. Usually theory and experimentation are interactive, and the earnings function regression provides a typical example. We ran the regression in the first place because economic theory tells us to expect earnings to be affected by schooling. The regression result confirmed this intuition since we rejected the null hypothesis $\beta_2 = 0$, but we were then left with something of a vacuum, since our theory is not strong enough to suggest that the true value of β_2 is equal to some specific number. However, we can now move in the opposite direction and ask ourselves the following question: given our regression result, what hypotheses would be compatible with it?

Obviously a hypothesis $\beta_2 = 1.073$ would be compatible, because then hypothesis and experimental result coincide. Also $\beta_2 = 1.072$ and $\beta_2 = 1.074$ would be compatible, because the difference between hypothesis and experimental result would be so small. The question is, how far can a hypothetical value differ from our experimental result before they become incompatible and we have to reject the null hypothesis?

We can answer this question by exploiting the previous analysis. From (3.50), we can see that regression coefficient b_2 and hypothetical value β_2 are incompatible if either

$$\frac{b_2 - \beta_2}{\text{s.e.}(b_2)} > t_{\text{crit}} \quad \text{or} \quad \frac{b_2 - \beta_2}{\text{s.e.}(b_2)} < -t_{\text{crit}}, \tag{3.54}$$

that is, if either

$$b_2 - \beta_2 > \text{s.e.}(b_2) \times t_{\text{crit}} \quad \text{or} \quad b_2 - \beta_2 < -\text{s.e.}(b_2) \times t_{\text{crit}}, \tag{3.55}$$

that is, if either

$$b_2 - \text{s.e.}(b_2) \times t_{\text{crit}} > \beta_2 \quad \text{or} \quad b_2 + \text{s.e.}(b_2) \times t_{\text{crit}} < \beta_2. \tag{3.56}$$

It therefore follows that a hypothetical β_2 is compatible with the regression result if both

$$b_2 - \text{s.e.}(b_2) \times t_{\text{crit}} \le \beta_2 \quad \text{and} \quad b_2 + \text{s.e.}(b_2) \times t_{\text{crit}} \ge \beta_2, \tag{3.57}$$

that is, if β_2 satisfies the double inequality *Confidence interval*

$$b_2 - \text{s.e.}(b_2) \times t_{\text{crit}} \le \beta_2 \le b_2 + \text{s.e.}(b_2) \times t_{\text{crit}}. \tag{3.58}$$

Any hypothetical value of β_2 that satisfies (3.58) will therefore automatically be compatible with the estimate b_2, that is, will not be rejected by it. The set of all such values, given by the interval between the lower and upper limits of the inequality, is known as the *confidence interval* for β_2.

Note that the center of the confidence interval is b_2 itself. The limits are equidistant on either side. Note also that, since the value of t_{crit} depends upon the choice of significance level, the limits will also depend on this choice. If the 5 percent significance level is adopted, the corresponding confidence interval is known as the 95 percent confidence interval. If the 1 percent level is chosen, one obtains the 99 percent confidence interval, and so on.

Since t_{crit} is greater for the 1 percent level than for the 5 percent level, for any given number of degrees of freedom, it follows that the 99 percent interval is wider than the 95 percent interval. Since they are both centered on b_2, the 99 percent interval encompasses all the hypothetical values of β_2 in the 95 percent confidence interval and some more on either side as well.

Example

In the earnings function output above, the coefficient of S was 1.073, its standard error was 0.132, and the critical value of t at the 5 percent significance level was

---

BOX 3.4   A second interpretation of a confidence interval

When you construct a confidence interval, the numbers you calculate for its upper and lower limits contain random components that depend on the values of the disturbance term in the observations in the sample. For example, in inequality (3.58), the upper limit is

$$b_2 + \text{s.e.}(b_2) \times t_{\text{crit}}$$

Both b_2 and $\text{s.e.}(b_2)$ are partly determined by the values of the disturbance term, and similarly for the lower limit. One hopes that the confidence interval will include the true value of the parameter, but sometimes it will be so distorted by the random element that it will fail to do so.

What is the probability that a confidence interval will capture the true value of the parameter? It can easily be shown, using elementary probability theory, that, in the case of a 95 percent confidence interval, the probability is 95 percent, provided that the model is correctly specified and that the Gauss–Markov conditions are satisfied. Similarly, in the case of a 99 percent confidence interval, the probability is 99 percent.

The estimated coefficient [for example, b_2 in inequality (3.58)] provides a point estimate of the parameter in question, but of course the probability of the true value being exactly equal to this estimate is infinitesimal. The confidence interval provides what is known as an *interval estimate* of the parameter, that is, a range of values that will include the true value with a high, predetermined probability. It is this interpretation that gives the confidence interval its name (for a detailed and lucid discussion, see Wonnacott and Wonnacott, 1990, Chapter 8).

---

about 1.97. The corresponding 95 percent confidence interval is therefore

$$1.073 - 0.132 \times 1.97 \leq \beta_2 \leq 1.073 + 0.132 \times 1.97, \tag{3.59}$$

that is,

$$0.813 \leq \beta_2 \leq 1.333. \tag{3.60}$$

We would therefore reject hypothetical values above 1.333 and below 0.813. Any hypotheses within these limits would not be rejected, given the regression result. This confidence interval actually appears as the final column in the output above. However, this is not a standard feature of a regression application, so you usually have to calculate the interval yourself.

Exercises

3.14   Calculate the 99 percent confidence interval for β_2 in the earnings function example ($b_2 = 1.073$, $\text{s.e.}(b_2) = 0.132$), and explain why it includes some values not included in the 95 percent confidence interval calculated in the previous section.

3.15   Calculate the 95 percent confidence interval for the slope coefficient in the earnings function fitted with your *EAEF* data set.

3.16* Calculate the 95 percent confidence interval for β_2 in the price inflation/wage inflation example:

$$\hat{p} = -1.21 + 0.82w.$$
$$\text{(0.05)} \ \text{(0.10)}$$

What can you conclude from this calculation?

3.9 One-tailed t tests

In our discussion of t tests, we started out with our null hypothesis H_0: $\beta_2 = \beta_2^0$ and tested it to see whether we should reject it or not, given the regression coefficient b_2. If we did reject it, then by implication we accepted the alternative hypothesis H_1: $\beta_2 \neq \beta_2^0$.

Thus far the alternative hypothesis has been merely the negation of the null hypothesis. However, if we are able to be more specific about the alternative hypothesis, we may be able to improve the testing procedure. We will investigate three cases: first, the very special case where there is only one conceivable alternative true value of β_2, which we will denote β_2^1; second, where, if β_2 is not equal to β_2^0, it must be greater than β_2^0; and third, where, if β_2 is not equal to β_2^0; it must be less than β_2^0.

H_0: $\beta_2 = \beta_2^0$, H_1: $\beta_2 = \beta_2^1$

In this case there are only two possible values of the true coefficient of X, β_2^0 and β_2^1. For sake of argument we will assume for the time being that β_2^1 is greater than β_2^0.

Suppose that we wish to test H_0 at the 5 percent significance level, and we follow the usual procedure discussed earlier in the chapter. We locate the limits of the upper and lower 2.5 percent tails under the assumption that H_0 is true, indicated by A and B in Figure 3.10, and we reject H_0 if the regression coefficient b_2 lies to the left of A or to the right of B.

Now, if b_2 does lie to the right of B, it is more compatible with H_1 than with H_0; the probability of it lying to the right of B is greater if H_1 is true than if H_0 is true. We should have no hesitation in rejecting H_0 in favor of H_1.

However, if b_2 lies to the left of A, the test procedure will lead us to a perverse conclusion. It tells us to reject H_0 in favor of H_1, even though the probability of b_2 lying to the left of A is negligible if H_1 is true. We have not even drawn the probability density function that far for H_1. If such a value of b_2 occurs only once in a million times when H_1 is true, but 2.5 percent of the time when H_0 is true, it is much more logical to assume that H_0 is true. Of course once in a million times you will make a mistake, but the rest of the time you will be right.

probability density
function of b_2

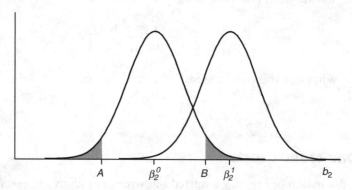

Figure 3.10 Distribution of b_2 under H_0 and H_1

Hence we will reject H_0 only if b_2 lies in the upper 2.5 percent tail, that is, to the right of B. We are now performing a one-tailed test, and we have reduced the probability of making a Type I error to 2.5 percent. Since the significance level is defined to be the probability of making a Type I error, it is now also 2.5 percent.

As we have seen, economists usually prefer 5 percent and 1 percent significance tests, rather than 2.5 percent tests. If you want to perform a 5 percent test, you move B to the left so that you have 5 percent of the probability in the tail and the probability of making a Type I error is increased to 5 percent. (*Question*: why would you deliberately choose to increase the probability of making a Type I error? Answer, because at the same time you are reducing the probability of making a Type II error, that is, of not rejecting the null hypothesis when it is false. Most of the time your null hypothesis is that the coefficient is 0, and you are trying to disprove this, demonstrating that the variable in question *does* have an effect. In such a situation, by using a one-tailed test, you reduce the risk of not rejecting a false null hypothesis, while holding the risk of a Type I error at 5 percent.)

If the standard deviation of b_2 is known (most unlikely in practice), so that the distribution is normal, B will be z standard deviations to the right of β_2^0, where z is given by $A(z) = 0.9500$ in Table A.1. This is true when z is 1.64. If the standard deviation is unknown and has been estimated as the standard error of b_2, you have to use a t distribution: you look up the critical value of t in Table A.2 for the appropriate number of degrees of freedom in the column headed 5 percent.

Similarly, if you want to perform a 1 percent test, you move B to the point where the right tail contains 1 percent of the probability. Assuming that you have had to calculate the standard error of b_2 from the sample data, you look up the critical value of t in the column headed 1 percent.

We have assumed in this discussion that β_2^1 is greater than β_2^0. Obviously, if it is less than β_2^0, we should use the same logic to construct a one-tailed test, but now we should use the left tail as the rejection region for H_0 and drop the right tail.

The power of a test

In this particular case we can calculate the probability of making a Type II error, that is, of accepting a false hypothesis. Suppose that we have adopted a false hypothesis H_0: $\beta_2 = \beta_2^0$ and that an alternative hypothesis H_1: $\beta_2 = \beta_2^1$ is in fact true. If we are using a two-tailed test, we will fail to reject H_0 if b_2 lies in the interval AB in Figure 3.11. Since H_1 is true, the probability of b_2 lying in that interval is given by the area under the curve for H_1 to the left of B, the lighter shaded area in the figure. If this probability is denoted γ, the power of the test, defined to be the probability of not making a Type II error, is $(1 - \gamma)$. Obviously, you have a trade-off between the power of the test and the significance level. The higher the significance level, the further B will be to the right, and so the larger γ will be, so the lower the power of the test will be.

In using a one-tailed instead of a two-tailed test, you are able to obtain greater power for any level of significance. As we have seen, you would move B in Figure 3.11 to the left if you were performing a one-tailed test at the 5 percent significance level, thereby reducing the probability of not rejecting H_0 if it happened to be false.

H_0: $\beta_2 = \beta_2^0$, H_1: $\beta_2 > \beta_2^0$

We have discussed the case in which the alternative hypothesis involved a *specific* hypothetical value β_2^1, with β_2^1 greater than β_2^0. Clearly, the logic that led us to use a one-tailed test would still apply even if H_1 were more general and merely asserted that $\beta_2^1 > \beta_2^0$, without stating any particular value.

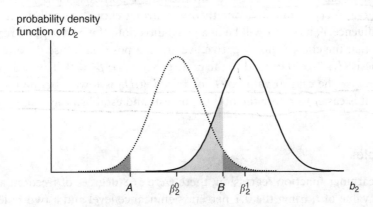

Figure 3.11 Probability of not rejecting H_0 when it is false, two-tailed test

We would still wish to eliminate the left tail from the rejection region because a low value of b_2 is more probable under H_0: $\beta_2 = \beta_2^0$ than under H_1: $\beta_2 > \beta_2^0$, and this would be evidence in favor of H_0, not against it. Therefore, we would still prefer a one-tailed t test, using the right tail as the rejection region, to a two-tailed test. Note that, since β_2^1 is not defined, we now have no way of calculating the power of such a test. However, we can still be sure that, for any given significance level, the power of a one-tailed test will be greater than that of the corresponding two-tailed test.

H_0: $\beta_2 = \beta_2^0$, H_1: $\beta_2 < \beta_2^0$

Similarly if the alternative hypothesis were H_0: $\beta_2 < \beta_2^0$, we would prefer a one-tailed test using the left tail as the rejection region.

Justification of the use of a one-tailed test

The use of a one-tailed test has to be justified beforehand on the grounds of theory, common sense, or previous experience. When stating the justification, you should be careful not to exclude the possibility that the null hypothesis is true. For example, suppose that you are relating household expenditure on clothing to household income. You would of course expect a significant positive effect, given a large sample. But your justification should not be that, on the basis of theory and common sense, the coefficient should be positive. This is too strong, for it eliminates the null hypothesis of no effect, and there is nothing to test. Instead, you should say that, on the basis of theory and common sense, you would exclude the possibility that income has a *negative* effect. This then leaves the possibility that the effect is 0 and the alternative that it is positive.

One-tailed tests are very important in practice in econometrics. As we have seen, the usual way of establishing that an explanatory variable really does influence a dependent variable is to set up the null hypothesis H_0: $\beta_2 = 0$ and try to refute it. Very frequently, our theory is strong enough to tell us that, if X does influence Y, its effect will be in a given direction. If we have good reason to believe that the effect is not negative, we are in a position to use the alternative hypothesis H_1: $\beta_2 > 0$ instead of the more general H_1: $\beta_2 \neq 0$. This is an advantage because the critical value of t for rejecting H_0 is lower for the one-tailed test, so it is easier to refute the null hypothesis and establish the relationship.

Examples

In the earnings function regression, there were 568 degrees of freedom and the critical value of t, using the 0.1 percent significance level and a two-tailed test, is approximately 3.31. If we take advantage of the fact that it is reasonable to expect schooling not to have a negative effect on earnings, we could use a one-tailed test and the critical value is reduced to approximately 3.10. The t statistic is in fact equal to 8.10, so in this case the refinement makes no difference. The estimated coefficient is so large relative to its standard error that we reject the null hypothesis regardless of whether we use a two-tailed or a one-tailed test, even using a 0.1 percent test.

In the price inflation/wage inflation example, exploiting the possibility of using a one-tailed test does make a difference. The null hypothesis was that wage inflation is reflected fully in price inflation and we have H_0: $\beta_2 = 1$. The main reason why the types of inflation may be different is that improvements in labor productivity may cause price inflation to be lower than wage inflation. Certainly improvements in productivity will not cause price inflation to be greater than wage inflation and so in this case we are justified in ruling out $\beta_2 > 1$. We are left with H_0: $\beta_2 = 1$ and H_1: $\beta_2 < 1$. Given a regression coefficient 0.82 and a standard error 0.10, the t statistic for the null hypothesis is -1.80. This was not high enough, in absolute terms, to cause H_0 to be rejected at the 5 percent level using a two-tailed test (critical value 2.10). However, if we use a one-tailed test, as we are entitled to, the critical value falls to 1.73 and we *can* reject the null hypothesis. In other words, we can conclude that price inflation is significantly lower than wage inflation.

Exercises

3.17 Explain whether it would have been possible to perform one-tailed tests instead of two-tailed tests in Exercise 3.9. If you think that one-tailed tests are justified, perform them and state whether the use of a one-tailed test makes any difference.

3.18* Explain whether it would have been possible to perform one-tailed tests instead of two-tailed tests in Exercise 3.10. If you think that one-tailed tests are justified, perform them and state whether the use of a one-tailed test makes any difference.

3.19* Explain whether it would have been possible to perform one-tailed tests instead of two-tailed tests in Exercise 3.11. If you think that one-tailed tests are justified, perform them and state whether the use of a one-tailed test makes any difference.

3.10 The *F* test of goodness of fit

Even if there is no relationship between Y and X, in any given sample of observations there may appear to be one, if only a faint one. Only by coincidence will the sample covariance be *exactly* equal to 0. Accordingly, only by coincidence will the correlation coefficient and R^2 be *exactly* equal to 0. So how do we know if the value of R^2 for the regression reflects a true relationship or if it has arisen as a matter of chance?

We could in principle adopt the following procedure. Suppose that the regression model is

$$Y_i = \beta_1 + \beta_2 X_i + u_i. \tag{3.61}$$

We take as our null hypothesis that there is no relationship between Y and X, that is, H_0: $\beta_2 = 0$. We calculate the value that would be exceeded by R^2 as a matter of chance, 5 percent of the time. We then take this figure as the critical level of R^2 for a 5 percent significance test. If it is exceeded, we reject the null hypothesis in favor of H_1: $\beta_2 \neq 0$.

Such a test, like the t test on a coefficient, would not be foolproof. Indeed, at the 5 percent significance level, one would risk making a Type I error, rejecting the null hypothesis when it is in fact true, 5 percent of the time. Of course you could cut down on this risk by using a higher significance level, for example, the 1 percent level. The critical level of R^2 would then be that which would be exceeded by chance only 1 percent of the time, so it would be higher than the critical level for the 5 percent test.

How does one find the critical level of R^2 at either significance level? Well, there is a small problem. There is no such thing as a table of critical levels of R^2. The traditional procedure is to use an indirect approach and perform what is known as an F test based on analysis of variance.

Suppose that, as in this case, you can decompose the variance of the dependent variable into 'explained' and 'unexplained' components using (2.46):

$$\text{Var}(Y) = \text{Var}(\hat{Y}) + \text{Var}(e). \tag{3.62}$$

Using the definition of sample variance, and multiplying through by n, we can rewrite the decomposition as

$$\sum_{i=1}^{n} (Y_i - \bar{Y})^2 = \sum_{i=1}^{n} (\hat{Y}_i - \bar{Y})^2 + \sum_{i=1}^{n} e_i^2. \tag{3.63}$$

(Remember that $\bar{e}$ is 0 and that the sample mean of $\hat{Y}$ is equal to the sample mean of Y.)

The left side is TSS, the total sum of squares of the values of the dependent variable about its sample mean. The first term on the right side is ESS, the explained sum of squares, and the second term is RSS, the unexplained, residual sum of squares:

$$TSS = ESS + RSS. \tag{3.64}$$

The F statistic for the goodness of fit of a regression is written as the explained sum of squares, per explanatory variable, divided by the residual sum of squares, per degree of freedom remaining:

$$F = \frac{ESS/(k-1)}{RSS/(n-k)},$$ (3.65)

where k is the number of parameters in the regression equation (intercept and $k-1$ slope coefficients).

By dividing both the numerator and the denominator of the ratio by TSS, this F statistic may equivalently be expressed in terms of R^2:

$$F = \frac{(ESS/TSS)/(k-1)}{(RSS/TSS)/(n-k)} = \frac{R^2/(k-1)}{(1-R^2)/(n-k)}.$$ (3.66)

In the present context, k is 2, so (3.66) becomes

— important.

$$F = \frac{R^2}{(1-R^2)/(n-2)}.$$ (3.67)

Having calculated F from your value of R^2, you look up F_{crit}, the critical level of F, in the appropriate table. If F is greater than F_{crit}, you reject the null hypothesis and conclude that the 'explanation' of Y is better than is likely to have arisen by chance.

Table A.3 gives the critical levels of F at the 5 percent, 1 percent and 0.1 percent significance levels. In each case the critical level depends on the number of explanatory variables, $k-1$, which is read from along the top of the table, and the number of degrees of freedom, $n-k$, which is read off down the side. In the present context, we are concerned with simple regression analysis, k is 2, and we should use the first column of the table.

In the earnings function example, R^2 was 0.1036. Since there were 570 observations, the F statistic is equal to $R^2/[(1-R^2)/568] = 0.1036/[0.8964/568] = 65.65$. At the 0.1 percent significance level, the critical level of F for 1 and 500 degrees of freedom (looking at the first column, row 500) is 10.96. The critical value for 1 and 568 degrees of freedom must be lower, so we have no hesitation in rejecting the null hypothesis in this particular example. In other words, the underlying value of R^2 is so high that we reject the suggestion that it could have arisen by chance. In practice the F statistic is always computed for you, along with R^2, so you never actually have to use (3.66) yourself.

Why do people bother with this indirect approach? Why not have a table of critical levels of R^2? The answer is that the F table is useful for testing many forms of analysis of variance, of which R^2 is only one. Rather than have a specialized table for each application, it is more convenient (or, at least, it saves a lot of paper) to have just one general table, and make transformations like (3.66) when necessary.

Of course you could derive critical levels of R^2 if you were sufficiently interested. The critical level of R^2 would be related to the critical level of F by

$$F_{\text{crit}} = \frac{R^2_{\text{crit}}/(k-1)}{(1 - R^2_{\text{crit}})/(n-k)}, \tag{3.68}$$

which yields

$$R^2_{\text{crit}} = \frac{(k-1)F_{\text{crit}}}{(k-1)F_{\text{crit}} + (n-k)}. \tag{3.69}$$

In the earnings function example, the critical value of F at the 1 percent significance level was approximately 11.38. Hence in this case, with $k = 2$,

$$R^2_{\text{crit}} = \frac{11.38}{11.38 + 568} = 0.020. \tag{3.70}$$

Although it is low, our R^2 is greater than 0.020, so a direct comparison of R^2 with its critical value confirms the conclusion of the F test that we should reject the null hypothesis.

Exercises

3.20 In Exercise 2.1, in the regression of employment growth rates on growth rates of GDP using a sample of 25 OECD countries, R^2 was 0.5909. Calculate the corresponding F statistic and check that it is equal to 33.22, the value printed in the output. Perform the F test at the 5 percent, 1 percent, and 0.1 percent significance levels. Is it necessary to report the results of the tests at all three levels?

3.21 Similarly, calculate the F statistic from the value of R^2 obtained in the earnings function fitted using your *EAEF* data set and check that it is equal to the value printed in the output. Perform an appropriate F test.

3.11 Relationship between the *F* test of goodness of fit and the *t* test on the slope coefficient in simple regression analysis

In the context of simple regression analysis (and *only* simple regression analysis) the F test on R^2 and the two-tailed t test on the slope coefficient both have H_0: $\beta_2 = 0$ as the null hypothesis and H_1: $\beta_2 \neq 0$ as the alternative hypothesis. This gives rise to the possibility that they might lead to different conclusions. Fortunately, they are in fact equivalent. The F statistic is equal to the square of the t statistic, and the critical value of F, at any given significance level, is equal to the square of the critical value of t. Starting with the definition of F in (3.67),

$$F = \frac{R^2}{(1 - R^2)/(n - 2)} = \frac{\dfrac{\text{Var}(\hat{Y})}{\text{Var}(Y)}}{\left\{ 1 - \dfrac{\text{Var}(\hat{Y})}{\text{Var}(Y)} \right\}/(n - 2)}$$

$$= \frac{\dfrac{\text{Var}(\hat{Y})}{\text{Var}(Y)}}{\left\{ \dfrac{\text{Var}(Y) - \text{Var}(\hat{Y})}{\text{Var}(Y)} \right\}/(n - 2)} = \frac{\text{Var}(\hat{Y})}{\text{Var}(e)/(n - 2)}$$

$$= \frac{\text{Var}(b_1 + b_2 X)}{\left\{ \dfrac{1}{n} \displaystyle\sum_{i=1}^{n} e_i^2 \right\}/(n - 2)} = \frac{b_2^2 \text{Var}(X)}{\dfrac{1}{n} s_u^2} = \frac{b_2^2}{\dfrac{s_u^2}{n\text{Var}(X)}} = \frac{b_2^2}{[s.e.(b_2)]^2} = t^2. \quad (3.71)$$

The proof that the critical value of F is equal to the square of the critical value of t for a two-tailed t test is more complicated and will be omitted. When we come to multiple regression analysis, we will see that the F test and the t tests have different roles and different null hypotheses. However, in simple regression analysis the fact that they are equivalent means that there is no point in performing both. Indeed, you would look ignorant if you did. Obviously, provided that it is justifiable, a one-tailed t test would be preferable to either.

Exercises

3.22 Verify that the F statistic in the earnings function regression run by you using your *EAEF* data set is equal to the square of the t statistic for the slope coefficient, and that the critical value of F at the 1 percent significance level is equal to the square of the critical value of t.

3.23 In Exercise 2.6 both researchers obtained values of R^2 equal to 0.10 in their regressions. Was this a coincidence?

4 Multiple regression analysis

In this chapter least squares regression analysis is generalized to cover the case in which there are several or many explanatory variables in the regression model, rather than just one. Two new topics are discussed. One is the problem of discriminating between the effects of different explanatory variables, a problem that, when particularly severe, is known as multicollinearity. The other is the evaluation of the joint explanatory power of the independent variables, as opposed to their individual marginal effects.

4.1 Illustration: a model with two explanatory variables

Multiple regression analysis is an extension of simple regression analysis to cover cases in which the dependent variable is hypothesized to depend on more than one explanatory variable. Much of the analysis will be a straightforward extension of the simple regression model, but we will encounter two new problems. First, when evaluating the influence of a given explanatory variable on the dependent variable, we now have to face the problem of discriminating between its effects and the effects of the other explanatory variables. Second, we shall have to tackle the problem of model specification. Frequently a number of variables might be thought to influence the behavior of the dependent variable; however, they might be irrelevant. We shall have to decide which should be included in the regression equation and which should be excluded. The second problem will be discussed in Chapter 7. In this chapter, we will assume that the model specification is correct. For much of it, we will confine ourselves to the basic case where there are only two explanatory variables.

We will begin by considering an example, the determinants of earnings. We will extend the earlier model to allow for the possibility that earnings are influenced by cognitive ability as well as education and assume that the true relationship can be expressed as

$$EARNINGS = \beta_1 + \beta_2 S + \beta_3 ASVABC + u, \qquad (4.1)$$

where $EARNINGS$ is hourly earnings, S is years of schooling (highest grade completed), $ASVABC$ is composite score on the cognitive tests in the Armed

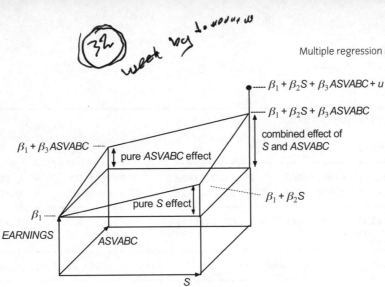

Figure 4.1 True model with two explanatory variables: earnings as a function of schooling and ability

Services Vocational Aptitude Battery, and u is a disturbance term. This model is still of course a great simplification, both in terms of the explanatory variables included in the relationship and in terms of its mathematical specification.

To illustrate the relationship geometrically, one needs a three-dimensional diagram with separate axes for $EARNINGS$, S, and $ASVABC$ as in Figure 4.1. The base of Figure 4.1 shows the axes for S and $ASVABC$, and, if one neglects the effect of the disturbance term for the moment, the tilted plane above it shows the value of $EARNINGS$ corresponding to any $(S, ASVABC)$ combination, measured by the vertical height of the plane above the base at that point. Since earnings may be expected to increase with both schooling and ability, the diagram has been drawn on the assumption that β_2 and β_3 are both positive. Literally, the intercept β_1 gives the predicted earnings for 0 schooling and 0 ability score. However, such an interpretation would be dangerous because the ASVABC score is scaled in such a way as to make it impossible to score less than 20. Furthermore, there was nobody with no schooling in the NLSY data set. Indeed very few individuals failed to complete eight years of schooling. Mathematically (4.1) implies that, if $ASVABC$ were 0, for any positive S, earnings would be equal to $\beta_1 + \beta_2 S$, the increase $\beta_2 S$ being marked 'pure S effect' in the figure. Keeping S at 0, the equation implies that for any positive value of $ASVABC$, earnings would be equal to $\beta_1 + \beta_3 ASVABC$, the increase $\beta_3 ASVABC$ being marked 'pure $ASVABC$ effect'. The combined effect of schooling and ability, $\beta_2 S + \beta_3 ASVABC$, is also indicated.

We have thus far neglected the disturbance term. If it were not for the presence of this in (4.1), the values of $EARNINGS$ in a sample of observations on $EARNINGS$, S, and $ASVABC$ would lie exactly on the tilted plane and it would be a trivial matter to deduce the exact values of β_1, β_2, and β_3 (not trivial geometrically, unless you are a genius at constructing three-dimensional models, but easy enough algebraically).

Table 4.1

```
. reg EARNINGS S ASVABC

   Source |       SS        df       MS              Number of obs =     570
----------+------------------------------           F( 2,    567) =   39.98
    Model | 4745.74965       2  2372.87483           Prob > F      =  0.0000
 Residual | 33651.2874      567  59.3497133          R-squared     =  0.1236
----------+------------------------------           Adj R-squared =  0.1205
    Total | 38397.0371      569  67.4816117          Root MSE      =  7.7039


------------------------------------------------------------------------------
 EARNINGS |    Coef.   Std. Err.      t    P>|t|     [95% Conf. Interval]
----------+-------------------------------------------------------------------
        S |  .7390366  .1606216    4.601   0.000    .4235506    1.054523
   ASVABC |  .1545341  .0429486    3.598   0.000    .0701764    .2388918
    _cons | -4.624749  2.0132     -2.297   0.022   -8.578989   -.6705095
------------------------------------------------------------------------------
```

The disturbance term causes the actual value of earnings to be sometimes above and sometimes below the value indicated by the tilted plane. Consequently one now has a three-dimensional counterpart to the two-dimensional problem illustrated in Figure 2.2. Instead of locating a line to fit a two-dimensional scatter of points, we now have to locate a plane to fit a three-dimensional scatter. The equation of the fitted plane will be

$$\widehat{EARNINGS} = b_1 + b_2 S + b_3 ASVABC \tag{4.2}$$

and its location will depend on the choice of $b_1, b_2,$ and b_3, the estimates of $\beta_1, \beta_2,$ and β_3, respectively. Using *EAEF* Data Set 21, we obtain the regression output as shown in Table 4.1.

The equation should be interpreted as follows. For every additional grade completed, holding the ability score constant, hourly earnings increase by $0.74. For every point increase in the ability score, holding schooling constant, earnings increase by $0.15. The constant has no meaningful interpretation. Literally, it suggests that a respondent with 0 years of schooling (no respondent had less than six) and an *ASVABC* score of 0 (impossible) would earn *minus* $4.62 per hour.

4.2 Derivation and interpretation of the multiple regression coefficients

As in the simple regression case, we choose the values of the regression coefficients to make the fit as good as possible in the hope that we will obtain the most satisfactory estimates of the unknown true parameters. As before, our definition of goodness of fit is the minimization of *RSS*, the sum of squares of the residuals:

$$RSS = \sum_{i=1}^{n} e_i^2, \tag{4.3}$$

where e_i is the residual in observation i, the difference between the actual value Y_i in that observation and the value $\hat{Y}_i$ predicted by the regression equation:

$$\hat{Y}_i = b_1 + b_2 X_{2i} + b_3 X_{3i}. \tag{4.4}$$

$$e_i = Y_i - \hat{Y}_i = Y_i - b_1 - b_2 X_{2i} - b_3 X_{3i}. \tag{4.5}$$

Note that the X variables now have two subscripts. The first identifies the X variable and the second identifies the observation.

Using (4.5), we can write

$$RSS = \sum_{i=1}^{n} e_i^2 = \sum_{i=1}^{n} (Y_i - b_1 - b_2 X_{2i} - b_3 X_{3i})^2. \tag{4.6}$$

The first-order conditions for a minimum, $\partial RSS/\partial b_1 = 0, \partial RSS/\partial b_2 = 0$, and $\partial RSS/\partial b_3 = 0$, yield the following equations:

$$\frac{\partial RSS}{\partial b_1} = -2 \sum_{i=1}^{n} (Y_i - b_1 - b_2 X_{2i} - b_3 X_{3i}) = 0. \tag{4.7}$$

$$\frac{\partial RSS}{\partial b_2} = -2 \sum_{i=1}^{n} X_{2i}(Y_i - b_1 - b_2 X_{2i} - b_3 X_{3i}) = 0. \tag{4.8}$$

$$\frac{\partial RSS}{\partial b_3} = -2 \sum_{i=1}^{n} X_{3i}(Y_i - b_1 - b_2 X_{2i} - b_3 X_{3i}) = 0. \tag{4.9}$$

Hence we have three equations in the three unknowns, b_1, b_2, and b_3. The first can easily be rearranged to express b_1 in terms of b_2, b_3, and the data on Y, X_2, and X_3:

$$b_1 = \overline{Y} - b_2 \overline{X}_2 - b_3 \overline{X}_3. \tag{4.10}$$

Using this expression and the other two equations, with a little work one can obtain the following expression for b_2:

$$b_2 = \frac{\text{Cov}(X_2, Y)\text{Var}(X_3) - \text{Cov}(X_3, Y)\text{Cov}(X_2, X_3)}{\text{Var}(X_2)\text{Var}(X_3) - [\text{Cov}(X_2, X_3)]^2}. \tag{4.11}$$

A parallel expression for b_3 can be obtained by interchanging X_2 and X_3 in (4.11).

The intention of this discussion is to press home two basic points. First, the principles behind the derivation of the regression coefficients are the same for multiple regression as for simple regression. Second, the expressions, however, are different, and so you should not try to use expressions derived for simple regression in a multiple regression context.

The general model

In the preceding example, we were dealing with only two explanatory variables. When there are more than two, it is no longer possible to give a geometrical representation of what is going on, but the extension of the algebra is in principle quite straightforward.

We assume that a variable Y depends on $k-1$ explanatory variables $X_2, \ldots, X_k$ according to a true, unknown relationship

$$Y_i = \beta_1 + \beta_2 X_{2i} + \cdots + \beta_k X_{ki} + u_i. \tag{4.12}$$

Given a set of n observations on $Y, X_2, \ldots, X_k$, we use least squares regression analysis to fit the equation

$$\hat{Y}_i = b_1 + b_2 X_{2i} + \cdots + b_k X_{ki}. \tag{4.13}$$

This again means minimizing the sum of the squares of the residuals, which are given by

$$e_i = Y_i - \hat{Y}_i = Y_i - b_1 - b_2 X_{2i} - \cdots - b_k X_{ki}. \tag{4.14}$$

(4.14) is the generalization of (4.5). We now choose $b_1, \ldots, b_k$ so as to minimize RSS, the sum of the squares of the residuals, $\sum_{i=1}^{n} e_i^2$. We obtain k first-order conditions $\partial RSS/\partial b_1 = 0, \ldots, \partial RSS/\partial b_k = 0$, and these provide k equations for solving for the k unknowns. It can readily be shown that the first of

---

BOX 4.1   **Whatever happened to X_1?**

You may have noticed that X_1 is missing from the general regression model

$$Y_i = \beta_1 + \beta_2 X_{2i} + \cdots + \beta_k X_{ki} + u_i.$$

Why so? The reason is to make the notation consistent with that found in texts using linear algebra (matrix algebra), and your next course in econometrics will almost certainly use such a text. For analysis using linear algebra, it is essential that every term on the right side of the equation should consist of the product of a parameter and a variable. When there is an intercept in the model, as here, the anomaly is dealt with by writing the equation

$$Y_i = \beta_1 X_{1i} + \beta_2 X_{2i} + \cdots + \beta_k X_{ki} + u_i,$$

where X_{1i} is equal to 1 in every observation. In analysis using ordinary algebra, there is usually no point in introducing X_1 explicitly, and so it has been suppressed. The one occasion in this text where it can help is in the discussion of the dummy variable trap in Chapter 6.

these equations yields a counterpart to (4.10) in the case with two explanatory variables:

$$b_1 = \bar{Y} - b_2\bar{X}_2 - \cdots - b_k\bar{X}_k. \tag{4.15}$$

The expressions for $b_2, \ldots, b_k$ become very complicated and the mathematics will not be presented explicitly here. The analysis should be done with matrix algebra.

Interpretation of the multiple regression coefficients

Multiple regression analysis allows one to discriminate between the effects of the explanatory variables, making allowance for the fact that they may be correlated. The regression coefficient of each X variable provides an estimate of its influence on Y, controlling for the effects of all the other X variables.

This can be demonstrated in two ways. One is to show that the estimators are unbiased, if the model is correctly specified and the Gauss–Markov conditions are fulfilled. We shall do this in the next section for the case where there are only two explanatory variables. A second method is to run a simple regression of Y on one of the X variables, having first purged both Y and the X variable of the components that could be accounted for by the other explanatory variables. The estimate of the slope coefficient and its standard error thus obtained are exactly the same as in the multiple regression, a result that is proved by the Frisch–Waugh theorem (Frisch and Waugh, 1933). It follows that a scatter diagram plotting the purged Y against the purged X variable will provide a valid graphical representation of their relationship that can be obtained in no other way. This result will not be proved but it will be illustrated using the earnings function in Section 4.1:

$$EARNINGS = \beta_1 + \beta_2 S + \beta_3 ASVABC + u. \tag{4.16}$$

Suppose that we are particularly interested in the relationship between earnings and schooling and that we would like to illustrate it graphically. A straightforward plot of EARNINGS on S, as in Figure 2.8, would give a distorted view of the relationship because ASVABC is positively correlated with S. As a consequence, as S increases, (1) EARNINGS will tend to increase, because β_2 is positive; (2) ASVABC will tend to increase, because S and ASVABC are positively correlated; and (3) EARNINGS will receive a boost due to the increase in ASVABC and the fact that β_3 is positive. In other words, the variations in EARNINGS will exaggerate the apparent influence of S because in part they will be due to associated variations in ASVABC. As a consequence, in a simple regression the estimator of β_2 will be biased. We will investigate the bias analytically in Section 7.2.

In this example, there is only one other explanatory variable, ASVABC. To purge EARNINGS and S of their ASVABC components, we first regress them

Table 4.2

```
. reg EEARN ES

  Source |       SS       df       MS              Number of obs =     570
---------+------------------------------           F(  1,    568) =   21.21
   Model |  1256.44239     1  1256.44239           Prob > F      =  0.0000
Residual |  33651.2873   568  59.2452241           R-squared     =  0.0360
---------+------------------------------           Adj R-squared =  0.0343
   Total |  34907.7297   569  61.3492613           Root MSE      =  7.6971


-----------------------------------------------------------------------------
   EEARN |    Coef.   Std. Err.     t     P>|t|    [95% Conf. Interval]
---------+-------------------------------------------------------------------
      ES |  .7390366   .1604802   4.605   0.000    .4238296   1.054244
   _cons | -5.99e-09   .3223957   0.000   1.000   -.6332333    .6332333
-----------------------------------------------------------------------------
```

on $ASVABC$:

$$\widehat{EARNINGS} = c_1 + c_2 ASVABC. \tag{4.17}$$

$$\hat{S} = d_1 + d_2 ASVABC. \tag{4.18}$$

We then subtract the fitted values from the actual values:

$$EEARN = EARNINGS - \widehat{EARNINGS}. \tag{4.19}$$

$$ES = S - \hat{S}. \tag{4.20}$$

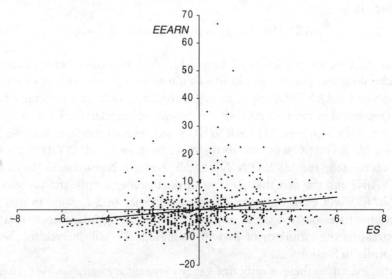

Figure 4.2 Regression of *EARNINGS* residuals on *S* residuals

The purged variables *EEARN* and *ES* are of course just the residuals from the regressions (4.17) and (4.18). We now regress *EEARN* on *ES* and obtain the output shown in Table 4.2.

You can verify that the coefficient of *ES* is identical to that of *S* in the multiple regression in Section 4.1. Figure 4.2 shows the regression line in a scatter diagram. The dotted line in the figure is the regression line from a simple regression of *EARNINGS* on *S*, shown for comparison.

The estimate of the intercept in the regression uses a common convention for fitting very large numbers or very small ones into a predefined field. $e+n$ indicates that the coefficient should be multiplied by 10^n. Similarly $e-n$ indicates that it should be multiplied by 10^{-n}. Thus in this regression the intercept is effectively 0.

Exercises

4.1 The result of fitting an educational attainment function, regressing *S* on *ASVABC*, *SM*, and *SF*, years of schooling (highest grade completed) of the respondent's mother and father, respectively, using *EAEF* Data Set 21 is shown below. Give an interpretation of the regression coefficients.

```
. reg S ASVABC SM SF

  Source |       SS       df       MS              Number of obs =     570
---------+------------------------------           F(  3,   566) =  110.83
   Model | 1278.24153        3  426.080508         Prob > F      =  0.0000
Residual | 2176.00584      566  3.84453329         R-squared     =  0.3700
---------+------------------------------           Adj R-squared =  0.3667
   Total | 3454.24737      569  6.07073351         Root MSE      =  1.9607


       S |    Coef.   Std. Err.     t     P>|t|    [95% Conf. Interval]
---------+--------------------------------------------------------------
  ASVABC |  .1295006  .0099544   13.009   0.000    .1099486   .1490527
      SM |  .069403   .0422974    1.641   0.101   -.013676    .152482
      SF |  .1102684  .0311948    3.535   0.000    .0489967   .1715401
   _cons |  4.914654  .5063527    9.706   0.000    3.920094   5.909214
```

4.2 Fit an educational attainment function parallel to that in Exercise 4.1, using your *EAEF* data set, and give an interpretation of the coefficients.

4.3 Fit an earnings function parallel to that in Section 4.1, using your *EAEF* data set, and give an interpretation of the coefficients.

4.4 Using your *EAEF* data set, make a graphical representation of the relationship between *S* and *SM* using the technique described above, assuming that the true model is as in Exercise 4.2. To do this, regress *S* on *ASVABC* and *SF* and save the residuals. Do the same with *SM*. Plot the *S* and *SM* residuals. Also regress the former on the latter, and verify that the slope coefficient is the same as that obtained in Exercise 4.2.

4.5* Explain why the intercept in the regression of *EEARN* on *ES* is equal to 0.

4.3 Properties of the multiple regression coefficients

As in the case of simple regression analysis, the regression coefficients should be thought of as special kinds of random variables whose random components are attributable to the presence of the disturbance term in the model. Each regression coefficient is calculated as a function of the values of Y and the explanatory variables in the sample, and Y in turn is determined by the explanatory variables and the disturbance term. It follows that the regression coefficients are really determined by the values of the explanatory variables and the disturbance term and that their properties depend critically upon the properties of the latter.

We shall continue to assume that the Gauss–Markov conditions are satisfied, namely (1) that the expected value of u in any observation is 0, (2) that the population variance of its distribution is the same for all observations, (3) that the population covariance of its values in any two observations is 0, and (4) that it is distributed independently of any explanatory variable. The first three conditions are the same as for simple regression analysis and (4) is a generalization of its counterpart. For the time being we shall adopt a stronger version of (4) and assume that the explanatory variables are nonstochastic.

There are two further practical requirements. First, there must be enough data to fit the regression line; that is, there must be at least as many (independent) observations as there are parameters to be estimated. Second, as we shall see in Section 4.4, there must not be an exact linear relationship among the explanatory variables.

Unbiasedness

We will first show that b_2 is an unbiased estimator of β_2 in the case where there are two explanatory variables. The proof can easily be generalized, using matrix algebra, to any number of explanatory variables. As one can see from (4.11), b_2 is calculated as a function of X_2, X_3, and Y. Y in turn is generated by X_2, X_3, and u. Hence b_2 depends in fact on the values of X_2, X_3, and u in the sample (provided that you understand what is going on, you may skip the details of the mathematical working):

$$
\begin{aligned}
b_2 &= \frac{\mathrm{Cov}(X_2, Y)\mathrm{Var}(X_3) - \mathrm{Cov}(X_3, Y)\mathrm{Cov}(X_2, X_3)}{\mathrm{Var}(X_2)\mathrm{Var}(X_3) - [\mathrm{Cov}(X_2, X_3)]^2} \\[2mm]
&= \frac{1}{\Delta}\left\{ \begin{array}{l} \mathrm{Cov}(X_2, [\beta_1 + \beta_2 X_2 + \beta_3 X_3 + u])\mathrm{Var}(X_3) \\ -\mathrm{Cov}(X_3, [\beta_1 + \beta_2 X_2 + \beta_3 X_3 + u])\mathrm{Cov}(X_2, X_3) \end{array} \right\} \\[2mm]
&= \frac{1}{\Delta}\left\{ \begin{array}{l} [\mathrm{Cov}(X_2, \beta_2 X_2) + \mathrm{Cov}(X_2, \beta_3 X_3) + \mathrm{Cov}(X_2, u)]\mathrm{Var}(X_3) \\ -[\mathrm{Cov}(X_3, \beta_2 X_2) + \mathrm{Cov}(X_3, \beta_3 X_3) + \mathrm{Cov}(X_3, u)]\mathrm{Cov}(X_2, X_3) \end{array} \right\},
\end{aligned}
$$

$$(4.21)$$

where Δ is $\text{Var}(X_2)\text{Var}(X_3) - [\text{Cov}(X_2, X_3)]^2$, since $\text{Cov}(X_2, \beta_1)$ and $\text{Cov}(X_3, \beta_1)$ are both 0, using Covariance Rule 3, because β_1 is a constant. $\text{Cov}(X_2, \beta_2 X_2)$ is $\beta_2 \text{Var}(X_2)$, using Covariance Rule 2 and the fact that $\text{Cov}(X_2, X_2)$ is the same as $\text{Var}(X_2)$. Similarly $\text{Cov}(X_3, \beta_3 X_3)$ is $\beta_3 \text{Var}(X_3)$. Hence

$$b_2 = \frac{1}{\Delta} \left\{ \begin{array}{l} [\beta_2 \text{Var}(X_2) + \beta_3 \text{Cov}(X_2, X_3) + \text{Cov}(X_2, u)]\text{Var}(X_3) \\ -[\beta_2 \text{Cov}(X_2, X_3) + \beta_3 \text{Var}(X_3) + \text{Cov}(X_3, u)]\text{Cov}(X_2, X_3) \end{array} \right\}$$

$$= \frac{1}{\Delta} \left\{ \begin{array}{l} \beta_2 \text{Var}(X_2)\text{Var}(X_3) + \beta_3 \text{Cov}(X_2, X_3)\text{Var}(X_3) \\ +\text{Cov}(X_2, u)\text{Var}(X_3) - \beta_2 [\text{Cov}(X_2, X_3)]^2 \\ -\beta_3 \text{Var}(X_3)\text{Cov}(X_2, X_3) - \text{Cov}(X_3, u)\text{Cov}(X_2, X_3) \end{array} \right\}$$

$$= \frac{1}{\Delta} \left\{ \begin{array}{l} \beta_2 \left(\text{Var}(X_2)\text{Var}(X_3) - [\text{Cov}(X_2, X_3)]^2 \right) \\ +\text{Cov}(X_2, u)\text{Var}(X_3) - \text{Cov}(X_3, u)\text{Cov}(X_2, X_3) \end{array} \right\}$$

$$= \frac{1}{\Delta} [\beta_2 \Delta + \text{Cov}(X_2, u)\text{Var}(X_3) - \text{Cov}(X_3, u)\text{Cov}(X_2, X_3)]$$

$$= \beta_2 + \frac{1}{\Delta} [\text{Cov}(X_2, u)\text{Var}(X_3) - \text{Cov}(X_3, u)\text{Cov}(X_2, X_3)]. \qquad (4.22)$$

Thus b_2 has two components: the true value β_2 and an error component. If we take expectations, we have

$$E(b_2) = \beta_2 + \frac{1}{\Delta}\text{Var}(X_3)E[\text{Cov}(X_2, u)] - \frac{1}{\Delta}\text{Cov}(X_2, X_3)E[\text{Cov}(X_3, u)]$$

$$= \beta_2 \qquad (4.23)$$

provided that X_2 and X_3 are nonstochastic. (The proofs that $E[\text{Cov}(X_2, u)]$ and $E[\text{Cov}(X_3, u)]$ are 0 are parallel to that for $E[\text{Cov}(X, u)]$ being 0 in Chapter 3.)

Efficiency

The Gauss–Markov theorem proves that, for multiple regression analysis, as for simple regression analysis, the ordinary least squares (OLS) technique yields the most efficient linear estimators, in the sense that it is impossible to find other unbiased estimators with lower variances, using the same sample information, provided that the Gauss–Markov conditions are satisfied. We will not attempt to prove this theorem since matrix algebra is required.

Precision of the multiple regression coefficients

We will investigate the factors governing the likely precision of the regression coefficients for the case where there are two explanatory variables. Similar considerations apply in the more general case, but with more than two variables the analysis becomes complex and one needs to switch to matrix algebra.

If the true relationship is

$$Y_i = \beta_1 + \beta_2 X_{2i} + \beta_3 X_{3i} + u_i, \tag{4.24}$$

and you fit the regression line

$$\hat{Y}_i = b_1 + b_2 X_{2i} + b_3 X_{3i}, \tag{4.25}$$

using appropriate data, $\sigma_{b_2}^2$, the population variance of the probability distribution of b_2, is given by *Variance of b_2.*

$$\sigma_{b_2}^2 = \frac{\sigma_u^2}{n\,\text{Var}(X_2)} \times \frac{1}{1 - r_{X_2X_3}^2}, \tag{4.26}$$

where σ_u^2 is the population variance of u and $r_{X_2X_3}$ is the correlation between X_2 and X_3. A parallel expression may be obtained for the population variance of b_3, replacing $\text{Var}(X_2)$ with $\text{Var}(X_3)$.

From (4.26) you can see that, as in the case of simple regression analysis, it is desirable for n and $\text{Var}(X_2)$ to be large and for σ_u^2 to be small. However, we now have the further term $(1 - r_{X_2X_3}^2)$ and clearly it is desirable that the correlation between X_2 and X_3 should be low.

It is easy to give an intuitive explanation of this. The greater the correlation, the harder it is to discriminate between the effects of the explanatory variables on Y, and the less accurate will be the regression estimates. This can be a serious problem and it is discussed in the next section.

The standard deviation of the distribution of b_2 is the square root of the variance. As in the simple regression case, the standard error of b_2 is the estimate of the standard deviation. For this we need to estimate σ_u^2. The variance of the residuals provides a biased estimator:

$$E[\text{Var}(e)] = \frac{n-k}{n}\sigma_u^2, \tag{4.27}$$

where k is the number of parameters in the regression equation. However, we can obtain an unbiased estimator, s_u^2, by neutralizing the bias:

$$s_u^2 = \frac{n}{n-k}\text{Var}(e). \tag{4.28}$$

The standard error is then given by

$$\text{s.e.}(b_2) = \sqrt{\frac{s_u^2}{n\,\text{Var}(X_2)} \times \frac{1}{1 - r_{X_2X_3}^2}}. \tag{4.29}$$

The determinants of the standard error will be illustrated by comparing them in earnings functions fitted to two subsamples of the respondents in *EAEF* Data Set 21, those who reported that their wages were set by collective bargaining and

Table 4.3

```
. reg EARNINGS S ASVABC if COLLBARG==1 .
```

Source	SS	df	MS		
Model	172.902083	2	86.4510417		
Residual	2012.88504	60	33.5480841		
Total	2185.78713	62	35.2546311		

Number of obs =	63
F(2, 60) =	2.58
Prob > F =	0.0844
R-squared =	0.0791
Adj R-squared =	0.0484
Root MSE =	5.7921

EARNINGS	Coef.	Std. Err.	t	P>|t|	[95% Conf. Interval]	
S	-.3872787	.3530145	-1.097	0.277	-1.093413	.3188555
ASVABC	.2309133	.1019211	2.266	0.027	.0270407	.4347858
_cons	8.291716	4.869209	1.703	0.094	-1.448152	18.03158

Table 4.4

```
. reg EARNINGS S ASVABC if COLLBARG==0
```

Source	SS	df	MS		
Model	4966.96516	2	2483.48258		
Residual	31052.2066	504	61.6115211		
Total	36019.1718	506	71.184134		

Number of obs =	507
F(2, 504) =	40.31
Prob > F =	0.0000
R-squared =	0.1379
Adj R-squared =	0.1345
Root MSE =	7.8493

EARNINGS	Coef.	Std. Err.	t	P>|t|	[95% Conf. Interval]	
S	.8891909	.1741617	5.106	0.000	.5470186	1.231363
ASVABC	.1398727	.0461806	3.029	0.003	.0491425	.2306029
_cons	-6.100961	2.15968	-2.825	0.005	-10.34404	-1.857877

the remainder. Regression output for the two subsamples is shown in Tables 4.3 and 4.4. In Stata, subsamples may be selected by adding an 'if' expression to a command. *COLLBARG* is a variable in the data set defined to be 1 for the collective bargaining subsample and 0 for the others. Note that in tests for equality, Stata requires the = sign to be duplicated.

The standard error of the coefficient of *S* is 0.1742 in the second regression and 0.3530, twice as large, in the first. We will investigate the reasons for the difference. It will be convenient to rewrite (4.29) in such a way as to isolate the contributions of the various factors:

$$\text{s.e.}(b_2) = s_u \times \frac{1}{\sqrt{n}} \times \frac{1}{\sqrt{\text{Var}(X_2)}} \times \frac{1}{\sqrt{1 - r_{X_2 X_3}^2}}. \qquad (4.30)$$

Table 4.5 Decomposition of the standard error of S

Component	s_u	n	$Var(S)$	$r_{S,ASVABC}$	s.e.
Collective bargaining	5.7921	63	6.0136	0.5380	0.3530
Not collective bargaining	7.8493	507	6.0645	0.5826	0.1742
Factor					
Collective bargaining	5.7921	0.1260	0.4078	1.1863	0.3531
Not collective bargaining	7.8493	0.0444	0.4061	1.2304	0.1741

The first element we need, s_u, can be obtained directly from the regression output. s_u^2 is equal to the sum of the squares of the residuals divided by $n - k$, here $n - 3$:

$$s_u^2 = \frac{n}{n-k}\text{Var}(e) = \frac{n}{n-k} \times \frac{1}{n}\sum_{i=1}^{n}(e_i - \bar{e})^2 = \frac{1}{n-k}\sum_{i=1}^{n}e_i^2 = \frac{1}{n-k}RSS. \quad (4.31)$$

(Note that $\bar{e}$ is equal to 0. This was proved for the simple regression model in Chapter 3, and the proof generalizes easily.) RSS is given in the top-left quarter of the regression output, as part of the decomposition of the total sum of squares into the explained sum of squares (in the Stata output denoted the model sum of squares) and the residual sum of squares. The value of $n - k$ is given to the right of RSS, and the ratio $RSS/(n-k)$ to the right of that. The square root, s_u, is listed as the Root MSE (root mean square error) in the top-right quarter of the regression output, 5.7921 for the collective bargaining subsample and 7.8493 for the regression with the other respondents.

The number of observations, 63 in the first regression and 507 in the second, is also listed in the top-right quarter of the regression output. The variances of S, 6.0136 and 6.0645, had to be calculated from the sample data. The correlations between S and $ASVABC$, 0.5380 and 0.5826 respectively, were calculated using the Stata 'cor' command. The factors of the standard error in equation (4.30) were then derived and are shown in the lower half of Table 4.5.

It can be seen that, in this example, the reason that the standard error of S in the collective bargaining subsample is relatively large is that the number of observations in that subsample is relatively small. The effect of the variance of S is neutral, and those of the other two factors are in the opposite direction, but not enough to make much difference.

t tests and confidence intervals

t tests on the regression coefficients are performed in the same way as for simple regression analysis. Note that when you are looking up the critical level of t at any given significance level, it will depend on the number of degrees of freedom, $n - k$: the number of observations minus the number of parameters estimated. The confidence intervals are also constructed in exactly the same way as in simple regression analysis, subject to the above comment about the number of degrees of freedom. As can be seen from the regression output, Stata automatically calculates confidence intervals for the coefficients (95 percent by default, other levels if desired), but this is not a standard feature of regression applications.

Consistency

Provided that the fourth Gauss–Markov condition is satisfied, OLS yields consistent estimates in the multiple regression model, as in the simple regression model. As n becomes large, the population variance of the estimator of each regression coefficient tends to 0 and the distribution collapses to a spike, one condition for consistency. Since the estimator is unbiased, the spike is located at the true value, the other condition for consistency.

Exercises

4.6   Perform t tests on the coefficients of the variables in the educational attainment function reported in Exercise 4.1.

4.7   Perform t tests on the coefficients of the variables in the educational attainment and earnings functions fitted by you in Exercises 4.2 and 4.3.

4.8   The following earnings functions were fitted separately for males and females, using *EAEF* Data Set 21 (standard errors in parentheses):

males

$$\widehat{EARNINGS} = -3.6121 + 0.7499S + 0.1558ASVABC.$$
$$(2.8420)\ (0.2434)\quad (0.0600)$$

females

$$\widehat{EARNINGS} = 5.9010 + 0.8803S + 0.1088ASVABC.$$
$$(2.6315)\ (0.1910)\quad (0.0577)$$

Using equation (4.30), explain why the standard errors of the coefficients of S and $ASVABC$ are greater for the male subsample than for the female subsample, and why the difference in the standard errors is relatively large for S.

Further data:

	males	females
s_u	8.47	6.23
n	325	245
$r_{S,ASVABC}$	0.61	0.55
Var(S)	5.88	6.26
Var($ASVABC$)	96.65	68.70

4.9*   Demonstrate that $\bar{e}$ is equal to 0 in multiple regression analysis. (*Note*: The proof is a generalization of the proof for the simple regression model, given in Section 2.7.)

4.10   Investigate whether you can extend the determinants of weight model using your *EAEF* data set, taking *WEIGHT94* as the dependent variable, and *HEIGHT* and other continuous variables in the data set as explanatory variables. Provide an interpretation of the coefficients and perform *t* tests on them.

4.4 Multicollinearity

In the previous section, in the context of a model with two explanatory variables, it was seen that the higher is the correlation between the explanatory variables, the larger are the population variances of the distributions of their coefficients, and the greater is the risk of obtaining erratic estimates of the coefficients. If the correlation causes the regression model to become unsatisfactory in this respect, it is said to be suffering from multicollinearity.

A high correlation does not necessarily lead to poor estimates. If all the other factors determining the variances of the regression coefficients are helpful, that is, if the number of observations and the sample variances of the explanatory variables are large, and the variance of the disturbance term small, you may well obtain good estimates after all. Multicollinearity therefore must be caused by a *combination* of a high correlation and one or more of the other factors being unhelpful. And it is a matter of *degree*, not kind. Any regression will suffer from it to some extent, unless all the explanatory variables are uncorrelated. You only start to talk about it when you think that it is affecting the regression results seriously.

It is an especially common problem in time-series regressions, that is, where the data consist of a series of observations on the variables over a number of time periods. If two or more of the explanatory variables have a strong time trend, they will be highly correlated and this condition may give rise to multicollinearity.

It should be noted that the presence of multicollinearity does not mean that the model is misspecified. Accordingly, the regression coefficients remain unbiased and the standard errors remain valid. The standard errors will be larger than they would have been in the absence of multicollinearity, warning you that the regression estimates are unreliable.

We will consider first the case of exact multicollinearity where the explanatory variables are perfectly correlated. Suppose that the true relationship is

$$Y = 2 + 3X_2 + X_3 + u. \tag{4.32}$$

Suppose that there is a linear relationship between X_2 and X_3:

$$X_3 = 2X_2 - 1, \tag{4.33}$$

Table 4.6

X_2	X_3	Y	Change in X_2	Change in X_3	Approximate change in Y
10	19	$51 + u_1$	1	2	5
11	21	$56 + u_2$	1	2	5
12	23	$61 + u_3$	1	2	5
13	25	$66 + u_4$	1	2	5
14	27	$71 + u_5$	1	2	5
15	29	$76 + u_6$	1	2	5

and suppose that X_2 increases by one unit in each observation. X_3 will increase by 2 units, and Y by approximately 5 units, for example as shown in Table 4.6.

Looking at the data, you could come to any of the following conclusions:

1. the correct one, that Y is determined by (4.32)
2. that X_3 is irrelevant and Y is determined by the relationship

$$Y = 1 + 5X_2 + u. \tag{4.34}$$

3. that X_2 is irrelevant and Y is determined by the relationship

$$Y = 3.5 + 2.5X_3 + u. \tag{4.35}$$

In fact these are not the only possibilities. Any relationship that is a weighted average of (4.34) and (4.35) would also fit the data. [(4.32) may be regarded as such a weighted average, being (4.34) multiplied by 0.6 plus (4.35) multiplied by 0.4.]

In such a situation it is impossible for regression analysis, or any other technique for that matter, to distinguish between these possibilities. You would not even be able to calculate the regression coefficients because both the numerator and the denominator of the regression coefficients would collapse to 0. This will be demonstrated with the general two-variable case. Suppose

$$Y = \beta_1 + \beta_2 X_2 + \beta_3 X_3 + u \tag{4.36}$$

and

$$X_3 = \lambda + \mu X_2. \tag{4.37}$$

Substituting for X_3 in (4.11), one obtains

$$
\begin{aligned}
b_2 &= \frac{\mathrm{Cov}(X_2, Y)\mathrm{Var}(X_3) - \mathrm{Cov}(X_3, Y)\mathrm{Cov}(X_2, X_3)}{\mathrm{Var}(X_2)\mathrm{Var}(X_3) - [\mathrm{Cov}(X_2, X_3)]^2} \\
&= \frac{\mathrm{Cov}(X_2, Y)\mathrm{Var}(\lambda + \mu X_2) - \mathrm{Cov}([\lambda + \mu X_2], Y)\mathrm{Cov}(X_2, [\lambda + \mu X_2])}{\mathrm{Var}(X_2)\mathrm{Var}(\lambda + \mu X_2) - [\mathrm{Cov}(X_2, [\lambda + \mu X_2])]^2} \\
&= \frac{\mathrm{Cov}(X_2, Y)\mathrm{Var}(\mu X_2) - \mathrm{Cov}(\mu X_2, Y)\mathrm{Cov}(X_2, \mu X_2)}{\mathrm{Var}(X_2)\mathrm{Var}(\mu X_2) - [\mathrm{Cov}(X_2, \mu X_2)]^2}.
\end{aligned}
\tag{4.38}
$$

By virtue of Variance Rule 4, the additive λ in the variances can be dropped. A similar rule could be developed for covariances, since an additive λ does not affect them either. Hence

$$
\begin{aligned}
b_2 &= \frac{\mathrm{Cov}(X_2, Y)\mu^2\mathrm{Var}(X_2) - \mu\mathrm{Cov}(X_2, Y)\mu\mathrm{Cov}(X_2, X_2)}{\mathrm{Var}(X_2)\mu^2\mathrm{Var}(X_2) - [\mu\mathrm{Cov}(X_2, X_2)]^2} \\
&= \frac{\mu^2\mathrm{Cov}(X_2, Y)\mathrm{Var}(X_2) - \mu^2\mathrm{Cov}(X_2, Y)\mathrm{Var}(X_2)}{\mu^2\mathrm{Var}(X_2)\mathrm{Var}(X_2) - [\mu\mathrm{Var}(X_2)]^2} = \frac{0}{0}.
\end{aligned}
\tag{4.39}
$$

It is unusual for there to be an exact relationship among the explanatory variables in a regression. When this occurs, it is typically because there is a logical error in the specification. An example is provided by Exercise 4.13. However, it often happens that there is an approximate relationship. Table 4.7 shows a regression of *EARNINGS* on *S*, *ASVABC*, and *ASVAB5*. *ASVAB5* is the score on a speed test of the ability to perform very simple arithmetical computations. Like *ASVABC*, the scores on this test were scaled so that they had mean 50 and standard deviation 10.

The regression result indicates that an extra year of schooling increases hourly earnings by $0.71. An extra point on *ASVABC* increases hourly earnings by $0.11. An individual with a score one standard deviation above the mean would therefore tend to earn an extra $1.10 per hour, compared with an individual at the mean. An extra point on the numerical computation speed test increases hourly earnings by $0.08.

Does *ASVAB5* belong in the earnings function? A *t* test reveals that its coefficient is just significantly different from 0 at the 5 percent level, using a one-tailed test. (A one-tailed test is justified by the fact that it is unlikely that a good score on this test would adversely affect earnings.) In this regression, the coefficient of *ASVABC* is significant only at the 5 percent level. In the regression without *ASVAB5*, reported in Section 4.1, its *t* statistic was 3.60, making it significantly different from 0 at the 0.1 percent level. The reason for the reduction in its *t* ratio is that it has a high correlation, 0.64, with *ASVAB5*. This makes it difficult to pinpoint the individual effects of *ASVABC* and *ASVAB5*. As a consequence the regression estimates tend to be erratic. The high correlation causes the standard errors to be larger than they would have been if *ASVABC* and *ASVAB5* had been less highly correlated, warning us that the point estimates are unreliable.

Table 4.7

```
. reg EARNINGS S ASVABC ASVAB5

    Source |       SS         df       MS              Number of obs =      570
-----------+------------------------------           F(  3,   566) =    27.66
     Model |  4909.11468       3  1636.37156          Prob > F      =   0.0000
  Residual |  33487.9224     566  59.1659406          R-squared     =   0.1279
-----------+------------------------------           Adj R-squared =   0.1232
     Total |  38397.0371     569  67.4816117          Root MSE      =   7.6919


----------------------------------------------------------------------------
  EARNINGS |     Coef.   Std. Err.      t     P>|t|    [95% Conf. Interval]
-----------+----------------------------------------------------------------
         S |   .7115506   .1612235    4.413   0.000    .3948811    1.02822
    ASVABC |   .1104595   .0504223    2.191   0.029    .0114219   .2094972
    ASVAB5 |   .0770794   .0463868    1.662   0.097   -.0140319   .1681908
     _cons |  -5.944977   2.161409   -2.751   0.006   -10.19034  -1.699616
----------------------------------------------------------------------------

. cor ASVABC ASVAB5
(obs=570)

           |   ASVABC   ASVAB5
-----------+------------------
    ASVABC |   1.0000
    ASVAB5 |   0.6371   1.0000
```

In this regression, multicollinearity is making it difficult to determine whether *ASVAB5* is a determinant of earnings. It is possible that it is not, and that its marginally significant *t* statistic has occurred as a matter of chance.

Multicollinearity in models with more than two explanatory variables

The foregoing discussion of multicollinearity was restricted to the case where there are two explanatory variables. In models with a greater number of explanatory variables, multicollinearity may be caused by an approximate linear relationship among them. It may be difficult to discriminate between the effects of one variable and those of a linear combination of the remainder. In the model with two explanatory variables, an approximate linear relationship automatically means a high correlation, but when there are three or more, this is not necessarily the case. A linear relationship does not inevitably imply high pairwise correlations between any of the variables. The effects of multicollinearity are the same as in the case with two explanatory variables, and, as in that case, the problem may not be serious if the population variance of the disturbance term is small, the number of observations large, and the variances of the explanatory variables large.

What can you do about multicollinearity?

The various ways of trying to alleviate multicollinearity fall into two categories: direct attempts to improve the four conditions responsible for the reliability of the regression estimates, and indirect methods.

First, you may try to reduce σ_u^2. The disturbance term is the joint effect of all the variables influencing Y that you have not included explicitly in the regression equation. If you can think of an important variable that you have omitted, and is therefore contributing to u, you will reduce the population variance of the disturbance term if you add it to the regression equation.

By way of illustration, we will take the earnings function discussed in the previous section, where a high correlation between ASVABC, the composite cognitive ability score, and ASVAB5, the score on a numerical computation speed test, gave rise to a problem of multicollinearity (Table 4.8). We now add three new variables that are often found to be determinants of earnings: length of tenure with the current employer, here measured in weeks, sex of respondent, and whether the respondent was living in an urban or a rural area. The last two variables are qualitative variables and their treatment will be explained in Chapter 6. All of these new variables have high t statistics and as a consequence the estimate of σ_u^2 falls, from 59.17 to 54.50 (see the calculation of the residual sum of squares divided by the number of degrees of freedom in the top-left quarter of the

Table 4.8

```
. reg EARNINGS S ASVABC ASVAB5 TENURE MALE URBAN

    Source |       SS       df       MS              Number of obs =     570
-----------+------------------------------           F(  6,    563) =   23.60
     Model |  7715.87322     6   1285.97887           Prob > F      =  0.0000
  Residual |  30681.1638   563   54.4958505           R-squared     =  0.2009
-----------+------------------------------           Adj R-squared =  0.1924
     Total |  38397.0371   569   67.4816117           Root MSE      =  7.3821


------------------------------------------------------------------------------
  EARNINGS |     Coef.   Std. Err.      t     P>|t|    [95% Conf. Interval]
-----------+------------------------------------------------------------------
         S |   .8137184   .1563975    5.203   0.000     .5065245    1.120912
     ASVABC |   .0442801    .049716    0.891   0.373    -.0533714    .1419317
     ASVAB5 |   .1113769   .0458757    2.428   0.016     .0212685    .2014853
     TENURE |    .287038   .0676471    4.243   0.000     .1541665    .4199095
       MALE |   3.123929     .64685    4.829   0.000     1.853395    4.394463
      URBAN |   2.061867   .7274286    2.834   0.005     .6330618    3.490672
      _cons |  -10.60023   2.195757   -4.828   0.000    -14.91311   -6.287358
------------------------------------------------------------------------------
```

regression output). However the joint contribution of the new variables to the explanatory power of the model is small, despite being highly significant, and the reduction in the standard errors of the coefficients of S, $ASVABC$, and $ASVAB5$ is negligible. They might even have increased. The new variables happen to have very low correlations with S, $ASVABC$, and $ASVAB5$. If they had been linearly related to one or more of the variables already in the equation, their inclusion could have made the problem of multicollinearity worse. Note how unstable the coefficients are, another sign of multicollinearity.

The next factor to consider is n, the number of observations. If you are working with cross-section data (individuals, households, enterprises, etc.) and you are undertaking a survey, you could increase the size of the sample by negotiating a bigger budget. Alternatively, you could make a fixed budget go further by using a technique known as clustering. You divide the country geographically into localities. For example, the National Longitudinal Survey of Youth, from which the $EAEF$ data are drawn, divides the country into counties, independent cities, and standard metropolitan statistical areas. You select a number of localities randomly, perhaps using stratified random sampling to make sure that metropolitan, other urban and rural areas are properly represented. You then confine the survey to the localities selected. This reduces the travel time of the fieldworkers, allowing them to interview a greater number of respondents.

If you are working with time-series data, you may be able to increase the sample by working with shorter time intervals for the data, for example quarterly or even monthly data instead of annual data. This is such an obvious thing to do that most researchers working with time series almost automatically use quarterly data, if they are available, instead of annual data, even if there does not appear to be a problem of multicollinearity, simply to minimize the population variances of the regression coefficients. There are, however, potential problems. You may introduce, or aggravate, autocorrelation (see Chapter 13), but this can be neutralized. Also you may introduce, or aggravate, measurement error bias (see Chapter 9) if the quarterly data are less accurately measured than the corresponding annual data. This problem is not so easily overcome, but it may be a minor one.

Table 4.9 shows the result of running the regression with all 2,868 observations in the $EAEF$ data set. Comparing this result with that using Data Set 21, we see that the standard errors are much smaller, as expected. As a consequence, the t statistics are higher. In the case of $ASVABC$, this is partly due to the fact that the point estimate of the coefficient is higher. However, in the case of $ASVAB5$, the t statistic is higher despite the fact that the coefficient is smaller.

A third possible way of reducing the problem of multicollinearity might be to increase the variance of the explanatory variables. This is possible only at the design stage of a survey. For example, if you were planning a household survey with the aim of investigating how expenditure patterns vary with income, you should make sure that the sample included relatively rich and relatively poor households as well as middle-income households by stratifying the sample. (For

Table 4.9

```
. reg EARNINGS S ASVABC ASVAB5

    Source |       SS        df       MS              Number of obs =    2868
-----------+------------------------------           F(  3,  2864) =  183.45
     Model | 36689.8765      3  12229.9588            Prob > F      =  0.0000
  Residual | 190928.139   2864  66.664853             R-squared     =  0.1612
-----------+------------------------------           Adj R-squared =  0.1603
     Total | 227618.016   2867  79.3924017            Root MSE      =  8.1649

------------------------------------------------------------------------------
  EARNINGS |     Coef.   Std. Err.      t    P>|t|     [95% Conf. Interval]
-----------+------------------------------------------------------------------
         S |  1.002693   .0787447   12.733   0.000    .8482905    1.157095
    ASVABC |  .1448345   .0241135    6.006   0.000    .097553     .1921161
    ASVAB5 |  .0483846   .0218352    2.216   0.027    .0055703    .091199
     _cons | -9.654593   1.033311   -9.343   0.000   -11.6807    -7.628485
------------------------------------------------------------------------------
```

a discussion of sampling theory and techniques, see, for example, Moser and Kalton, 1985, or Fowler, 1993.)

The fourth direct method is the most direct of all. If you are still at the design stage of a survey, you should do your best to obtain a sample where the explanatory variables are less related (more easily said than done, of course).

Next, indirect methods. If the correlated variables are similar conceptually, it may be reasonable to combine them into some overall index. That is precisely what has been done with the three cognitive ASVAB variables. *ASVABC* has been calculated as a weighted average of *ASVAB2* (arithmetic reasoning), *ASVAB3* (word knowledge), and *ASVAB4* (paragraph comprehension). Table 4.10 shows the result of a regression of *EARNINGS* on *S* and the three components of *ASVABC*. *ASVAB2* has a highly significant coefficient, but *ASVAB3* does not and the coefficient of *ASVAB4* has the wrong sign. This is not surprising, given the high correlations between the ASVAB variables.

Comparing this regression with the regression with *ASVABC*, it can be seen that the standard errors of the coefficients of *ASVAB2*, *ASVAB3*, and *ASVAB4* are larger than that of *ASVABC*, as you would expect. The *t* statistic of *ASVAB2* is larger than that of *ASVABC*, but that is because its coefficient is larger.

Another possible solution to the problem of multicollinearity is to drop some of the correlated variables, if they have insignificant coefficients. If we drop *ASVAB3* and *ASVAB4*, we obtain the output shown in Table 4.11. As expected, the standard error of the coefficient of *ASVAB2* is smaller than in the regression including *ASVAB3* and *ASVAB4*. However, this approach to alleviating the problem of multicollinearity involves the risk that some of the variables dropped may truly belong in the model and their omission may cause omitted variable bias (see Chapter 7).

Table 4.10

```
. reg EARNINGS S ASVAB2 ASVAB3 ASVAB4

  Source |       SS       df       MS              Number of obs =     570
---------+------------------------------          F(  4,   565) =   25.68
   Model | 5906.47726      4 1476.61931           Prob > F      =  0.0000
Residual | 32490.5598     565 57.5054156          R-squared     =  0.1538
---------+------------------------------          Adj R-squared =  0.1478
   Total | 38397.0371     569 67.4816117          Root MSE      =  7.5832


------------------------------------------------------------------------
EARNINGS |    Coef.   Std. Err.     t    P>|t|    [95% Conf. Interval]
---------+--------------------------------------------------------------
       S |  .7362439  .1586812    4.640  0.000    .4245668    1.047921
  ASVAB2 |  .2472668  .0472249    5.236  0.000     .154509    .3400246
  ASVAB3 |  .0137422   .058716    0.234  0.815   -.1015861    .1290705
  ASVAB4 | -.1051868  .0544682   -1.931  0.054   -.2121716     .001798
   _cons | -4.734303   2.06706   -2.290  0.022   -8.794363   -.6742428
------------------------------------------------------------------------

. cor ASVAB2 ASVAB3 ASVAB4
(obs=570)
         |  ASVAB2   ASVAB3   ASVAB4
---------+---------------------------
  ASVAB2 |  1.0000
  ASVAB3 |  0.6916   1.0000
  ASVAB4 |  0.6536   0.7628   1.0000
```

Table 4.11

```
. reg EARNINGS S ASVAB2

  Source |       SS       df       MS              Number of obs =     570
---------+------------------------------          F(  2,   567) =   48.81
   Model | 5639.37111      2 2819.68556           Prob > F      =  0.0000
Residual | 32757.666      567 57.7736613          R-squared     =  0.1469
---------+------------------------------          Adj R-squared =  0.1439
   Total | 38397.0371     569 67.4816117          Root MSE      =  7.6009


------------------------------------------------------------------------
EARNINGS |    Coef.   Std. Err.     t    P>|t|    [95% Conf. Interval]
---------+--------------------------------------------------------------
       S |  .6449415  .1519755    4.244  0.000    .3464378    .9434452
  ASVAB2 |  .2019724  .0376567    5.364  0.000    .1280086    .2759361
   _cons | -5.796398  1.957987   -2.960  0.003   -9.642191   -1.950605
------------------------------------------------------------------------
```

A further way of dealing with the problem of multicollinearity is to use extraneous information, if available, concerning the coefficient of one of the variables.

$$Y = \beta_1 + \beta_2 X + \beta_3 P + u. \qquad (4.40)$$

For example, suppose that Y in equation (4.40) is the aggregate demand for a category of consumer expenditure, X is aggregate disposable personal income, and P is a price index for the category. To fit a model of this type you would use time-series data. If X and P possess strong time trends and are therefore highly correlated, which is often the case with time-series variables, multicollinearity is likely to be a problem. Suppose, however, that you also have cross-section data on Y and X derived from a separate household survey. These variables will be denoted Y' and X' to indicate that the data are household data, not aggregate data. Assuming that all the households in the survey were paying roughly the same price for the commodity, one would fit the simple regression

$$\hat{Y}' = b_1' + b_2' X'. \qquad (4.41)$$

Now substitute b_2' for β_2 in the time-series model,

$$Y = \beta_1 + b_2' X + \beta_3 P + u, \qquad (4.42)$$

subtract $b_2' X$ from both sides,

$$Y - b_2' X = \beta_1 + \beta_3 P + u \qquad (4.43)$$

and regress $Z = Y - b_2' X$ on price. This is a simple regression, so multicollinearity has been eliminated.

There are, however, two possible problems with this technique. First, the estimate of β_3 in (4.43) depends on the accuracy of the estimate of b_2', and this of course is subject to sampling error. Second, you are assuming that the income coefficient has the same meaning in time-series and cross-section contexts, and this may not be the case. For many commodities the short-run and long-run effects of changes in income may differ because expenditure patterns are subject to inertia. A change in income can affect expenditure both directly, by altering the budget constraint, and indirectly, through causing a change in lifestyle, and the indirect effect is much slower than the direct one. As a first approximation, it is commonly argued that time-series regressions, particularly those using short sample periods, estimate short-run effects while cross-section regressions estimate long-run ones. For a discussion of this and related issues, see Kuh and Meyer (1957).

Last, but by no means least, is the use of a theoretical restriction, which is defined as a hypothetical relationship among the parameters of a regression model. It will be explained using an educational attainment model as an example. Suppose that we hypothesize that years of schooling, S, depends on $ASVABC$,

Table 4.12

```
. reg S ASVABC SM SF

  Source |       SS       df       MS              Number of obs =     570
---------+------------------------------           F(  3,    566) =  110.83
   Model | 1278.24153      3  426.080508           Prob > F       =  0.0000
Residual | 2176.00584    566  3.84453329           R-squared      =  0.3700
---------+------------------------------           Adj R-squared  =  0.3667
   Total | 3454.24737    569  6.07073351           Root MSE       =  1.9607


------------------------------------------------------------------------------
       S |     Coef.   Std. Err.      t    P>|t|     [95% Conf. Interval]
---------+--------------------------------------------------------------------
  ASVABC |   .1295006   .0099544   13.009   0.000     .1099486    .1490527
      SM |    .069403   .0422974    1.641   0.101     -.013676    .152482
      SF |   .1102684   .0311948    3.535   0.000     .0489967    .1715401
   _cons |   4.914654   .5063527    9.706   0.000     3.920094    5.909214
------------------------------------------------------------------------------
```

and the years of schooling of the respondent's mother and father, SM and SF, respectively:

$$S = \beta_1 + \beta_2 ASVABC + \beta_3 SM + \beta_4 SF + u. \tag{4.44}$$

Fitting the model using *EAEF* Data Set 21, we obtain the output shown in Table 4.12.

The regression coefficients imply that S increases by 0.13 years for every one-point increase in $ASVABC$, by 0.07 years for every extra year of schooling of the mother and by 0.11 years for every extra year of schooling of the father. Mother's education is generally held to be at least as important as father's education for educational attainment, so the relatively low coefficient of SM is unexpected. It is also surprising that the coefficient is not significant, even at the 5 percent level, using a one-tailed test. However assortive mating leads to a high correlation between SM and SF and the regression appears to be suffering from multicollinearity.

Suppose that we hypothesize that mother's and father's education are equally important. We can then impose the restriction $\beta_3 = \beta_4$. This allows us to write the equation as

$$S = \beta_1 + \beta_2 ASVABC + \beta_3(SM + SF) + u. \tag{4.45}$$

Defining SP to be the sum of SM and SF, the equation may be rewritten with $ASVABC$ and SP as the explanatory variables:

$$S = \beta_1 + \beta_2 ASVABC + \beta_3 SP + u. \tag{4.46}$$

Table 4.13

```
. g SP=SM+SF
. reg S ASVABC SP

  Source |       SS       df       MS              Number of obs =     570
---------+------------------------------          F( 2,   567) =  166.22
   Model | 1276.73764      2  638.368819           Prob > F      =  0.0000
Residual | 2177.50973    567  3.84040517           R-squared     =  0.3696
---------+------------------------------          Adj R-squared =  0.3674
   Total | 3454.24737    569  6.07073351           Root MSE      =  1.9597


       S |     Coef.   Std. Err.     t    P>|t|    [95% Conf. Interval]
---------+--------------------------------------------------------------
  ASVABC |  .1295653   .0099485  13.024  0.000    .1100249    .1491057
      SP |   .093741   .0165688   5.658  0.000    .0611973    .1262847
   _cons |  4.823123   .4844829   9.955  0.000    3.871523    5.774724
```

The estimate of β_3 is now 0.094. Not surprisingly, this is a compromise between the coefficients of *SM* and *SF* in the previous specification. The standard error of *SP* is much smaller than those of *SM* and *SF*, indicating that the use of the restriction has led to a gain in efficiency, and as a consequence the *t* statistic is very high. Thus the problem of multicollinearity has been eliminated. However, it is possible that the restriction may not be valid. We should test it. We shall see how to do this in Chapter 7.

Exercises

4.11   Using your *EAEF* data set, regress *S* on *SM*, *SF*, *ASVAB2*, *ASVAB3*, and *ASVAB4*, the three components of the *ASVABC* composite score. Compare the coefficients and their standard errors with those of *ASVABC* in a regression of *S* on *SM*, *SF*, and *ASVABC*. Calculate correlation coefficients for the three ASVAB components.

4.12   Investigate the determinants of family size by regressing *SIBLINGS* on *SM* and *SF* using your *EAEF* data set. *SM* and *SF* are likely to be highly correlated (find the correlation in your data set) and the regression may be subject to multicollinearity. Introduce the restriction that the theoretical coefficients of *SM* and *SF* are equal and run the regression a second time replacing *SM* and *SF* by their sum, *SP*. Evaluate the regression results.

4.13* A researcher investigating the determinants of the demand for public transport in a certain city has the following data for 100 residents for the previous calendar year: expenditure on public transport, *E*, measured in dollars; number of days worked, *W*; and number of days not worked, *NW*. By definition *NW* is equal to $365 - W$. He attempts to fit the following model

$$E = \beta_1 + \beta_2 W + \beta_3 NW + u.$$

Explain why he is unable to fit this equation. (Give both intuitive and technical explanations.) How might he resolve the problem?

4.14 Years of work experience in the labor force is generally found to be an important determinant of earnings. There is no direct measure of work experience in the *EAEF* data set, but potential work experience, *PWE*, defined by

$$PWE = AGE - S - 5$$

may approximate it. This is the maximum number of years since the completion of full-time education, assuming that an individual enters first grade at the age of 6. Using your *EAEF* data set, first regress *EARNINGS* on *S* and *PWE*, and then run the regression a second time adding *AGE* as well. Comment on the regression results.

4.5 Goodness of fit: R^2

As in simple regression analysis, the coefficient of determination, R^2, measures the proportion of the variance of Y explained by the regression and is defined equivalently by $\mathrm{Var}(\hat{Y})/\mathrm{Var}(Y)$, by $1 - [\mathrm{Var}(e)/\mathrm{Var}(Y)]$, or by the square of the correlation coefficient for Y and $\hat{Y}$. It can never decrease, and generally will increase, if you add another variable to a regression equation, provided that you retain all the previous explanatory variables. To see this, suppose that you regress Y on X_2 and X_3 and fit the equation

$$\hat{Y}_i = b_1 + b_2 X_{2i} + b_3 X_{3i}. \tag{4.47}$$

Next suppose that you regress Y on X_2 only and the result is

$$\hat{Y}_i = b_1^* + b_2^* X_{2i}. \tag{4.48}$$

This can be rewritten

$$\hat{Y}_i = b_1^* + b_2^* X_{2i} + 0 X_{3i}. \tag{4.49}$$

Comparing (4.47) and (4.49), the coefficients in the former have been determined freely by the OLS technique using the data for Y, X_2, and X_3 to give the best possible fit. In (4.49), however, the coefficient of X_3 has arbitrarily been set at 0, and the fit will be suboptimal unless, by coincidence, b_3 happens to be 0, in which case the fit will be the same. (b_1^* will then be equal to b_1, and b_2^* will be equal to b_2.) Hence, in general, the level of R^2 will be higher in (4.47) than in (4.49), and it can never be lower. Of course, if the new variable does not genuinely belong in the equation, the increase in R^2 is likely to be negligible.

You might think that, because R^2 measures the proportion of the variance jointly explained by the explanatory variables, it should be possible to deduce the individual contribution of each explanatory variable and thus obtain a measure of its relative importance. At least it would be very convenient if one could. Unfortunately, such a decomposition is impossible if the explanatory variables are correlated because their explanatory power will overlap. The problem will be discussed further in Section 7.2.

F tests

We saw in Section 3.10 that we could perform an F test of the explanatory power of the simple regression model

$$Y_i = \beta_1 + \beta_2 X_i + u_i, \qquad (4.50)$$

the null hypothesis being $H_0\colon \beta_2 = 0$ and the alternative being $H_1\colon \beta_2 \neq 0$. The null hypothesis was the same as that for a t test on the slope coefficient and it turned out that the F test was equivalent to a (two-tailed) t test. However, in the case of the multiple regression model the tests have different roles. The t tests test the significance of the coefficient of each variable individually, while the F test tests their joint explanatory power. The null hypothesis, which we hope to reject, is that the model has no explanatory power. The model will have no explanatory power if it turns out that Y is unrelated to any of the explanatory variables. Mathematically, therefore, if the model is

$$Y_i = \beta_1 + \beta_2 X_{2i} + \cdots + \beta_k X_{ki} + u_i, \qquad (4.51)$$

the null hypothesis is that all the slope coefficients $\beta_2, \ldots, \beta_k$ are 0:

$$H_0\colon \beta_2 = \cdots = \beta_k = 0. \qquad (4.52)$$

The alternative hypothesis H_1 is that at least one of the slope coefficients $\beta_2, \ldots, \beta_k$ is different from 0. The F statistic is defined as

$$F(k-1, n-k) = \frac{ESS/(k-1)}{RSS/(n-k)}, \qquad (4.53)$$

and the test is performed by comparing this with the critical level of F in the column corresponding to $k - 1$ degrees of freedom and the row corresponding to $n - k$ degrees of freedom in the appropriate part of Table A.3.

This F statistic may also be expressed in terms of R^2 by dividing both the numerator and denominator of (4.53) by TSS, the total sum of squares, and noting that ESS/TSS is R^2 and RSS/TSS is $(1 - R^2)$:

$$F(k-1, n-k) = \frac{R^2/(k-1)}{(1-R^2)/(n-k)}. \qquad (4.54)$$

Example

The educational attainment model will be used as an illustration. We will suppose that S depends on $ASVABC$, SM, and SF:

$$S = \beta_1 + \beta_2 ASVABC + \beta_3 SM + \beta_4 SF + u. \qquad (4.55)$$

The null hypothesis for the F test of goodness of fit is that all three slope coefficients are equal to 0:

$$H_0: \beta_2 = \beta_3 = \beta_4 = 0. \qquad (4.56)$$

The alternative hypothesis is that at least one of them is nonzero. The regression output using *EAEF* Data Set 21 is as shown in Table 4.14.

In this example, $k - 1$, the number of explanatory variables, is equal to 3 and $n - k$, the number of degrees of freedom, is equal to 566. The numerator of the F statistic is the explained sum of squares divided by $k - 1$. In the Stata output these numbers, 1278.2 and 3, respectively, are given in the Model row. The denominator is the residual sum of squares divided by the number of degrees of freedom remaining, 2176.0 and 566, respectively. Hence the F statistic is 110.8. All serious regression applications compute it for you as part of the diagnostics in the regression output:

$$F(3, 566) = \frac{1278.2/3}{2176.0/566} = 110.8. \qquad (4.57)$$

The critical value for $F(3, 566)$ is not given in the F tables, but we know it must be lower than $F(3, 500)$, which is given. At the 0.1 percent level, this is

Table 4.14

```
. reg S ASVABC SM SF

  Source |       SS       df       MS              Number of obs =     570
---------+------------------------------           F(  3,   566) =  110.83
   Model |  1278.24153     3   426.080508          Prob > F      =  0.0000
Residual |  2176.00584   566   3.84453329          R-squared     =  0.3700
---------+------------------------------           Adj R-squared =  0.3667
   Total |  3454.24737   569   6.07073351          Root MSE      =  1.9607


-------------------------------------------------------------------------
       S |     Coef.   Std. Err.     t    P>|t|    [95% Conf. Interval]
---------+---------------------------------------------------------------
  ASVABC |   .1295006   .0099544  13.009  0.000    .1099486    .1490527
      SM |    .069403   .0422974   1.641  0.101   -.013676     .152482
      SF |   .1102684   .0311948   3.535  0.000    .0489967    .1715401
   _cons |   4.914654   .5063527   9.706  0.000    3.920094    5.909214
-------------------------------------------------------------------------
```

5.51. Hence we reject H_0 at that significance level. This result could have been anticipated because both $ASVABC$ and SF have highly significant t statistics. So we knew in advance that both β_2 and β_4 were nonzero.

In general, the F statistic will be significant if any t statistic is. In principle, however, it might not be. Suppose that you ran a nonsense regression with 40 explanatory variables, none being a true determinant of the dependent variable. Then the F statistic should be low enough for H_0 not to be rejected. However, if you are performing t tests on the slope coefficients at the 5 percent level, with a 5 percent chance of a Type I error, on average 2 of the 40 variables could be expected to have 'significant' coefficients.

On the other hand it can easily happen that the F statistic is significant while the t statistics are not. Suppose you have a multiple regression model that is correctly specified and R^2 is high. You would be likely to have a highly significant F statistic. However, if the explanatory variables are highly correlated and the model is subject to severe multicollinearity, the standard errors of the slope coefficients could all be so large that none of the t statistics is significant. In this situation you would know that your model has high explanatory power, but you are not in a position to pinpoint the contributions made by the explanatory variables individually.

Further analysis of variance

Besides testing the equation as a whole, you can use an F test to see whether or not the joint marginal contribution of a group of variables is significant. Suppose that you first fit the model

$$Y = \beta_1 + \beta_2 X_2 + \cdots + \beta_k X_k + u, \qquad (4.58)$$

with explained sum of squares ESS_k. Next you add $m - k$ variables and fit the model

$$Y = \beta_1 + \beta_2 X_2 + \cdots + \beta_k X_k + \beta_{k+1} X_{k+1} + \cdots + \beta_m X_m + u, \qquad (4.59)$$

with explained sum of squares ESS_m. You have then explained an additional sum of squares equal to $ESS_m - ESS_k$ using up an additional $m - k$ degrees of freedom, and you want to see whether the increase is greater than is likely to have arisen by chance.

Again an F test is used and the appropriate F statistic may be expressed in verbal terms as

$$F = \frac{\text{Improvement in fit/Extra degrees of freedom used up}}{\text{Residual sum of squares remaining/Degrees of freedom remaining}}. \qquad (4.60)$$

Since RSS_m, the unexplained sum of squares in the second model, is equal to $TSS - ESS_m$, and RSS_k, the residual sum of squares in the first model, is equal

Table 4.15

	Sum of squares	Degrees of freedom	Sum of squares divided by degrees of freedom	F statistic
Explained by original variables	ESS_k	$k - 1$	$ESS_k/(k - 1)$	
				$\dfrac{ESS_k/(k - 1)}{RSS_k/(n - k)}$
Residual	$RSS_k = TSS - ESS_k$	$n - k$	$RSS_k/(n - k)$	
Explained by new variables	$ESS_m - ESS_k = RSS_k - RSS_m$	$m - k$	$(RSS_k - RSS_m)/ (m - k)$	
				$\dfrac{(RSS_k - RSS_m)/(m - k)}{RSS_m/(n - m)}$
Residual	$RSS_m = TSS - ESS_m$	$n - m$	$RSS_m/(n - m)$	

to $TSS - ESS_k$, the improvement in the fit when the extra variables are added, $ESS_m - ESS_k$, is equal to $RSS_k - RSS_m$. Hence the appropriate F statistic is

$$F(m - k, n - m) = \frac{(RSS_k - RSS_m)/(m - k)}{RSS_m/(n - m)}. \qquad (4.61)$$

Under the null hypothesis that the additional variables contribute nothing to the equation,

$$H_0: \beta_{k+1} = \beta_{k+2} = \cdots = \beta_m = 0. \qquad (4.62)$$

this F statistic is distributed with $m - k$ and $n - m$ degrees of freedom. The upper half of Table 4.15 gives the analysis of variance for the explanatory power of the original $k - 1$ variables. The lower half gives it for the joint marginal contribution of the new variables.

Example

We will illustrate the test with the educational attainment example (Table 4.16). The output shows the result of regressing S on $ASVABC$ using $EAEF$ Data Set 21. We make a note of the residual sum of squares, 2300.4.

Table 4.16

```
. reg S ASVABC

    Source |      SS          df        MS              Number of obs =     570
-----------+----------------------------------          F(  1,   568) =  284.89
     Model | 1153.80864        1   1153.80864           Prob > F      =  0.0000
  Residual | 2300.43873      568   4.05006818           R-squared     =  0.3340
-----------+----------------------------------          Adj R-squared =  0.3329
     Total | 3454.24737      569   6.07073351           Root MSE      =  2.0125


-------------------------------------------------------------------------------
         S |     Coef.   Std. Err.      t    P>|t|     [95% Conf. Interval]
-----------+-------------------------------------------------------------------
    ASVABC |   .1545378   .0091559    16.879  0.000     .1365543    .1725213
     _cons |   5.770845   .4668473    12.361  0.000     4.853888    6.687803
```

Table 4.17

```
. reg S ASVABC SM SF

    Source |      SS          df        MS              Number of obs =     570
-----------+----------------------------------          F(  3,   566) =  110.83
     Model | 1278.24153        3   426.080508           Prob > F      =  0.0000
  Residual | 2176.00584      566   3.84453329           R-squared     =  0.3700
-----------+----------------------------------          Adj R-squared =  0.3667
     Total | 3454.24737      569   6.07073351           Root MSE      =  1.9607


-------------------------------------------------------------------------------
         S |     Coef.   Std. Err.      t    P>|t|     [95% Conf. Interval]
-----------+-------------------------------------------------------------------
    ASVABC |   .1295006   .0099544    13.009  0.000     .1099486    .1490527
        SM |    .069403   .0422974     1.641  0.101     -.013676     .152482
        SF |   .1102684   .0311948     3.535  0.000     .0489967    .1715401
     _cons |   4.914654   .5063527     9.706  0.000     3.920094    5.909214
```

Now we add a group of two variables, the years of schooling of each parent (Table 4.17). Do these variables jointly make a significant contribution to the explanatory power of the model? Well, we can see that a t test would show that SF has a highly significant coefficient, but we will perform the F test anyway. We make a note of RSS, 2176.0.

The improvement in the fit on adding the parental schooling variables is the reduction in the residual sum of squares, $2300.4 - 2176.0$. The cost is two degrees of freedom because two additional parameters have been estimated. The residual sum of squares remaining unexplained after adding SM and SF is 2176.0. The number of degrees of freedom remaining after adding the new variables is $570 - 4 = 566$.

$$F(2, 570 - 4) = \frac{(2300.4 - 2176.0)/2}{2176.0/566} = 16.18. \quad (4.63)$$

Thus the F statistic is 16.18. The critical value of $F(2, 500)$ at the 0.1 percent level is 7.00. The critical value of $F(2, 566)$ must be lower, so we reject H_0 and conclude that the parental education variables do have significant joint explanatory power.

Relationship between F statistic and t statistic

Suppose that you are considering the following alternative model specifications:

$$Y = \beta_1 + \beta_2 X_2 + \cdots + \beta_{k-1} X_{k-1} + u, \quad (4.64)$$

and

$$Y = \beta_1 + \beta_2 X_2 + \cdots + \beta_{k-1} X_{k-1} + \beta_k X_k + u, \quad (4.65)$$

the only difference being the addition of X_k as an explanatory variable in (4.65). You now have two ways to test whether X_k belongs in the model. You could perform a t test on its coefficient when (4.65) is fitted. Alternatively, you could perform an F test of the type just discussed, treating X_k as a 'group' of just one variable, to test its marginal explanatory power. For the F test the null hypothesis will be H_0: $\beta_k = 0$, since only X_k has been added and this is the same null hypothesis as that for the t test. Thus it might appear that there is a risk that the outcomes of the two tests might conflict with each other.

Fortunately, this is impossible, since it can be shown that the F statistic must be equal to the square of the t statistic and that the critical value of F is equal to the square of the critical value of t (two-tailed test). This result means that the t test of the coefficient of a variable is in effect a test of its marginal explanatory power, *after all the other variables have been included in the equation*.

If the variable is correlated with one or more of the other variables, its marginal explanatory power may be quite low, even if it genuinely belongs in the model. If all the variables are correlated, it is possible for all of them to have low marginal explanatory power and for none of the t tests to be significant, even though the F test for their joint explanatory power is highly significant. If this is the case, the model is said to be suffering from the problem of multicollinearity discussed earlier in this chapter.

No proof of the equivalence will be offered here, but it will be illustrated with the educational attainment model (Table 4.18). In the first regression it has been hypothesized that S depends on $ASVABC$ and SM. In the second, it has been hypothesized that it depends on SF as well.

The improvement on adding SF is the reduction in the residual sum of squares, $2224.0 - 2176.0$. The cost is just the single degree of freedom lost when estimating the coefficient of SF. The residual sum of squares remaining after adding

Table 4.18

```
. reg S ASVABC SM                        |. reg S ASVABC SM SF
                                         |
 Source |    SS      df       MS         |  Source |    SS      df       MS
--------+---------------------------     | --------+---------------------------
  Model | 1230.2039    2   615.101949    |   Model | 1278.24153    3  426.080508
Residual |2224.04347  567   3.92247526   | Residual | 2176.00584  566  3.84453329
--------+---------------------------     | --------+---------------------------
  Total | 3454.24737  569   6.07073351   |   Total | 3454.24737  569  6.07073351
                                         |
-----------------------------------      | ------------------------------------
    S |   Coef.   Std. Err.    t         |     S |   Coef.   Std. Err.    t
--------+---------------------------     | ------------------------------------
ASVABC | .1381062  .0097494  14.166      | ASVABC |.1295006   .0099544   13.009
   SM |  .154783   .0350728   4.413      |    SM | .069403   .0422974    1.641
_cons |  4.791277  .5102431   9.390      |    SF |.1102684   .0311948    3.535
-----------------------------------      | _cons |4.914654   .5063527    9.706
                                         | ------------------------------------
                                         |
```

SF is 2176.0. The number of degrees of freedom remaining after adding *SF* is $570 - 4 = 566$. Hence the *F* statistic is 12.49.

$$F(1, 570 - 4) = \frac{(2224.0 - 2176.0)/1}{2176.0/566} = 12.49 . \tag{4.66}$$

The critical value of *F* at the 0.1 percent significance level with 500 degrees of freedom is 10.96. The critical value with 566 degrees of freedom must be lower, so we reject H_0 at the 0.1 percent level. The *t* statistic for the coefficient of *SF* in the second regression is 3.54. The critical value of *t* at the 0.1 percent level with 500 degrees of freedom is 3.31. The critical value with 566 degrees of freedom must be lower, so we also reject H_0 with the *t* test. The square of 3.54 is 12.53, equal to the *F* statistic, except for rounding error, and the square of 3.31 is 10.96, equal to the critical value of $F(1, 500)$. (The critical values shown are for 500 degrees of freedom, but this must also be true for 566 degrees of freedom.) Hence the conclusions of the two tests must coincide.

'Adjusted' R^2

If you look at regression output, you will almost certainly find near the R^2 statistic something called the 'adjusted' R^2. Sometimes it is called the 'corrected' R^2. However, 'corrected' makes it sound as if it is better than the ordinary one, and this is debatable.

As was noted in Section 4.5, R^2 can never fall, and generally increases, if you add another variable to a regression equation. The adjusted R^2, usually denoted $\bar{R}^2$, attempts to compensate for this automatic upward shift by imposing a penalty for increasing the number of explanatory variables. It is defined as

$$\bar{R}^2 = 1 - (1 - R^2)\frac{n-1}{n-k} = \frac{n-1}{n-k}R^2 - \frac{k-1}{n-k}$$

$$= R^2 - \frac{k-1}{n-k}(1 - R^2), \tag{4.67}$$

where $k-1$ is the number of explanatory variables. As k increases, $(k-1)/(n-k)$ increases, and so the negative adjustment to R^2 increases.

It can be shown that the addition of a new variable to a regression will cause $\bar{R}^2$ to rise if and only if the absolute value of its t statistic is greater than 1. Hence a rise in $\bar{R}^2$ when a new variable is added does not necessarily mean that its coefficient is significantly different from 0. It therefore does not follow, as is sometimes suggested, that a rise in $\bar{R}^2$ implies that the specification of an equation has improved.

This is one reason why $\bar{R}^2$ has lost favor as a diagnostic statistic. Another is the decrease in attention paid to R^2 itself. At one time there was a tendency for applied econometricians to regard R^2 as a key indicator of the success of model specification. In practice, however, as will be seen in the following chapters, even a very badly specified regression model may yield a high R^2, and recognition of this fact has led to the demotion of R^2 in importance. It is now regarded as just one of a whole set of diagnostic statistics that should be examined when evaluating a regression model. Consequently, there is little to be gained by fine tuning it with a 'correction' of dubious value.

Exercises

4.15 Using your *EAEF* data set, fit an educational attainment function, regressing S on ASVABC, *SM*, and *SF*. Calculate the F statistic using R^2 and perform a test of the explanatory power of the equation as a whole.

4.16 Fit an educational attainment function using the specification in Exercise 4.15, adding the ASVAB speed test scores *ASVAB5* and *ASVAB6*. Perform an F test of the joint explanatory power of *ASVAB5* and *ASVAB6*, using the results of this regression and that in Exercise 4.15.

4.17 Fit an educational attainment function, regressing S on ASVABC, *SM*, *SF*, and *ASVAB5*. Perform an F test of the explanatory power of *ASVAB6*, using the results of this regression and that in Exercise 4.16. Verify that it leads to the same conclusion as a two-tailed t test.

4.18* The researcher in Exercise 4.13 decides to divide the number of days not worked into the number of days not worked because of illness, I, and the number of days not worked for other reasons, O. The mean value of I in the sample is 2.1 and the mean value of O is 120.2. He fits the regression (standard errors in parentheses):

$$\hat{E} = -9.6 + 2.10W + 0.45O. \quad R^2 = 0.72$$
$$(8.3) \quad (1.98) \quad\quad (1.77)$$

Perform t tests on the regression coefficients and an F test on the goodness of fit of the equation. Explain why the t tests and F test have different outcomes.

5 Transformations of variables

Nonlinear relationships are more plausible than linear ones for many economic processes. In this chapter we will first define what is meant by linear regression analysis and then show how some apparently nonlinear relationships can be fitted by it. We will next see what can be done when linear methods cannot be used. The chapter ends with an exposition of a technique for discriminating statistically between linear and nonlinear relationships.

5.1 Basic procedure

One of the limitations of linear regression analysis is implicit in its very name, in that it can be used to fit only linear equations where every explanatory term, except the constant, is written in the form of a coefficient multiplied by variable:

$$Y = \beta_1 + \beta_2 X_2 + \beta_3 X_3 + \beta_4 X_4. \tag{5.1}$$

Equations such as

$$Y = \beta_1 + \frac{\beta_2}{X} \tag{5.2}$$

and

$$Y = \beta_1 X^{\beta_2} \tag{5.3}$$

are nonlinear.

However, both (5.2) and (5.3) have been suggested as suitable forms for Engel curves, the relationship between the demand for a particular commodity, Y, and income, X. Given data on Y and X, how could one estimate the parameters β_1 and β_2 in these equations?

Actually, in both cases, with a little preparation one can use linear regression analysis after all. First, note that (5.1) is linear in two senses. The right side is linear in variables because the variables are included exactly as defined, rather than as functions. It therefore consists of a weighted sum of the variables, the parameters being the weights. The right side is also linear in the parameters since it consists of a weighted sum of these as well, the X variables being the weights this time.

For the purpose of linear regression analysis, only the second type of linearity is important. Nonlinearity in the variables can always be sidestepped by using appropriate definitions. For example, suppose that the relationship were of the form

$$Y = \beta_1 + \beta_2 X_2^2 + \beta_3 \sqrt{X_3} + \beta_4 \log X_4 + \cdots \tag{5.4}$$

By defining $Z_2 = X_2^2, Z_3 = \sqrt{X_3}, Z_4 = \log X_4$, etc, the relationship can be rewritten

$$Y = \beta_1 + \beta_2 Z_2 + \beta_3 Z_3 + \beta_4 Z_4 + \cdots \tag{5.5}$$

and it is now linear in variables as well as in parameters. This type of transformation is only cosmetic, and you will usually see the regression equation presented with the variables written in their nonlinear form. This avoids the need for explanation and extra notation.

On the other hand an equation such as (5.3) is nonlinear in both parameters and variables and cannot be handled by a mere redefinition. (Do not be tempted to think that you can make it linear by defining $Z = X^{\beta_2}$ and replacing X^{β_2} with Z; since you do not know β_2, you have no way of calculating sample data for Z.) We will discuss the problem of fitting relationships that are nonlinear in parameters in the next section.

In the case of (5.2), however, all we have to do is to define $Z = 1/X$. Equation (5.2) now becomes

$$Y = \beta_1 + \beta_2 Z \tag{5.6}$$

and this is linear, so you regress Y on Z. The constant term in the regression will be an estimate of β_1 and the coefficient of Z will be an estimate of β_2.

Example

Suppose that you are investigating the relationship between annual consumption of bananas (boring, safe example) and annual income, and you have the observations shown in Table 5.1 for ten households (ignore Z for the time being):

These observations are plotted in Figure 5.1, together with the line obtained by regressing Y on X (standard errors in parentheses):

$$\hat{Y} = 4.62 + 0.84X. \quad R^2 = 0.69 \tag{5.7}$$
$$(1.26) \quad (0.20)$$

Now, if you look at Figure 5.1, you will see that the regression line does not fit the observations very well, despite the fact that the coefficient of income is significantly different from 0 at the 1 percent level. Quite obviously, the observations lie on a curve, while the regression equation is of course a straight line. In this case, it is easy to see that the functional relationship between Y and X has been misspecified. In the case of multiple regression analysis, nonlinearity might be detected using the graphical technique described in Section 4.2. Alternatively,

Table 5.1

Household	Bananas (lbs) Y	Income ($10,000) X	Z
1	1.71	1	1.000
2	6.88	2	0.500
3	8.25	3	0.333
4	9.52	4	0.250
5	9.81	5	0.200
6	11.43	6	0.167
7	11.09	7	0.143
8	10.87	8	0.125
9	12.15	9	0.111
10	10.94	10	0.100

an examination of the residuals may be sufficient to indicate that something is wrong. In this case the residuals are as shown in Table 5.2.

The residuals ought to be randomly positive or negative, large or small. Instead, they start out being negative, cross to being positive, reach a maximum, fall again, and cross back to being negative: very suspicious indeed.

The values of Y and X in this example were generated using the Monte Carlo technique, the true relationship being

$$Y = 12 - \frac{10}{X} + \text{disturbance term,} \tag{5.8}$$

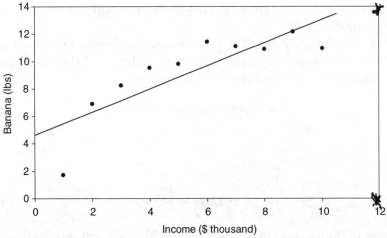

Figure 5.1 Regression of expenditure on bananas on income

Table 5.2

Household	Y	$\hat{Y}$	e	Household	Y	$\hat{Y}$	e
1	1.71	5.46	−3.75	6	11.43	9.69	1.74
2	6.88	6.31	0.57	7	11.09	10.53	0.55
3	8.25	7.15	1.10	8	10.87	11.38	−0.51
4	9.52	8.00	1.52	9	12.15	12.22	−0.07
5	9.81	8.84	0.97	10	10.94	13.07	−2.13

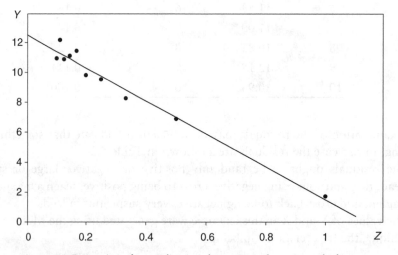

Figure 5.2 Regression of expenditure on bananas on the reciprocal of income

X taking the numbers from 1 to 10 and the values of the disturbance term being obtained using normally distributed random numbers with 0 mean and standard deviation equal to 0.5.

If we realize this and define $Z = 1/X$, this equation becomes of the linear form (5.6). Z for each household has already been calculated in Table 5.1. Regressing Y on Z, we obtain (standard errors in parentheses):

$$\hat{Y} = 12.48 - 10.99Z. \quad R^2 = 0.97 \tag{5.9}$$
$$(0.26) \quad (0.65)$$

Substituting $Z = 1/X$, this becomes

$$\hat{Y} = 12.48 - \frac{10.99}{X}. \tag{5.10}$$

In view of the excellent fit obtained with (5.9), it is not surprising that (5.10) is close to the true equation (5.8). The regression relationship, together with the

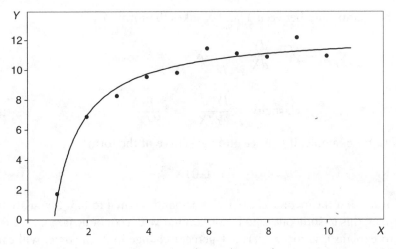

Figure 5.3 Nonlinear regression of expenditure on bananas on income

observations on Y, X, and Z, is shown in Figures 5.2 and 5.3. The improvement in the fit, as measured by R^2, is clear from a comparison of Figures 5.1 and 5.3.

5.2 Logarithmic transformations

Next we will tackle functions such as (5.3), which are nonlinear in parameters as well as variables:

$$Y = \beta_1 X^{\beta_2}. \tag{5.11}$$

When you see such a function, you can immediately say that the elasticity of Y with respect to X is constant and equal to β_2. This is easily demonstrated. Regardless of the mathematical relationship connecting Y and X, or the definitions of Y and X, the elasticity of Y with respect to X is defined to be the proportional change in Y for a given proportional change in X:

$$\text{elasticity} = \frac{dY/Y}{dX/X}. \tag{5.12}$$

Thus, for example, if Y is demand and X is income, the above expression defines the income elasticity of demand for the commodity in question.

The expression may be rewritten

$$\text{elasticity} = \frac{dY/dX}{Y/X}. \tag{5.13}$$

In the case of the demand example, this may be interpreted as the marginal propensity to consume the commodity divided by the average propensity to consume it.

If the relationship between Y and X takes the form (5.11),

$$\frac{dY}{dX} = \beta_1\beta_2 X^{\beta_2-1} = \beta_2\frac{Y}{X}. \tag{5.14}$$

Hence

$$\text{elasticity} = \frac{dY/dX}{Y/X} = \frac{\beta_2 Y/X}{Y/X} = \beta_2. \tag{5.15}$$

Thus, for example, if you see an Engel curve of the form

$$Y = 0.01X^{0.3}, \tag{5.16}$$

this means that the income elasticity of demand is equal to 0.3. If you are trying to explain this to someone who is not familiar with economic jargon, the easiest way to explain it is to say that a 1 percent change in X (income) will cause a 0.3 percent change in Y (demand).

A function of this type can be converted into a linear equation by using logarithms. You will certainly have encountered logarithms in a basic mathematics course. You probably thought that when that course was finished, you could forget about them, writing them off as one of those academic topics that never turn out to be of practical use. No such luck. In econometric work they are indispensable, so if you are unsure about their use, you should review your notes from that basic math course. The main properties of logarithms are given in Box 5.1.

In the box it is shown that (5.11) may be linearized as

$$\log Y = \log \beta_1 + \beta_2 \log X. \tag{5.17}$$

If we write $Y' = \log Y$, $Z = \log X$, and $\beta_1' = \log \beta_1$, the equation may be rewritten

$$Y' = \beta_1' + \beta_2 Z. \tag{5.18}$$

The regression procedure is now as follows. First calculate Y' and Z for each observation, taking the logarithms of the original data. Your regression application will almost certainly do this for you, given the appropriate instructions. Second, regress Y' on Z. The coefficient of Z will be a direct estimate of β_2. The constant term will be an estimate of β_1', that is, of $\log \beta_1$. To obtain an estimate of β_1, you have to take the antilog, that is, calculate $\exp(\beta_1')$.

Example: Engel curve

Figure 5.4 plots annual household expenditure on food eaten at home, *FDHO*, and total annual household expenditure, both measured in dollars, for 869 representative households in the United States in 1995, the data being taken from the Consumer Expenditure Survey.

When analyzing household expenditure data, it is usual to relate types of expenditure to total household expenditure rather than income, the reason

---

BOX 5.1 **Use of logarithms**

First, some basic rules:

1. If $Y = XZ$, $\log Y = \log X + \log Z$.
2. If $Y = X/Z$, $\log Y = \log X - \log Z$.
3. If $Y = X^n$, $\log Y = n \log X$.

These rules can be combined to transform more complicated expressions. For example, take equation (5.11): if $Y = \beta_1 X^{\beta_2}$,

$$\log Y = \log \beta_1 + \log X^{\beta_2} \quad \text{using Rule 1}$$
$$= \log \beta_1 + \beta_2 \log X \quad \text{using Rule 3}.$$

Thus far we have not specified whether we are taking logarithms to base e or to base 10. Throughout this text we shall be using e as the base, and so we shall be using what are known as 'natural' logarithms. This is standard in econometrics. Purists sometimes write ln instead of log to emphasize that they are working with natural logarithms, but this is now unnecessary. Nobody uses logarithms to base 10 anymore. They were tabulated in the dreaded log tables that were universally employed for multiplying or dividing large numbers until the early 1970s. When the pocket calculator was invented, they became redundant. They are not missed.

With e as base, we can state another rule:

4. If $Y = e^X$, $\log Y = X$.

e^X, also sometimes written $\exp(X)$, is familiarly known as the antilog of X. One can say that $\log e^X$ is the log of the antilog of X, and since log and antilog cancel out, it is not surprising that $\log e^X$ turns out just to be X.

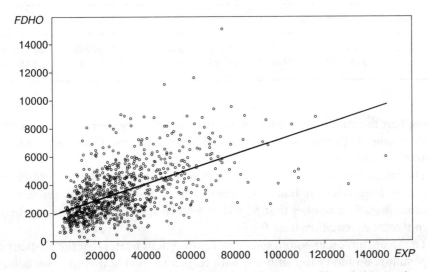

Figure 5.4 Regression of expenditure on food eaten at home on total household expenditure

Table 5.3

```
. reg FDHO EXP

    Source |       SS         df       MS                Number of obs =     869
-----------+-------------------------------              F(  1,   867) =  381.47
     Model |  915843574       1   915843574              Prob > F      =  0.0000
  Residual | 2.0815e+09      867  2400831.16             R-squared     =  0.3055
-----------+-------------------------------              Adj R-squared =  0.3047
     Total | 2.9974e+09      868  3453184.55             Root MSE      =  1549.5


------------------------------------------------------------------------------
      FDHO |     Coef.   Std. Err.      t    P>|t|     [95% Conf. Interval]
-----------+------------------------------------------------------------------
       EXP |  .0528427   .0027055    19.531   0.000     .0475325    .0581529
     _cons |  1916.143   96.54591    19.847   0.000     1726.652    2105.634
------------------------------------------------------------------------------
```

Table 5.4

```
. g LGFDHO = ln(FDHO)
. g LGEXP = ln(EXP)
. reg LGFDHO LGEXP

    Source |       SS         df       MS                Number of obs =     868
-----------+-------------------------------              F(  1,   866) =  396.06
     Model | 84.4161692       1  84.4161692              Prob > F      =  0.0000
  Residual | 184.579612      866  .213140429             R-squared     =  0.3138
-----------+-------------------------------              Adj R-squared =  0.3130
     Total | 268.995781      867  .310260416             Root MSE      =  .46167


------------------------------------------------------------------------------
    LGFDHO |     Coef.   Std. Err.      t    P>|t|     [95% Conf. Interval]
-----------+------------------------------------------------------------------
     LGEXP |  .4800417   .0241212    19.901   0.000     .4326988    .5273846
     _cons |  3.166271    .244297    12.961   0.000     2.686787    3.645754
------------------------------------------------------------------------------
```

being that the relationship with expenditure tends to be more stable than that with income. The outputs from linear and logarithmic regressions are shown in Tables 5.3 and 5.4.

The linear regression indicates that 5.3 cents out of the marginal dollar are spent on food eaten at home. Interpretation of the intercept is problematic because literally it implies that $1,916 would be spent on food eaten at home even if total expenditure were 0.

The logarithmic regression, shown in Figure 5.5, indicates that the elasticity of expenditure on food eaten at home with respect to total household expenditure is 0.48. Is this figure plausible? Yes, because food eaten at home is a necessity

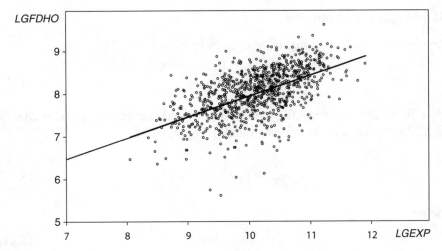

Figure 5.5 Logarithmic regression of expenditure on food eaten at home on total household expenditure

rather than a luxury, so one would expect the elasticity to be less than 1. The intercept has no economic meaning. Figure 5.6 plots the logarithmic regression line in the original diagram. While there is not much difference between the regression lines over the middle part of the range of observations, it is clear that the logarithmic regression gives a better fit for very low and very high levels of household expenditure.

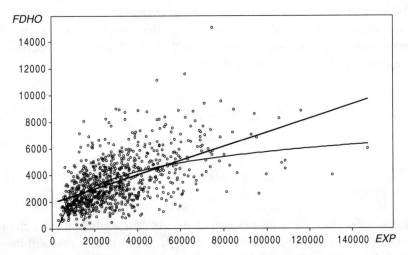

Figure 5.6 Linear and logarithmic regressions of expenditure on food eaten at home on total household expenditure

Semi-logarithmic models

Another common functional form is given by equation (5.19):

$$Y = \beta_1 e^{\beta_2 X}, \tag{5.19}$$

Here β_2 should be interpreted as the proportional change in Y per *unit* change in X. Again, this is easily demonstrated. Differentiating,

$$\frac{dY}{dX} = \beta_1 \beta_2 e^{\beta_2 X} = \beta_2 Y, \tag{5.20}$$

Hence

$$\frac{dY/Y}{dX} = \beta_2. \tag{5.21}$$

In practice it is often more natural to speak of the percentage change in Y, rather than the proportional change, per unit change in X, in which case one multiplies the estimate of β_2 by 100.

The function can be converted into a model that is linear in parameters by taking the logarithms of both sides:

$$\begin{aligned} \log Y = \log \beta_1 e^{\beta_2 X} &= \log \beta_1 + \log e^{\beta_2 X} \\ &= \log \beta_1 + \beta_2 X \log e \\ &= \log \beta_1 + \beta_2 X. \end{aligned} \tag{5.22}$$

Note that only the left side is logarithmic in variables, and for this reason the model is described as semi-logarithmic.

The interpretation of β_2 as the proportional change in Y per unit change in X is valid only when β_2 is small. When β_2 is large, the interpretation may be a little more complex. Suppose that Y is related to X by (5.19) and that X increases by one unit to X'. Then Y', the new value of Y is given by

$$\begin{aligned} Y' = \beta_1 e^{\beta_2 X'} &= \beta_1 e^{\beta_2 (X+1)} \\ &= \beta_1 e^{\beta_2 X} e^{\beta_2} = Y e^{\beta_2} \\ &= Y \left(1 + \beta_2 + \frac{\beta_2^2}{2} + \cdots \right). \end{aligned} \tag{5.23}$$

Thus the proportional change per unit change in X is actually greater than β_2. However, if β_2 is small (say, less than 0.1), β_2^2 and further terms will be very small and can be neglected. In that case, the right side of the equation simplifies to $Y(1 + \beta_2)$ and the original marginal interpretation of β_2 still applies.

Example: Semi-logarithmic earnings function

For fitting earnings functions, the semi-logarithmic model is generally considered to be superior to the linear model. We will start with the simplest possible version:

$$EARNINGS = \beta_1 e^{\beta_2 S}, \tag{5.24}$$

where $EARNINGS$ is hourly earnings, measured in dollars, and S is years of schooling. After taking logarithms, the result is shown in Table 5.5.

$$LGEARN = \beta_1' + \beta_2 S, \tag{5.25}$$

where $LGEARN$ is the natural logarithm of $EARNINGS$ and β_1' is the logarithm of β_1.

The regression output, which uses $EAEF$ Data Set 21, indicates that every extra year of schooling increases earnings by a proportion 0.079, that is, 7.9 percent, as a first approximation. Strictly speaking, a whole extra year of schooling is not marginal, so it would be more accurate to calculate $e^{0.079}$, which is 1.082. Thus a more accurate interpretation is that an extra year of schooling raises earnings by 8.2 percent.

The scatter diagram for the semi-logarithmic regression is shown in Figure 5.7. For the purpose of comparison, it is plotted together with the linear regression in a plot with the untransformed variables in Figure 5.8. The two regression lines do not differ greatly in their overall fit, but the semi-logarithmic specification has the advantages of not predicting negative earnings for individuals with low levels of schooling and of allowing the increase in earnings per year of schooling to increase with schooling.

Table 5.5

```
. reg LGEARN S
```

Source	SS	df	MS		Number of obs =	570
					F(1, 568) =	93.21
Model	21.681253	1	21.681253		Prob > F =	0.0000
Residual	132.12064	568	.23260676		R-squared =	0.1410
					Adj R-squared =	0.1395
Total	153.801893	569	.270302096		Root MSE =	.48229

LGEARN	Coef.	Std. Err.	t	P>|t|	[95% Conf. Interval]	
S	.0792256	.0082061	9.655	0.000	.0631077	.0953435
_cons	1.358919	.1127785	12.049	0.000	1.137406	1.580433

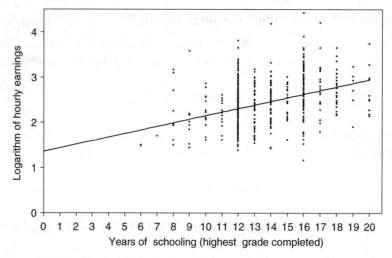

Figure 5.7 Semi-logarithmic regression of earnings on schooling

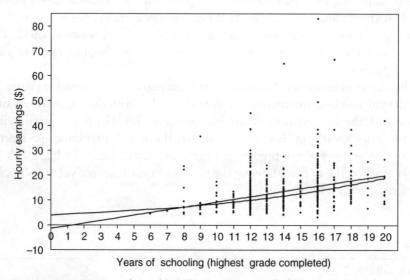

Figure 5.8 Linear and semi-logarithmic regressions of earnings on schooling

Exercises

Note: For all of these exercises, you should discuss the plausibility of the estimated coefficients.

5.1   Download the *CES* data set from the website and fit linear and (double) logarithmic regressions for your commodity on total household expenditure, *EXP*, excluding observations with 0 expenditure on your commodity. Interpret the regressions and perform appropriate tests.

5.2   Repeat the logarithmic regression in Exercise 5.1, adding the logarithm of the size of the household as an additional explanatory variable. Interpret the results and perform appropriate tests.

5.3 Using your *EAEF* data set, regress the (natural) logarithm of *WEIGHT85* on the logarithm of *HEIGHT*. Interpret the regression results and perform appropriate tests.

5.4 Using your *EAEF* data set, regress the logarithm of earnings on *S* and *ASVABC*. Interpret the regression results and perform appropriate tests.

5.5* Download from the website the OECD data set on employment growth rates and GDP growth rates tabulated in Exercise 2.1, plot a scatter diagram and investigate whether a nonlinear specification might be superior to a linear one.

5.3 The disturbance term

Thus far, nothing has been said about how the disturbance term is affected by these transformations. Indeed, in the discussion above it has been left out altogether.

The fundamental requirement is that the disturbance term should appear in the transformed equation as an additive term ($+u$) that satisfies the Gauss–Markov conditions. If it does not, the least squares regression coefficients will not have the usual properties, and the tests will be invalid.

For example, it is highly desirable that (5.6) should be of the form

$$Y = \beta_1 + \beta_2 Z + u \tag{5.26}$$

when we take the random effect into account. Working backwards, this implies that the original (untransformed) equation should be of the form

$$Y = \beta_1 + \frac{\beta_2}{X} + u. \tag{5.27}$$

In this particular case, if it is true that in the original equation the disturbance term is additive and the Gauss–Markov conditions are satisfied, it will also be true in the transformed equation. No problem here.

What happens when we start off with a model such as

$$Y = \beta_1 X_2^{\beta_2}? \tag{5.28}$$

As we have seen, the regression model, after linearization by taking logarithms, is

$$\log Y = \log \beta_1 + \beta_2 \log X + u \tag{5.29}$$

when the disturbance term is included. Working back to the original equation, this implies that (5.28) should be rewritten

$$Y = \beta_1 X_2^{\beta_2} v, \tag{5.30}$$

where v and u are related by $\log v = u$. Hence to obtain an additive disturbance term in the regression equation for this model, we must start with a multiplicative disturbance term in the original equation.

The disturbance term v modifies $\beta_1 X_2^{\beta_2}$ by increasing it or reducing it by a random *proportion*, rather than by a random amount. Note that u is equal to 0 when $\log v$ is equal to 0, which occurs when v is equal to 1. The random factor will be 0 in the estimating equation (5.29) if v happens to be equal to 1. This makes sense, since if v is equal to 1 it is not modifying $\beta_1 X_2^{\beta_2}$ at all.

For the t tests and the F tests to be valid, u must be normally distributed. This means that $\log v$ must be normally distributed, which will occur only if v is lognormally distributed.

What would happen if we assumed that the disturbance term in the original equation was additive, instead of multiplicative?

$$Y = \beta_1 X_2^{\beta_2} + u. \qquad (5.31)$$

The answer is that when you take logarithms, there is no mathematical way of simplifying $\log(\beta_1 X_2^{\beta_2} + u)$. The transformation does not lead to a linearization. You would have to use a nonlinear regression technique, for example, of the type discussed in the next section.

Example

The central limit theorem suggests that the disturbance term should have a normal distribution. It can be demonstrated that if the disturbance term has a normal distribution, so also will the residuals, provided that the regression equation is correctly specified. An examination of the distribution of the residuals thus provides indirect evidence of the adequacy of the specification of a regression model.

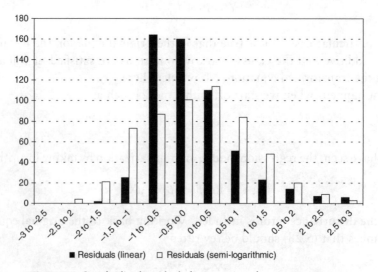

Figure 5.9 Standardized residuals from earnings function regressions

Figure 5.9 shows the residuals from linear and semi-logarithmic regressions of *EARNINGS* on *S* using *EAEF* Data Set 21, standardized so that they have standard deviation equal to 1, for comparison. The distribution of the semi-logarithmic residuals is much closer to a normal distribution than that of the linear regression, suggesting that the semi-logarithmic specification is preferable. Its distribution is right skewed, but not nearly as sharply as that of the linear regression.

5.4 Nonlinear regression

Suppose you believe that a variable Y depends on a variable X according to the relationship

$$Y = \beta_1 + \beta_2 X^{\beta_3} + u, \tag{5.32}$$

and you wish to obtain estimates of β_1, β_2, and β_3 given data on Y and X. There is no way of transforming (5.32) to obtain a linear relationship, and so it is not possible to apply the usual regression procedure.

Nevertheless one can still use the principle of minimizing the sum of the squares of the residuals to obtain estimates of the parameters. The procedure is best described as a series of steps:

1. You start by guessing plausible values for the parameters.
2. You calculate the predicted values of Y from the data on X, using these values of the parameters.
3. You calculate the residual for each observation in the sample, and hence *RSS*, the sum of the squares of the residuals.
4. You then make small changes to one or more of your estimates of the parameters.
5. You calculate the new predicted values of Y, residuals, and *RSS*.
6. If *RSS* is smaller than before, your new estimates of the parameters are better than the old ones and you take them as your new starting point.
7. You repeat steps 4, 5, and 6 again and again until you are unable to make any changes in the estimates of the parameters that would reduce *RSS*.
8. You conclude that you have minimized *RSS*, and you can describe the final estimates of the parameters as the least squares estimates.

Example

We will return to the bananas example in Section 5.1, where Y and X are related by

$$Y = \beta_1 + \frac{\beta_2}{X} + u. \tag{5.33}$$

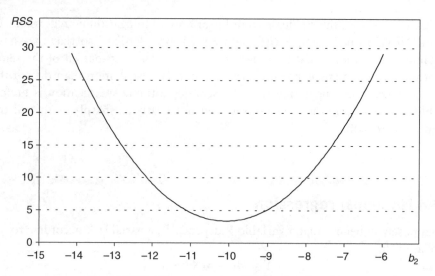

Figure 5.10 Nonlinear regression, *RSS* as a function of b_2

To keep things as simple as possible, we will assume that we know that β_1 is equal to 12, so we have only one unknown parameter to estimate. We will suppose that we have guessed that the relationship is of the form (5.33), but we are too witless to think of the transformation discussed in Section 5.1. We instead use nonlinear regression.

Figure 5.10 shows the value of *RSS* that would result from any choice of b_2, given the values of *Y* and *X* in Table 5.1. Suppose we started off with a guess of -6.0 for b_2. Our provisional equation would be

$$Y = 12 - \frac{6}{X}. \tag{5.34}$$

We would calculate the predicted values of *Y* and the residuals, and from the latter calculate a value of 29.17 for *RSS*.

Next we try $b_2 = -7$. *RSS* is now 18.08, which is lower. We are going in the right direction. So we next try $b_2 = -8$. *RSS* is 10.08. We keep going. Putting $b_2 = -9$, *RSS* is 5.19. Putting $b_2 = -10$, *RSS* is 3.39. Putting $b_2 = -11$, *RSS* is 4.70.

Clearly with $b_2 = -11$ we have overshot, because *RSS* has started rising again. We start moving backwards, but with smaller steps, say 0.1, trying -10.9, -10.8, etc. We keep moving backwards until we overshoot again, and then start moving forwards, with even smaller steps, say 0.01. Each time we overshoot, we reverse direction, cutting the size of the step. We continue doing this until we have achieved the desired accuracy in the calculation of the estimate of β_2. Table 5.6 shows the steps in this example.

Table 5.6

b_2	RSS	b_2	RSS	b_2	RSS	b_2	RSS
−6	29.17	−10.8	4.19	−10.1	3.38	−10.06	3.384
−7	18.08	−10.7	3.98	−10.0	3.393	−10.07	3.384
−8	10.08	−10.6	3.80	−10.01	3.391	−10.08	3.383
−9	5.19	−10.5	3.66	−10.02	3.389	−10.09	3.384
−10	3.39	−10.4	3.54	−10.03	3.387		
−11	4.70	−10.3	3.46	−10.04	3.386.		
−10.9	4.43	−10.2	3.41	−10.05	3.385		

The process shown in Table 5.6 was terminated after twenty-five iterations, by which time it is clear that the estimate, to two decimal places, is −10.08. Obviously, greater precision would have been obtained by continuing the iterative process further.

Note that the estimate is not exactly the same as the estimate obtained in equation (5.9), which was −10.99. In principle the two sets of results should be identical, because both are minimizing the sum of the squares of the residuals. The discrepancy is caused by the fact that we have cheated slightly in the nonlinear case. We have assumed that β_1 is equal to its true value, 12, instead of estimating it. If we had really failed to spot the transformation that allows us to use linear regression analysis, we would have had to use a nonlinear technique hunting for the best values of b_1 and b_2 simultaneously, and the final values of b_1 and b_2 would have been 12.48 and −10.99, respectively, as in equation (5.9).

In practice, the algorithms used for minimizing the residual sum of squares in a nonlinear model are mathematically far more sophisticated than the simple trial-and-error method described above. Nevertheless, until fairly recently a major problem with the fitting of nonlinear regressions was that it was very slow compared with linear regression, especially when there were several parameters to be estimated, and the high computing cost discouraged the use of nonlinear regression. This has changed as the speed and power of computers have increased. As a consequence more interest is being taken in the technique and some regression applications now incorporate user-friendly nonlinear regression features.

5.5 Choice of function: Box–Cox tests

The possibility of fitting nonlinear models, either by means of a linearizing transformation or by the use of a nonlinear regression algorithm, greatly increases the flexibility of regression analysis, but it also makes your task as a researcher more complex. You have to ask yourself whether you should start off with a linear relationship or a nonlinear one, and if the latter, what kind.

A graphical inspection, using the technique described in Section 4.2 in the case of multiple regression analysis, might help you decide. In the illustration in Section 5.1, it was obvious that the relationship was nonlinear, and it should not have taken much effort to discover that an equation of the form (5.2) would give a good fit. Usually, however, the issue is not so clear-cut. It often happens that several different nonlinear forms might approximately fit the observations if they lie on a curve.

When considering alternative models with the same specification of the dependent variable, the selection procedure is straightforward. The most sensible thing to do is to run regressions based on alternative plausible functions and choose the function that explains the greatest proportion of the variance of the dependent variable. If two or more functions are more or less equally good, you should present the results of each. Looking again at the illustration in Section 5.1, you can see that the linear function explained 69 percent of the variance of Y, whereas the hyperbolic function (5.2) explained 97 percent. In this instance we have no hesitation in choosing the latter.

However, when alternative models employ different functional forms for the dependent variable, the problem of model selection becomes more complicated because you cannot make direct comparisons of R^2 or the sum of the squares of the residuals. In particular—and this is the most common example of the problem—you cannot compare these statistics for linear and logarithmic dependent variable specifications.

For example, in Section 2.6, the linear regression of earnings on schooling has an R^2 of 0.104, and RSS is 34,420. For the semi-logarithmic version in Section 5.2, the corresponding figures are 0.141 and 132. RSS is much smaller for the logarithmic version, but this means nothing at all. The values of $LGEARN$ are much smaller than those of $EARNINGS$, so it is hardly surprising that the residuals are also much smaller. Admittedly R^2 is unit-free, but it is referring to different concepts in the two equations. In one equation it is measuring the proportion of the variance of earnings explained by the regression, and in the other it is measuring the proportion of the variance of the logarithm of earnings explained. If R^2 is much greater for one model than for the other, you would probably be justified in selecting it without further fuss. But if R^2 is similar for the two models, simple eyeballing will not do.

The standard procedure in these circumstances is to perform what is known as a Box–Cox test (Box and Cox, 1964). If you are interested only in comparing models using Y and $\log Y$ as the dependent variable, you can use a version developed by Zarembka (1968). It involves scaling the observations on Y so that the residual sums of squares in the linear and logarithmic models are rendered directly comparable. The procedure has the following steps:

1. You calculate the geometric mean of the values of Y in the sample. This is equal to the exponential of the mean of log Y, so it is easy to calculate:

$$e^{\frac{1}{n}\sum \log Y_i} = e^{\frac{1}{n}\log(Y_1 \times \cdots \times Y_n)} = e^{\log(Y_1 \times \cdots \times Y_n)^{\frac{1}{n}}} = (Y_1 \times \cdots \times Y_n)^{\frac{1}{n}}. \qquad (5.35)$$

2. You scale the observations on Y by dividing by this figure. So

$$Y_i^* = Y_i/\text{geometric mean of } Y, \qquad (5.36)$$

where Y_i^* is the scaled value in observation i.

3. You then regress the linear model using Y^* instead of Y as the dependent variable, and the logarithmic model using log Y^* instead of log Y, but otherwise leaving the models unchanged. The residual sums of squares of the two regressions are now comparable, and the model with the lower sum is providing the better fit.

4. To see if one model is providing a *significantly* better fit, you calculate $(n/2) \log Z$ where Z is the ratio of the residual sums of squares in the scaled regressions and n is the number of observations, and take the absolute value (that is, ignore a minus sign if present). Under the null hypothesis that there is no difference, this statistic is distributed as a chi-squared statistic with 1 degree of freedom. If it exceeds the critical level of chi-squared at the chosen significance level, you conclude that there is a significant difference in the fit.

Example

The test will be performed for the alternative specifications of the earnings function. The mean value of *LGEARN* is 2.430133. The scaling factor is therefore $\exp(2.430133) = 11.3604$. The residual sum of squares in a regression of the Zarembka-scaled earnings on S is 266.7; the residual sum of squares in a regression of the logarithm of Zarembka-scaled earnings is 132.1. Hence the test statistic is

$$\frac{570}{2} \log_e \frac{266.7}{132.1} = 200.2. \qquad (5.37)$$

The critical value of chi-squared with 1 degree of freedom at the 0.1 percent level is 10.8. Hence there is no doubt, according to this test, that the semi-logarithmic specification provides a better fit.

  Note: the Zarembka-scaled regressions are solely for deciding which model you prefer. You should *not* pay any attention to their coefficients, only to their residual sums of squares. You obtain the coefficients by fitting the unscaled version of the preferred model.

Exercises

5.6 Perform a Box–Cox test parallel to that described in this section using your *EAEF* data set.

5.7 Linear and logarithmic Zarembka-scaled regressions of expenditure on food at home on total household expenditure were fitted using the CES data set in Section 5.2. The residual sums of squares were 225.1 and 184.6, respectively. The number of observations was 868, the household reporting no expenditure on food at home being dropped. Perform a Box–Cox test and state your conclusion.

5.8 Perform a Box–Cox test for your commodity in the CES data set, dropping households reporting no expenditure on your commodity.

Appendix 5.1

A More General Box–Cox Test

(*Note:* This section contains relatively advanced material that can safely be omitted at a first reading.)

The original Box–Cox procedure is more general than the version described in Section 5.5. Box and Cox noted that $Y - 1$ and $\log Y$ are special cases of the function $(Y^\lambda - 1)/\lambda$, $Y - 1$ being the function when λ is equal to 1, $\log Y$ being the (limiting form of the) function as λ tends to 0. There is no reason to suppose that either of these values of λ is optimal, and hence it makes sense to try a range of values and see which yields the minimum value of *RSS* (after performing the Zarembka scaling). This exercise is known as a grid search. There is no purpose-designed facility for it in the typical regression application, but nevertheless it is not hard to execute. If you are going to try ten values of λ, you generate within the regression application ten new dependent variables using the functional form and

Table 5.7

λ	*RSS*	λ	*RSS*
1.0	225.1	0.4	176.4
0.9	211.2	0.3	175.5
0.8	199.8	0.2	176.4
0.7	190.9	0.1	179.4
0.6	184.1	0.0	184.6
0.5	179.3		

the different values of λ, after first performing the Zarembka scaling. You then regress each of these separately on the explanatory variables. Table 5.7 gives the results for food expenditure at home, using the CES data set, for various values of λ. The regressions were run with disposable personal income being transformed in the same way as Y, except for the Zarembka scaling. This is not necessary; you can keep the right-side variable or variables in linear form if you wish if you think this appropriate, or you could execute a simultaneous, separate grid search for a different value of λ for them.

The results indicate that the optimal value of λ is about 0.3. In addition to obtaining a point estimate for λ, one may also obtain a confidence interval, but the procedure is beyond the level of this text. (Those interested should consult Spitzer, 1982.)

6 Dummy variables

It frequently happens that some of the factors that you would like to introduce into a regression model are qualitative in nature and therefore not measurable in numerical terms. Some examples are the following.

1. You are investigating the relationship between schooling and earnings, and you have both males and females in your sample. You would like to see if the sex of the respondent makes a difference.

2. You are investigating the relationship between income and expenditure in Belgium, and your sample includes both Flemish-speaking and French-speaking households. You would like to find out whether the ethnic difference is relevant.

3. You have data on the growth rate of GDP per capita and foreign aid per capita for a sample of developing countries, of which some are democracies and some are not. You would like to investigate whether the impact of foreign aid on growth is affected by the type of government.

In each of these examples, one solution would be to run separate regressions for the two categories and see if the coefficients are different. Alternatively, you could run a single regression using all the observations together, measuring the effect of the qualitative factor with what is known as a dummy variable. This has the two important advantages of providing a simple way of testing whether the effect of the qualitative factor is significant and, provided that certain assumptions are valid, making the regression estimates more efficient.

6.1 Illustration of the use of a dummy variable

We will illustrate the use of a dummy variable with a series of regressions investigating how the cost of running a secondary school varies with the number of students and the type of school. We will take as our starting point the model

$$COST = \beta_1 + \beta_2 N + u, \tag{6.1}$$

Table 6.1

```
. reg COST N

  Source |       SS          df       MS              Number of obs =      74
---------+-----------------------------------         F(  1,    72) =    46.82
   Model |   5.7974e+11     1    5.7974e+11           Prob > F       =   0.0000
Residual |   8.9160e+11    72    1.2383e+10           R-squared      =   0.3940
---------+-----------------------------------         Adj R-squared  =   0.3856
   Total |   1.4713e+12    73    2.0155e+10           Root MSE       = 1.1e+05


----------------------------------------------------------------------------
   COST |    Coef.   Std. Err.     t     P>|t|       [95% Conf. Interval]
--------+-------------------------------------------------------------------
      N |  339.0432  49.55144   6.842    0.000        240.2642    437.8222
  _cons |   23953.3  27167.96   0.882    0.381       -30205.04    78111.65
----------------------------------------------------------------------------
```

where $COST$ is the annual recurrent expenditure incurred by a school and N is the number of students attending it. Fitting a regression to a sample of seventy-four secondary schools in Shanghai in the mid-1980s (for details, see the website), the Stata output is as shown in Figure 6.1.

The regression equation is thus (standard errors in parentheses):

$$\widehat{COST} = 24{,}000 + 339N, \quad R^2 = 0.39 \tag{6.2}$$
$$(27{,}000) \quad (50)$$

the cost being measured in yuan, one yuan being worth about 20 cents US at the time of the survey. The equation implies that the marginal cost per student is 339 yuan and that the annual overhead cost (administration and maintenance) is 24,000 yuan.

This is just the starting point. Next we will investigate the impact of the type of school on the cost. Occupational schools aim to provide skills for specific occupations and they tend to be relatively expensive to run because they need to maintain specialized workshops. We could model this by having two equations

$$COST = \beta_1 + \beta_2 N + u, \tag{6.3}$$

and

$$COST = \beta_1' + \beta_2 N + u, \tag{6.4}$$

the first equation relating to regular schools and the second to the occupational schools. Effectively, we are hypothesizing that the annual overhead cost is different for the two types of school, but the marginal cost is the same. The marginal cost assumption is not very plausible and we will relax it in due course. Let us define δ to be the difference in the intercepts: $\delta = \beta_1' - \beta_1$. Then $\beta_1' = \beta_1 + \delta$ and

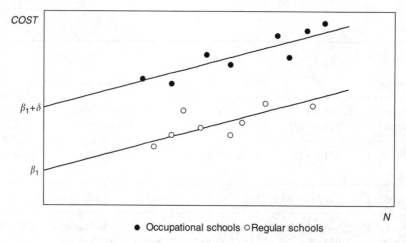

Figure 6.1 Cost functions for regular and occupational schools

we can rewrite the cost function for occupational schools as

$$COST = \beta_1 + \delta + \beta_2 N + u. \tag{6.5}$$

The model is illustrated in Figure 6.1. The two lines show the relationship between the cost and the number of students, neglecting the disturbance term. The line for the occupational schools is the same as that for the regular schools, except that it has been shifted up by an amount δ.

The object of the present exercise is to estimate this unknown shift factor, and we shall do this by introducing what is known as a dummy variable. We shall rewrite the model

$$COST = \beta_1 + \delta OCC + \beta_2 N + u, \tag{6.6}$$

where OCC is a dummy variable, an artificial variable with two possible values, 0 and 1. If OCC is equal to 0, the cost function becomes (6.3), that for regular schools. If OCC is equal to 1, the cost function becomes (6.5), that for occupational schools. Hence, instead of two separate regressions for the different types of school, we can run just one regression using the whole sample. Using the whole sample in a single regression will reduce the population variances of the coefficients, and this should be reflected by smaller standard errors. We will also obtain a single estimate of β_2, instead of two separate ones that are likely to conflict. The price we have to pay is that we have to assume that β_2 is the same for both subsamples. We will relax this assumption in due course.

Data for the first ten schools in the sample are shown in Table 6.2. Note how OCC varies with the type of school.

The data are fed into the computer regression program and multiple regression is used to regress $COST$ on N and OCC. OCC is treated exactly like an ordinary variable, even though it consists only of 0s and 1s.

The Stata output in Table 6.3 gives the results of the regression, using the full sample of seventy-four schools. In equation form, we have (standard errors in

Table 6.2 Recurrent expenditure, number of students, and type of school

School	Type	COST	N	OCC
1	Occupational	345,000	623	1
2	Occupational	537,000	653	1
3	Regular	170,000	400	0
4	Occupational	526,000	663	1
5	Regular	100,000	563	0
6	Regular	28,000	236	0
7	Regular	160,000	307	0
8	Occupational	45,000	173	1
9	Occupational	120,000	146	1
10	Occupational	61,000	99	1

parentheses):

$$\widehat{COST} = -34{,}000 + 133{,}000\,OCC + 331N. \quad R^2 = 0.62 \qquad (6.7)$$
$$(24{,}000) \quad (21{,}000) \qquad\quad (40)$$

Putting OCC equal to 0 and 1, respectively, we can obtain the implicit cost functions for the two types of school.

$$\textit{Regular schools}: \quad \widehat{COST} = -34{,}000 + 331N. \qquad (6.8)$$

$$\textit{Occupational schools}: \quad \widehat{COST} = -34{,}000 + 133{,}000 + 331N$$
$$= 99{,}000 + 331N. \qquad (6.9)$$

Table 6.3

```
. reg COST N OCC

   Source |       SS        df       MS              Number of obs =      74
----------+----------------------------------       F( 2,    71) =   56.86
    Model | 9.0582e+11       2  4.5291e+11           Prob > F      =  0.0000
 Residual | 5.6553e+11      71  7.9652e+09           R-squared     =  0.6156
----------+----------------------------------       Adj R-squared =  0.6048
    Total | 1.4713e+12      73  2.0155e+10           Root MSE      =   89248


------------------------------------------------------------------------------
     COST |     Coef.   Std. Err.      t    P>|t|     [95% Conf. Interval]
----------+-------------------------------------------------------------------
        N |  331.4493   39.75844    8.337   0.000    252.1732    410.7254
      OCC |  133259.1   20827.59    6.398   0.000    91730.06    174788.1
    _cons | -33612.55   23573.47   -1.426   0.158   -80616.71    13391.61
------------------------------------------------------------------------------
```

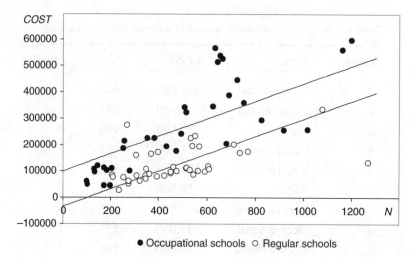

Figure 6.2 Cost functions for regular and occupational schools in Shanghai

The regression implies that the marginal cost per student per year is 331 yuan and that the annual overhead cost of a regular school is −34,000 yuan. Obviously having a negative intercept does not make any sense at all and it suggests that the model is misspecified in some way. We will come back to this later. The coefficient of the dummy variable, 133,000, is an estimate of the extra annual overhead cost of an occupational school. The marginal cost of an occupational school is the same as that for a regular school—it must be, given the model specification. Figure 6.2 shows the data and the cost functions derived from the regression results.

Standard errors and hypothesis testing

In addition to the estimates of the coefficients, the regression results include standard errors and the usual diagnostic statistics. We will perform a t test on the coefficient of the dummy variable. Our null hypothesis is $H_0: \delta = 0$ and our alternative hypothesis is $H_1: \delta \neq 0$. In words, our null hypothesis is that there is no difference in the overhead costs of the two types of school. The t statistic is 6.40, so it is rejected at the 0.1 percent significance level. We can perform t tests on the other coefficients in the usual way. The t statistic for the coefficient of N is 8.34, so we conclude that the marginal cost is (very) significantly different from 0. In the case of the intercept, the t statistic is −1.43, so we do not reject the null hypothesis $H_0: \beta_1 = 0$. Thus one explanation of the nonsensical negative overhead cost of regular schools might be that they do not actually have any overheads and our estimate is a random number. A more realistic version of this hypothesis is that β_1 is positive but small (as you can see, the 95 percent confidence interval includes positive values) and the disturbance term is responsible for the negative estimate. As already noted, a further possibility is that the model is misspecified in some way.

Exercises

6.1   Using your *EAEF* data set, regress *S* on *ASVABC*, *SM*, *SF*, and *MALE*, a dummy variable that is 1 for male respondents and 0 for female ones. Interpret the coefficients and perform *t* tests. Is there any evidence that the educational attainment of males is different from that of females?

6.2*   The Stata output shows the result of regressing weight on height, first with a linear specification, then with a double-logarithmic one, including a dummy variable *MALE*, defined as in Exercise 6.1, in both cases. Give an interpretation of the equations and perform appropriate statistical tests.

```
. g LGWEIGHT=ln(WEIGHT85)
(20 missing values generated)
. g LGHEIGHT=ln(HEIGHT)
(19 missing values generated)

. reg WEIGHT85 HEIGHT MALE

      Source |       SS       df       MS              Number of obs =     550
-------------+------------------------------           F(  2,   547) =  179.27
       Model |  252465.351      2  126232.675          Prob > F      =  0.0000
    Residual |  385164.642    547  704.140113          R-squared     =  0.3959
-------------+------------------------------           Adj R-squared =  0.3937
       Total |  637629.993    549  1161.43897          Root MSE      =  26.536


------------------------------------------------------------------------------
    WEIGHT85 |      Coef.   Std. Err.      t    P>|t|     [95% Conf. Interval]
-------------+----------------------------------------------------------------
      HEIGHT |   4.389971   .4313611    10.177   0.000     3.542644    5.237298
        MALE |   10.74783   3.408249     3.153   0.002     4.05297    17.44269
       _cons |  -147.6628   27.9497     -5.283   0.000    -202.5647   -92.76089
------------------------------------------------------------------------------

. reg LGWEIGHT LGHEIGHT MALE

      Source |       SS       df       MS              Number of obs =     550
-------------+------------------------------           F(  2,   547) =  216.63
       Model |  10.9693142      2  5.48465712          Prob > F      =  0.0000
    Residual |  13.8491387    547  .025318352          R-squared     =  0.4420
-------------+------------------------------           Adj R-squared =  0.4399
       Total |  24.8184529    549  .045206654          Root MSE      =  .15912


------------------------------------------------------------------------------
    LGWEIGHT |      Coef.   Std. Err.      t    P>|t|     [95% Conf. Interval]
-------------+----------------------------------------------------------------
    LGHEIGHT |   1.901986   .1747121    10.886   0.000     1.558797    2.245174
        MALE |   .077839    .020447      3.807   0.000     .0376748    .1180032
       _cons |  -3.033228   .7283617    -4.164   0.000    -4.463957    -1.6025
------------------------------------------------------------------------------
```

6.3   Using your *EAEF* data set, regress *LGEARN* on *S*, *ASVABC*, and *MALE*. Interpret the coefficients and perform *t* tests. (See Section 3 of the *EAEF* manual for help with the interpretation of the coefficient of a dummy variable in a semi-logarithmic regression.)

6.2 Extension to more than two categories and to multiple sets of dummy variables

In the previous section we used a dummy variable to differentiate between regular and occupational schools when fitting a cost function. In actual fact there are two types of regular secondary school in Shanghai. There are general schools, which provide the usual academic education, and vocational schools. As their name implies, the vocational schools are meant to impart occupational skills as well as give an academic education. However, the vocational component of the curriculum is typically quite small and the schools are similar to the general schools. Often they are just general schools with a couple of workshops added. Likewise there are two types of occupational school. There are technical schools training technicians and skilled workers' schools training craftsmen.

Thus now the qualitative variable has four categories and we need to develop a more elaborate set of dummy variables. The standard procedure is to choose one category as the reference category to which the basic equation applies, and then to define dummy variables for each of the other categories. In general it is good practice to select the dominant or most normal category, if there is one, as the reference category. In the Shanghai sample it is sensible to choose the general schools. They are the most numerous and the other schools are variations of them.

Accordingly we will define dummy variables for the other three types. *TECH* will be the dummy variable for the technical schools: *TECH* is equal to 1 if the observation relates to a technical school, 0 otherwise. Similarly we will define dummy variables *WORKER* and *VOC* for the skilled workers' schools and the vocational schools. The regression model is now

$$COST = \beta_1 + \delta_T TECH + \delta_W WORKER + \delta_V VOC + \beta_2 N + u, \qquad (6.10)$$

where δ_T, δ_W, and δ_V are coefficients that represent the extra overhead costs of the technical, skilled workers', and vocational schools, relative to the cost of a general school. Note that you do not include a dummy variable for the reference category, and that is the reason that the reference category is usually described as the omitted category. Note that we do not make any prior assumption about the size, or even the sign, of the δ coefficients. They will be estimated from the sample data.

Table 6.4 gives the data for the first ten of the seventy-four schools. Note how the values of the dummy variables *TECH*, *WORKER*, and *VOC* are determined by the type of school in each observation.

Table 6.4 Recurrent expenditure, number of students, and type of school

School	Type	COST	N	TECH	WORKER	VOC
1	Technical	345,000	623	1	0	0
2	Technical	537,000	653	1	0	0
3	General	170,000	400	0	0	0
4	Skilled workers'	526,000	663	0	1	0
5	General	100,000	563	0	0	0
6	Vocational	28,000	236	0	0	1
7	Vocational	160,000	307	0	0	1
8	Technical	45,000	173	1	0	0
9	Technical	120,000	146	1	0	0
10	Skilled workers'	61,000	99	0	1	0

The Stata output in Table 6.5 gives the regression results for this model. In equation form, we have (standard errors in parentheses):

$$\widehat{COST} = -55{,}000 + 154{,}000\,TECH + 143{,}000\,WORKER$$
$$\phantom{\widehat{COST} = } (27{,}000) \quad (27{,}000) \qquad\quad (28{,}000)$$
$$+\, 53{,}000\,VOC + 343N. \quad R^2 = 0.63 \qquad\qquad (6.11)$$
$$ (31{,}000) \qquad\; (40)$$

Table 6.5

```
. reg COST N TECH WORKER VOC

      Source |       SS       df       MS              Number of obs =      74
-------------+------------------------------          F(  4,     69) =   29.63
       Model |  9.2996e+11        4   2.3249e+11       Prob > F       =  0.0000
    Residual |  5.4138e+11       69   7.8461e+09       R-squared      =  0.6320
-------------+------------------------------          Adj R-squared  =  0.6107
       Total |  1.4713e+12       73   2.0155e+10       Root MSE       =   88578


        COST |      Coef.   Std. Err.      t    P>|t|     [95% Conf. Interval]
-------------+----------------------------------------------------------------
           N |   342.6335    40.2195    8.519   0.000     262.3978    422.8692
        TECH |   154110.9    26760.41   5.759   0.000     100725.3    207496.4
      WORKER |   143362.4     27852.8   5.147   0.000     87797.57    198927.2
         VOC |   53228.64   31061.65    1.714   0.091    -8737.646    115194.9
       _cons |  -54893.09   26673.08   -2.058   0.043    -108104.4   -1681.748
```

The coefficient of N indicates that the marginal cost per student per year is 343 yuan. The constant indicates that the annual overhead cost of a general academic school is −55,000 yuan per year. Obviously this is nonsense and indicates that something is wrong with the model. The coefficients of *TECH*, *WORKER*, and *VOC* indicate that the overhead costs of technical, skilled workers', and vocational schools are 154,000 yuan, 143,000 yuan, and 53,000 yuan greater than the cost of a general school.

From this equation we can obtain the implicit cost functions for the four types of school. First, putting the three dummy variables equal to 0, we obtain the cost function for general schools:

$$\text{General schools:} \quad \widehat{COST} = -55{,}000 + 343N. \tag{6.12}$$

Next, putting *TECH* equal to 1 and *WORKER* and *VOC* to 0, we obtain the cost function for technical schools:

$$\text{Technical schools:} \quad \widehat{COST} = -55{,}000 + 154{,}000 + 343N = 99{,}000 + 343N. \tag{6.13}$$

And similarly we obtain the cost functions for skilled workers' and vocational schools:

Skilled workers' schools:

$$\widehat{COST} = -55{,}000 + 143{,}000 + 343N = 88{,}000 + 343N. \tag{6.14}$$

Vocational schools:

$$\widehat{COST} = -55{,}000 + 53{,}000 + 343N = -2{,}000 + 343N. \tag{6.15}$$

Note that in each case the annual marginal cost per student is estimated at 343 yuan. The model specification assumes that this figure does not differ according to type of school. The four cost functions are illustrated in Figure 6.3.

We can perform *t* tests on the coefficients in the usual way. The *t* statistic for N is 8.52, so the marginal cost is (very) significantly different from 0, as we would expect. The *t* statistic for the technical school dummy is 5.76, indicating that the annual overhead cost of a technical school is (very) significantly greater than that of a general school, again as expected. Similarly for skilled workers' schools, the *t* statistic being 5.15. In the case of vocational schools, however, the *t* statistic is only 1.71, indicating that the overhead cost of such a school is not significantly greater than that of a general school. This is not surprising, given that the vocational schools are not much different from the general schools. Note that the null hypotheses for the tests on the coefficients of the dummy variables are that the overhead costs of the other schools are not different from the overhead cost of a general school.

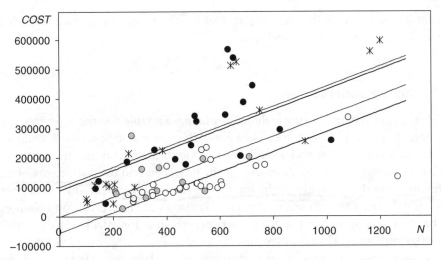

Technical schools ● Workers' schools ✗ Vocational schools ◐ General schools ○

Figure 6.3

Joint explanatory power of a group of dummy variables

Finally we will perform an F test of the joint explanatory power of the dummy variables as a group. The null hypothesis is $H_0\colon \delta_T = \delta_W = \delta_V = 0$. The alternative hypothesis H_1 is that at least one δ is different from 0. The residual sum of squares in the specification including the dummy variables is 5.41×10^{11}. (In the Stata output, it appears as $5.4138e + 11$. The $e + 11$ means that the coefficient should be multiplied by 10^{11}.) The residual sum of squares in the original specification excluding the dummy variables was 8.92×10^{11} (see Table 6.1). The reduction in RSS when we include the dummies is therefore $(8.92 - 5.41) \times 10^{11}$. We will check whether this reduction is significant with the usual F test.

The numerator in the F ratio is the reduction in RSS divided by the cost, which is the 3 degrees of freedom given up when we estimate three additional coefficients (the coefficients of the dummies). The denominator is RSS for the specification including the dummy variables, divided by the number of degrees of freedom remaining after they have been added. The F ratio is therefore given by

$$F(3, 69) = \frac{(8.9160 \times 10^{11} - 5.4138 \times 10^{11})/3}{5.4138 \times 10^{11}/69} = \frac{1.1674}{0.07846} = 14.9. \quad (6.16)$$

Note that the ratios were calculated to four significant figures. This will ensure that the F statistic will be correct to three significant figures. The critical value of $F(3, 69)$ will be a little below 6.17, the critical value for $F(3, 60)$ at the 0.1 percent significance level, so we can reject H_0 at this level. This is only to be expected because t tests showed that δ_T and δ_W were both significantly different from 0, and it is rare (but not impossible) for the F test not to reject H_0 when one or more coefficients is significant.

The dummy variable trap

What would happen if you included a dummy variable for the reference category? There would be two consequences. First, were it possible to compute regression coefficients, you would not be able to give them an interpretation. The coefficient b_1 is a basic estimate of the intercept, and the coefficients of the dummies are the estimates of the increase in the intercept from this basic level, but now there is no definition of what is basic, so the interpretation collapses. The other consequence is that the numerical procedure for calculating the regression coefficients will break down and the computer will simply send you an error message (or possibly, in sophisticated applications, drop one of the dummies for you). Suppose that there are m dummy categories and you define dummy variables $D_1, \ldots, D_m$. Then, in observation i, $\sum_{j=1}^{m} D_{ji} = 1$ because one of the dummy variables will be equal to 1 and all the others will be equal to 0. But the intercept β_1 is really the product of the parameter β_1 and a special variable whose value is 1 in all observations (see Box 4.1). Hence, for all observations, the sum of the dummy variables is equal to this special variable, and one has an exact linear relationship among the variables in the regression model. As a consequence the model is subject to a special case of exact multicollinearity, making it impossible to compute regression coefficients.

Change of reference category

The skilled workers' schools are considerably less academic than the others, even the technical schools. Suppose that we wish to investigate whether their costs are significantly different from the others. The easiest way to do this is to make them the omitted category (reference category). Then the coefficients of the dummy variables become estimates of the differences between the overhead costs of the other types of school and those of the skilled workers' schools. Since skilled workers' schools are now the reference category, we need a dummy variable, which will be called GEN, for the general academic schools. The model becomes

$$COST = \beta_1 + \delta_T TECH + \delta_V VOC + \delta_G GEN + \beta_2 N + u, \qquad (6.17)$$

where δ_T, δ_V, and δ_G are the extra costs of technical, vocational, and general schools relative to skilled workers' schools. The data table for the first ten schools is now as shown in Table 6.6. The Stata output is shown in Table 6.7.

Table 6.6 Recurrent expenditure, enrolments, and type of school

School	Type	COST	N	TECH	GEN	VOC
1	Technical	345,000	623	1	0	0
2	Technical	537,000	653	1	0	0
3	General	170,000	400	0	1	0
4	Skilled workers'	526,000	663	0	0	0
5	General	100,000	563	0	1	0
6	Vocational	28,000	236	0	0	1
7	Vocational	160,000	307	0	0	1
8	Technical	45,000	173	1	0	0
9	Technical	120,000	146	1	0	0
10	Skilled workers'	61,000	99	0	0	0

The regression equation is therefore (standard errors in parentheses):

$$\widehat{COST} = 88,000 + 11,000TECH - 143,000GEN$$
$$\phantom{\widehat{COST} = 8}(29,000)\ (30,000)(28,000)$$

$$- 90,000VOC + 343N. \quad R^2 = 0.63 \qquad (6.18)$$
$$(34,000)(40)$$

Table 6.7

```
. reg COST N TECH VOC GEN

  Source |       SS         df       MS              Number of obs =      74
---------+------------------------------            F( 4,    69) =   29.63
   Model | 9.2996e+11        4  2.3249e+11           Prob > F      =  0.0000
Residual | 5.4138e+11       69  7.8461e+09           R-squared     =  0.6320
---------+------------------------------            Adj R-squared =  0.6107
   Total | 1.4713e+12       73  2.0155e+10           Root MSE      =   88578


---------------------------------------------------------------------------
    COST |    Coef.    Std. Err.     t     P>|t|   [95% Conf. Interval]
---------+-----------------------------------------------------------------
       N |  342.6335    40.2195    8.519   0.000    262.3978    422.8692
    TECH |  10748.51    30524.87   0.352   0.726   -50146.93    71643.95
     VOC | -90133.74    33984.22  -2.652   0.010   -157930.4   -22337.07
     GEN | -143362.4    27852.8   -5.147   0.000   -198927.2   -87797.57
   _cons |  88469.29    28849.56   3.067   0.003    30916.01    146022.6
---------------------------------------------------------------------------
```

From this equation we can again obtain the implicit cost functions the four types of school. Putting all the dummy variables equal to 0, we obtain the cost function for skilled workers' schools:

Skilled workers' schools : $\widehat{COST} = 88,000 + 343N.$

$$(6.19)$$

Then, putting *TECH, WORKER,* and *GEN* equal to 1 and the other two to 0, we derive the cost functions for the other types of school:

Technical schools: $\widehat{COST} = 88,000 + 11,000 + 343N = 99,000 + 343N.$

$$(6.20)$$

Vocational schools: $\widehat{COST} = 88,000 - 90,000 + 343N = -2,000 + 343N.$

$$(6.21)$$

General schools: $\widehat{COST} = 88,000 - 143,000 + 343N = -55,000 + 343N.$

$$(6.22)$$

Note that these equations are identical to those obtained when general schools were the reference category. The choice of omitted category does not affect the substance of the regression results. The only components that change are the standard errors and the interpretation of the t tests. R^2, the coefficients of the other variables, the t statistics for the other variables, and the F statistic for the equation as a whole do not alter. And of course the diagram representing the four cost functions is the same as before.

Multiple sets of dummy variables

It may happen that you wish to include more than one set of dummy variables in your regression equation. This is especially common when working with cross-section data, when you may have gathered data on a number of qualitative as well as quantitative characteristics. There is no problem in extending the use of dummy variables in this way, provided that the framework is defined clearly.

We will illustrate the procedure using the school cost data. Many of the occupational schools and some of the regular schools are residential. We will investigate the extra cost of running a residential school, controlling for number of students and type of school. To do this, we introduce a dummy variable, *RES*, which is equal to 1 for residential schools and 0 for the others. For the sake of simplicity we will revert to the occupational/regular classification of school type. The model now becomes

$$COST = \beta_1 + \delta OCC + \varepsilon RES + \beta_2 N + u, \qquad (6.23)$$

where ε is the extra cost of a residential school. The reference category now has two dimensions, one for each qualitative characteristic. In this case it is a nonresidential ($RES = 0$), regular ($OCC = 0$) school. Table 6.8 presents the

Table 6.8 Recurrent expenditure, number of students, school type and whether residential

School	Type	COST	N	OCC	RES
1	Occupational, nonresidential	345,000	623	1	0
2	Occupational, residential	537,000	653	1	1
3	Regular, nonresidential	170,000	400	0	0
4	Occupational, residential	526,000	663	1	1
5	Regular, nonresidential	100,000	563	0	0
6	Regular, nonresidential	28,000	236	0	0
7	Regular, residential	160,000	307	0	1
8	Occupational, nonresidential	45,000	173	1	0
9	Occupational, nonresidential	120,000	146	1	0
10	Occupational, nonresidential	61,000	99	1	0

data for the first ten schools in the sample. The second, fourth, and seventh are residential schools and so RES is set equal to 1, while for the others it is 0.

The Stata regression results are as shown in Table 6.9. The regression equation is therefore (standard errors in parentheses):

$$\widehat{COST} = -29,000 + 110,000 OCC + 58,000 RES + 322 N. \quad R^2 = 0.63$$
$$(23,000) \quad (24,000) \quad\quad (31,000) \quad\quad (39) \quad\quad\quad\quad (6.24)$$

Table 6.9

```
. reg COST N OCC RES

      Source |       SS       df       MS              Number of obs =      74
-------------+------------------------------           F(  3,    70) =   40.43
       Model |  9.3297e+11     3  3.1099e+11           Prob > F      =  0.0000
    Residual |  5.3838e+11    70  7.6911e+09           R-squared     =  0.6341
-------------+------------------------------           Adj R-squared =  0.6184
       Total |  1.4713e+12    73  2.0155e+10           Root MSE      =   87699


------------------------------------------------------------------------------
        COST |      Coef.   Std. Err.      t    P>|t|     [95% Conf. Interval]
-------------+----------------------------------------------------------------
           N |    321.833   39.40225     8.168   0.000    243.2477    400.4183
         OCC |   109564.6   24039.58     4.558   0.000    61619.15      157510
         RES |   57909.01   30821.31     1.879   0.064   -3562.137    119380.2
       _cons |  -29045.27   23291.54    -1.247   0.217   -75498.78    17408.25
------------------------------------------------------------------------------
```

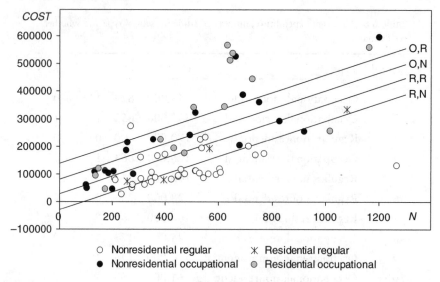

Figure 6.4

Using the four combinations of *OCC* and *RES*, one may obtain the following subequations:

$$\text{Regular, nonresidential:} \quad \widehat{COST} = -29{,}000 + 322N. \tag{6.25}$$

$$\text{Occupational, nonresidential:} \quad \widehat{COST} = -29{,}000 + 110{,}000 + 322N$$
$$= 81{,}000 + 322N. \tag{6.26}$$

$$\text{Regular, residential:} \quad \widehat{COST} = -29{,}000 + 58{,}000 + 322N$$
$$= 29{,}000 + 322N. \tag{6.27}$$

$$\text{Occupational, residential:} \quad \widehat{COST} = -29{,}000 + 110{,}000$$
$$+ 58{,}000 + 322N$$
$$= 139{,}000 + 322N. \tag{6.28}$$

The cost functions are illustrated in Figure 6.4. Note that the model incorporates the (plausible) assumption that the extra cost of a residential school is the same for regular and occupational schools.

The *t* statistic for the residential dummy is only 1.88. However, we can perform a one-tailed test because it is reasonable to exclude the possibility that residential schools cost less to run than nonresidential ones, and so we can reject the null hypothesis of no difference in the costs at the 5 percent level.

The procedure may be generalized, with no limit on the number of qualitative characteristics in the model or the number of categories defined for each characteristic.

Exercises

6.4* Does ethnicity affect educational attainment? In your *EAEF* data set you will find the following ethnic dummy variables:

ETHHISP	1 if hispanic, 0 otherwise
ETHBLACK	1 if black, 0 otherwise
ETHWHITE	1 if not hispanic or black, 0 otherwise.

Regress *S* on *ASVABC*, *MALE*, *SM*, *SF*, *ETHBLACK*, and *ETHHISP*. (In this specification *ETHWHITE* has been chosen as the reference category, and so it is omitted.) Interpret the regression results and perform *t* tests on the coefficients.

6.5 `reg LGEARN EDUCPROF EDUCPHD EDUCMAST EDUCBA EDUCAA EDUCGED`
`EDUCDO ASVABC MALE`

```
      Source |       SS       df       MS              Number of obs =     570
-------------+------------------------------           F(  9,   560) =   17.67
       Model |  34.0164091      9  3.77960101           Prob > F      =  0.0000
    Residual |  119.785484    560  .213902649           R-squared     =  0.2212
-------------+------------------------------           Adj R-squared =  0.2087
       Total |  153.801893    569  .270302096           Root MSE      =   .4625


      LGEARN |      Coef.   Std. Err.      t    P>|t|     [95% Conf. Interval]
-------------+----------------------------------------------------------------
    EDUCPROF |   .3860621   .1789987     2.157   0.031    .0344711    .737653
     EDUCPHD |  -.3376001   .4654787    -0.725   0.469  -1.251898    .5766974
    EDUCMAST |   .3539022   .0876093     4.040   0.000    .1818193    .5259851
      EDUCBA |   .2917556   .0563315     5.179   0.000    .1811087    .4024026
      EDUCAA |   .0671492   .0727099     0.924   0.356   -.0756682    .2099665
     EDUCGED |  -.1448539   .0819881    -1.767   0.078   -.3058956    .0161879
      EDUCDO |  -.0924651   .0782349    -1.182   0.238   -.2461348    .0612046
      ASVABC |   .0110694   .0026095     4.242   0.000    .0059439    .016195
        MALE |   .2103497   .0394895     5.327   0.000    .1327841    .2879153
       _cons |   1.685005   .1294621    13.015   0.000    1.430714   1.939295
```

The Stata output shows the result of a semilogarithmic regression of earnings on highest educational qualification obtained, *ASVABC* score, and the sex of the respondent, the educational qualifications being a professional degree, a PhD, a Master's degree, a Bachelor's degree, an Associate of Arts degree, a general equivalence diploma, and no qualification (high school drop-out). The GED is a qualification equivalent to a high school diploma. The high school diploma was the reference category. Provide an interpretation of the coefficients and perform *t* tests.

6.6 Are earnings subject to ethnic discrimination? Using your *EAEF* data set, regress *LGEARN* on *S*, *ASVABC*, *MALE*, *ETHHISP*, and *ETHBLACK*. Interpret the regression results and perform *t* tests on the coefficients.

6.7 Does belonging to a union have an impact on earnings? In the output below, *COLLBARG* is a dummy variable defined to be 1 for workers whose wages are determined by collective bargaining and 0 for the others. Provide an interpretation of the regression coefficients and perform appropriate statistical tests.

```
. reg LGEARN S ASVABC MALE COLLBARG

      Source |       SS       df       MS              Number of obs =     570
-------------+------------------------------           F(  4,   565) =   40.65
       Model |  34.3688209     4  8.59220523           Prob > F      =  0.0000
    Residual |  119.433072   565  .211385968           R-squared     =  0.2235
-------------+------------------------------           Adj R-squared =  0.2180
       Total |  153.801893   569  .270302096           Root MSE      =  .45977


------------------------------------------------------------------------------
      LGEARN |      Coef.   Std. Err.      t    P>|t|     [95% Conf. Interval]
-------------+----------------------------------------------------------------
           S |   .0597083   .0096328     6.198   0.000     .0407879    .0786287
      ASVABC |   .0100311    .002574     3.897   0.000     .0049753    .0150868
        MALE |   .2148213   .0391191     5.491   0.000     .1379846     .291658
    COLLBARG |   .1927604   .0614425     3.137   0.002     .0720769     .313444
       _cons |   .9759561   .1225332     7.965   0.000     .7352799    1.216632
------------------------------------------------------------------------------
```

6.8* Evaluate whether the ethnicity dummies as a group have significant explanatory power for educational attainment by comparing the residual sums of squares in the regressions in Exercises 6.1 and 6.4.

6.9 Evaluate whether the ethnicity dummies as a group have significant explanatory power for earnings by comparing the residual sums of squares in the regressions in Exercises 6.3 and 6.6.

6.10* Repeat Exercise 6.4 making *ETHBLACK* the reference category. Evaluate the impact on the interpretation of the coefficients and the statistical tests.

6.11 Repeat Exercise 6.6 making *ETHBLACK* the reference category. Evaluate the impact on the interpretation of the coefficients and the statistical tests.

6.3 Slope dummy variables

We have so far assumed that the qualitative variables we have introduced into the regression model are responsible only for shifts in the intercept of the regression line. We have implicitly assumed that the slope of the regression line is the same for each category of a qualitative variable. This is not necessarily a plausible assumption, and we will now see how to relax it, and test it, using the device known as a slope dummy variable (also sometimes known as an interactive dummy variable).

To illustrate this, we will return to the school cost example. The assumption that the marginal cost per student is the same for occupational and regular schools is unrealistic because occupational schools incur expenditure on training materials related to the number of students and the staff–student ratio has to be higher in occupational schools because workshop groups cannot be, or at least should not be, as large as academic classes. We can relax the assumption by introducing the slope dummy variable, NOCC, defined as the product of N and OCC:

$$COST = \beta_1 + \delta OCC + \beta_2 N + \lambda NOCC + u. \tag{6.29}$$

If this is rewritten

$$COST = \beta_1 + \delta OCC + (\beta_2 + \lambda OCC)N + u, \tag{6.30}$$

it can be seen that the effect of the slope dummy variable is to allow the coefficient of N for occupational schools to be λ greater than that for regular schools. If OCC is 0, so is NOCC and the equation becomes

$$COST = \beta_1 + \beta_2 N + u. \tag{6.31}$$

If OCC is 1, NOCC is equal to N and the equation becomes

$$COST = \beta_1 + \delta + (\beta_2 + \lambda)N + u. \tag{6.32}$$

λ is thus the incremental marginal cost associated with occupational schools, in the same way that δ is the incremental overhead cost associated with them. Table 6.10 gives the data for the first ten schools in the sample.

Table 6.10 Recurrent expenditure, number of students, and school type

School	Type	COST	N	OCC	NOCC
1	Occupational	345,000	623	1	623
2	Occupational	537,000	653	1	653
3	Regular	170,000	400	0	0
4	Occupational	526,000	663	1	663
5	Regular	100,000	563	0	0
6	Regular	28,000	236	0	0
7	Regular	160,000	307	0	0
8	Occupational	45,000	173	1	173
9	Occupational	120,000	146	1	146
10	Occupational	61,000	99	1	99

Table 6.11

```
. g NOCC=N*OCC

. reg COST N OCC NOCC

    Source |       SS          df        MS              Number of obs =        74
-----------+----------------------------------           F(  3,    70) =     49.64
     Model | 1.0009e+12        3    3.3363e+11           Prob > F      =    0.0000
  Residual | 4.7045e+11       70    6.7207e+09           R-squared     =    0.6803
-----------+----------------------------------           Adj R-squared =    0.6666
     Total | 1.4713e+12       73    2.0155e+10           Root MSE      =     81980


------------------------------------------------------------------------------
      COST |      Coef.   Std. Err.      t    P>|t|     [95% Conf. Interval]
-----------+------------------------------------------------------------------
         N |   152.2982   60.01932     2.537   0.013     32.59349    272.003
       OCC | -3501.177    41085.46    -0.085   0.932    -85443.55    78441.19
      NOCC |   284.4786   75.63211     3.761   0.000     133.6351    435.3221
     _cons |   51475.25   31314.84     1.644   0.105    -10980.24    113930.7
------------------------------------------------------------------------------
```

From the Stata output we obtain the regression equation (standard errors in parentheses):

$$\widehat{COST} = 51,000 - 4,000OCC + 152N + 284NOCC. \quad R^2 = 0.68 \quad (6.33)$$
$$(31,000)(41,000) \qquad (60) \qquad (76)$$

Putting OCC, and hence NOCC, equal to 0, we get the cost function for a regular school. We estimate that the annual overhead cost is 51,000 yuan and the annual marginal cost per student is 152 yuan.

$$Regular\ schools: \qquad \widehat{COST} = 51,000 + 152N. \qquad (6.34)$$

Putting OCC equal to 1, and hence NOCC equal to N, we estimate that the annual overhead cost of an occupational school is 47,000 yuan and the annual marginal cost per student is 436 yuan.

$$Occupational\ schools: \quad \widehat{COST} = 51,000 - 4,000 + 152N + 284N$$
$$= 47,000 + 436N. \qquad (6.35)$$

The two cost functions are shown in Figure 6.5. You can see that they fit the data much better than before and that the real difference is in the marginal cost, not the overhead cost. We can now see why we had a nonsensical negative estimate of the overhead cost of a regular school in previous specifications. The assumption of the same marginal cost led to an estimate of the marginal cost that was a compromise between the marginal costs of occupational and regular

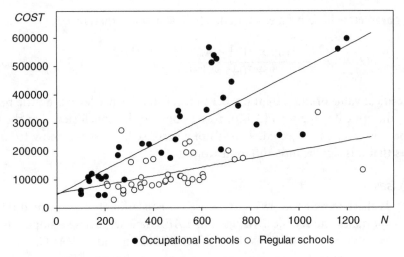

Figure 6.5 School cost functions with a slope dummy variable

schools. The cost function for regular schools was too steep and as a consequence the intercept was underestimated, actually becoming negative and indicating that something was wrong with the specification of the model.

We can perform t tests as usual. The t statistic for the coefficient of $NOCC$ is 3.76, so the marginal cost per student in an occupational school is significantly higher than that in a regular school. The coefficient of OCC is now negative, suggesting that the overhead cost of an occupational school is actually lower than that of a regular school. This is unlikely. However, the t statistic is only -0.09, so we do not reject the null hypothesis that the overhead costs of the two types of school are the same.

Joint explanatory power of the intercept and slope dummy variables

The joint explanatory power of the intercept and slope dummies can be tested with the usual F test for a group of variables, comparing RSS when the dummy variables are included with RSS when they are not. The null hypothesis is $H_0: \delta = \lambda = 0$. The alternative hypothesis is that one or both are nonzero. The numerator of the F statistic is the reduction in RSS when the dummies are added, divided by the cost in terms of degrees of freedom. RSS in the regression without the dummy variables was 8.9160×10^{11}, and in the regression with the dummy variables it was 4.7045×10^{11}. The cost is 2 because two extra parameters, the coefficients of the dummy variables, have been estimated. The denominator of the F statistic is RSS after the dummies have been added, divided by the number of degrees of freedom remaining. This is 70 because there are seventy-four observations and four parameters have been estimated. The F statistic is therefore

$$F(2,70) = \frac{(8.9160 \times 10^{11} - 4.7045 \times 10^{11})/2}{4.7045 \times 10^{11}/70} = 31.3. \qquad (6.36)$$

The critical value of $F(2,70)$ at the 0.1 percent significance level is a little below 7.77, the critical value for $F(2,60)$, so we come to the conclusion that the null hypothesis should be rejected. This is not a surprise because we know from the t tests that λ is significantly different from 0.

Exercises

6.12* Is the effect of the *ASVABC* score on educational attainment different for males and females? Using your *EAEF* data set, define a slope dummy variable *MALEASVC* as the product of *MALE* and *ASVABC*:

$$MALEASVC = MALE * ASVABC.$$

Regress S on *ASVABC*, *SM*, *SF*, *ETHBLACK*, *ETHHISP*, *MALE*, and *MALEASVC*, interpret the equation and perform appropriate statistical tests.

6.13 Is the effect of education on earnings different for members of a union? In the output below, *COLLBARG* is a dummy variable defined to be 1 for workers whose wages are determined by collective bargaining and 0 for the others. *SBARG* is a slope dummy variable defined as the product of S and *COLLBARG*. Provide an interpretation of the regression coefficients, comparing them with those in Exercise 6.7, and perform appropriate statistical tests.

```
. g SBARG=S*COLLBARG

. reg LGEARN S ASVABC MALE COLLBARG SBARG

      Source |       SS       df       MS              Number of obs =     570
-------------+------------------------------           F(  5,   564) =   35.40
       Model |  36.7418126     5  7.34836253           Prob > F      =  0.0000
    Residual |  117.06008    564  .207553333           R-squared     =  0.2389
-------------+------------------------------           Adj R-squared =  0.2321
       Total |  153.801893   569  .270302096           Root MSE      =  .45558

------------------------------------------------------------------------------
      LGEARN |      Coef.   Std. Err.      t    P>|t|     [95% Conf. Interval]
-------------+----------------------------------------------------------------
           S |   .0695614   .0099799    6.970   0.000     .049959    .0891637
      ASVABC |   .0097345   .0025521    3.814   0.000    .0047218    .0147472
        MALE |   .2153046   .0387631    5.554   0.000    .1391668    .2914423
    COLLBARG |   1.334913   .3432285    3.889   0.000    .6607513    2.009076
       SBARG |  -.0839265   .0248208   -3.381   0.001   -.1326789    -.035174
       _cons |   .8574219   .1263767    6.785   0.000    .6091955    1.105648
------------------------------------------------------------------------------
```

6.14   Is the effect of education on earnings different for males and females? Using your *EAEF* data set, define a slope dummy variable *MALES* as the product of *MALE* and *S*:

$$MALES = MALE * S.$$

Regress *LGEARN* on *S*, *ASVABC*, *ETHBLACK*, *ETHHISP*, *MALE*, and *MALES*, interpret the equation and perform appropriate statistical tests.

6.15   Are there ethnic variations in the effect of the sex of a respondent on educational attainment? A special case of a slope dummy variable is the interactive dummy variable defined as the product of two dummy variables. Using your *EAEF* data set, define interactive dummy variables *MALEBLAC* and *MALEHISP* as the product of *MALE* and *ETHBLACK*, and of *MALE* and *ETHHISP*, respectively:

$$MALEBLAC = MALE * ETHBLACK.$$

$$MALEHISP = MALE * ETHHISP.$$

Regress *S* on *ASVABC*, *SM*, *SF*, *MALE*, *ETHBLACK*, *ETHHISP*, *MALE-BLAC*, and *MALEHISP*. Interpret the regression results and perform appropriate statistical tests.

6.4 **The Chow test**

It sometimes happens that your sample of observations consists of two or more subsamples, and you are uncertain about whether you should run one combined regression or separate regressions for each subsample. Actually, in practice the choice is not usually as stark as this, because there may be some scope for combining the subsamples, using appropriate dummy and slope dummy variables to relax the assumption that all the coefficients must be the same for each subsample. This is a point to which we shall return.

Suppose that we have a sample consisting of two subsamples and that you are wondering whether to combine them in a pooled regression, P, or to run separate regressions, A and B. We will denote the residual sums of squares for the subsample regressions RSS_A and RSS_B. We will denote RSS_A^P and RSS_B^P the sum of the squares of the residuals in the pooled regression for the observations belonging to the two subsamples. Since the subsample regressions minimize RSS for their observations, they must fit them at least as well as, and generally better than, the pooled regression. Thus $RSS_A \leq RSS_A^P$ and $RSS_B \leq RSS_B^P$, and so $(RSS_A + RSS_B) \leq RSS_P$, where RSS_P, the total sum of the squares of the residuals in the pooled regression, is equal to the sum of RSS_A^P and RSS_B^P.

Equality between RSS_P and $(RSS_A + RSS_B)$ will occur only when the regression coefficients for the pooled and subsample regressions coincide. In general, there

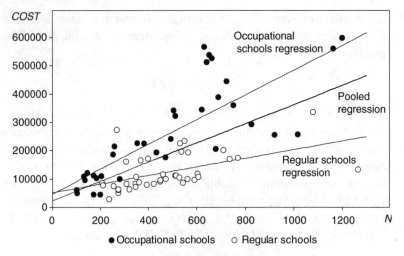

Figure 6.6 Pooled and subsample regression lines

will be an improvement $(RSS_P - RSS_A - RSS_B)$ when the sample is split up. There is a price to pay, in that k extra degrees of freedom are used up, since instead of k parameters for one combined regression we now have to estimate $2k$ in all. After breaking up the sample, we are still left with $(RSS_A + RSS_B)$ (unexplained) sum of squares of the residuals, and we have $n - 2k$ degrees of freedom remaining.

We are now in a position to see whether the improvement in fit when we split the sample is significant. We use the F statistic

$$F(k, n - 2k) = \frac{\text{improvement in } RSS/\text{degress of freedom used up}}{\text{remaining } RSS/\text{degrees of freedom remaining}}$$

$$= \frac{(RSS_P - RSS_A - RSS_B)/k}{(RSS_A + RSS_B)/(n - 2k)}, \tag{6.37}$$

which is distributed with k and $n - 2k$ degrees of freedom under the null hypothesis of no significant improvement in fit.

We will illustrate the test with reference to the school cost function data, making a simple distinction between regular and occupational schools. We need to run three regressions. In the first we regress $COST$ on N using the whole sample of seventy-four schools. We have already done this in Section 6.1. This is the pooled regression. We make a note of RSS for it, 8.9160×10^{11}. In the second and third we run the same regression for the two subsamples of regular and occupational schools separately and again make a note of RSS. The regression lines are shown in Figure 6.6.

RSS is 1.2150×10^{11} for the regular schools and 3.4895×10^{11} for the occupational schools. The total RSS from the subsample regressions is therefore 4.7045×10^{11}. The numerator of the F test is the improvement in fit on splitting the sample, divided by the cost (having to estimate two sets of parameters instead of only one). In this case it is $(8.9160 - 4.7045) \times 10^{11}$ divided by 2

Table 6.12

```
. reg COST N if OCC==0

      Source |       SS          df       MS              Number of obs =       40
-------------+------------------------------              F(  1,    38) =     13.53
       Model |  4.3273e+10        1   4.3273e+10          Prob > F      =    0.0007
    Residual |  1.2150e+11       38   3.1973e+09          R-squared     =    0.2626
-------------+------------------------------              Adj R-squared =    0.2432
       Total |  1.6477e+11       39   4.2249e+09          Root MSE      =    56545


        COST |      Coef.   Std. Err.      t     P>|t|     [95% Conf. Interval]
-------------+----------------------------------------------------------------
           N |   152.2982   41.39782     3.679   0.001     68.49275    236.1037
       _cons |   51475.25   21599.14     2.383   0.022     7750.064    95200.43
-------------+----------------------------------------------------------------


. reg COST N if OCC==1

      Source |       SS          df       MS              Number of obs =       34
-------------+------------------------------              F(  1,    32) =     55.52
       Model |  6.0538e+11        1   6.0538e+11          Prob > F      =    0.0000
    Residual |  3.4895e+11       32   1.0905e+10          R-squared     =    0.6344
-------------+------------------------------              Adj R-squared =    0.6229
       Total |  9.5433e+11       33   2.8919e+10          Root MSE      =   1.0e+05


        COST |      Coef.   Std. Err.      t     P>|t|     [95% Conf. Interval]
-------------+----------------------------------------------------------------
           N |   436.7769   58.62085     7.451   0.000     317.3701    556.1836
       _cons |   47974.07   33879.03     1.416   0.166    -21035.26    116983.4
```

(we have had to estimate two intercepts and two slope coefficients, instead of only one of each). The denominator is the joint *RSS* remaining after splitting the sample, divided by the joint number of degrees of freedom remaining. In this case it is 4.7045×10^{11} divided by 70 (seventy-four observations, less 4 degrees of freedom because two parameters were estimated in each equation). When we calculate the *F* statistic the 10^{11} factors cancel out and we have

$$F(2, 70) = \frac{4.2115 \times 10^{11}/2}{4.7045 \times 10^{11}/70} = 31.3. \qquad (6.38)$$

The critical value of $F(2, 70)$ at the 0.1 percent significance level is a little below 7.77, the critical value for $F(2, 60)$, so we come to the conclusion that there is a significant improvement in the fit on splitting the sample and that we should not use the pooled regression.

Relationship between the Chow test and the *F* test of the explanatory power of a set of dummy variables

In this chapter we have used both dummy variables and a Chow test to investigate whether there are significant differences in a regression model for different categories of a qualitative characteristic. Could the two approaches have led to different conclusions? The answer is no, provided that a full set of dummy variables for the qualitative characteristic has been included in the regression model, a full set being defined as an intercept dummy, assuming that there is an intercept in the model, and a slope dummy for each of the other variables. The Chow test is then equivalent to an *F* test of the explanatory power of the dummy variables as a group.

To simplify the discussion, we will suppose that there are only two categories of the qualitative characteristic, as in the example of the cost functions for regular and occupational schools. Suppose that you start with the basic specification with no dummy variables. The regression equation will be that of the pooled regression in the Chow test, with every coefficient a compromise for the two categories of the qualitative variable. If you then add a full set of dummy variables, the intercept and the slope coefficients can be different for the two categories. The basic coefficients will be chosen so as to minimize the sum of the squares of the residuals relating to the reference category, and the intercept dummy and slope dummy coefficients will be chosen so as to minimize the sum of the squares of the residuals for the other category. Effectively, the outcome of the estimation of the coefficients is the same as if you had run separate regressions for the two categories.

In the school cost function example, the implicit cost functions for regular and operational schools with a full set of dummy variables (in this case just an intercept dummy and a slope dummy for *N*), shown in Figure 6.5, are identical to the cost functions for the subsample regressions in the Chow test, shown in Figure 6.6. It follows that the improvement in the fit, as measured by the reduction in the residual sum of squares, when one adds the dummy variables to the basic specification is identical to the improvement in fit on splitting the sample and running subsample regressions. The cost, in terms of degrees of freedom, is also the same. In the dummy variable approach you have to add an intercept dummy and a slope dummy for each variable, so the cost is k if there are $k - 1$ variables in the model. In the Chow test, the cost is also k because you have to estimate $2k$ parameters instead of k when you split the sample. Thus the numerator of the *F* statistic is the same for both tests. The denominator is also the same because in both cases it is the residual sum of squares for the subsample regressions divided by $n - 2k$. In the case of the Chow test, $2k$ degrees of freedom are used up when fitting the separate regressions. In the case of the dummy variable group test, k degrees of freedom are used up when estimating the original intercept and slope coefficients, and a further k degrees of freedom are used up estimating the intercept dummy and the slope dummy coefficients.

What are the advantages and disadvantages of the two approaches? The Chow test is quick. You just run the three regressions and compute the test statistic. But it does not tell you how the functions differ, if they do. The dummy variable approach involves more preparation because you have to define a dummy variable for the intercept and for each slope coefficient. However, it is more informative because you can perform t tests on the individual dummy coefficients and they may indicate where the functions differ, if they do.

Exercises

6.16* Are educational attainment functions different for males and females? Using your *EAEF* data set, regress S on *ASVABC*, *ETHBLACK*, *ETHHISP*, *SM*, and *SF* (do not include *MALE*). Repeat the regression using only the male respondents. Repeat it again using only the female respondents. Perform a Chow test.

6.17 Are earnings functions different for males and females? Using your *EAEF* data set, regress *LGEARN* on S, *ASVABC*, *ETHBLACK*, and *ETHHISP* (do not include *MALE*). Repeat the regression using only the male respondents. Repeat it again using only the female respondents. Perform a Chow test.

6.18* Are there differences in male and female educational attainment functions? This question has been answered by Exercise 6.16 but nevertheless it is instructive to investigate the issue using the dummy variable approach. Using your *EAEF* data set, define the following slope dummies combining *MALE* with the parental education variables:

$$MALESM = MALE * SM$$
$$MALESF = MALE * SF,$$

and regress S on *ETHBLACK*, *ETHHISP*, *ASVABC*, *SM*, *SF*, *MALE*, *MALEBLAC*, *MALEHISP* (defined in Exercise 6.15), *MALEASVC* (defined in Exercise 6.12), *MALESM*, and *MALESF*. Next regress S on *ETHBLACK*, *ETHHISP*, *ASVABC*, *SM*, and *SF* only. Perform an F test of the joint explanatory power of *MALE* and the slope dummy variables as a group (verify that the F statistic is the same as in Exercise 6.16) and perform t tests on the coefficients of the slope dummy variables in the first regression.

6.19 Where are the differences in male and female earnings functions? Using your *EAEF* data set, regress *LGEARN* on S, *ASVABC*, *ETHBLACK*, *ETHHISP*, *MALE*, *MALES*, *MALEASVC*, *MALEBLAC*, and *MALEHISP*. Next regress *LGEARN* on S, *ASVABC*, *ETHBLACK*, and *ETHHISP* only. Calculate the correlation matrix for *MALE* and the slope dummies. Perform an F test of the joint explanatory power of *MALE* and the slope dummies (verify that the F statistic is the same as in Exercise 6.17) and perform t tests on the coefficients of the dummy variables.

7 Specification of regression variables: a preliminary skirmish

What are the consequences of including in the regression model a variable that should not be there? What are the consequences of leaving out a variable that should be included? What happens if you have difficulty finding data on a variable and use a proxy instead? This chapter is a preliminary skirmish with these issues in the sense that it focuses on the consequences of variable misspecification, rather than on procedures for model selection, a much more complex subject that is left to later in the text. The chapter concludes by showing how simple restrictions on the parameters can be tested.

7.1 Model specification

The construction of an economic model involves the specification of the relationships that constitute it, the specification of the variables that participate in each relationship, and the mathematical function representing each relationship. The last element was discussed in Chapter 5. In this chapter, we will consider the second element, and we will continue to assume that the model consists of just one equation. We will discuss the application of regression analysis to models consisting of systems of simultaneous relationships in Chapter 10.

If we know exactly which explanatory variables ought to be included in the equation when we undertake regression analysis, our task is limited to calculating estimates of their coefficients, confidence intervals for these estimates, and so on. In practice, however, we can never be sure that we have specified the equation correctly. Economic theory ought to provide a guide, but theory is never perfect. Without being aware of it, we might be including some variables that ought not to be in the model, and we might be leaving out others that ought to be included.

The properties of the regression estimates of the coefficients depend crucially on the validity of the specification of the model. The consequences of misspecification of the variables in a relationship are summarized in Table 7.1.

1. If you leave out a variable that ought to be included, the regression estimates are in general (but not always) biased. The standard errors of the coefficients and the corresponding *t* tests are in general invalid.

Table 7.1 Consequences of variable specification

Fitted model	True model	
	$Y = \beta_1 + \beta_2 X_2 + u$	$Y = \beta_1 + \beta_2 X_2 + \beta_3 X_3 + u$
$\hat{Y} = b_1 + b_2 X_2$	Correct specification, no problems	Coefficients are biased (in general). Standard errors are invalid
$\hat{Y} = b_1 + b_2 X_2 + b_3 X_3$	Coefficients are unbiased (in general) but inefficient. Standard errors are valid (in general)	Correct specification, no problems

2. If you include a variable that ought not to be in the equation, the regression coefficients are in general (but not always) inefficient but not biased. The standard errors are in general valid but, because the regression estimation is inefficient, they will be needlessly large.

We will begin by discussing these two cases and then come to some broader issues of model specification.

7.2 The effect of omitting a variable that ought to be included

The problem of bias

Suppose that the dependent variable Y depends on two variables X_2 and X_3 according to a relationship

$$Y = \beta_1 + \beta_2 X_2 + \beta_3 X_3 + u, \tag{7.1}$$

but you are unaware of the importance of X_3. Thinking that the model should be

$$Y = \beta_1 + \beta_2 X_2 + u, \tag{7.2}$$

you use regression analysis to fit

$$\hat{Y} = b_1 + b_2 X_2, \tag{7.3}$$

and you calculate b_2 using the expression $\text{Cov}(X_2, Y)/\text{Var}(X_2)$, instead of the correct expression

$$b_2 = \frac{\text{Cov}(X_2, Y)\text{Var}(X_3) - \text{Cov}(X_3, Y)\text{Cov}(X_2, X_3)}{\text{Var}(X_2)\text{Var}(X_3) - [\text{Cov}(X_2, X_3)]^2}. \tag{7.4}$$

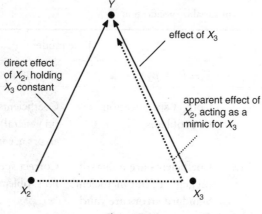

Figure 7.1

By definition, b_2 is an unbiased estimator of β_2 if and only if $E(b_2)$ is equal to β_2. In fact, if (7.1) is true,

$$E\left[\frac{\text{Cov}(X_2, Y)}{\text{Var}(X_2)}\right] = \beta_2 + \beta_3 \frac{\text{Cov}(X_2, X_3)}{\text{Var}(X_2)}. \tag{7.5}$$

We shall give first an intuitive explanation of this and then a formal proof.

If X_3 is omitted from the regression model, X_2 will appear to have a double effect, as illustrated in Figure 7.1. It will have a direct effect and also a proxy effect when it mimics the effect of X_3. The apparent indirect effect of X_2 on Y depends on two factors: the apparent ability of X_2 to mimic X_3, and the effect of X_3 on Y.

The apparent ability of X_2 to explain X_3 is determined by the slope coefficient h in the pseudo-regression

$$\hat{X}_3 = g + hX_2. \tag{7.6}$$

h of course is given by the usual simple regression formula, in this case $\text{Cov}(X_2, X_3)/\text{Var}(X_2)$. The effect of X_3 on Y is β_3, so the mimic effect via X_3 may be written $\beta_3 \text{Cov}(X_2, X_3)/\text{Var}(X_2)$. The direct effect of X_2 on Y is β_2, and hence when Y is regressed on X_2, omitting X_3, the coefficient of X_2 is given by

$$\beta_2 + \beta_3 \frac{\text{Cov}(X_2, X_3)}{\text{Var}(X_2)} + \text{sampling error}. \tag{7.7}$$

Provided that X_2 and X_3 are nonstochastic, the expected value of the coefficient will be the sum of the first two terms. The presence of the second term implies that in general the expected value of the coefficient will be different from the true value β_2 and therefore biased.

The formal proof of (7.5) is straightforward. We begin by making a theoretical expansion of the estimator b_2:

$$b_2 = \frac{\text{Cov}(X_2, Y)}{\text{Var}(X_2)} = \frac{\text{Cov}(X_2, [\beta_1 + \beta_2 X_2 + \beta_3 X_3 + u])}{\text{Var}(X_2)}$$

$$= \frac{1}{\text{Var}(X_2)}[\text{Cov}(X_2, \beta_1) + \text{Cov}(X_2, \beta_2 X_2) + \text{Cov}(X_2, \beta_3 X_3) + \text{Cov}(X_2, u)]$$

$$= \frac{1}{\text{Var}(X_2)}[0 + \beta_2 \text{Var}(X_2) + \beta_3 \text{Cov}(X_2, X_3) + \text{Cov}(X_2, u)]$$

$$= \beta_2 + \beta_3 \frac{\text{Cov}(X_2, X_3)}{\text{Var}(X_2)} + \frac{\text{Cov}(X_2, u)}{\text{Var}(X_2)}. \tag{7.8}$$

Provided that X_2 and X_3 are nonstochastic, the first two terms are unaffected when we take expectations and the third is 0. Hence we obtain (7.5).

This confirms our earlier intuitive conclusion that b_2 is biased by an amount $\beta_3 \text{Cov}(X_2, X_3)/\text{Var}(X_2)$. The direction of the bias will depend on the signs of β_3 and $\text{Cov}(X_2, X_3)$. For example, if β_3 is positive and the covariance is positive, the bias will be positive and b_2 will tend to overestimate β_2. There is, however, one exceptional case where b_2 is unbiased after all. That is when the sample covariance between X_2 and X_3 happens to be exactly 0. If $\text{Cov}(X_2, X_3)$ is 0, the bias term disappears. Indeed, the regression coefficient obtained using simple regression will be exactly the same as if you had used a properly specified multiple regression. Of course, the bias term would also be 0 if β_3 were 0, but then the model is not misspecified.

Invalidation of the statistical tests

Another serious consequence of omitting a variable that ought to be included in the regression is that the standard errors of the coefficients and the test statistics are in general invalidated. This means of course that you are not in principle able to test any hypotheses with your regression results.

Example

The problem of omitted variable bias will first be illustrated with the educational attainment function using *EAEF* Data Set 21. For the present purposes, it will be assumed that the true model is

$$S = \beta_1 + \beta_2 ASVABC + \beta_3 SM + u, \tag{7.9}$$

although obviously this is a great oversimplification. The first part of the regression output in Table 7.2 shows the result of this regression. The second and third parts of the output then show the effects of omitting *SM* and *ASVABC*, respectively.

Table 7.2

```
. reg S ASVABC SM

    Source |       SS         df        MS                Number of obs =      570
-----------+------------------------------                F(  2,   567) =   156.81
     Model |  1230.2039       2   615.101949              Prob > F      =   0.0000
  Residual |  2224.04347     567   3.92247526             R-squared     =   0.3561
-----------+------------------------------                Adj R-squared =   0.3539
     Total |  3454.24737     569   6.07073351             Root MSE      =   1.9805


         S |    Coef.    Std. Err.      t     P>|t|     [95% Conf. Interval]
-----------+----------------------------------------------------------------
    ASVABC |  .1381062   .0097494    14.166   0.000     .1189567    .1572556
        SM |   .154783   .0350728     4.413   0.000     .0858946    .2236715
     _cons |  4.791277   .5102431     9.390   0.000     3.78908     5.793475
```

```
. reg S ASVABC

    Source |       SS         df        MS                Number of obs =      570
-----------+------------------------------                F(  1,   568) =   284.89
     Model |  1153.80864      1   1153.80864              Prob > F      =   0.0000
  Residual |  2300.43873     568   4.05006818             R-squared     =   0.3340
-----------+------------------------------                Adj R-squared =   0.3329
     Total |  3454.24737     569   6.07073351             Root MSE      =   2.0125


         S |    Coef.    Std. Err.      t     P>|t|     [95% Conf. Interval]
-----------+----------------------------------------------------------------
    ASVABC |  .1545378   .0091559    16.879   0.000     .1365543    .1725213
     _cons |  5.770845   .4668473    12.361   0.000     4.853888    6.687803
```

```
. reg S SM

    Source |       SS         df        MS                Number of obs =      570
-----------+------------------------------                F(  1,   568) =    83.59
     Model |  443.110436      1   443.110436              Prob > F      =   0.0000
  Residual |  3011.13693     568   5.30129742             R-squared     =   0.1283
-----------+------------------------------                Adj R-squared =   0.1267
     Total |  3454.24737     569   6.07073351             Root MSE      =   2.3025


         S |    Coef.    Std. Err.      t     P>|t|     [95% Conf. Interval]
-----------+----------------------------------------------------------------
        SM |  .3445198   .0376833     9.142   0.000     .2705041    .4185354
     _cons |  9.506491   .4495754    21.145   0.000     8.623458    10.38952
```

When *SM* is omitted,

$$E(b_2) = \beta_2 + \beta_3 \frac{\text{Cov}(ASVABC, SM)}{\text{Var}(ASVABC)}. \tag{7.10}$$

The correlation between *ASVABC* and *SM* is positive (0.38). Therefore the covariance term is positive. Since variances are always positive (unless equal to 0), the only other relevant factor for determining the sign of the bias is β_3. It is reasonable to assume that this is positive, and the fact that its estimate in the first regression is indeed positive and highly significant provides overwhelming corroborative evidence. One would therefore anticipate that the coefficient of *ASVABC* will be upwards biased when *SM* is omitted, and you can see that it — *why?* is indeed higher. Not all of the difference should be attributed to bias. Part of it may be attributable to the effects of the disturbance term, which could go either way.

Similarly, when *ASVABC* is omitted,

why?

$$E(b_3) = \beta_3 + \beta_2 \frac{\text{Cov}(ASVABC, SM)}{\text{Var}(SM)}. \tag{7.11}$$

Since β_2 is also likely to be positive, the coefficient of *SM* in the third regression should be upwards biased. The estimate in the third regression is indeed higher than that in the first. *why?*

In this example, the omission of one explanatory variable causes the coefficient of the other to be overestimated. However, the bias could just as easily be negative. The sign of the bias depends on the sign of the true coefficient of the omitted variable and on the sign of the sample covariance between the included and omitted variables, and these will depend on the nature of the model being investigated.

It should be emphasized that the analysis above applies only to the case where the true model is a multiple regression model with two explanatory variables. When there are more explanatory variables, it may be difficult to predict the impact of omitted variable bias mathematically. Nevertheless it may be possible to conclude that the estimates of the coefficients of some of the variables may have been inflated or deflated by the bias.

R^2 in the presence of omitted variable bias

In Section 4.5 it was asserted that in general it is impossible to determine the contribution to R^2 of each explanatory variable in multiple regression analysis, and we are now in a position to see why.

We will discuss the issue first with reference to the educational attainment model above. In the regression of *S* on *ASVABC* alone, R^2 was 0.33. In the regression on *SM* alone, it was 0.13. Does this mean that *ASVABC* explains 33 percent of the variance in *S*, and *SM* 13 percent? No, because this would

Table 7.3

```
. reg LGEARN S MALE

  Source |       SS       df       MS              Number of obs =     570
---------+------------------------------           F(  2,   567) =   65.74
   Model |  28.951332      2   14.475666           Prob > F      =  0.0000
Residual | 124.850561    567   .220194992          R-squared     =  0.1882
---------+------------------------------           Adj R-squared =  0.1854
   Total | 153.801893    569   .270302096          Root MSE      =  .46925


------------------------------------------------------------------------------
  LGEARN |    Coef.   Std. Err.      t     P>|t|    [95% Conf. Interval]
---------+--------------------------------------------------------------------
       S |  .0818944   .0079976   10.240   0.000    .0661858    .097603
    MALE |  .2285156   .0397695    5.746   0.000    .1504021    .3066291
   _cons |  1.19254    .1134845   10.508   0.000    .9696386    1.415441
------------------------------------------------------------------------------


. reg LGEARN S

  Source |       SS       df       MS              Number of obs =     570
---------+------------------------------           F(  1,   568) =   93.21
   Model |  21.681253      1   21.681253           Prob > F      =  0.0000
Residual | 132.12064     568   .23260676           R-squared     =  0.1410
---------+------------------------------           Adj R-squared =  0.1395
   Total | 153.801893    569   .270302096          Root MSE      =  .48229


------------------------------------------------------------------------------
  LGEARN |    Coef.   Std. Err.      t     P>|t|    [95% Conf. Interval]
---------+--------------------------------------------------------------------
       S |  .0792256   .0082061    9.655   0.000    .0631077    .0953435
   _cons |  1.358919   .1127785   12.049   0.000    1.137406    1.580433
------------------------------------------------------------------------------


. reg LGEARN MALE

  Source |       SS       df       MS              Number of obs =     570
---------+------------------------------           F(  1,   568) =   22.51
   Model |  5.86288165     1   5.86288165          Prob > F      =  0.0000
Residual | 147.939011    568   .260456005          R-squared     =  0.0381
---------+------------------------------           Adj R-squared =  0.0364
   Total | 153.801893    569   .270302096          Root MSE      =  .51035


------------------------------------------------------------------------------
  LGEARN |    Coef.   Std. Err.      t     P>|t|    [95% Conf. Interval]
---------+--------------------------------------------------------------------
    MALE |  .2048652   .0431797    4.744   0.000    .1200538    .2896767
   _cons |  2.313324   .032605    70.950   0.000    2.249282    2.377365
------------------------------------------------------------------------------
```

imply that together they would explain 46 percent of the variance, and this conflicts with the finding in the multiple regression that their joint explanatory power is 0.36.

The explanation is that in the simple regression of S on ASVABC, ASVABC is acting partly as a variable in its own right and partly as a proxy for the missing SM, as in Figure 7.1. R^2 for that regression therefore reflects the combined explanatory power of ASVABC in both of these roles, and not just its direct explanatory power. Hence 0.33 overestimates the latter.

Similarly, in the simple regression of S on SM, SM is acting partly as a proxy for the missing ASVABC, and the level of R^2 in that regression reflects the combined explanatory power of SM in both those roles, and not just its direct explanatory power.

In this example, the explanatory power of the two variables overlapped, with the consequence that R^2 in the multiple regression was less than the sum of R^2 in the individual simple regressions. However it is also possible for R^2 in the multiple regression to be greater than the sum of R^2 in the individual simple regressions, as is shown in the regression output in Table 7.3 for an earnings function model. It is assumed that the true model is

$$LGEARN = \beta_1 + \beta_2 S + \beta_3 MALE + u, \qquad (7.12)$$

where MALE is a dummy variable equal to 1 for males and 0 for females. The first part of the regression output shows the result of fitting (7.12), and the second and third parts show the results of omitting, first MALE, and then S. R^2 in the multiple regression is 0.188, while it is 0.141 and 0.038 in the simple regressions, the sum being 0.179. As in the previous example, it can be assumed that both β_2 and β_3 are positive. However S and MALE are negatively correlated, so in this case the coefficients of S and MALE in the second and third regressions may be expected to be biased downwards. As a consequence, the apparent explanatory power of S and MALE in the simple regressions is underestimated.

Exercises

7.1 Using your EAEF data set, regress LGEARN (1) on S and ASVABC, (2) on S only, and (3) on ASVABC only. Calculate the correlation between S and ASVABC. Compare the coefficients of S in regressions (1) and (2). Give both mathematical and intuitive explanations of the direction of the change. Also compare the coefficients of ASVABC in regressions (1) and (3) and explain the direction of the change.

7.2* The table gives the results of multiple and simple regressions of LGFDHO, the logarithm of annual household expenditure on food eaten at home, on LGEXP, the logarithm of total annual household expenditure, and LGSIZE, the logarithm of the number of persons in the household, using a sample of 868 households in the 1995 Consumer Expenditure Survey. The correlation coefficient for LGEXP and LGSIZE was 0.45. Explain the variations in the regression coefficients.

	(1)	(2)	(3)
LGEXP	0.29	0.48	—
	(0.02)	(0.02)	
LGSIZE	0.49	—	0.63
	(0.03)		(0.02)
constant	4.72	3.17	7.50
	(0.22)	(0.24)	(0.02)
R^2	0.52	0.31	0.42

7.3 Suppose that Y is determined by X_2 and X_3 according to the relationship

$$Y = \beta_1 + \beta_2 X_2 + \beta_3 X_3 + u,$$

and that $\text{Cov}(X_2, X_3)$ is 0. Use this to simplify the multiple regression coefficient b_2 given by

$$b_2 = \frac{\text{Cov}(X_2, Y)\text{Var}(X_3) - \text{Cov}(X_3, Y)\text{Cov}(X_2, X_3)}{\text{Var}(X_2)\text{Var}(X_3) - [\text{Cov}(X_2, X_3)]^2}$$

and show that it reduces to the simple regression expression. What are the implications for the specification of the regression equation?

7.4 In a Monte Carlo experiment, a variable Y was generated as a linear function of two variables X_2 and X_3:

$$Y = 10.0 + 10.0X_2 + 0.5X_3 + u,$$

where X_2 was the sequence of integers $1, 2, \ldots, 30$, X_3 was generated from X_2 by adding random numbers, and u was a normally distributed disturbance term with mean 0 and standard deviation 100. The correlation between X_2 and X_3 was 0.95. The sample variance of X_2 was 74.92 and that of X_3 was 82.67. The sample covariance between X_2 and X_3 was 74.94. The table shows the result of fitting the following regressions for ten samples:

Model A $\hat{Y} = b_1 + b_2 X_2 + b_3 X_3$.

Model B $\hat{Y} = b_1 + b_2 X_2$.

Comment on all aspects of the regression results, giving full explanations of what you observe.

Sample	Model A					Model B		
	b_2	s.e.(b_2)	b_3	s.e.(b_3)	R^2	b_2	s.e.(b_2)	R^2
1	10.68	6.05	0.60	5.76	0.5800	11.28	1.82	0.5799
2	7.52	7.11	3.74	6.77	0.5018	11.26	2.14	0.4961
3	7.26	6.58	2.93	6.26	0.4907	10.20	1.98	0.4865
4	11.47	8.60	0.23	8.18	0.4239	11.70	2.58	0.4239
5	13.07	6.07	−3.04	5.78	0.5232	10.03	1.83	0.5183
6	16.74	6.63	−4.01	6.32	0.5966	12.73	2.00	0.5906
7	15.70	7.50	−4.80	7.14	0.4614	10.90	2.27	0.4523
8	8.01	8.10	1.50	7.71	0.3542	9.51	2.43	0.3533
9	1.08	6.78	9.52	6.45	0.5133	10.61	2.11	0.4740
10	13.09	7.58	−0.87	7.21	0.5084	12.22	2.27	0.5081

7.3 The effect of including a variable that ought not to be included

Suppose that the true model is

$$Y = \beta_1 + \beta_2 X_2 + u \tag{7.13}$$

and you think it is

$$Y = \beta_1 + \beta_2 X_2 + \beta_3 X_3 + u, \tag{7.14}$$

and you estimate b_2 using (7.4) instead of $\text{Cov}(X_2, Y)/\text{Var}(X_2)$.

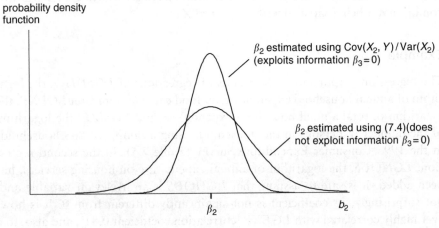

Figure 7.2

Table 7.4

Simple regression	Multiple regression
$\sigma_{b_2}^2 = \dfrac{\sigma_u^2}{n\text{Var}(X_2)}$	$\sigma_{b_2}^2 = \dfrac{\sigma_u^2}{n\text{Var}(X_2)}\dfrac{1}{1 - r_{X_2X_3}^2}$

In general there is no problem of bias, even though b_2 has been calculated incorrectly. $E(b_2)$ will still be equal to β_2, but in general b_2 will be an inefficient estimator. It will be more erratic, in the sense of having a larger variance about β_2, than if it had been calculated correctly. This is illustrated in Figure 7.2.

This is easy to explain intuitively. The true model may be rewritten

$$Y = \beta_1 + \beta_2X_2 + 0X_3 + u. \tag{7.15}$$

So if you regress Y on X_2 and X_3, b_2 will be an unbiased estimator of β_2 and b_3 will be an unbiased estimator of 0, provided that the Gauss–Markov conditions are satisfied. Effectively, you are discovering for yourself that β_3 is 0. If you realized beforehand that β_3 is 0, you would be able to exploit this information to exclude X_3 and use simple regression, which in this context is more efficient.

The loss of efficiency caused by including X_3 when it ought not to be included depends on the correlation between X_2 and X_3. Compare the expressions for the variances of b_2 using simple and multiple regression in Table 7.4. The variance will in general be larger in the case of multiple regression, and the difference will be the greater the closer the correlation coefficient is to plus or minus 1. The one exception to the loss of efficiency occurs when the correlation coefficient happens to be exactly equal to 0. In that case the estimator b_2 for multiple regression will be identical to that for simple regression. The proof of this will be left as an easy exercise.

There is one exception to the unbiasedness conclusion that ought to be kept in mind. If X_3 is correlated with u, the regression coefficients will be biased after all. Writing the model as (7.15), this amounts to the fourth Gauss–Markov condition not being satisfied with respect to X_3.

Example

The regression output shows the results of regressions of $LGFDHO$, the logarithm of annual household expenditure on food eaten at home, on $LGEXP$, the logarithm of total annual household expenditure, and $LGSIZE$, the logarithm of the number of persons in the household, using a sample of 868 households in the 1995 Consumer Expenditure Survey (Table 7.5). In the second regression, $LGHOUS$, the logarithm of annual expenditure on housing services, has been added. It is safe to assume that $LGHOUS$ is an irrelevant variable and, not surprisingly, its coefficient is not significantly different from 0. It is however highly correlated with $LGEXP$ (correlation coefficient 0.81), and also, to a

Table 7.5

```
. reg LGFDHO LGEXP LGSIZE

  Source |      SS         df        MS              Number of obs =     868
---------+------------------------------           F(  2,   865) =  460.92
   Model | 138.776549      2   69.3882747           Prob > F      =  0.0000
Residual | 130.219231    865   .150542464           R-squared     =  0.5159
---------+------------------------------           Adj R-squared =  0.5148
   Total | 268.995781    867   .310260416           Root MSE      =    .388


  LGFDHO |    Coef.    Std. Err.      t     P>|t|    [95% Conf. Interval]
---------+------------------------------------------------------------------
   LGEXP |  .2866813   .0226824    12.639   0.000    .2421622    .3312003
  LGSIZE |  .4854698   .0255476    19.003   0.000    .4353272    .5356124
   _cons |  4.720269   .2209996    21.359   0.000    4.286511    5.154027


. reg LGFDHO LGEXP LGSIZE LGHOUS

  Source |      SS         df        MS              Number of obs =     868
---------+------------------------------           F(  3,   864) =  307.22
   Model | 138.841976      3   46.2806586           Prob > F      =  0.0000
Residual | 130.153805    864   .150640978           R-squared     =  0.5161
---------+------------------------------           Adj R-squared =  0.5145
   Total | 268.995781    867   .310260416           Root MSE      =  .38812


  LGFDHO |    Coef.    Std. Err.      t     P>|t|    [95% Conf. Interval]
---------+------------------------------------------------------------------
   LGEXP |  .2673552   .0370782     7.211   0.000    .1945813     .340129
  LGSIZE |  .4868228   .0256383    18.988   0.000    .4365021    .5371434
  LGHOUS |  .0229611   .0348408     0.659   0.510   -.0454214    .0913436
   _cons |  4.708772   .2217592    21.234   0.000    4.273522    5.144022
```

lesser extent, with *LGSIZE* (correlation coefficient 0.33). Its inclusion does not cause the coefficients of those variables to be biased but it does increase their standard errors, particularly that of *LGEXP*, as you would expect, given the loss of efficiency.

Exercises

7.5* A social scientist thinks that the level of activity in the shadow economy, Y, depends either positively on the level of the tax burden, X, or negatively on the level of government expenditure to discourage shadow economy activity, Z. Y might also depend on both X and Z. International cross-section data on Y, X, and Z, all measured in US\$ million, are obtained for a sample of thirty industrialized countries and a second sample of thirty developing countries. The social scientist regresses (1) log Y on both log X and log Z, (2) log Y on log X alone, and (3) log Y on log Z alone, for each sample, with the results as shown in the table (standard errors in parentheses).

	Industrialized countries			Developing countries		
	(1)	(2)	(3)	(1)	(2)	(3)
log X	0.699	0.201	—	0.806	0.727	—
	(0.154)	(0.112)		(0.137)	(0.090)	
log Z	−0.646	—	−0.053	−0.091	—	0.427
	(0.162)		(0.124)	(0.117)		(0.116)
constant	−1.137	−1.065	1.230	−1.122	−1.024	2.824
	(0.863)	(1.069)	(0.896)	(0.873)	(0.858)	(0.835)
R^2	0.44	0.10	0.01	0.71	0.70	0.33

X was positively correlated with Z in both samples. Having carried out the appropriate statistical tests, write a short report advising the social scientist how to interpret these results.

7.6   Regress *LGEARN* on *S*, *ASVABC*, *MALE*, *ETHHISP*, and *ETHBLACK* using your *EAEF* data set. Repeat the regression, adding *SIBLINGS*. Calculate the correlations between *SIBLINGS* and the other explanatory variables. Compare the results of the two regressions.

7.4 Proxy variables

It frequently happens that you are unable to obtain data on a variable that you would like to include in a regression equation. Some variables, such as socioeconomic status and quality of education, are so vaguely defined that it may be impossible even in principle to measure them. Others might be measurable, but require so much time and energy that in practice they have to be abandoned. Sometimes you are frustrated because you are using survey data collected by someone else, and an important variable (from your point of view) has been omitted.

Whatever the reason, it is usually a good idea to use a proxy for the missing variable, rather than leave it out entirely. For socioeconomic status, you might use income as a substitute if data on it are available. For quality of education, you might use the staff–student ratio or expenditure per student. For a variable omitted in a survey, you will have to look at the data actually collected to see if there is a suitable substitute.

There are two good reasons for trying to find a proxy. First, if you simply leave the variable out, your regression is likely to suffer from omitted variable bias of the type described in Section 7.2, and the statistical tests will be invalidated. Second, the results from your proxy regression may indirectly shed light on the influence of the missing variable.

Suppose that the true model is

$$Y = \beta_1 + \beta_2 X_2 + \beta_3 X_3 + \cdots + \beta_k X_k + u. \tag{7.16}$$

Suppose that we have no data for X_2, but another variable Z is an ideal proxy for it in the sense that there exists an exact linear relationship between X_2 and Z:

$$X_2 = \lambda + \mu Z. \tag{7.17}$$

λ and μ being fixed, but unknown, constants. (Note that if λ and μ were known, we could calculate X_2 from Z, and so there would be no need to use Z as a proxy. Note further that we cannot estimate λ and μ by regression analysis, because to do that we need data on X_2.)

Substituting for X_2 from (7.17) into (7.16), the model may be rewritten

$$Y = \beta_1 + \beta_2(\lambda + \mu Z) + \beta_3 X_3 + \cdots + \beta_k X_k + u$$
$$= \beta_1 + \beta_2 \lambda + \beta_2 \mu Z + \beta_3 X_3 + \cdots + \beta_k X_k + u. \tag{7.18}$$

The model is now formally correctly specified in terms of observable variables, and if we fit it, the following results will obtain:

1. The coefficients of $X_3, \ldots, X_k$, their standard errors, and their t statistics will be the same as if X_2 had been used instead of Z.
2. R^2 will be the same as if X_2 had been used instead of Z.
3. The coefficient of Z will be an estimate of $\beta_2 \mu$ and so it will not be possible to obtain an estimate of β_2, unless you are able to guess the value of μ.
4. However, the t statistic for Z will be the same as that which would have been obtained for X_2, and so you are able to assess the significance of X_2, even though you are not able to estimate its coefficient.
5. It will not be possible to obtain an estimate of β_1, since the intercept is now $(\beta_1 + \beta_2 \lambda)$, but usually the intercept is of secondary interest, anyway.

With regard to the third point, suppose that you are investigating migration from country A to country B and you are using the (very naïve) model

$$M = \beta_1 + \beta_2 W + u, \tag{7.19}$$

where M is the rate of migration of a certain type of worker from A to B, and W is the ratio of the wage rate in B to the wage rate in A. The higher the relative wage rate, you think the higher is migration. But suppose that you only have data on GDP per capita, not wages. You might define a proxy variable G that is the ratio of GDP per capita in B to GDP per capita in A.

In this case it might be reasonable to assume, as a first approximation, that relative wages are proportional to relative GDP per capita. If that were true, one could write (7.17) with λ equal to 0 and μ equal to 1. In this case the coefficient of relative GDP per capita would yield a direct estimate of the coefficient of relative wages. Since variables in regression analysis are frequently defined in relative terms, this special case actually has quite a wide application.

In this discussion we have assumed that Z is an ideal proxy for X_2, and the validity of all the foregoing results depends on this condition. In practice it is unusual to find a proxy that is exactly linearly related to the missing variable, but if the relationship is close the results will hold approximately. A major problem is posed by the fact that there is never any means of testing whether the condition is or is not approximated satisfactorily. One has to justify the use of the proxy subjectively.

Example

The main determinants of educational attainment appear to be the cognitive ability of an individual and the support and motivation provided by the family background. The NLSY data set is exceptional in that cognitive ability measures are available for virtually all the respondents, the data being obtained when the Department of Defense, needing to re-norm the Armed Services Vocational Aptitude Battery scores, sponsored the administration of the tests. However, there are no data that bear directly on support and motivation provided by the family background. This factor is difficult to define and probably has several dimensions. Accordingly, it is unlikely that a single proxy could do justice to it. The NLSY data set includes data on parental educational attainment and the number of siblings of the respondent, both of which could be used as proxies, the rationale for the latter being that parents who are ambitious for their children tend to limit the family size in order to concentrate resources. The data set also contains three dummy variables specifically intended to capture family background effects: whether anyone in the family possessed a library card, whether anyone in the family bought magazines, and whether anyone in the family bought newspapers, when the respondent was aged 14. However the explanatory power of these variables appears to be very limited.

The regression output in Table 7.6 shows the results of regressing S on $ASVABC$ only and on $ASVABC$, parental education, number of siblings, and the library card dummy variable. $ASVABC$ is positively correlated with SM, SF, and $LIBRARY$ (correlation coefficients 0.38, 0.42, and 0.22, respectively), and negatively correlated with $SIBLINGS$ (correlation coefficient -0.19). Its coefficient is therefore unambiguously biased upwards in the first regression. However, there

Table 7.6

```
. reg S ASVABC

   Source |       SS       df       MS              Number of obs =     570
----------+------------------------------           F( 1,    568) =  284.89
    Model | 1153.80864       1  1153.80864          Prob > F       =  0.0000
 Residual | 2300.43873     568  4.05006818          R-squared      =  0.3340
----------+------------------------------           Adj R-squared  =  0.3329
    Total | 3454.24737     569  6.07073351          Root MSE       =  2.0125


------------------------------------------------------------------------------
        S |     Coef.    Std. Err.      t     P>|t|     [95% Conf. Interval]
----------+-------------------------------------------------------------------
   ASVABC | .1545378    .0091559    16.879   0.000     .1365543     .1725213
    _cons | 5.770845    .4668473    12.361   0.000     4.853888     6.687803
------------------------------------------------------------------------------

. reg S ASVABC SM SF LIBRARY SIBLINGS

   Source |       SS       df       MS              Number of obs =     570
----------+------------------------------           F( 5,    564) =   66.87
    Model | 1285.58208       5  257.116416          Prob > F       =  0.0000
 Residual | 2168.66529     564  3.84515122          R-squared      =  0.3722
----------+------------------------------           Adj R-squared  =  0.3666
    Total | 3454.24737     569  6.07073351          Root MSE       =  1.9609


------------------------------------------------------------------------------
        S |     Coef.    Std. Err.      t     P>|t|     [95% Conf. Interval]
----------+-------------------------------------------------------------------
   ASVABC | .1277852    .010054     12.710   0.000     .1080373     .147533
       SM | .0619975    .0427558     1.450   0.148    -.0219826     .1459775
       SF | .1045035    .0314928     3.318   0.001     .042646      .166361
  LIBRARY | .1151269    .1969844     0.584   0.559    -.2717856     .5020394
 SIBLINGS | -.0509486   .039956     -1.275   0.203    -.1294293     .027532
    _cons | 5.236995    .5665539     9.244   0.000     4.124181     6.349808
------------------------------------------------------------------------------
```

may still be an element of bias in the second, given the weakness of the proxy variables.

Unintentional Proxies

It sometimes happens that you use a proxy without realizing it. You think that Y depends upon Z, but in reality it depends upon X.

If the correlation between Z and X is low, the results will be poor, so you may realize that something is wrong, but, if the correlation is good, the results may appear to be satisfactory (R^2 up to the anticipated level, etc) and you may remain blissfully unaware that the relationship is false.

Does this matter? Well, it depends on why you are running the regression in the first place. If the purpose of fitting the regression line is to predict future values of Y, the use of a proxy will not matter much, provided of course that the correlation remains high and was not a statistical fluke in the sample period. However, if your intention is to use the explanatory variable as a policy instrument for influencing the dependent variable, the consequences could be serious. Unless there happens to be a functional connection between the proxy and the true explanatory variable, manipulating the proxy will have no effect at all on the dependent variable. If the motive for your regression is scientific curiosity, the outcome is equally unsatisfactory.

Unintentional proxies are especially common in time-series analysis, particularly in macroeconomic models. If the true explanatory variable is subject to a time trend, you will probably get a good fit if you substitute (intentionally or otherwise) any other variable with a time trend. Even if you relate changes in your dependent variable to changes in your explanatory variable, you are likely to get similar results whether you are using the correct explanatory variable or a proxy, since macroeconomic variables tend to change in concert over the trade cycle.

Exercises

7.7   Length of work experience is generally found to be an important determinant of earnings. The data set does not contain this variable, but *TENURE*, tenure with the current employer, could be taken as a proxy. An alternative is to calculate years of potential work experience, *PWE*, as a proxy. This is defined to be current age, *AGE*, less age of completion of full-time education. The latter can be estimated as years of schooling plus 5, assuming that schooling begins at the age of 6. Hence

$$PWE = AGE - S - 5.$$

Using your *EAEF* data set, regress *LGEARN* on *S*, *ASVABC*, *MALE*, *ETHBLACK*, *ETHHISP*, and *PWE*. Compare the results with the corresponding regression without *PWE*. You are likely to find that the coefficient of *S* is greater than before. Can you explain why?

The data set includes *TENURE*, tenure with current employer. This allows one to divide *PWE* into two components: potential work experience with previous employers, *PWEBEF*, and *TENURE*. Define *PWEBEF* as

$$PWEBEF = PWE - TENURE$$

and regress *LGEARN* on the variables as before, replacing *PWE* by *PWEBEF* and *TENURE*. Compare the result with that of the previous regression.

Variation: *PWE* is not likely to be a satisfactory proxy for work experience for females because it does not take into account time spent out of the labor force rearing children. Investigate this by running the regressions with *PWE* for the male and female subsamples separately. You must drop the *MALE* dummy from the specification (explain why). Do the same for the regressions with *PWEBEF* and *TENURE*.

7.8* A researcher has data on output per worker, *Y*, and capital per worker, *K*, both measured in thousands of dollars, for fifty firms in the textiles industry in 2001. She hypothesizes that output per worker depends on capital per worker and perhaps also the technological sophistication of the firm, *TECH*:

$$Y = \beta_1 + \beta_2 K + \beta_3 TECH + u,$$

where *u* is a disturbance term. She is unable to measure *TECH* and decides to use expenditure per worker on research and development in 2001, *R&D*, as a proxy for it. She fits the following regressions (standard errors in parentheses):

$$\hat{Y} = 1.02 + 0.32K. \quad R^2 = 0.79$$
$$\phantom{\hat{Y} = } (0.45) \ (0.04)$$

$$\hat{Y} = 0.34 + 0.29K + 0.05R\&D. \quad R^2 = 0.750$$
$$\phantom{\hat{Y} = } (0.61) \ (0.22) \quad (0.15)$$

The correlation coefficient for *K* and *R&D* was 0.92. Discuss these regression results (1) assuming that *Y* does depend on both *K* and *TECH*, (2) assuming that *Y* depends only on *K*.

7.5 Testing a linear restriction

In Section 4.4 it was demonstrated that you can reduce the number of explanatory variables in a regression equation by one if you believe that there exists a linear relationship between the parameters in it. By exploiting the information about the relationship, you will make the regression estimates more efficient. If there was previously a problem of multicollinearity, it may be alleviated. Even if the original model was not subject to this problem, the gain in efficiency may yield a welcome improvement in the precision of the estimates, as reflected by their standard errors.

The example discussed in Section 4.4 was an educational attainment model with *S* related to *ASVABC*, *SM*, and *SF* (Table 7.7).

Somewhat surprisingly, the coefficient of *SM* is not significant, even at the 5 percent level, using a one-tailed test. However assortive mating leads to a high correlation between *SM* and *SF* and the regression appeared to be suffering from multicollinearity.

We then hypothesized that mother's and father's education are equally important for educational attainment, allowing us to impose the restriction $\beta_3 = \beta_4$

Table 7.7

```
. reg S ASVABC SM SF
```

Source	SS	df	MS		
Model	1278.24153	3	426.080508		
Residual	2176.00584	566	3.84453329		
Total	3454.24737	569	6.07073351		

Number of obs = 570
F(3, 566) = 110.83
Prob > F = 0.0000
R-squared = 0.3700
Adj R-squared = 0.3667
Root MSE = 1.9607

S	Coef.	Std. Err.	t	P>|t|	[95% Conf. Interval]	
ASVABC	.1295006	.0099544	13.009	0.000	.1099486	.1490527
SM	.069403	.0422974	1.641	0.101	-.013676	.152482
SF	.1102684	.0311948	3.535	0.000	.0489967	.1715401
_cons	4.914654	.5063527	9.706	0.000	3.920094	5.909214

and rewrite the equation as

$$S = \beta_1 + \beta_2 ASVSABC + \beta_3(SM + SF) + u$$
$$= \beta_1 + \beta_2 ASVSABC + \beta_3 SP + u, \qquad (7.20)$$

where SP is the sum of SM and SF.

The standard error of SP in Table 7.8 is much smaller than those of SM and SF, indicating that the use of the restriction has led to a gain in efficiency, and as a consequence the t statistic is very high. Thus the problem of multicollinearity has

Table 7.8

```
. g SP=SM+SF
. reg S ASVABC SP
```

Source	SS	df	MS		
Model	1276.73764	2	638.368819		
Residual	2177.50973	567	3.84040517		
Total	3454.24737	569	6.07073351		

Number of obs = 570
F(2, 567) = 166.22
Prob > F = 0.0000
R-squared = 0.3696
Adj R-squared = 0.3674
Root MSE = 1.9597

S	Coef.	Std. Err.	t	P>|t|	[95% Conf. Interval]	
ASVABC	.1295653	.0099485	13.024	0.000	.1100249	.1491057
SP	.093741	.0165688	5.658	0.000	.0611973	.1262847
_cons	4.823123	.4844829	9.955	0.000	3.871523	5.774724

been eliminated. However, we are obliged to test the validity of the restriction, and there are two equivalent procedures.

F test of a restriction

Run the regression in both the restricted and the unrestricted forms and denote the sum of the squares of the residuals RSS_R in the restricted case and RSS_U in the unrestricted case. Since the imposition of the restriction makes it more difficult to fit the regression equation to the data, RSS_R cannot be less than RSS_U and will in general be greater. We would like to test whether the improvement in the fit on going from the restricted to the unrestricted version is significant. If it is, the restriction should be rejected.

For this purpose we can use an F test whose structure is the same as that described in Section 4.5:

$$F = \frac{\text{Improvement in fit/Extra degrees of freedom used up}}{\text{Residual sum of squares remaining/Degrees of freedom remaining}}.$$
(7.21)

In this case the improvement on going from the restricted to the unrestricted version is $(RSS_R - RSS_U)$, one extra degree of freedom is used up in the unrestricted version (because there is one more parameter to estimate), and the residual sum of squares remaining after the shift from the restricted to the unrestricted version is RSS_U. Hence the F statistic is in this case

$$F(1, n - k) = \frac{RSS_R - RSS_U}{RSS_U/(n - k)},$$
(7.22)

where k is the number of parameters in the unrestricted version. It is distributed with 1 and $n-k$ degrees of freedom under the null hypothesis that the restriction is valid.

In the case of the educational attainment function, the null hypothesis was $H_0: \beta_3 = \beta_4$, where β_3 is the coefficient of SM and β_4 is the coefficient of SF. The residual sum of squares was 2177.51 in the restricted version and 2176.01 in the unrestricted version. Hence the F statistic is

$$F(1, n - k) = \frac{2177.51 - 2176.01}{2176.01/566} = 0.39.$$
(7.23)

Since the F statistic is less than 1, it is not significant at any significance level and we do not reject the null hypothesis that the coefficients of SM and SF are equal.

t test of a restriction

Linear restrictions can also be tested using a t test. This involves writing down the model for the restricted version and adding the term that would convert it back to the unrestricted version. The test evaluates whether this additional term is needed. To find the conversion term, we write the restricted version of the model under the unrestricted version and subtract:

$$S = \beta_1 + \beta_2 ASVABC + \beta_3 SM + \beta_4 SF + u. \qquad (7.24)$$

$$S = \beta_1 + \beta_2 ASVABC + \beta_3 SP + u. \qquad (7.25)$$

$$0 = \beta_3 SM + \beta_4 SF - \beta_3 SP$$
$$= \beta_3 SM + \beta_4 SF - \beta_3 (SM + SF)$$
$$= (\beta_4 - \beta_3)SF. \qquad (7.26)$$

We add this term to the restricted model and investigate whether it is needed.

$$S = \beta_1 + \beta_2 ASVABC + \beta_3 SP + (\beta_4 - \beta_3)SF + u. \qquad (7.27)$$

The null hypothesis, $H_0: \beta_4 - \beta_3 = 0$, is that the coefficient of the conversion term is 0, and the alternative hypothesis is that it is different from 0. Of course the null hypothesis is that the restriction is valid. If it is valid, the conversion term is not needed, and the restricted version is an adequate representation of the data.

Table 7.9 presents the corresponding regression for the educational attainment example. We see that the coefficient of SF is not significantly different from 0, indicating that the term is not needed and that the restricted version is an adequate representation of the data.

Why is the t test approach equivalent to that of the F test? Well the F test tests the improvement in fit when you go from the restricted version to the unrestricted version. This is accomplished by adding the conversion term, but, as we know, an F test on the improvement in fit when you add an extra term is equivalent to the t test on the coefficient of that term (see Section 4.5).

Table 7.9

```
. reg S ASVABC SP SF

      Source |       SS       df       MS              Number of obs =     570
-------------+------------------------------           F(  3,   566) =  110.83
       Model |  1278.24153      3  426.080508           Prob > F      =  0.0000
    Residual |  2176.00584    566  3.84453329           R-squared     =  0.3700
-------------+------------------------------           Adj R-squared =  0.3667
       Total |  3454.24737    569  6.07073351           Root MSE      =  1.9607


           S |     Coef.   Std. Err.      t    P>|t|     [95% Conf. Interval]
-------------+----------------------------------------------------------------
      ASVABC |   .1295006   .0099544    13.009  0.000     .1099486    .1490527
          SP |    .069403   .0422974     1.641  0.101    -.013676     .152482
          SF |   .0408654   .0653386     0.625  0.532    -.0874704    .1692012
       _cons |   4.914654   .5063527     9.706  0.000     3.920094    5.909214
```

Exercises

7.9   You will have found in Exercise 7.7 that the estimates of the coefficients of *PWEBEF* and *TENURE* are different. This raises the issue of whether the difference is due to random factors or whether the coefficients are significantly different. Set up the null hypothesis H_0: $\delta_1 = \delta_2$, where δ_1 is the coefficient of *PWEBEF* and δ_2 is the coefficient of *TENURE*. Explain why the regression with *PWE* is the correct specification if H_0 is true, while the regression with *PWEBEF* and *TENURE* should be used if H_0 is false. Perform an *F* test of the restriction using *RSS* for the two regressions. Do this for the combined sample and also for males and females separately.

7.10* The first regression shows the result of regressing *LGFDHO*, the logarithm of annual household expenditure on food eaten at home, on *LGEXP*, the logarithm of total annual household expenditure, and *LGSIZE*, the logarithm of the number of persons in the household,

```
. reg LGFDHO LGEXP LGSIZE

    Source |       SS       df       MS                Number of obs =     868
-----------+------------------------------             F(  2,   865) =  460.92
     Model | 138.776549        2  69.3882747           Prob > F      =  0.0000
  Residual | 130.219231      865  .150542464           R-squared     =  0.5159
-----------+------------------------------             Adj R-squared =  0.5148
     Total | 268.995781      867  .310260416           Root MSE      =    .388


    LGFDHO |      Coef.   Std. Err.       t     P>|t|     [95% Conf. Interval]
-----------+--------------------------------------------------------------------
     LGEXP |   .2866813   .0226824    12.639    0.000      .2421622    .3312003
    LGSIZE |   .4854698   .0255476    19.003    0.000      .4353272    .5356124
     _cons |   4.720269   .2209996    21.359    0.000      4.286511    5.154027


. reg LGFDHOPC LGEXPPC

    Source |       SS       df       MS                Number of obs =     868
-----------+------------------------------             F(  1,   866) =  313.04
     Model | 51.4364364        1  51.4364364           Prob > F      =  0.0000
  Residual | 142.293973      866  .164311747           R-squared     =  0.2655
-----------+------------------------------             Adj R-squared =  0.2647
     Total |  193.73041      867  .223449146           Root MSE      =  .40535


  LGFDHOPC |      Coef.   Std. Err.       t     P>|t|     [95% Conf. Interval]
-----------+--------------------------------------------------------------------
   LGEXPPC |    .376283   .0212674    17.693    0.000      .3345414    .4180246
     _cons |   3.700667   .1978925    18.700    0.000      3.312262    4.089072
```

```
. reg LGFDHOPC LGEXPPC LGSIZE

    Source |       SS       df       MS              Number of obs =     868
-----------+------------------------------           F(  2,   865) =  210.94
     Model |  63.5111811      2  31.7555905          Prob > F      =  0.0000
  Residual |  130.219229    865  .150542461          R-squared     =  0.3278
-----------+------------------------------           Adj R-squared =  0.3263
     Total |   193.73041    867  .223449146          Root MSE      =    .388


  LGFDHOPC |     Coef.   Std. Err.      t    P>|t|     [95% Conf. Interval]
-----------+----------------------------------------------------------------
   LGEXPPC |   .2866813   .0226824   12.639   0.000     .2421622    .3312004
    LGSIZE |  -.2278489   .0254412   -8.956   0.000    -.2777826   -.1779152
     _cons |   4.720269   .2209996   21.359   0.000     4.286511    5.154027
```

using a sample of 868 households in the 1995 Consumer Expenditure Survey. In the second regression, $LGFDHOPC$, the logarithm of food expenditure per capita ($FDHO/SIZE$), is regressed on $LGEXPPC$, the logarithm of total expenditure per capita ($EXP/SIZE$). In the third regression $LGFDHOPC$ is regressed on $LGEXPPC$ and $LGSIZE$.

1. Explain why the second model is a restricted version of the first, stating the restriction.

2. Perform an F test of the restriction.

3. Perform a t test of the restriction.

4. Summarize your conclusions from the analysis of the regression results.

7.11 In his classic article, Nerlove (1963) derives the following cost function for electricity generation:

$$C = \beta_1 Y^{\beta_2} P_1^{\gamma_1} P_2^{\gamma_2} P_3^{\gamma_3} v,$$

where C is total production cost, Y is output (measured in kilowatt hours), P_1 is the price of labor input, P_2 is the price of capital input, P_3 is the price of fuel (all measured in appropriate units), and v is a disturbance term. Theoretically, the sum of the price elasticities should be 1:

$$\gamma_1 + \gamma_2 + \gamma_3 = 1,$$

and hence the cost function may be rewritten

$$\frac{C}{P_3} = \beta_1 Y^{\beta_2} \left(\frac{P_1}{P_3}\right)^{\gamma_1} \left(\frac{P_2}{P_3}\right)^{\gamma_2} v.$$

The two versions of the cost function are fitted to the twenty-nine medium-sized firms in Nerlove's sample, with the following results (standard errors in parentheses):

$$\widehat{\log C} = -4.93 + 0.94 \log Y + 0.31 \log P_1 - 0.26 \log P_2 + 0.44 \log P_3.$$
$$\phantom{\widehat{\log C} =} (1.62) \quad (0.11) \qquad (0.23) \qquad\quad (0.29) \qquad\quad (0.07)$$

$$RSS = 0.336$$

$$\widehat{\log \frac{C}{P_3}} = -6.55 + 0.91 \log Y + 0.51 \log \frac{P_1}{P_3} + 0.09 \log \frac{P_2}{P_3}.$$
$$\phantom{\widehat{\log \frac{C}{P_3}} =} (0.16) \quad (0.11) \qquad (0.23) \qquad\quad (0.19)$$

$$RSS = 0.364$$

Compare the regression results for the two equations and perform a test of the validity of the restriction.

7.6 Getting the most out of your residuals

There are two ways of looking at the residuals obtained after fitting a regression equation to a set of data. If you are pessimistic and passive, you will simply see them as evidence of failure. The bigger the residuals, the worse is your fit, and the smaller is R^2. The whole object of the exercise is to fit the regression equation in such a way as to minimize the sum of the squares of the residuals. However, if you are enterprising, you will also see the residuals as a potentially fertile source of new ideas, perhaps even new hypotheses. They offer both a challenge and constructive criticism. The challenge is that providing the stimulus for most scientific research: evidence of the need to find a better explanation of the facts. The constructive criticism comes in because the residuals, taken individually, indicate when and where and by how much the existing model is failing to fit the facts.

Taking advantage of this constructive criticism requires patience on the part of the researcher. If the sample is small enough, you should look carefully at every observation with a large positive or negative residual, and try to hypothesize explanations for them. Some of these explanations may involve special factors specific to the observations in question. These are not of much use to the theorist. Other factors, however, may appear to be associated with the residuals in several observations. As soon as you detect a regularity of this kind, you have the makings of progress. The next step is to find a sensible way of quantifying the factor and of including it in the model.

8 Heteroscedasticity

Medicine is traditionally divided into the three branches of anatomy, physiology, and pathology—what a body is made of, how it works, and what can go wrong with it. It is time to start discussing the pathology of least squares regression analysis. The properties of the estimators of the regression coefficients depend on the properties of the disturbance term in the regression model. In this and the next two chapters we shall be looking at some of the problems that arise when the Gauss–Markov conditions, the assumptions relating to the disturbance term, are not satisfied.

8.1 Heteroscedasticity and its implications

The second of the Gauss–Markov conditions listed in Section 3.3 states that the variance of the disturbance term in each observation should be constant. This sounds peculiar and needs a bit of explanation. The disturbance term in each observation has only *one* value, so what can be meant by its 'variance'?

What we are talking about is its *potential* behavior *before* the sample is generated. When we write the model

$$Y = \beta_1 + \beta_2 X + u, \tag{8.1}$$

the first two Gauss–Markov conditions state that the disturbance terms $u_1, \ldots, u_n$ in the n observations are drawn from probability distributions that have 0 mean and the same variance. Their *actual* values in the sample will sometimes be positive, sometimes negative, sometimes relatively far from 0, sometimes relatively close, but there will be no a priori reason to anticipate a particularly erratic value in any given observation. To put it another way, the probability of u reaching a given positive (or negative) value will be the same in all observations. This condition is known as homoscedasticity, which means 'same dispersion'.

Figure 8.1 provides an illustration of homoscedasticity. To keep the diagram simple, the sample contains only five observations. Let us start with the first observation, where X has the value X_1. If there were no disturbance term in the model, the observation would be represented by the circle vertically above

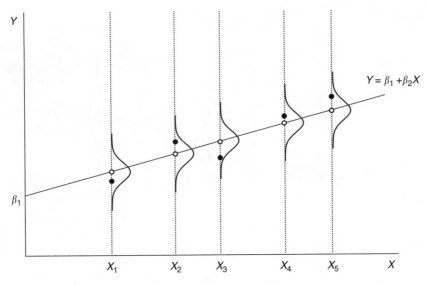

Figure 8.1 Homoscedasticity

X_1 on the line $Y = \beta_1 + \beta_2 X$. The effect of the disturbance term is to shift the observation upwards or downwards vertically. The *potential* distribution of the disturbance term, before the observation has been generated, is shown by the normal distribution centered on the circle. The actual value of the disturbance term for this observation turned out to be negative, the observation being represented by the solid marker. The potential distribution of the disturbance term, and the actual outcome, are shown in a similar way for the other four observations.

Although homoscedasticity is often taken for granted in regression analysis, in some contexts it may be more reasonable to suppose that the potential distribution of the disturbance term is different for different observations in the sample. This is illustrated in Figure 8.2, where the variance of the potential distribution of the disturbance term is increasing as X increases. This does not mean that the disturbance term will *necessarily* have a particularly large (positive or negative) value in an observation where X is large, but it does mean that the a priori *probability* of having an erratic value will be relatively high. This is an example of heteroscedasticity, which means 'differing dispersion'. Mathematically, homoscedasticity and heteroscedasticity may be defined:

Homoscedasticity: $\sigma_{u_i}^2 = \sigma_u^2$, same for all observations
Heteroscedasticity: $\sigma_{u_i}^2$ not the same for all observations

Figure 8.3 illustrates how a typical scatter diagram would look if Y were an increasing function of X and the heteroscedasticity were of the type shown in Figure 8.2. You can see that, although the observations are not necessarily further away from the nonstochastic component of the relationship, represented by the line $Y = \beta_1 + \beta_2 X$, there is a tendency for their dispersion to increase as

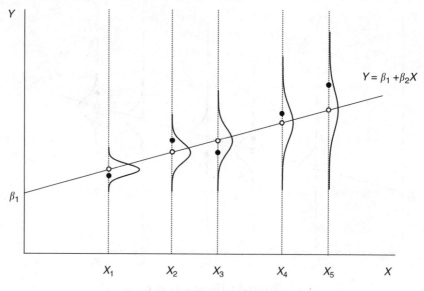

Figure 8.2 Heteroscedasticity

X increases. (You should be warned that heteroscedasticity is not necessarily of the type shown in Figure 8.2 and 8.3. The term refers to any case in which the variance of the probability distribution of the disturbance term is not the same in all observations.)

Why does heteroscedasticity matter? This particular Gauss–Markov condition does not appear to have been used anywhere in the analysis so far, so it might

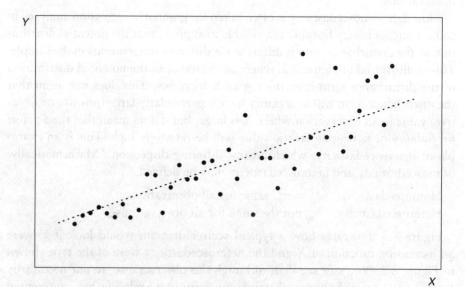

Figure 8.3 Model with a heteroscedastic disturbance term

seem almost irrelevant. In particular, the proofs of the unbiasedness of the OLS regression coefficients did not use this condition.

There are two reasons. The first concerns the variances of the regression coefficients. You want these to be as small as possible so that, in a probabilistic sense, you have maximum precision. If there is no heteroscedasticity, and if the other Gauss–Markov conditions are satisfied, the OLS regression coefficients have the lowest variances of all the unbiased estimators that are linear functions of the observations of Y. If heteroscedasticity is present, the OLS estimators are inefficient because you could, at least in principle, find other estimators that have smaller variances and are still unbiased.

The second, equally important, reason is that the estimators of the standard errors of the regression coefficients will be wrong. They are computed on the assumption that the distribution of the disturbance term is homoscedastic. If this is not the case, they are biased, and as a consequence the t tests, and also the usual F tests, are invalid. It is quite likely that the standard errors will be underestimated, so the t statistics will be overestimated and you will have a misleading impression of the precision of your regression coefficients. You may be led to believe that a coefficient is significantly different from 0, at a given significance level, when in fact it is not.

The inefficiency property can be explained intuitively quite easily. Suppose that heteroscedasticity of the type displayed in Figures 8.2 and 8.3 is present. An observation where the potential distribution of the disturbance term has a small standard deviation, like the first observation in Figure 8.2, will tend to lie close to the line $Y = \beta_1 + \beta_2 X$ and hence will be a good guide to the location of that line. By contrast, an observation where the potential distribution has a large standard deviation, like that for the fifth observation in Figure 8.2, will be an unreliable guide to the location of the line. OLS does not discriminate between the quality of the observations, giving equal weight to each, irrespective of whether they are good or poor guides to the location of the line. It follows that if we can find a way of giving more weight to the high-quality observations and less to the unreliable ones, we are likely to obtain a better fit. In other words, our estimators of β_1 and β_2 will be more efficient. We shall see how to do this below.

Possible causes of heteroscedasticity

Heteroscedasticity is likely to be a problem when the values of the variables in the sample vary substantially in different observations. If the true relationship is given by $Y = \beta_1 + \beta_2 X + u$, it may well be the case that the variations in the omitted variables and the measurement errors that are jointly responsible for the disturbance term will be relatively small when Y and X are small and large when they are large, economic variables tending to move in size together.

For example, suppose that you are using the simple regression model to investigate the relationship between value added in manufacturing, $MANU$, and gross domestic product, GDP, in cross-country data, and that you have collected the

Table 8.1 Manufacturing value added, GDP, and population for a sample of countries, 1994

Country	MANU	GDP	POP	MANU/POP	GDP/POP
Belgium	44517	232006	10.093	4411	22987
Canada	112617	547203	29.109	3869	18798
Chile	13096	50919	13.994	936	3639
Denmark	25927	151266	5.207	4979	29050
Finland	21581	97624	5.085	4244	19199
France	256316	1330998	57.856	4430	23005
Greece	9392	98861	10.413	902	9494
Hong Kong	11758	130823	6.044	1945	21645
Hungary	7227	41506	10.162	711	4084
Ireland	17572	52662	3.536	4970	14893
Israel	11349	74121	5.362	2117	13823
Italy	145013	1016286	57.177	2536	17774
Korea, S.	161318	380820	44.501	3625	8558
Kuwait	2797	24848	1.754	1595	14167
Malaysia	18874	72505	19.695	958	3681
Mexico	55073	420788	89.564	615	4698
Netherlands	48595	334286	15.382	3159	21732
Norway	13484	122926	4.314	3126	28495
Portugal	17025	87352	9.824	1733	8892
Singapore	20648	71039	3.268	6318	21738
Slovakia	2720	13746	5.325	511	2581
Slovenia	4520	14386	1.925	2348	7473
Spain	80104	483652	39.577	2024	12221
Sweden	34806	198432	8.751	3977	22675
Switzerland	57503	261388	7.104	8094	36794
Syria	3317	44753	13.840	240	3234
Turkey	31115	135961	59.903	519	2270
UK	244397	1024609	58.005	4213	17664

Source: UNIDO *Yearbook 1997*
Note: MANU and GDP are measured in US$ million. POP is measured in million.
MANU/POP and GDP/POP are measured in US$

sample of observations given in Table 8.1, which includes small economies such as Slovenia and Slovakia as well as large ones such as France, the UK, and Italy. Manufacturing output tends to account for 15 to 25 percent of GDP, variations being caused by comparative advantage and historical economic development.

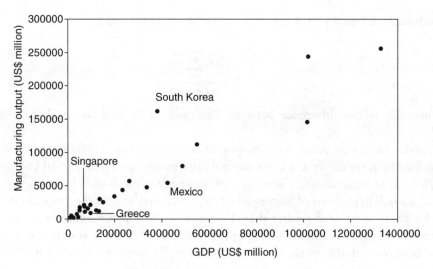

Figure 8.4 Manufacturing output and GDP

Clearly, when GDP is large, a 1 percent variation will make a great deal more difference, in absolute terms, than when it is small.

South Korea and Mexico are both countries with relatively large GDP. The manufacturing sector is relatively important in South Korea, so its observation is far above the trend line. The opposite was the case for Mexico, at least in 1997. Singapore and Greece are another pair of countries with relatively large and small manufacturing sectors. However, because the GDP of both countries is small, their variations from the trend relationship are also small.

8.2 Detection of heteroscedasticity

In principle there is no limit to the possible different types of heteroscedasticity and accordingly a large number of different tests appropriate for different circumstances have been proposed. We will confine our attention to three tests that hypothesize a relationship between the variance of the disturbance term and the size of the explanatory variable(s): the Spearman rank correlation test, the Goldfeld–Quandt test, and the Glejser test.

The Spearman rank correlation test

The Spearman rank correlation test assumes that the variance of the disturbance term is either increasing or decreasing as X increases and that therefore there will be a correlation between the absolute size of the residuals and the size of X in an OLS regression. The data on X and the absolute values of the residuals are both ranked, and the rank correlation coefficient is defined as

$$r_{Xe} = 1 - \frac{6 \sum\limits_{i=1}^{n} D_i^2}{n(n^2 - 1)}, \qquad (8.2)$$

where D_i is the difference between the rank of X and the rank of e in observation i.

Under the assumption that the population correlation coefficient is 0, the rank correlation coefficient has a normal distribution with 0 mean and variance $1/(n-1)$ in large samples. The appropriate test statistic is therefore $r_{Xe}\sqrt{n-1}$ and the null hypothesis of homoscedasticity will be rejected at the 5 percent level if its absolute value is greater than 1.96 and at the 1 percent level if its absolute value is greater than 2.58, using two-tailed tests. If there is more than one explanatory variable in the model, the test may be performed with any one of them.

Example

Using the data in Table 8.1, an OLS regression of manufacturing output on GDP yields the following result (standard errors in parentheses):

$$\widehat{MANU} = 604 + 0.194GDP. \quad R^2 = 0.89 \qquad (8.3)$$
$$\phantom{\widehat{MANU} = } (5700) \ (0.013)$$

Table 8.2

GDP	Rank	$|e|$	Rank	D	D^2	GDP	Rank	$|e|$	Rank	D	D^2
13746	1	547	2	−1	1	130823	15	14185	23	−8	64
14386	2	1130	4	−2	4	135961	16	4176	12	4	16
24848	3	2620	8	−5	25	151266	17	3976	11	6	36
41506	4	1417	5	−1	1	198432	18	4233	14	4	16
44753	5	5955	15	−10	100	232006	19	1025	3	16	256
50919	6	2629	9	−3	9	261388	20	6270	17	3	9
52662	7	6768	19	−12	144	334286	21	16758	24	−3	9
71039	8	6284	18	−10	100	380820	22	86952	28	−6	36
72505	9	4227	13	−4	16	420788	23	27034	25	−2	4
74121	10	3611	10	0	0	483652	24	14180	22	2	4
87352	11	499	1	10	100	547203	25	6024	16	9	81
97624	12	2067	6	6	36	1016286	26	52439	27	−1	1
98861	13	10360	20	−7	49	1024609	27	45333	26	1	1
122926	14	10929	21	−7	49	1330998	28	2093	7	21	441

This implies that manufacturing accounts for $194,000 out of every $1 million increase in *GDP* in the cross-section. The residuals from the regression and GDP are both ranked in Table 8.2 and D_i and D_i^2 are computed. The sum of the latter came to 1608. The rank correlation coefficient is thus

$$1 - \frac{6 \times 1608}{28 \times 783} = 0.56 \tag{8.4}$$

and the test statistic is $0.56\sqrt{27} = 2.91$. This is above 2.58 and hence the null hypothesis of homoscedasticity is rejected at the 1 percent level.

The Goldfeld–Quandt test

Perhaps the most common formal test for heteroscedasticity is that of Goldfeld and Quandt (1965). It assumes that σ_{u_i}, the standard deviation of the probability distribution of the disturbance term in observation i, is proportional to the size of X_i. It also assumes that the disturbance term is normally distributed and satisfies the other Gauss–Markov conditions.

The n observations in the sample are ordered by the magnitude of X and separate regressions are run for the first n' and for the last n' observations, the middle $(n - 2n')$ observations being dropped entirely. If heteroscedasticity is present, and if the assumption concerning its nature is true, the variance of u in the last n' observations will be greater than that in the first n', and this will be reflected in the residual sums of squares in the two subregressions. Denoting these by RSS_1 and RSS_2 for the subregressions with the first n' and the last n' observations, respectively, the ratio RSS_2/RSS_1 will be distributed as an F statistic with $(n' - k)$ and $(n' - k)$ degrees of freedom, where k is the number of parameters in the equation, under the null hypothesis of homoscedasticity. The power of the test depends on the choice of n' in relation to n. As a result of some experiments undertaken by them, Goldfeld and Quandt suggest that n' should be about 11 when n is 30 and about 22 when n is 60, suggesting that n' should be about three-eighths of n. If there is more than one explanatory variable in the model, the observations should be ordered by that which is hypothesized to be associated with σ_{u_i}.

The null hypothesis for the test is that RSS_2 is not significantly greater than RSS_1, and the alternative hypothesis is that it is significantly greater. If RSS_2 turns out to be *smaller* than RSS_1, you are not going to reject the null hypothesis and there is no point in computing the test statistic RSS_2/RSS_1. However, the Goldfeld–Quandt test can also be used for the case where the standard deviation of the disturbance term is hypothesized to be inversely proportional to X_i. The procedure is the same as before, but the test statistic is now RSS_1/RSS_2, and it will again be distributed as an F statistic with $(n' - k)$ and $(n' - k)$ degrees of freedom under the null hypothesis of homoscedasticity.

Example

Using the data in Table 8.1, OLS regressions were run using the observations for the eleven countries with smallest GDP and for the eleven countries with largest GDP. The residual sum of squares in the first regression was 157×10^6, and in the second it was $13,518 \times 10^6$. The ratio RSS_2/RSS_1 was therefore 86.1. The critical value of $F(9,9)$ at the 0.1 percent level is 10.1, and the null hypothesis of homoscedasticity was therefore rejected.

The Glejser test

The Glejser test allows you to explore the nature of the heteroscedasticity a little more closely. We relax the assumption that σ_{u_i} is proportional to X_i and investigate whether some other functional form may be more appropriate, for example

$$\sigma_{u_i} = \beta_1 + \beta_2 X_i^{\gamma}. \tag{8.5}$$

To use the procedure, you regress Y on X using OLS and then fit the absolute values of the residuals, $|e|$, to the function for a given value of γ. You may fit several such functions, varying the choice of γ. In each case the null hypothesis of homoscedasticity will be rejected if the estimate of β_2 is significantly different from 0. If more than one function gives rise to a significant estimate of β_2, that with the best fit may be a guide to the nature of the heteroscedasticity.

Example

Using the data on GDP and $|e|$ in Table 8.2, (8.5) was fitted using values of γ from -1.0 to 1.5. The results are summarized in Table 8.3.

Note that the different estimates of β_2 are not comparable because the definition of the explanatory variable, X^{γ}, is different in each case. However, the levels of R^2 are comparable because the dependent variable is the same in each case. Significant coefficients, at the 1 percent level, are obtained for the middle

Table 8.3

γ	b_2	s.e.(b_2)	R^2
-1.0	-3.51×10^8	1.94×10^8	0.11
-0.5	-4.21×10^6	1.71×10^6	0.19
-0.25	0.56×10^6	0.20×10^6	0.23
0.25	1640	520	0.28
0.5	36.1	11.8	0.27
1.0	0.026	0.010	0.21
1.5	19.8×10^{-6}	9.3×10^{-6}	0.15

three values of γ. The best fits are obtained with γ equal to 0.25 and 0.5, so the standard deviation of the distribution of u does appear to be increasing with GDP but not in the same proportion.

Exercises

8.1 The table gives data on government recurrent expenditure, G, investment, I, gross domestic product, Y, and population, P, for thirty countries in 1997 (source: 1999 International Monetary Fund *Yearbook*). G, I, and Y are measured in US\$ billion and P in million. A researcher investigating whether government expenditure tends to crowd out investment fits the regression (standard errors in parentheses):

$$\hat{I} = 18.10 - 1.07G + 0.36Y. \quad R^2 = 0.99$$
$$\quad (7.79) \ (0.14) \quad (0.02)$$

Country	I	G	Y	P	Country	I	G	Y	P
Australia	94.5	75.5	407.9	18.5	Netherlands	73.0	49.9	360.5	15.6
Austria	46.0	39.2	206.0	8.1	New Zealand	12.9	9.9	65.1	3.8
Canada	119.3	125.1	631.2	30.3	Norway	35.3	30.9	153.4	4.4
Czech Republic	16.0	10.5	52.0	10.3	Philippines	20.1	10.7	82.2	78.5
Denmark	34.2	42.9	169.3	5.3	Poland	28.7	23.4	135.6	38.7
Finland	20.2	25.0	121.5	5.1	Portugal	25.6	19.9	102.1	9.8
France	255.9	347.2	1409.2	58.6	Russia	84.7	94.0	436.0	147.1
Germany	422.5	406.7	2102.7	82.1	Singapore	35.6	9.0	95.9	3.7
Greece	24.0	17.7	119.9	10.5	Spain	109.5	86.0	532.0	39.3
Iceland	1.4	1.5	7.5	0.3	Sweden	31.2	58.8	227.8	8.9
Ireland	14.3	10.1	73.2	3.7	Switzerland	50.2	38.7	256.0	7.1
Italy	190.8	189.7	1145.4	57.5	Thailand	48.1	15.0	153.9	60.6
Japan	1105.9	376.3	3901.3	126.1	Turkey	50.2	23.3	189.1	62.5
Korea	154.9	49.3	442.5	46.0	UK	210.1	230.7	1256.0	58.2
Malaysia	41.6	10.8	97.3	21.0	USA	1517.7	1244.1	8110.9	267.9

She sorts the observations by increasing size of Y and runs the regression again for the eleven countries with smallest Y and the eleven countries with largest Y. *RSS* for these regressions is 321 and 28101, respectively. Perform a Goldfeld–Quandt test for heteroscedasticity.

8.2 Fit an earnings function using your *EAEF* data set, taking *EARNINGS* as the dependent variable and S, *ASVABC*, and *MALE* as the explanatory variables, and perform a Goldfeld–Quandt test for heteroscedasticity in the S dimension. (Remember to sort the observations by S first.)

8.3* The following regressions were fitted using the Shanghai school cost data introduced in Section 6.1 (standard errors in parentheses):

$$\widehat{COST} = 24{,}000 + 339N. \quad R^2 = 0.39$$
$$\phantom{\widehat{COST} = }(27{,}000) \quad (50)$$

$$\widehat{COST} = 51{,}000 - 4{,}000\ OCC + 152N + 284\ NOCC. \quad R^2 = 0.68$$
$$\phantom{\widehat{COST} = }(31{,}000)\,(41{,}000) \qquad\quad (60) \qquad (76)$$

where $COST$ is the annual cost of running a school, N is the number of students, OCC is a dummy variable defined to be 0 for regular schools and 1 for occupational schools, and $NOCC$ is a slope dummy variable defined as the product of N and OCC. There are seventy-four schools in the sample. With the data sorted by N, the regressions are fitted again for the twenty-six smallest and twenty-six largest schools, the residual sum of squares being as shown in the table.

	26 smallest	26 largest
First regression	7.8×10^{10}	54.4×10^{10}
Second regression	6.7×10^{10}	13.8×10^{10}

Perform a Goldfeld–Quandt test for heteroscedasticity for the two models and, with reference to Figure 6.5, explain why the problem of heteroscedasticity is less severe in the second model.

8.4* The file educ.dta in the heteroscedastic data sets folder on the website contains international cross-section data on aggregate expenditure on education, $EDUC$, gross domestic product, GDP, and population, POP, for a sample of thirty-eight countries in 1997. $EDUC$ and GDP are measured in US\$ million and POP is measured in thousands. Download the data set, plot a scatter diagram of $EDUC$ on GDP, and comment on whether the data set appears to be subject to heteroscedasticity. Sort the data set by GDP and perform a Goldfeld–Quandt test for heteroscedasticity, running regressions using the subsamples of fourteen countries with the smallest and greatest GDP.

8.3 What can you do about heteroscedasticity?

Suppose that the true relationship is

$$Y_i = \beta_1 + \beta_2 X_i + u_i. \tag{8.6}$$

Let the standard deviation of the disturbance term in observation i be σ_{u_i}. If you happened to know for each observation, you could eliminate the heteroscedasticity by dividing each observation by its value of σ. The model becomes

$$\frac{Y_i}{\sigma_{u_i}} = \beta_1 \frac{1}{\sigma_{u_i}} + \beta_2 \frac{X_i}{\sigma_{u_i}} + \frac{u_i}{\sigma_{u_i}}. \tag{8.7}$$

The disturbance term u_i/σ_{u_i} is homoscedastic because its population variance is

$$E\left\{\left(\frac{u_i}{\sigma_{u_i}}\right)^2\right\} = \frac{1}{\sigma_{u_i}^2} E(u_i^2) = \frac{1}{\sigma_{u_i}^2} \sigma_{u_i}^2 = 1. \tag{8.8}$$

Therefore, every observation will have a disturbance term drawn from a distribution with population variance 1, and the model will be homoscedastic. The revised model may be rewritten

$$Y_i' = \beta_1 H_i + \beta_2 X_i' + u_i', \tag{8.9}$$

where $Y_i' = Y_i/\sigma_{u_i}$, $X_i' = X_i/\sigma_{u_i}$, H is a new variable whose value in observation i is $1/\sigma_{u_i}$, and $u_i' = u_i/\sigma_{u_i}$. Note that there should not be a constant term in the equation. By regressing Y' on H and X', you will obtain efficient estimates of β_1 and β_2 with unbiased standard errors.

A mathematical demonstration that the revised model will yield more efficient estimates than the original one is beyond the scope of this text, but it is easy to give an intuitive explanation. Those observations with the smallest values of σ_{u_i} will be the most useful for locating the true relationship between Y and X because they will tend to have the smallest disturbance terms. We are taking advantage of this fact by performing what is sometimes called a weighted regression. The fact that observation i is given weight $1/\sigma_{u_i}$ automatically means that the better its quality, the greater the weight that it receives.

The snag with this procedure is that it is most unlikely that you will know the actual values of the σ_{u_i}. However, if you can think of something that is proportional to it in each observation, and divide the equation by that, this will work just as well.

Suppose that you can think of such a variable, which we shall call Z, and it is reasonable to suppose that σ_{u_i} is proportional to Z_i:

$$\sigma_{u_i} = \lambda Z_i \tag{8.10}$$

for some constant, λ. If we divide the original equation through by Z, we have

$$\frac{Y_i}{Z_i} = \beta_1 \frac{1}{Z_i} + \beta_2 \frac{X_i}{Z_i} + \frac{u_i}{Z_i}. \tag{8.11}$$

The model is now homoscedastic because the population variance of u_i/Z_i is

$$E\left\{\left(\frac{u_i}{Z_i}\right)^2\right\} = \frac{1}{Z_i^2} E\left(u_i^2\right) = \frac{1}{Z_i^2} \sigma_{u_i}^2 = \frac{\lambda^2 Z_i^2}{Z_i^2} = \lambda^2. \tag{8.12}$$

We do not need to know the value of λ, and indeed in general will not know it. It is enough that it should be constant for all observations.

In particular, it may be reasonable to suppose that σ_{u_i} is roughly proportional to X_i, as is assumed in the Goldfeld–Quandt test. If you then divide each observation by its value of X, the model becomes

$$\frac{Y_i}{X_i} = \beta_1 \frac{1}{X_i} + \beta_2 + \frac{u_i}{X_i}, \tag{8.13}$$

and, with a little bit of luck, the new disturbance term u_i/X_i will have constant variance. You now regress Y/X on $1/X$, including a constant term in the regression. The coefficient of $1/X$ will be an efficient estimate of β_1 and the constant will be an efficient estimate of β_2. In the case of the manufacturing output example in the previous section, the dependent variable would be manufacturing output as a proportion of GDP, and the explanatory variable would be the reciprocal of GDP.

Sometimes there may be more than one variable that might be used for scaling the equation. In the case of the manufacturing output example, an alternative candidate would be the size of the population of the country, POP. Dividing the original model through by POP, one obtains

$$\frac{Y_i}{POP_i} = \beta_1 \frac{1}{POP_i} + \beta_2 \frac{X_i}{POP_i} + \frac{u_i}{POP_i}, \tag{8.14}$$

and again one hopes that the disturbance term, u_i/POP_i, will have constant variance across observations. Thus now one is regressing manufacturing output per capita on GDP per capita and the reciprocal of the size of the population, this time without a constant term.

In practice it may be a good idea to try several variables for scaling the observations and to compare the results. If the results are roughly similar each time, and tests fail to reject the null hypothesis of homoscedasticity, your problem should be at an end.

Examples

In the previous section it was found that a linear regression of $MANU$ on GDP using the data in Table 8.1 and the model

$$MANU = \beta_1 + \beta_2 GDP + u \tag{8.15}$$

was subject to severe heteroscedasticity. One possible remedy might be to scale the observations by population, the model becoming

$$\frac{MANU}{POP} = \beta_1 \frac{1}{POP} + \beta_2 \frac{GDP}{POP} + \frac{u}{POP}, \tag{8.16}$$

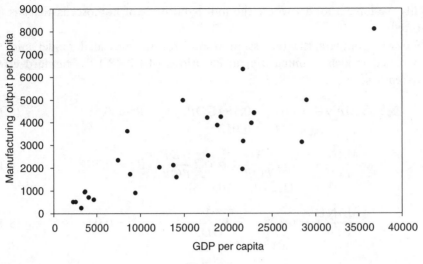

Figure 8.5

Figure 8.5 provides a plot of *MANU/POP* on *GDP/POP*. Despite scaling, the plot still looks heteroscedastic. When (8.16) is fitted using the eleven countries with smallest GDP per capita and the eleven countries with the greatest, the residual sums of squares are 5,378,000 and 17,362,000. The ratio, and hence the F statistic, is 3.23. If the subsamples are small, it is possible to obtain high ratios under the null hypothesis of homoscedasticity. In this case, the null hypothesis is just rejected at the 5 percent level, the critical value of $F(9,9)$ being 3.18.

Figure 8.6 shows the result of scaling through by GDP itself, manufacturing as a share of GDP being plotted against the reciprocal of GDP. In this case the residual sums of squares for the subsamples are 0.065 and 0.070, and so

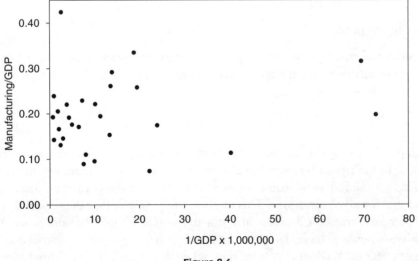

Figure 8.6

finally we have a model where the null hypothesis of homoscedasticity is not rejected.

We will compare the regression results for the unscaled model and the two scaled models, summarized in equations (8.17)–(8.19) (standard errors in parentheses):

$$\widehat{MANU} = 604 + 0.194GDP. \qquad R^2 = 0.89 \qquad (8.17)$$
$$(5,700) \quad (0.013)$$

$$\frac{\widehat{MANU}}{POP} = 612\frac{1}{POP} + 0.182\frac{GDP}{POP}. \quad R^2 = 0.70 \qquad (8.18)$$
$$(1,370) \quad (0.016)$$

$$\frac{\widehat{MANU}}{GDP} = 0.189 + 533\frac{1}{GDP}. \qquad R^2 = 0.02 \qquad (8.19)$$
$$(0.019) \ (841)$$

First, note that the estimate of the coefficient of GDP is much the same in the three regressions: 0.194, 0.182, and 0.189 (remember that it becomes the intercept when scaling through by the X variable). One would not expect dramatic shifts since heteroscedasticity does not give rise to bias. The estimator in the third estimate should have the smallest variance and therefore ought to have a tendency to be the most accurate. Perhaps surprisingly, its standard error is the largest, but then the standard errors in the first two regressions should be disregarded because they are invalidated by the heteroscedasticity.

In this model the intercept does not have any sensible economic interpretation. In any case its estimate in the third equation, where it has become the coefficient of $1/GDP$, is not significantly different from 0. The only apparent problem with the third model is that R^2 is very low. We will return to this in the next subsection.

Nonlinear models

Heteroscedasticity, or perhaps apparent heteroscedasticity, may be a consequence of misspecifying the model mathematically. Suppose that the true model is nonlinear, for example

$$Y = \beta_1 X^{\beta_2} v, \qquad (8.20)$$

with (for sake of argument) β_1 and β_2 positive so that Y is an increasing function of X. The multiplicative disturbance term v has the effect of increasing or reducing Y by a random proportion. Suppose that the probability distribution of v is the same for all observations. This implies, for example, that the probability of a 5 percent increase or decrease in Y due to its effects is just the same when X is small as when X is large. However, in absolute terms a 5 percent increase has a larger effect on Y when X is large than when X is small. If Y is plotted against

X, the scatter of observations will therefore tend to be more widely dispersed about the true relationship as X increases, and a linear regression of Y on X may therefore exhibit heteroscedasticity.

The solution, of course, is to run a logarithmic regression instead:

$$\log Y = \log \beta_1 + \beta_2 \log X + \log v. \tag{8.21}$$

Not only would this be a more appropriate mathematical specification, but it makes the regression model homoscedastic. $\log v$ now affects the dependent variable, $\log Y$, additively, so the absolute size of its effect is independent of the magnitude of $\log X$.

Figure 8.7 shows the logarithm of manufacturing output plotted against the logarithm of GDP using the data in Table 8.1. At first sight at least, the plot does not appear to exhibit heteroscedasticity. Logarithmic regressions using the sub-samples of eleven countries with smallest and greatest GDP yield residual sums of squares 2.14 and 1.04, respectively. In this case the conventional Goldfeld–Quandt test is superfluous. Since the second *RSS* is *smaller* than the first, it cannot be significantly *greater*. However the Goldfeld–Quandt test can also be used to test for heteroscedasticity where the standard deviation of the distribution of the disturbance term is inversely proportional to the size of the X variable. The F statistic is the same, with RSS_1 and RSS_2 interchanged. In the present case the F statistic if 2.06, which is lower than the critical value of F at the 5 percent level, and we do not reject the null hypothesis of homoscedasticity. Running the regression with the complete sample, we obtain (standard errors in parentheses):

$$\widehat{\log MANU} = -1.694 + 0.999 \log GDP \quad R^2 = 0.90 \tag{8.22}$$
$$(0.785) \quad (0.066)$$

implying that the elasticity of *MANU* with respect to *GDP* is equal to 1.

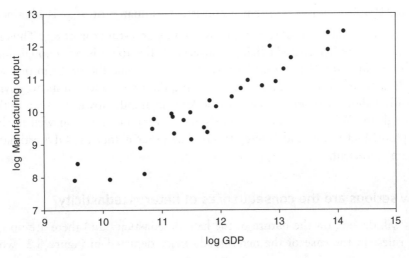

Figure 8.7

We now have two models free from heteroscedasticity, (8.19) and (8.22). The latter might seem more satisfactory, given that it has a very high R^2 and (8.19) a very low one, but in fact, in this particular case, they happen to be equivalent. (8.22) is telling us that manufacturing output increases proportionally with GDP in the cross-section of countries in the sample. In other words, manufacturing output accounts for a constant proportion of GDP. To work out this proportion, we rewrite the equation as

$$\widehat{MANU} = e^{-1.694}GDP^{0.99} = 0.184GDP^{0.999}. \tag{8.23}$$

(8.19) is telling us that the ratio $MANU/GDP$ is effectively a constant, since the $1/GDP$ term appears to be redundant, and that the constant is 0.189. Hence in substance the interpretations coincide.

White's heteroscedasticity-consistent standard errors

It can be shown that the population variance of the slope coefficient in a simple OLS regression with a heteroscedastic disturbance term is given by

$$\sigma^2_{b_2^{OLS}} = \frac{\sum_{i=1}^{n} w_i \sigma^2_{u_i}}{n\text{Var}(X)}, \tag{8.24}$$

where $\sigma^2_{u_i}$ is the variance of the disturbance term in observation i and w_i, its weight in the numerator, is given by

$$w_i = \frac{(X_i - \bar{X})^2}{\sum_{i=1}^{n} (X_j - \bar{X})^2}. \tag{8.25}$$

White (1980) demonstrated that a consistent estimator of $\sigma^2_{b_2^{OLS}}$ is obtained if the squared residual in observation i is used as an estimator of $\sigma^2_{u_i}$. Thus in a situation where heteroscedasticity is suspected, but there is not enough information to identify its nature, it is possible to overcome the problem of biased standard errors, at least in large samples, and the t tests and F tests are asymptotically valid. Two points, need to be kept in mind, however. One is that, although the White estimator is consistent, it may not perform well in finite samples (MacKinnon and White, 1985). The other is that the OLS estimators remain inefficient.

How serious are the consequences of heteroscedasticity?

This will depend on the nature of the heteroscedasticity and there are no general rules. In the case of the heteroscedasticity depicted in Figure 8.3, where the standard deviation of the disturbance term is proportional to X and the values of X are the integers from 5 to 44, the population variance of the OLS estimator of the slope coefficient is approximately double that of the estimator using equation (8.13), where the heteroscedasticity has been eliminated by dividing through by X. Further, the standard errors of the OLS estimators are underestimated, giving a misleading impression of the precision of the OLS coefficients.

Exercises

8.5   The researcher mentioned in Exercise 8.1 runs the following regressions as alternative specifications of her model (standard errors in parentheses):

$$\frac{\hat{I}}{P} = -0.03\frac{1}{P} - 0.69\frac{G}{P} + 0.34\frac{Y}{P}. \quad R^2 = 0.97 \tag{1}$$
$$\quad\quad (0.28)\quad (0.16)\quad\quad (0.03)$$

$$\frac{\hat{I}}{Y} = 0.39 + 0.03\frac{1}{Y} - 0.93\frac{G}{Y}. \quad R^2 = 0.78 \tag{2}$$
$$\quad\quad (0.04)\ (0.42)\quad\ (0.22)$$

$$\widehat{\log I} = -2.44 - 0.63\log G + 1.60\log Y. \quad R^2 = 0.98 \tag{3}$$
$$\quad\quad (0.26)\ (0.12)\quad\quad\ (0.12)$$

She sorts the sample by Y/P, G/Y, and $\log Y$, respectively, and in each case runs the regression again for the subsamples of observations with the eleven smallest and eleven greatest values of the sorting variable. The residual sums of squares are as shown in the table:

	11 smallest	11 largest
(1)	1.43	12.63
(2)	0.0223	0.0155
(3)	0.573	0.155

Perform a Goldfeld–Quandt test for each model specification and discuss the merits of each specification. Is there evidence that investment is an inverse function of government expenditure?

8.6   Using your *EAEF* data set, repeat Exercise 8.2 with *LGEARN* as the dependent variable. Is there evidence that this is a preferable specification?

8.7* Repeat Exercise 8.4, using the Goldfeld–Quandt test to investigate whether scaling by population or by GDP, or whether running the regression in logarithmic form, would eliminate the heteroscedasticity. Compare the results of regressions using the entire sample and the alternative specifications.

9 Stochastic regressors and measurement errors

In the basic least squares regression model, it is assumed that the explanatory variables are nonstochastic. This is typically an unrealistic assumption, and it is important to know the consequences of relaxing it. We shall see that in some contexts we can continue to use OLS, but in others, for example when one or more explanatory variables are subject to measurement error, it is a biased and inconsistent estimator. The chapter ends by introducing an alternative technique, instrumental variables estimation, that may have more desirable properties.

9.1 Stochastic regressors

So far we have assumed that the regressors—the explanatory variables—in the regression model are nonstochastic. This means that they do not have random components and that their values in the sample are fixed and unaffected by the way the sample is generated. Perhaps the best example of a nonstochastic variable is time, which, as we will see when we come to time-series analysis, is sometimes included in the regression model as a proxy for variables that are difficult to measure, such as technical progress or changes in tastes. Nonstochastic explanatory variables are actually unusual in regression analysis. In the *EAEF* data sets provided for practical work, there are similar numbers of individuals with different amounts of schooling, but the numbers do vary from sample to sample and hence when an earnings function is fitted it has to be conceded that the schooling variable has a random component. However, if stratified random sampling has been used to generate a sample, then the variable that has been used for stratification may be nonstochastic. For example, the sex variable in the *EAEF* data sets is nonstochastic because by construction each sample has exactly 325 males and 245 females. But such examples are relatively uncommon and nearly always confined to dummy variables.

The reason for making the nonstochasticity assumption has been the technical one of simplifying the analysis of the properties of the regression estimators. For example, we saw that in the regression model

$$Y = \beta_1 + \beta_2 X + u, \tag{9.1}$$

the OLS estimator of the slope coefficient may be decomposed as follows:

$$b_2 = \frac{\text{Cov}(X, Y)}{\text{Var}(X)} = \beta_2 + \frac{\text{Cov}(X, u)}{\text{Var}(X)}. \tag{9.2}$$

Now, if X is nonstochastic, so is $\text{Var}(X)$, and the expected value of the error term can be written $E[\text{Cov}(X, u)]/\text{Var}(X)$. Furthermore, if X is nonstochastic, $E[\text{Cov}(X, u)]$ is 0. Hence we have no trouble proving that b_2 is an unbiased estimator of β_2. Although a proof was not supplied, the nonstochasticity assumption was also used in deriving the expression for the population variance of the coefficient.

Fortunately, the desirable properties of the OLS estimators remain unchanged even if the explanatory variables have stochastic components, provided that these components are distributed independently of the disturbance term, and provided that their distributions do not depend on the parameters β_1, β_2, or σ_u. We will demonstrate the unbiasedness and consistency properties and as usual take efficiency on trust.

Unbiasedness

If X is stochastic, $\text{Var}(X)$ cannot be treated as a scalar, so we cannot rewrite $E[\text{Cov}(X, u)/\text{Var}(X)]$ as $E[\text{Cov}(X, u)]/\text{Var}(X)$. Hence the previous proof of unbiasedness is blocked. However, we can find another route by decomposing the error term:

$$
\begin{aligned}
\frac{\text{Cov}(X, u)}{\text{Var}(X)} &= \frac{\dfrac{1}{n} \displaystyle\sum_{i=1}^{n} (X_i - \overline{X})(u_i - \overline{u})}{\text{Var}(X)} \\
&= \frac{1}{n} \sum_{i=1}^{n} \left(\frac{X_i - (\overline{X})}{\text{Var}(X)} \right)(u_i - \overline{u}) \\
&= \frac{1}{n} \sum_{i=1}^{n} f(X_i)(u_i - \overline{u}),
\end{aligned} \tag{9.3}
$$

where $f(X_i) = (X_i - \overline{X})/\text{Var}(X)$. Now, if X and u are independently distributed, $E[f(X_i)(u_i - \overline{u})]$ may be decomposed as the product of $E[f(x_i)]$ and $E(u_i - \overline{u})$ (see the definition of independence in the Review). Hence

$$E[f(X_i)(u_i - \overline{u})] = E[f(X_i)]E(u_i - \overline{u}) = E[f(X_i)] \times 0, \tag{9.4}$$

since $E(u_i)$ is 0 in each observation, by assumption. (This implies, of course, that $E(\overline{u})$ is also 0.) Hence, when we take the expectation of $\dfrac{1}{n} \displaystyle\sum_{i=1}^{n} f(X_i)(u_i - \overline{u})$, each term within the summation has expected value 0. Thus the error term as a whole has expected value 0 and b_2 is an unbiased estimator of β_2.

Consistency

We know that, in general, plim (A/B) is equal to $\text{plim}(A)/\text{plim}(B)$, where A and B are any two stochastic quantities, provided that both $\text{plim}(A)$ and $\text{plim}(B)$ exist and that $\text{plim}(B)$ is nonzero (see the Review; 'plim' simply means 'the limiting value as the sample size becomes large'). We also know that sample expressions tend to their population counterparts as the sample size becomes large, so plim $\text{Cov}(X, u)$ is the population covariance of X and u and plim $\text{Var}(X)$ is σ_X^2, the population variance of X. If X and u are independent, the population covariance of X and u is 0 and hence

$$\text{plim } b_2 = \beta_2 + \frac{\text{plim Cov}(X, u)}{\text{plim Var}(X)} = \beta_2 + \frac{0}{\sigma_X^2} = \beta_2. \tag{9.5}$$

9.2 The consequences of measurement errors

It frequently happens in economics that, when you are investigating a relationship, the variables involved have been measured defectively. For example, surveys often contain errors caused by the person being interviewed not remembering properly or not understanding the question correctly. However, misreporting is not the only source of inaccuracy. It sometimes happens that you have defined a variable in your model in a certain way, but the available data correspond to a slightly different definition. Friedman's critique of the conventional consumption function, discussed in Section 9.3, is a famous case of this.

Measurement errors in the explanatory variable(s)

Let us suppose that a variable Y depends on a variable Z according to the relationship

$$Y_i = \beta_1 + \beta_2 Z_i + v_i, \tag{9.6}$$

where v is a disturbance term with mean 0 and variance σ_v^2, distributed independently of Z. We shall suppose that Z cannot be measured absolutely accurately, and we shall use X to denote its measured value. In observation i, X_i is equal to the true value, Z_i, plus the measurement error, w_i:

$$X_i = Z_i + w_i. \tag{9.7}$$

We shall suppose that w has mean 0 and variance σ_w^2, that Z has population variance σ_Z^2, and that w is distributed independently of Z and v.

Substituting from (9.7) into (9.6), we obtain

$$Y_i = \beta_1 + \beta_2(X_i - w_i) + v_i = \beta_1 + \beta_2 X_i + v_i - \beta_2 w_i. \tag{9.8}$$

This equation has two random components, the original disturbance term v and the measurement error (multiplied by $-\beta_2$). Together they form a composite disturbance term, which we shall call u:

$$u_i = v_i - \beta_2 w_i. \tag{9.9}$$

(9.8) may then be written

$$Y_i = \beta_1 + \beta_2 X_i + u_i. \tag{9.10}$$

You have your data on Y (which, for the time being, we shall assume has been measured accurately) and X, and you unsuspectingly regress Y on X.

As usual, the regression coefficient b_2 is given by

$$b_2 = \frac{\text{Cov}(X, Y)}{\text{Var}(X)} = \beta_2 + \frac{\text{Cov}(X, u)}{\text{Var}(X)}. \tag{9.11}$$

Looking at the error term, we can see that it is going to behave badly. By virtue of (9.7) and (9.9), both X_i and u_i depend on w_i. The population covariance between X and u is nonzero and so b_2 is an inconsistent estimator of β_2. Even if you had a very large sample, your estimate would be inaccurate. In the limit it would underestimate β_2 by an amount

$$\frac{\sigma_w^2}{\sigma_Z^2 + \sigma_w^2} \beta_2. \tag{9.12}$$

A proof of this is given below. First we will note its implications, which are fairly obvious. The bigger the population variance of the measurement error, relative to the population variance of Z, the bigger will be the bias. For example, if σ_w^2 were equal to $0.25\ \sigma_Z^2$, the bias would be

$$-\frac{0.25\ \sigma_Z^2}{1.25\ \sigma_Z^2} \beta_2 \tag{9.13}$$

which is $-0.2\beta_2$. Even if the sample were very large, your estimate would tend to be 20 percent below the true value if β_2 were positive, 20 percent above it if β_2 were negative.

Figure 9.1 illustrates how measurement errors give rise to biased regression coefficients, using the model represented by (9.6) and (9.7). The circles represent the observations on Z and Y, the values of Y being generated by a process of type (9.6), the true relationship being given by the dashed line. The solid markers represent the observations on X and Y, the measurement error in each case causing a horizontal shift marked by a dotted line. Positive measurement errors tend to cause the observations to lie under the true relationship, and negative ones tend to cause the observations to lie above it. This causes the scatter of observations on X and Y to look flatter than that for Z and Y and the best-fitting regression line will tend to underestimate the slope of the true relationship. The greater the variance of the measurement error relative to that of Z, the greater will be the flattening effect and the worse the bias.

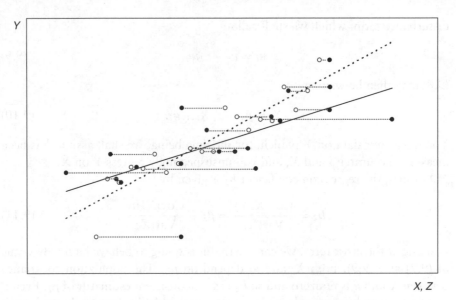

Figure 9.1 Effect of errors of measurement of the explanatory variable

Imperfect proxy variables

In Chapter 7 it was shown that, if we are unable to obtain data on one of the explanatory variables in a regression model and we run the regression without it, the coefficients of the other variables will in general be biased and their standard errors will be invalid. However, in Section 7.4 we saw that if we are able to find a perfect proxy for the missing variable, that is, another variable that has an exact linear relationship with it, and use that in its place in the regression, most of the regression results will be saved. Thus, the coefficients of the other variables will not be biased, their standard errors and associated t tests will be valid, and R^2 will be the same as if we had been able to include the unmeasurable variable directly. We will not be able to obtain an estimate of the coefficient of the latter, but the t statistic for the proxy variable will be the same as the t statistic for the unmeasurable variable.

Unfortunately, it is unusual to find a perfect proxy. Generally the best that you can hope for is a proxy that is approximately linearly related to the missing variable. The consequences of using an imperfect proxy instead of a perfect one are parallel to those of using a variable subject to measurement error instead of one that is free from it. It will cause the regression coefficients to be biased, the standard errors to be invalid, and so on, after all.

You may nevertheless justify the use of a proxy if you have reason to believe that the degree of imperfection is not so great as to cause the bias to be serious and the standard errors to be misleading. Since there is normally no way of testing whether the degree of imperfection is great or small, the case for using a proxy has to be made on subjective grounds in the context of the model.

Proof of the inconsistency expression

Since X and u are not distributed independently of each other, there is no simple way of summarizing the behavior of the term $\text{Cov}(X,u)/\text{Var}(X)$ in small samples. We cannot even obtain an expression for its expected value. Rewriting it as (9.3) does not help because $E[f(X_i)(u_i-\bar{u})]$ cannot be decomposed as $E[f(X_i)E(u_i-\bar{u})]$. The most we can do is to predict how it would behave if the sample were very large. It will tend to plim $\text{Cov}(X,u)$ divided by plim $\text{Var}(X)$. We will look at these separately.

Using the definitions of X and u, the sample variance between them may be decomposed as follows:

$$\text{Cov}(X,u) = \text{Cov}[(Z+w),(v-\beta_2 w)]$$
$$= \text{Cov}(Z,v) + \text{Cov}(w,v) - \text{Cov}(Z,\beta_2 w) - \text{Cov}(w,\beta_2 w), \quad (9.14)$$

using the covariance rules. In large samples, sample covariances and variances tend towards their population counterparts. Since we have assumed that v and w are distributed independently of each other and Z, the population covariances of v and w, Z and v, and Z and $\beta_2 w$ are all 0. This leaves us with the population covariance of w and $\beta_2 w$, which is $\beta_2\sigma_w^2$. Hence

$$\text{plim Cov}(X,u) = -\beta_2\sigma_w^2. \quad (9.15)$$

Now for plim $\text{Var}(X)$. Since X is equal to $(Z+w)$,

$$\text{plim Var}(X) = \text{plim Var}(Z+w)$$
$$= \text{plim Var}(Z) + \text{plim Var}(w) + 2\,\text{plim Cov}(Z,w)$$
$$= \sigma_Z^2 + \sigma_w^2. \quad (9.16)$$

The sample variances tend to their population counterparts and the sample covariance tends to 0 if Z and w are distributed independently. Thus

$$\text{plim } b_2^{\text{OLS}} = \beta_2 + \frac{\text{plim Cov}(X,u)}{\text{plim Var}(X)} = \beta_2 - \frac{\beta_2\sigma_w^2}{\sigma_Z^2+\sigma_w^2}. \quad (9.17)$$

Note that we have assumed that w is distributed independently of v and Z. The first assumption is usually plausible because in general there is no reason for any measurement error in an explanatory variable to be correlated with the disturbance term. However, we may have to relax the second assumption. If we do, b_2^{OLS} remains inconsistent, but the expression for the bias becomes more complex. See Exercise 9.4.

Measurement errors in the dependent variable

Measurement errors in the dependent variable do not matter as much. In practice they can be thought of as contributing to the disturbance term. They are undesirable, because anything that increases the noise in the model will tend to make the regression estimates less accurate, but they will not cause the regression estimates to be biased.

Let the true value of the dependent variable be Q, and the true relationship be

$$Q_i = \beta_1 + \beta_2 X_i + v_i, \tag{9.18}$$

where v is a disturbance term. If Y_i is the measured value of the dependent variable in observation i, and r_i is the measurement error,

$$Y_i = Q_i + r_i. \tag{9.19}$$

Hence the relationship between the observed value of the dependent variable and X is given by

$$Y_i - r_i = \beta_1 + \beta_2 X_i + v_i, \tag{9.20}$$

which may be rewritten

$$Y_i = \beta_1 + \beta_2 X_i + u_i, \tag{9.21}$$

where u is the composite disturbance term $(v + r)$.

The only difference from the usual model is that the disturbance term in (9.21) has two components: the original disturbance term and the error in measuring Y. The important thing is that the explanatory variable X has not been affected. Hence OLS still yields unbiased estimates, provided that X is nonstochastic or that it is distributed independently of v and r. The population variance of the slope coefficient will be given by

$$\sigma_{b_2}^2 = \frac{\sigma_u^2}{n\sigma_X^2} = \frac{\sigma_v^2 + \sigma_r^2}{n\sigma_X^2} \tag{9.22}$$

and so will be greater than it would have been in the absence of measurement error, reducing the precision of the estimator. The standard errors remain valid but will be larger than they would have been in the absence of the measurement error, reflecting the loss of precision.

Exercises

9.1 In a certain industry, firms relate their stocks of finished goods, Y, to their expected annual sales, X^e, according to a linear relationship

$$Y = \beta_1 + \beta_2 X^e.$$

Actual sales, X, differ from expected sales by a random quantity u, that is distributed with mean 0 and constant variance:

$$X = X^e + u.$$

u is distributed independently of X^e. An investigator has data on Y and X (but not on X^e) for a cross-section of firms in the industry. Describe the problems that would be encountered if OLS were used to estimate β_1 and β_2, regressing Y on X.

9.2   In a similar industry, firms relate their *intended* stocks of finished goods, Y^*, to their expected annual sales, X^e, according to a linear relationship

$$Y^* = \beta_1 + \beta_2 X^e.$$

Actual sales, X, differ from expected sales by a random quantity u, which is distributed with mean 0 and constant variance:

$$X = X^e + u.$$

u is distributed independently of X^e. Since unexpected sales lead to a reduction in stocks, actual stocks are given by

$$Y = Y^* - u.$$

An investigator has data on Y and X (but not on Y^* or X^e) for a cross-section of firms in the industry. Describe analytically the problems that would be encountered if OLS were used to estimate β_1 and β_2, regressing Y on X. [*Note*: You are warned that the standard expression for measurement error bias is not valid in this case.]

9.3* A variable Q is determined by the model

$$Q = \beta_1 + \beta_2 X + v,$$

where X is a variable and v is a disturbance term that satisfies the Gauss–Markov conditions. The dependent variable is subject to measurement error and is measured as Y where

$$Y = Q + r$$

and r is the measurement error, distributed independently of v. Describe analytically the consequences of using OLS to fit this model if

(1) The expected value of r is not equal to 0 (but r is distributed independently of Q),

(2) r is not distributed independently of Q (but its expected value is 0).

9.4* A variable Y is determined by the model

$$Y = \beta_1 + \beta_2 Z + v,$$

where Z is a variable and v is a disturbance term that satisfies the Gauss–Markov conditions. The explanatory variable is subject to measurement error and is measured as X where

$$X = Z + w$$

and w is the measurement error, distributed independently of v.

Describe analytically the consequences of using OLS to fit this model if

(1) The expected value of w is not equal to 0 (but w is distributed independently of Z),

(2) w is not distributed independently of Z (but its expected value is 0).

9.5* A researcher investigating the shadow economy using international cross-section data for twenty-five countries hypothesizes that consumer expenditure on shadow goods and services, Q, is related to total consumer expenditure, Z, by the relationship

$$Q = \beta_1 + \beta_2 Z + v,$$

where v is a disturbance term that satisfies the Gauss–Markov conditions. Q is part of Z and any error in the estimation of Q affects the estimate of Z by the same amount. Hence

$$Y_i = Q_i + w_i$$

and

$$X_i = Z_i + w_i,$$

where Y_i is the estimated value of Q_i, X_i is the estimated value of Z_i, and w_i is the measurement error affecting both variables in observation i. It is assumed that the expected value of w is 0 and that v and w are distributed independently of Z and of each other.

(1) Derive an expression for the large-sample bias in the estimate of β_2 when OLS is used to regress Y on X, and determine its sign if this is possible. [*Note*: You are warned that the standard expression for measurement error bias is not valid in this case.]

Sample	b_1	s.e.(b_1)	b_2	s.e.(b_2)	R^2
1	−0.85	1.09	0.42	0.07	0.61
2	−0.37	1.45	0.36	0.10	0.36
3	−2.85	0.88	0.49	0.06	0.75
4	−2.21	1.59	0.54	0.10	0.57
5	−1.08	1.43	0.47	0.09	0.55
6	−1.32	1.39	0.51	0.08	0.64
7	−3.12	1.12	0.54	0.07	0.71
8	−0.64	0.95	0.45	0.06	0.74
9	0.57	0.89	0.38	0.05	0.69
10	−0.54	1.26	0.40	0.08	0.50

(2) In a Monte Carlo experiment based on the model above, the true relationship between Q and Z is

$$Q = 2.0 + 0.2Z.$$

A sample of twenty-five observations is generated using the integers $1, 2, \ldots, 25$ as data for Z. The variance of Z is 52.0. A normally distributed random variable with mean 0 and variance 25 is used to generate the values of the measurement error in the dependent and explanatory variables. The results with ten samples are summarized in the table. Comment on the results, stating whether or not they support your theoretical analysis.

(3) The figure shows plots the points (Q, Z) and (Y, X) for the first sample, with each (Q, Z) point linked to the corresponding (Y, X) point. Comment on this graph, given your answers to parts (1) and (2).

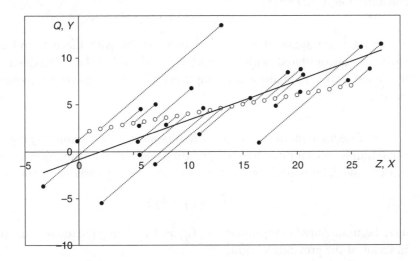

9.3 Friedman's critique of the conventional consumption function

Now we come to the most celebrated application of measurement error analysis in the whole of economic theory: Friedman's critique of the use of OLS to fit a consumption function (Friedman, 1957). We discuss here Friedman's analysis of the problem and in Section 12.3 we will discuss his solution.

In Friedman's model, the consumption of individual (or household) i is related, not to actual (measured) current income Y_i, but to permanent income, which will be denoted Y_i^P. Permanent income is to be thought of as a medium-term notion of income: the amount that the individual can more or less depend on for the foreseeable future, taking into account possible fluctuations. It is subjectively determined by recent experience and by expectations about the future, and because it is subjective it cannot be measured directly. Actual income at any moment may be higher or lower than permanent income depending on the influence of short-run random factors. The difference between actual and permanent income caused by these factors is described as transitory income, Y_i^T. Thus

$$Y_i = Y_i^P + Y_i^T. \tag{9.23}$$

In the same way, Friedman makes a distinction between actual consumption, C_i, and permanent consumption, C_i^P. Permanent consumption is the level of consumption justified by the level of permanent income. Actual consumption may differ from it as special, unforeseen circumstances arise (unanticipated medical bills, for example) or as a consequence of impulse purchases. The difference between actual and permanent consumption is described as transitory consumption, C_i^T. Thus

$$C_i = C_i^P + C_i^T. \tag{9.24}$$

Y_i^T and C_i^T are assumed to be random variables with mean 0 and constant variance, uncorrelated with Y_i^P and C_i^P and each other. Friedman further hypothesizes that permanent consumption is directly proportional to permanent income:

$$C_i^P = \beta_2 Y_i^P. \tag{9.25}$$

If the Friedman model is correct, what happens if you ignorantly try to fit the usual simple consumption function, relating measured consumption to measured income? Well, both the dependent and the explanatory variables in the regression

$$\hat{C}_i = b_1 + b_2 Y_i \tag{9.26}$$

have been measured inappropriately, C_i^T and Y_i^T being the measurement errors. In terms of the previous section,

$$Z_i = Y_i^P, \quad w_i = Y_i^T, \quad Q_i = C_i^P, \quad r_i = C_i^T. \tag{9.27}$$

As we saw in that section, the only effect of the measurement error in the dependent variable is to increase the variance of the disturbance term. The use of the wrong income concept is more serious. It causes the estimate of β_2 to be inconsistent. From (9.11), we can see that in large samples

$$\text{plim } b_2 = \beta_2 - \frac{\sigma_{Y^T}^2}{\sigma_{Y^P}^2 + \sigma_{Y^T}^2}\beta_2, \tag{9.28}$$

where $\sigma_{Y^T}^2$ is the population variance of Y^T and $\sigma_{Y^P}^2$ is the population variance of Y^P. It implies that, even in large samples, the apparent marginal propensity to consume (your estimate b_2) will be lower than the value of β_2 in the true relationship (9.25). The size of the bias depends on the ratio of the variance of transitory income to that of permanent income. It will be highest for those occupations whose earnings are most subject to fluctuations. An obvious example is farming. Friedman's model predicts that, even if farmers have the same β_2 as the rest of the population, an OLS estimate of their marginal propensity to consume will be relatively low, and this is consistent with the facts (Friedman, 1957: 57 ff.).

An illustration

The Friedman analysis will be illustrated with a Monte Carlo experiment. It was supposed that a sample of twenty individuals had permanent incomes 2000, 2100, 2200, ..., 3900. It was also assumed that each individual had transitory income equal to 200 times a random number drawn from a normal population with mean 0 and unit variance. Measured income for each individual was the sum of permanent and transitory income. It was assumed that the true value of β_2 was 0.9, so that permanent consumption was 0.9 times the corresponding permanent income. There was no provision for a transitory component for consumption, so measured consumption was equal to permanent consumption. When measured consumption was regressed on measured income, the result was (standard errors in parentheses)

$$\hat{C} = 443 + 0.75Y. \quad R^2 = 0.89 \tag{9.29}$$
$$\text{(179)} \quad \text{(0.06)}$$

As anticipated, the estimated marginal propensity to consume is below the true value. Indeed, if you construct a 95 percent confidence interval using the regression results, the true value lies outside it and would therefore be rejected at the 5 percent significance level. With 18 degrees of freedom, the critical level of t is 2.10, so the confidence interval would be calculated as

$$0.75 - 2.10 \times 0.06 \leq \beta_2 \leq 0.75 + 2.10 \times 0.06, \tag{9.30}$$

that is,

$$0.62 \leq \beta_2 \leq 0.88. \tag{9.31}$$

Therefore you would make a Type I error. Actually, the presence of measurement errors makes the standard error of Y, and hence the confidence interval, invalid. A further side effect is that the constant term, which ought to have been 0 since there was no intercept in the model, appears to be significantly positive at the 5 percent level. The experiment was repeated nine further times and the results are summarized in Table 9.1, set A.

b_2 clearly gives a downward-biased estimate of the marginal propensity to consume. It is lower than the true value of 0.90 in nine of the ten samples. We will check whether the results support the analysis leading to equation (9.28).

Table 9.1 Experiments with measurement error

Sample	Experiment A				Experiment B			
	b_1	s.e.(b_1)	b_2	s.e.(b_2)	b_1	s.e.(b_1)	b_2	s.e.(b_2)
1	443	179	0.75	0.06	1001	251	0.56	0.08
2	152	222	0.83	0.07	755	357	0.62	0.11
3	101	222	0.89	0.08	756	376	0.68	0.13
4	195	179	0.83	0.06	668	290	0.66	0.09
5	319	116	0.78	0.04	675	179	0.64	0.06
6	371	200	0.78	0.07	982	289	0.57	0.10
7	426	161	0.74	0.05	918	229	0.56	0.07
8	−146	275	0.93	0.09	625	504	0.66	0.16
9	467	128	0.74	0.04	918	181	0.58	0.06
10	258	153	0.80	0.05	679	243	0.65	0.08

In this example $\sigma^2_{Y^T}$ is 40,000, since Y^T has standard deviation 200. We will assume that in large samples Y^P takes the values 2,000, 2,100,..., 3,900 with equal probability, and hence that $\sigma^2_{Y^P}$ is the variance of these numbers, which is 332,500. Hence in large samples β_2 would be underestimated by an amount

$$\frac{\sigma^2_{Y^T}}{\sigma^2_{Y^P} + \sigma^2_{Y^T}}\beta_2 = \frac{40,000}{332,500 + 40,000} \times 0.90 = 0.11 \times 0.90 = 0.10. \qquad (9.32)$$

It should be stressed that this is valid only for large samples, and that we are not entitled to say anything about the behavior of b_2 in small samples. However, in this case we can see that it does in fact provide a good guide. Looking at the estimates of b_2 in the ten samples, we see that they appear to be randomly distributed about 0.80, instead of 0.90, and that there is thus a downwards bias of about 0.10.

A consequence of the underestimation of β_2 is that β_1 is overestimated, appearing to be positive even though its true value is 0. Indeed in four cases a t test would indicate that it is significantly different from 0 at the 5 percent significance level. However, in these conditions the t tests are invalid because the failure of the fourth Gauss–Markov condition to be satisfied causes the standard errors, and hence the t statistics, to be estimated wrongly.

What would happen if we increased the variance of Y^T, keeping everything else the same? In set B in Table 9.1 the original random numbers were multiplied by 400 instead of 200, so $\sigma^2_{Y^T}$ is now 160,000 instead of 40,000. The error term in expression (9.28) is now equal to 160,000/(332,500 + 160,000), which is 0.32, so we would anticipate that b_2 would tend to (0.9 − 0.32 × 0.9), which is 0.61, in large samples. Again, we see that this is a good guide to the actual behavior of b_2, even though each sample has only 20 observations. As should be predicted, the estimates of β_1 are even greater than in set A.

Policy implications

There are two separate and opposite implications for the multiplier. First, if Friedman is right, a regression of actual consumption on actual income will yield an underestimate of the marginal propensity to consume and hence an underestimate of the multiplier. In the illustration in the previous section, the true value of β_2 was 0.90, so the true value of the multiplier was 10. But in set A the estimate of β_2 was tending to 0.80, implying a multiplier of only 5. In set B, it would have been lower still. The estimate of β_2 was tending to 0.61, giving a multiplier of 2.6.

If the government underestimates the multiplier, it will underestimate the effects of fiscal policy. For example, an increase in government expenditure intended to reduce unemployment may in fact lead to an excessive increase in effective demand and an increase in the rate of inflation.

The second implication is that the multiplier applies only to that part of a change in income that is perceived as permanent, because (according to Friedman) consumption depends only on permanent income. Thus, if the increase in government expenditure is thought to be temporary, it will not affect consumption at all (as a first approximation), and the multiplier associated with it will be 1.

These remarks must however be qualified by a consideration of the form in which individuals hold their savings. We have implicitly assumed so far that they take them in the form of financial assets (bank deposits, bonds, and so on). However, in the Friedman model, expenditure on consumer durables is considered to be a form of saving. An increase in transitory income will not be spent on ordinary consumer goods, but it may be partly saved in the form of purchases of consumer durables, and the increase in the demand for these will give rise to a multiplier effect. The multiplier for transitory income may not be so low after all.

This discussion has been confined to consumption theory, the original application of Friedman's concept of permanent income. But the concept can be, and has been, used in other fields. In particular, in monetary theory it can be argued that the transactions demand for cash should be related to permanent, rather than actual, income, and in investment theory it can be argued that the accelerator should be related to changes in permanent income rather than changes in actual income. The seminal contributions are Friedman (1959) and Eisner (1967).

Exercises

9.6   In a certain economy the variance of transitory income is 0.5 that of permanent income, the propensity to consume nondurables out of permanent income is 0.6, and there is no expenditure on durables. What would be the value of the multiplier derived from a naïve regression of consumption on income, and what would be the true value?

9.7 In his definition of permanent consumption, Friedman includes the consumption of services provided by durables. Purchases of durables are classified as a form of saving. In an economy similar to that in Exercise 9.6, the variance of transitory income is 0.5 that of permanent income, the propensity to consume nondurables out of permanent income is 0.6, and half of current saving (actual income minus expenditure on nondurables) takes the form of expenditure on durables. What would be the value of the multiplier derived from a naïve regression of consumption on income, and what would be the true value?

9.4 Instrumental variables

What can be done about measurement errors? If the measurement errors are due to inaccuracy in the recording of the data, not much. If they arise because the variable being measured is conceptually different from the true variable in the relationship, the obvious answer is to attempt to obtain more appropriate data. Often, however, this is not possible. In the case of Friedman's Permanent Income Hypothesis, there is no way of obtaining data directly on permanent income since it is a subjective concept. Sometimes the problem can be sidestepped. Friedman's own approach will be discussed in Section 12.3. Another technique, known as instrumental variables (IV), will be discussed here. IV is a major variation on OLS and it will be of great importance when we come to the fitting of models comprising several simultaneous equations.

Essentially IV consists of semi-replacing a defective explanatory variable with one that is not correlated with the disturbance term. The discussion will be confined to the simple regression case

$$Y_i = \beta_1 + \beta_2 X_i + u_i \tag{9.33}$$

and we shall suppose that for some reason X_i has a random component that depends on u_i. A straightforward OLS regression of Y on X would then lead to inconsistent estimates of the parameters.

Suppose, however, that we can think of another variable Z that is correlated with X but not correlated with u. We shall show that the instrumental variables estimator of β_2, defined as

$$b_2^{IV} = \frac{\text{Cov}(Z, Y)}{\text{Cov}(Z, X)} \tag{9.34}$$

is consistent, provided that σ_{ZX}, the population covariance of Z and X, is nonzero.

Before doing this, it is instructive to compare b_2^{IV} with the OLS estimator, which will be denoted b_2^{OLS}.

$$b_2^{OLS} = \frac{\text{Cov}(X, Y)}{\text{Var}(X)} = \frac{\text{Cov}(X, Y)}{\text{Cov}(X, X)} \tag{9.35}$$

since $\text{Cov}(X, X)$ and $\text{Var}(X)$ are the same thing. The IV estimator, in simple regression analysis, is obtained by substituting the instrument Z for the X in the numerator and for one X (but not both) in the denominator.

Substituting for Y from (9.33), we can expand the expression for b_2^{IV}:

$$
\begin{aligned}
b_2^{IV} &= \frac{\text{Cov}(Z, Y)}{\text{Cov}(Z, X)} = \frac{\text{Cov}(Z, [\beta_1 + \beta_2 X + u])}{\text{Cov}(Z, X)} \\
&= \frac{\text{Cov}(Z, \beta_1) + \text{Cov}(Z, \beta_2 X) + \text{Cov}(Z, u)}{\text{Cov}(Z, X)} \\
&= \beta_2 + \frac{\text{Cov}(Z, u)}{\text{Cov}(Z, X)},
\end{aligned}
\tag{9.36}
$$

since $\text{Cov}(Z, \beta_1)$ is 0 (β_1 being a constant), and $\text{Cov}(Z, \beta_2 X)$ is equal to $\beta_2 \, \text{Cov}(Z, X)$.

We can see therefore that the instrumental variable estimator is equal to the true value plus an error term $\text{Cov}(Z, u)/\text{Cov}(Z, X)$. In large samples, the error term will vanish, for

$$\text{plim} \, b_2^{IV} = \beta_2 + \frac{\text{plim} \, \text{Cov}(Z, u)}{\text{plim} \, \text{Cov}(Z, X)} = \beta_2 + \frac{0}{\sigma_{ZX}} = \beta_2, \tag{9.37}$$

provided that we are correct in supposing that Z is distributed independently of u. Hence in large samples b_2^{IV} will tend to the true value β_2.

Nothing much can be said about the distribution of b_2^{IV} in small samples, but as n increases, the distribution will converge on a normal one with mean β_2 and variance $\sigma_{b_2^{IV}}^2$ given by

$$\sigma_{b_2^{IV}}^2 = \frac{\sigma_u^2}{n\sigma_X^2} \times \frac{1}{r_{XZ}^2}, \tag{9.38}$$

where r_{XZ} is the sample correlation between X and Z.

Compare this with the variance of the OLS estimator:

$$\sigma_{b_2^{OLS}}^2 = \frac{\sigma_u^2}{n\sigma_X^2}. \tag{9.39}$$

The difference is that the variance of b_2^{IV} is multiplied by the factor $1/r_{XZ}^2$. The greater the correlation between X and Z, the smaller will be this factor, and hence the smaller will be the variance of b_2^{IV}.

We are now in a position to state the three requirements of an instrument:

1. It should be correlated with the variable being instrumented, and the higher the correlation, the better, provided that the second requirement is satisfied.

2. It should not be correlated with the disturbance term. If it is stochastic, its random component should be distributed independently of the disturbance term. Otherwise plim $\text{Cov}(Z, u)$ in (9.37) will not be 0. Thus it would not be desirable to use an instrument that is perfectly correlated with X, even if you could find one, because then it would automatically be correlated with u as well and you would still obtain inconsistent estimates.

3. It should not be an explanatory variable in its own right.

What should you do if you cannot find an instrumental variable highly correlated with X? Well, you may wish to stick with OLS after all. If, for example, your criterion for selecting an estimator is its mean square error, you may find that the OLS estimator is preferable to an IV estimator, despite the bias, because its variance is smaller.

Example: Use of IV to fit the Friedman consumption function

The pioneering use of IV in the context of the Friedman permanent income hypothesis is Liviatan (1963). Liviatan had data on the consumption and income of the same 883 households for two consecutive years. We will denote consumption and income in the first year C_1 and Y_1, and in the second year C_2 and Y_2.

Liviatan observed that if Friedman's theory is correct, Y_2 can act as an instrument for Y_1. Obviously it is likely to be highly correlated with Y_1, so the first requirement of a good instrument is satisfied. If the transitory component of measured income is uncorrelated from one year to the next, as hypothesized by Friedman, Y_2 will be uncorrelated with the disturbance term in the relationship between C_1 and Y_1, and so the second condition is satisfied. Finally, C_1 is likely to be related to Y_1 rather than Y_2, so the third condition is satisfied. The instrumental variable estimator is then given by

$$b_2^{IV} = \frac{\text{Cov}(Y_2, C_1)}{\text{Cov}(Y_2, Y_1)}. \tag{9.40}$$

Alternatively, one could use C_2 as an instrument for Y_1. It will be highly correlated with Y_2, and therefore with Y_1, and also not correlated with the disturbance term in the relationship between C_1 and Y_1 if, as Friedman hypothesized, the transitory components of consumption are uncorrelated.

Similarly one could run regressions using the data for year 2, using Y_1 and C_1 as instruments for Y_2. Liviatan tried all four combinations, separating his sample into employees and self-employed. He found that four of the estimates of the marginal propensity to consume were significantly greater than those obtained by straightforward OLS at the 1 percent level; one was significantly greater at the 5 percent level, and in the other three cases the difference was not significant, evidence that on the whole corroborates the permanent income hypothesis. However, the marginal propensity to consume was generally not as high as the average propensities; therefore, his results did not support the hypothesis of a unit elasticity of consumption with respect to permanent income, which is implicit in equation (9.25).

Example: Use of IV to fit an earnings function

In some data sets up to 10 percent of the variance of measured years of schooling is thought to be attributable to measurement error. Accordingly, the coefficient of schooling in an earnings function may be underestimated. The regression output in Table 9.2 gives first the output from an OLS regression of the logarithm of hourly earnings on years of schooling and the $ASVABC$ score, and then the output from an IV regression with mother's years of schooling used as an instrument for years of schooling. SM is likely to be a suitable instrument because it is correlated with S, unlikely to be correlated with the disturbance term, and unlikely to be a direct determinant of earnings.

The coefficient of schooling is much larger in the IV regression, suggesting that measurement error may have led to a downwards bias in its coefficient in the OLS regression. However, note that its standard error is also much larger than in the OLS regression. This is because the correlation between S and SM, 0.36, is not very high. It is possible that the difference in the OLS and IV estimates of the coefficient may be due to chance. We will improve the IV estimation by drawing on a group of family background variables, instead of just SM, to instrument for S, and then we will perform a formal test of the difference in the coefficients.

First, however, some practical notes. The example used here is a multiple regression model, and you should be aware that the expressions for IV coefficients in a multiple regression model are more complex than those in a simple regression model, in the same way that OLS multiple regression coefficients are more complex than OLS simple regression coefficients. However, the expressions are straightforward in a treatment using matrix algebra. A facility for performing IV regressions is a standard feature of all regression applications. A typical procedure is to state the variables for the regression in the usual way and append a list of non-instrumented variables and instrument(s) in parentheses. The output used version 6 of Stata, which departs from this convention in two ways. The command for IV regressions is different from that for OLS regressions ('ivreg' instead of 'reg'), and the list of variables in parentheses is in the form of an equation with the instrumented variable(s) to the left of the = sign and the instruments to the right of it.

Table 9.2

```
. reg LGEARN S ASVABC

    Source |       SS       df       MS                Number of obs =      570
-----------+------------------------------            F( 2,    567) =    57.45
     Model | 25.9166749        2 12.9583374           Prob > F      =   0.0000
  Residual | 127.885218      567 .225547121           R-squared     =   0.1685
-----------+------------------------------            Adj R-squared =   0.1656
     Total | 153.801893      569 .270302096           Root MSE      =   .47492


------------------------------------------------------------------------------
    LGEARN |      Coef.   Std. Err.       t    P>|t|     [95% Conf. Interval]
-----------+------------------------------------------------------------------
         S |   .0544266   .0099018    5.497   0.000      .034978    .0738753
    ASVABC |   .0114733   .0026476    4.333   0.000     .0062729    .0166736
     _cons |   1.118832    .124107    9.015   0.000     .8750665    1.362598
------------------------------------------------------------------------------


. ivreg LGEARN ASVABC (S=SM)

Instrumental variables (2SLS) regression

    Source |       SS       df       MS                Number of obs =      570
-----------+------------------------------            F( 2,    567) =    41.48
     Model | 15.5448371        2 7.77241854           Prob > F      =   0.0000
  Residual | 138.257056      567 .243839604           R-squared     =   0.1011
-----------+------------------------------            Adj R-squared =   0.0979
     Total | 153.801893      569 .270302096           Root MSE      =    .4938


------------------------------------------------------------------------------
    LGEARN |      Coef.   Std. Err.       t    P>|t|     [95% Conf. Interval]
-----------+------------------------------------------------------------------
         S |    .121573   .0564962    2.152   0.032     .0106057    .2325403
    ASVABC |   .0010966   .0090152    0.122   0.903    -.0166106    .0188039
     _cons |   .7313408   .3455687    2.116   0.035     .0525898    1.410092
------------------------------------------------------------------------------
Instrumented:  S
Instruments:   ASVABC SM
```

Multiple instruments

Father's years of schooling, number of siblings, and possession of a library card are other factors that may be associated with years of schooling of the respondent but are not likely to be direct determinants of earnings. Thus we have four potential instruments for S and, for reasons that will be explained in the next chapter, IV estimation is more efficient if they are used as a group rather than individually. To do this, you include all of them in the list of instruments in the regression command. The corresponding regression output is shown in Table 9.3.

Table 9.3

```
. ivreg LGEARN ASVABC (S=SM SF SIBLINGS LIBRARY)

Instrumental variables (2SLS) regression

  Source |       SS       df       MS              Number of obs =     570
---------+------------------------------           F( 2,   567) =   43.58
   Model | 20.3209223      2  10.1604612           Prob > F      =  0.0000
Residual | 133.48097     567  .235416173           R-squared     =  0.1321
---------+------------------------------           Adj R-squared =  0.1291
   Total | 153.801893    569  .270302096           Root MSE      =  .4852


------------------------------------------------------------------------------
  LGEARN |     Coef.   Std. Err.      t    P>|t|     [95% Conf. Interval]
---------+--------------------------------------------------------------------
       S |   .1037467   .0422673     2.455   0.014     .0207272    .1867663
  ASVABC |   .0038515   .0068948     0.559   0.577    -.009691     .0173939
   _cons |   .8342134   .2686343     3.105   0.002     .3065736    1.361853
------------------------------------------------------------------------------
Instrumented:  S
Instruments:   ASVABC SM SF SIBLINGS LIBRARY
```

The smaller standard error indicates that there has been a modest gain in efficiency, but it is still much larger than that for the original OLS regression and it is possible that the difference in the OLS and IV estimates of the coefficient of S is purely random. We will perform a formal test.

The Durbin–Wu–Hausman specification test

Most economic data are subject to some element of measurement error and a recurring issue, as in the present case, is whether it is potentially serious enough to require the use of IV instead of OLS to fit a model. It has been shown that if measurement error is serious, OLS estimates will be inconsistent and IV is to be preferred. However, if there is no measurement error, both OLS and IV will be consistent and OLS will be preferred because it is more efficient. The Durbin–Wu–Hausman specification test (sometimes described as the Hausman test: the standard reference is Hausman (1978), but Durbin (1954) and Wu (1973) made important contributions to its development) can be used in this context to discriminate between the two possibilities. We will assume that the regression model is given by

$$Y = \beta_1 + \beta_2 X_2 + \cdots + \beta_k X_k + u, \qquad (9.41)$$

where one or more of the explanatory variables are potentially subject to measurement error. Under the null hypothesis that there is no measurement error, the OLS and IV coefficients will not be systematically different. The test statistic is based on the differences between the OLS and IV coefficients (all of them, not just those of the variables potentially subject to measurement error) and it has a chi-squared distribution with degrees of freedom equal to the number of instrumented variables under the null hypothesis of no significant difference. Its computation is too complex to be reproduced here and you would be well advised to employ a regression application such as Stata version 6 or EViews version 3 that will do it for you.

We will perform the test for the earnings function example using Stata. We first run the IV regression of the logarithm of earnings on the *ASVABC* score, dummy variables for male sex and black and hispanic ethnicity, and years of schooling instrumented with multiple instruments: mother's and father's years of schooling, number of siblings, and a dummy variable equal to 1 if anyone in the family possessed a library card, 0 otherwise, when the respondent was 14. After this we give the command 'hausman, save'. We then run the corresponding OLS regression and follow with the command 'hausman, constant sigmamore'. This produces the output shown in Table 9.4.

The chi-squared statistic is 1.27, lower than 3.84, the critical value of chi-squared at the 5 percent significance level with one degree of freedom, and so we do not reject the null hypothesis of no difference in the OLS and IV estimates.

Table 9.4

```
. ivreg LGEARN ASVABC MALE ETHBLACK ETHHISP (S=SM SF SIBLINGS LIBRARY)

Instrumental variables (2SLS) regression

   Source |       SS       df       MS                Number of obs =     570
----------+------------------------------            F(  5,    564) =   23.49
    Model | 29.1540126      5  5.83080252            Prob > F       =  0.0000
 Residual |  124.64788    564   .22100688            R-squared      =  0.1896
----------+------------------------------            Adj R-squared  =  0.1824
    Total | 153.801893    569  .270302096            Root MSE       =  .47011


-----------------------------------------------------------------------------
   LGEARN |      Coef.   Std. Err.       t     P>|t|    [95% Conf. Interval]
----------+------------------------------------------------------------------
        S |   .1026815   .0381431     2.692    0.007    .0277615    .1776014
   ASVABC |   .0025508   .0067323     0.379    0.705   -.0106727    .0157743
     MALE |   .2280404   .0422514     5.397    0.000     .145051    .3110298
 ETHBLACK |    -.15289   .0882356    -1.733    0.084   -.3262005    .0204204
  ETHHISP |   .0463734    .085714     0.541    0.589   -.1219842     .214731
    _cons |   .7939315   .2347929     3.381    0.001    .3327562    1.255107
-----------------------------------------------------------------------------
Instrumented:  S
Instruments:   ASVABC MALE ETHBLACK ETHHISP SM SF SIBLINGS LIBRARY
-----------------------------------------------------------------------------
```

Table 9.4 *(Continued)*

```
. hausman, save

. reg LGEARN S ASVABC MALE ETHBLACK ETHHISP

      Source |       SS          df       MS              Number of obs =     570
-------------+------------------------------           F(  5,   564) =   30.63
       Model | 32.8416113        5  6.56832227           Prob > F      =  0.0000
    Residual | 120.960281       564  .214468584          R-squared     =  0.2135
-------------+------------------------------           Adj R-squared =  0.2066
       Total | 153.801893       569  .270302096          Root MSE      =  .46311


------------------------------------------------------------------------------
      LGEARN |     Coef.    Std. Err.      t     P>|t|     [95% Conf. Interval]
-------------+----------------------------------------------------------------
           S |   .0618848   .0098386     6.290   0.000     .04256     .0812097
       ASVABC |  .0093287   .0027721     3.365   0.001     .0038838   .0147737
        MALE |   .2130222   .0394229     5.404   0.000     .1355886   .2904557
    ETHBLACK |  -.1019355   .0741871    -1.374   0.170    -.2476523   .0437813
     ETHHISP |   .0537519   .0841815     0.639   0.523    -.1115956   .2190993
       _cons |   1.009459   .1295912     7.790   0.000     .7549185   1.263999
------------------------------------------------------------------------------

. hausman, constant sigmamore

                 ---- Coefficients ----
             |      (b)          (B)            (b-B)     sqrt(diag(V_b-V_B))
             |     Prior       Current        Difference        S.E.
-------------+----------------------------------------------------------------
           S |   .1026815     .0618848        .0407967        .0362637
       ASVABC |  .0025508     .0093287       -.0067779        .0060248
        MALE |   .2280404     .2130222        .0150182        .0133495
    ETHBLACK |  -.15289      -.1019355       -.0509546        .045293
     ETHHISP |   .0463734     .0537519       -.0073784        .0065586
       _cons |   .7939315     1.009459       -.2155273        .1915801
-------------+----------------------------------------------------------------
             b = less efficient estimates obtained previously from ivreg.
             B = more efficient estimates obtained from regress.

Test:  Ho:  difference in coefficients not systematic

             chi2(  1) = (b-B)' [(V_b-V_B)^(-1)](b-B)
                       =    1.27
             Prob>chi2 =    0.2606
```

We infer that it is safe to use OLS rather than IV, and we are happy to do so because the OLS standard errors, particularly those of the coefficients of *S* and *ASVABC*, are smaller than their IV counterparts. This is likely to be the correct conclusion. The schooling histories are recorded in great detail in the NLSY data set and accordingly the measurement error is almost certainly minimal.

The Hausman test can be used in any comparison of OLS and IV estimators where both are consistent, but OLS more efficient, under a null hypothesis, and OLS is inconsistent under the alternative hypothesis. We will encounter another application in the next chapter. With the usage of the test becoming more common, a facility for performing it is becoming a standard feature of regression applications.

Exercises

9.8   In Exercise 9.1, the amount of labor, L, employed by the firms is also a linear function of expected sales:

$$L = \delta_1 + \delta_2 X^e.$$

Explain how this relationship might be exploited by the investigator to counter the problem of measurement error bias.

9.9*   It is possible that the $ASVABC$ test score is a poor measure of the kind of ability relevant for earnings. Accordingly, perform an OLS regression of the logarithm of hourly earnings on years of schooling and the $ASVABC$ score using your $EAEF$ data set and an IV regression using SM, SF, $SIBLINGS$, and $LIBRARY$ as instruments for $ASVABC$. Perform a Durbin–Wu–Hausman test to evaluate whether $ASVABC$ appears to be subject to measurement error.

9.10*   What is the difference between an instrumental variable and a proxy variable (as described in Section 7.4)? When would you use one and when would you use the other?

10 Simultaneous equations estimation

If you employ OLS to estimate the parameters of an equation that is embedded in a simultaneous equations model, it is likely that the estimates will be biased and inconsistent and that the statistical tests will be invalid. This is demonstrated in the first part of this chapter. The second part discusses how these problems may be overcome by using instrumental variables estimation.

10.1 Simultaneous equations models: structural and reduced form equations

Measurement error is not the only possible reason why the fourth Gauss–Markov condition may not be satisfied. Simultaneous equations bias is another, and it is best explained with an example.

Suppose that you are investigating the determinants of price inflation and wage inflation. We will start with a very simple model that supposes that p, the annual rate of growth of prices, is related to w, the annual rate of growth of wages, it being hypothesized that increases in wage costs force prices upwards:

$$p = \beta_1 + \beta_2 w + u_p. \tag{10.1}$$

At the same time w is related to p and U, the rate of unemployment, workers protecting their real wages by demanding increases in wages as prices rise, but their ability to do so being the weaker, the higher the rate of unemployment ($\alpha_3 < 0$):

$$w = \alpha_1 + \alpha_2 p + \alpha_3 U + u_w. \tag{10.2}$$

u_p and u_w are disturbance terms.

By its very specification, this simultaneous equations model involves a certain amount of circularity: w determines p in the first equation, and in turn p helps to determine w in the second. To cut through the circularity we need to make a distinction between *endogenous* and *exogenous* variables. *Endo-* and *exo-* are Greek prefixes that mean within and outside, respectively. Endogenous variables are variables whose values are determined by the interaction of the relationships in the model. Exogenous ones are those whose values are determined externally.

Thus in the present case p and w are both endogenous and U is exogenous. The exogenous variables and the disturbance terms ultimately determine the values of the endogenous variables, once one has cut through the circularity. The mathematical relationships expressing the endogenous variables in terms of the exogenous variables and disturbance terms are known as the reduced form equations. The original equations that we wrote down when specifying the model are described as the structural equations. We will derive the reduced form equations for p and w. To obtain that for p, we take the structural equation for p and substitute for w from the second equation:

$$p = \beta_1 + \beta_2 w + u_p$$
$$= \beta_1 + \beta_2(\alpha_1 + \alpha_2 p + \alpha_3 U + u_w) + u_p. \tag{10.3}$$

Hence

$$(1 - \alpha_2\beta_2)p = \beta_1 + \alpha_1\beta_2 + \alpha_3\beta_2 U + u_p + \beta_2 u_w \tag{10.4}$$

and so

$$p = \frac{\beta_1 + \alpha_1\beta_2 + \alpha_3\beta_2 U + u_p + \beta_2 u_w}{1 - \alpha_2\beta_2}. \tag{10.5}$$

Similarly we obtain the reduced form equation for w:

$$w = \alpha_1 + \alpha_2 p + \alpha_3 U + u_w$$
$$= \alpha_1 + \alpha_2(\beta_1 + \beta_2 w + u_p) + \alpha_3 U + u_w. \tag{10.6}$$

Hence

$$(1 - \alpha_2\beta_2)w = \alpha_1 + \alpha_2\beta_1 + \alpha_3 U + u_w + \alpha_2 u_p \tag{10.7}$$

and so

$$w = \frac{\alpha_1 + \alpha_2\beta_1 + \alpha_3 U + u_w + \alpha_2 u_p}{1 - \alpha_2\beta_2}. \tag{10.8}$$

Exercise

10.1* A simple macroeconomic model consists of a consumption function and an income identity:

$$C = \beta_1 + \beta_2 Y + u$$
$$Y = C + I,$$

where C is aggregate consumption, I is aggregate investment, Y is aggregate income, and u is a disturbance term. On the assumption that I is exogenous, derive the reduced form equations for C and Y.

10.2 **Simultaneous equations bias**

In many (but by no means all) simultaneous equations models, the reduced form equations express the endogenous variables in terms of all the exogenous variables and all the disturbance terms. You can see that this is the case with the price inflation/wage inflation model. In this model, there is only one exogenous variable, U. w depends on it directly; p does not depend on it directly but does so indirectly because it is determined by w. Similarly, both p and w depend on u_p, p directly and w indirectly. And both depend on u_w, w directly and p indirectly.

The dependence of w on u_p means that OLS would yield inconsistent estimates if used to fit equation (10.1), the structural equation for p. w is a stochastic regressor and its random component is not distributed independently of the disturbance term u_p. Similarly the dependence of p on u_w means that OLS would yield inconsistent estimates if used to fit (10.2). Since (10.1) is a simple regression equation, it is easy to analyze the large-sample bias in the OLS estimator of β_2 and we will do so. After writing down the expression for b_2^{OLS}, the first step, as usual, is to substitute for p. Here we have to make a decision. We now have two equations for p, the structural equation (10.1) and the reduced form equation (10.5). Ultimately it does not matter which we use, but the algebra is a little more straightforward if we use the structural equation because the expression for b_2^{OLS} decomposes immediately into the true value and the error term. We can then concentrate on the error term.

$$b_2^{OLS} = \frac{\mathrm{Cov}(p, w)}{\mathrm{Var}(w)} = \frac{\mathrm{Cov}([\beta_1 + \beta_2 w + u_p], w)}{\mathrm{Var}(w)}$$

$$= \frac{\mathrm{Cov}(\beta_1, w) + \mathrm{Cov}(\beta_2 w, w) + \mathrm{Cov}(u_p, w)}{\mathrm{Var}(w)} = \beta_2 + \frac{\mathrm{Cov}(u_p, w)}{\mathrm{Var}(w)}. \quad (10.9)$$

The error term is a nonlinear function of both u_p and u_w (remember that w depends on both) and it is not possible to obtain an analytical expression for its expected value. Instead we will investigate its probability limit, using the rule that the probability limit of a ratio is equal to the probability limit of the numerator divided by the probability limit of the denominator, provided that both exist. We will first focus on $\mathrm{plim}\ \mathrm{Cov}(u_p, w)$. We need to substitute for w and again have two choices: the structural equation (10.2) and the reduced form equation (10.8). We choose (10.8) because (10.2) would reintroduce p and we would find ourselves going round in circles.

$$\mathrm{plim}\ \mathrm{Cov}(u_p, w) = \mathrm{plim}\ \mathrm{Cov}\left(u_p, \frac{1}{1 - \alpha_2 \beta_2}(\alpha_1 + \alpha_2 \beta_1 + \alpha_3 U + u_w + \alpha_2 u_p)\right)$$

$$= \frac{1}{1 - \alpha_2 \beta_2}\left(\begin{array}{l} \mathrm{plim}\ \mathrm{Cov}(u_p, [\alpha_1 + \alpha_2 \beta_1]) + \alpha_3 \mathrm{plim}\ \mathrm{Cov}(u_p, U) \\ + \mathrm{plim}\ \mathrm{Cov}(u_p, u_w) + \alpha_2 \mathrm{plim}\ \mathrm{Cov}(u_p, u_p) \end{array}\right).$$

$$(10.10)$$

$\text{Cov}(u_w, [\alpha_1 + \alpha_2\beta_1])$ is 0 since $[\alpha_1 + \alpha_2\beta_1]$ is a constant. plim $\text{Cov}(u_p, U)$ will be 0 if U is truly exogenous, as we have assumed. plim $\text{Cov}(u_p, u_w)$ will be 0 provided that the disturbance terms in the structural equations are independent. But plim $\text{Cov}(u_p, u_p)$ is nonzero because it is plim $\text{Var}(u_p)$ and the limiting value of the sample variance of u_p is its population variance, $\sigma_{u_p}^2$. Hence

$$\text{plim Cov}(u_p, w) = \frac{\alpha_2 \sigma_{u_p}^2}{1 - \alpha_2\beta_2} \tag{10.11}$$

Now for plim $\text{Var}(w)$:

$$\text{plim Var}(w) = \text{plim Var}\left(\frac{\alpha_1 + \alpha_2\beta_1}{1 - \alpha_2\beta_2} + \frac{\alpha_3 U + u_w + \alpha_2 u_p}{1 - \alpha_2\beta_2}\right)$$

$$= \text{plim Var}\left(\frac{\alpha_3 U + u_w + \alpha_2 u_p}{1 - \alpha_2\beta_2}\right) \tag{10.12}$$

since $(\alpha_1 + \alpha_2\beta_1)/(1 - \alpha_2\beta_2)$ is an additive constant. So

$$\text{plim Var}(w) = \frac{1}{(1 - \alpha_2\beta_2)^2}\begin{pmatrix}\text{plim Var}(\alpha_3 U) + \text{plim Var}(u_w) + \text{plim Var}(\alpha_2 u_p) \\ + 2\text{plim Cov}(\alpha_3 U, u_w) + 2\text{plim Cov}(\alpha_3 U, \alpha_2 u_p) \\ + 2\text{plim Cov}(u_w, \alpha_2 u_p)\end{pmatrix}. \tag{10.13}$$

Now if U, u_p, and u_w are independently distributed, the limiting values of the three covariance terms are 0. The limiting values of the variance terms are the corresponding population variances. Hence

$$\text{plim Var}(w) = \frac{1}{(1 - \alpha_2\beta_2)^2}\left(\alpha_3^2 \sigma_U^2 + \sigma_{u_w}^2 + \alpha_2^2 \sigma_{u_p}^2\right). \tag{10.14}$$

Thus

$$\text{plim } b_2^{\text{OLS}} = \beta_2 + (1 - \alpha_2\beta_2)\frac{\alpha_2 \sigma_{u_p}^2}{\alpha_3^2 \sigma_U^2 + \sigma_{u_w}^2 + \alpha_2^2 \sigma_{u_p}^2} \tag{10.15}$$

and so b_2^{OLS} is an inconsistent estimator of β_2.

The direction of simultaneous equations bias depends on the structure of the model being fitted. Can one say anything about it in this case? Variances are always positive, if not 0, and α_2 should be positive, so it depends on the sign of $(1 - \alpha_2\beta_2)$. Looking at the reduced form equation (10.8), it is reasonable to suppose that w will be negatively influenced by U. Since it is also reasonable to suppose that α_3 is negative, one may infer that $(1 - \alpha_2\beta_2)$ is positive. Actually, this is a condition for equilibrium in this model. Consider the effect of a change ΔU in U. In view of (10.2), its immediate effect is to change w, in the opposite direction, by an amount $\alpha_3\Delta U$. Looking at (10.1), this in turn changes p by an amount $\alpha_3\beta_2\Delta U$. Returning to (10.2), this causes a secondary change in w of $\alpha_2\alpha_3\beta_2\Delta U$, and hence, returning to (10.1), a secondary change in p equal to

$\alpha_2\alpha_3\beta_2^2\Delta U$. Returning again to (10.2), this causes a further change in w equal to $\alpha_2^2\alpha_3\beta_2^2\Delta U$. The total change in w will therefore be

$$\Delta w = (1 + \alpha_2\beta_2 + \alpha_2^2\beta_2^2 + \alpha_2^3\beta_2^3 + \cdots)\alpha_3\Delta U \qquad (10.16)$$

and this will be finite only if $\alpha_2\beta_2 < 1$.

A Monte Carlo experiment

This section reports on a Monte Carlo experiment that investigates the performance of OLS and, later, IV when fitting the price inflation equation in the price inflation/wage inflation model. Numerical values were assigned to the parameters of the equations as follows:

$$p = 1.5 + 0.5w + u_p. \qquad (10.17)$$

$$w = 2.5 + 0.5p - 0.4U + u_w. \qquad (10.18)$$

U was assigned the values 2, 2.25, increasing by steps of 0.25 to 6.75. u_p was generated as a normal random variable with 0 mean and unit variance, scaled by a factor 0.8. The disturbance term u_w is not responsible for bias when OLS is used to fit the price inflation equation and so, to keep things simple, it was suppressed. Each replication of the experiment used a sample of twenty observations. Using the expression derived above, plim b_2^{OLS} is equal to 0.87 when the price inflation equation is fitted with OLS. The experiment was replicated ten times with the results shown in the Table 10.1.

It is evident that the estimates are heavily biased. Every estimate of the slope coefficient is above the true value of 0.5, and every estimate of the intercept is below the true value of 1.5. The mean of the slope coefficients is 0.96, not far

Table 10.1

Sample	b_1	s.e.(b_1)	b_2	s.e.(b_2)
1	0.36	0.39	1.11	0.22
2	0.45	0.38	1.06	0.17
3	0.65	0.27	0.94	0.12
4	0.41	0.39	0.98	0.19
5	0.92	0.46	0.77	0.22
6	0.26	0.35	1.09	0.16
7	0.31	0.39	1.00	0.19
8	1.06	0.38	0.82	0.16
9	−0.08	0.36	1.16	0.18
10	1.12	0.43	0.69	0.20

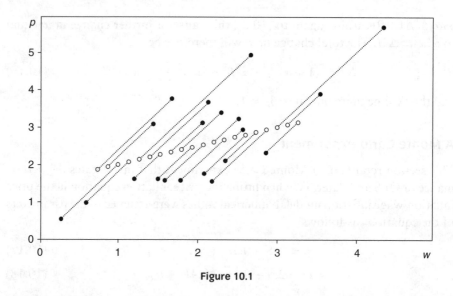

Figure 10.1

from the theoretical plim for the OLS estimate. Figure 10.1 shows how the bias arises. The hollow circles show what the relationship between p and w would look like in the absence of the disturbance terms, for twenty observations. The disturbance term u_p alters the values of both p and w in each observation when it is introduced. As can be seen from the reduced form equations, it increases p by an amount $u_p/(1-\alpha_2\beta_2)$ and w by an amount $\alpha_2 u_p/(1-\alpha_2\beta_2)$. It follows that the shift is along a line with slope $1/\alpha_2$. The solid circles are the actual observations, after u_p has been introduced. The shift line has been drawn for each observation. As can be seen, the overall effect is to skew the pattern of observations, with the result that the OLS slope coefficient is a compromise between the slope of the true relationship, β_2, and the slope of the shift lines, $1/\alpha_2$. This can be demonstrated mathematically be rewriting equation (10.15):

$$\text{plim } b_2^{\text{OLS}} = \beta_2 + (1 - \alpha_2\beta_2)\frac{\alpha_2\sigma_{u_p}^2}{\alpha_3^2\sigma_U^2 + \sigma_{u_w}^2 + \alpha_2^2\sigma_{u_p}^2}$$

$$= \beta_2 + \left(\frac{1}{\alpha_2} - \beta_2\right)\frac{\alpha_2^2\sigma_{u_p}^2}{\alpha_3^2\sigma_U^2 + \sigma_{u_w}^2 + \alpha_2^2\sigma_{u_p}^2}$$

$$= \beta_2\left(\frac{\alpha_3^2\sigma_U^2 + \sigma_{u_w}^2}{\alpha_3^2\sigma_U^2 + \sigma_{u_w}^2 + \alpha_2^2\sigma_{u_p}^2}\right) + \frac{1}{\alpha_2}\left(\frac{\alpha_2^2\sigma_{u_p}^2}{\alpha_3^2\sigma_U^2 + \sigma_{u_w}^2 + \alpha_2^2\sigma_{u_p}^2}\right).$$

$$(10.19)$$

plim b_2^{OLS} is thus a weighted average of β_2 and $1/\alpha_2$, the bias being proportional to the variance of u_p.

Exercises

10.2* In the simple macroeconomic model

$$C = \beta_1 + \beta_2 Y + u$$
$$Y = C + I,$$

described in Exercise 10.1, demonstrate that OLS would yield inconsistent results if used to fit the consumption function, and investigate the direction of the bias in the slope coefficient.

10.3 A researcher is investigating the impact of advertising on sales using cross-section data from firms producing recreational goods. For each firm there are data on sales, S, and expenditure on advertising, A, both measured in suitable units, for a recent year. The researcher proposes the following model:

$$S = \beta_1 + \beta_2 A + u_S$$
$$A = \alpha_1 + \alpha_2 S + u_A,$$

where u_S and u_A are disturbance terms. The first relationship reflects the positive effect of advertising on sales, and the second the fact that largest firms, as measured by sales, tend to spend most on advertising. Give a mathematical analysis of what would happen if the researcher tried to fit the model using OLS.

10.3 Instrumental variables estimation

As we saw in the discussion of measurement error, the instrumental variables approach may offer a solution to the problems caused by a violation of the fourth Gauss–Markov condition. In the present case, when we fit the structural equation for p, the fourth Gauss–Markov condition is violated because w is not distributed independently of u_p. We need a variable that is correlated with w but not with u_p, and does not already appear in the equation in its own right. The reduced form equation for w gave us some bad news—it revealed that w was dependent on u_p. But it also gives us some good news—it shows that w is correlated with U, which is exogenous and thus independent of u_p. So we can fit the equation using U as an instrument for w. Recalling that, for simple regression analysis, the instrumental variables estimator of the slope coefficient is given by the covariance of the instrument with the dependent variable divided by the covariance of the instrument with the explanatory variable, the IV estimator of β_2 is given by

$$b_2^{IV} = \frac{\text{Cov}(U, p)}{\text{Cov}(U, w)}. \tag{10.20}$$

We will demonstrate that it is consistent. Substituting from the structural equation for p,

$$b_2^{IV} = \frac{\text{Cov}(U, [\beta_1 + \beta_2 w + u_p])}{\text{Cov}(U, w)} = \frac{\text{Cov}(U, \beta_1) + \text{Cov}(U, \beta_2 w) + \text{Cov}(U, u_p)}{\text{Cov}(U, w)}$$

$$= \beta_2 + \frac{\text{Cov}(U, u_p)}{\text{Cov}(U, w)} \qquad (10.21)$$

since the first covariance in the numerator is 0 and the second is equal to $\beta_2 \text{Cov}(U, w)$. Now plim $\text{Cov}(U, u_p)$ is 0 if U is exogenous and so distributed independently of u_p. plim $\text{Cov}(U, w)$ is nonzero because U is a determinant of w. Hence the instrumental variable estimator is a consistent estimator of β_2.

Table 10.2 shows the results when IV is used to fit the model described in Section 10.2. In contrast to the OLS estimates, the IV estimates are distributed around the true values, the mean of the estimates of the slope coefficient (true value 0.5) being 0.37 and of those of the intercept (true value 1.5) being 1.69. There is no point in comparing the standard errors using the two approaches. Those for OLS may appear to be slightly smaller, but the simultaneous equations bias renders them invalid.

In this example, IV definitely gave better results than OLS, but that outcome was not inevitable. In Table 10.2 the distribution of the OLS estimates of the slope coefficient is more concentrated than that of the IV estimates. The standard deviation of the estimates (calculated directly from the estimates, ignoring the standard errors) is 0.15. For the IV estimates it is 0.20. So if the bias had been smaller, it is possible that OLS might have yielded superior estimates according

Table 10.2

Sample	OLS				IV			
	b_1	s.e.(b_1)	b_2	s.e.(b_2)	b_1	s.e.(b_1)	b_2	s.e.(b_2)
1	0.36	0.39	1.11	0.22	2.33	0.97	0.16	0.45
2	0.45	0.38	1.06	0.17	1.53	0.57	0.53	0.26
3	0.65	0.27	0.94	0.12	1.13	0.32	0.70	0.15
4	0.41	0.39	0.98	0.19	1.55	0.59	0.37	0.30
5	0.92	0.46	0.77	0.22	2.31	0.71	0.06	0.35
6	0.26	0.35	1.09	0.16	1.24	0.52	0.59	0.25
7	0.31	0.39	1.00	0.19	1.52	0.62	0.33	0.32
8	1.06	0.38	0.82	0.16	1.95	0.51	0.41	0.22
9	−0.08	0.36	1.16	0.18	1.11	0.62	0.45	0.33
10	1.12	0.43	0.69	0.20	2.26	0.61	0.13	0.29

to a criterion like the mean square error that allows a trade-off between bias and variance.

Underidentification

If OLS were used to fit the wage inflation equation

$$w = \alpha_1 + \alpha_2 p + \alpha_3 U + u_w, \tag{10.22}$$

the estimates would be subject to simultaneous equations bias caused by the (indirect) dependence of p on u_w. However, in this case it is not possible to use the instrumental variables approach to obtain consistent estimates, and the relationship is said to be underidentified. The only determinant of p, apart from the disturbance terms, is U, and it is already in the model in its own right. An attempt to use it as an instrument for p would lead to a form of exact multi-collinearity and it would be impossible to obtain estimates of the parameters. Using the expression in Box 10.1, we would have

$$
\begin{aligned}
a_2^{IV} &= \frac{\text{Cov}(Z,w)\text{Var}(U) - \text{Cov}(U,w)\text{Cov}(Z,U)}{\text{Cov}(Z,p)\text{Var}(U) - \text{Cov}(p,U)\text{Cov}(Z,U)} \\
&= \frac{\text{Cov}(U,w)\text{Var}(U) - \text{Cov}(U,w)\text{Cov}(U,U)}{\text{Cov}(U,p)\text{Var}(U) - \text{Cov}(p,U)\text{Cov}(U,U)}
\end{aligned}
\tag{10.23}
$$

and the numerator and denominator both reduce to 0.

However, suppose that the rate of price inflation were hypothesized to be determined by the rate of growth of the money supply, m, as well as the rate of

---

BOX 10.1   Instrumental variables estimation in a model with two explanatory variables

Suppose that the true model is

$$Y = \beta_1 + \beta_2 X_2 + \beta_3 X_3 + u,$$

that X_2 is not distributed independently of u, and that Z is being used as an instrument for X_2. Then the IV estimators of β_2 and β_3 are given by

$$b_2^{IV} = \frac{\text{Cov}(Z,Y)\text{Var}(X_3) - \text{Cov}(X_3,Y)\text{Cov}(Z,X_3)}{\text{Cov}(Z,X_2)\text{Var}(X_3) - \text{Cov}(X_2,X_3)\text{Cov}(Z,X_3)}$$

$$b_3^{IV} = \frac{\text{Cov}(X_3,Y)\text{Cov}(Z,X_2) - \text{Cov}(Z,Y)\text{Cov}(X_2,X_3)}{\text{Cov}(Z,X_2)\text{Var}(X_3) - \text{Cov}(X_2,X_3)\text{Cov}(Z,X_3)}.$$

growth of wages, and that m were assumed to be exogenous:

$$p = \beta_1 + \beta_2 w + \beta_3 m + u_p. \tag{10.24}$$

The reduced form equations become

$$p = \frac{\beta_1 + \alpha_1 \beta_2 + \alpha_3 \beta_2 U + \beta_3 m + u_p + \beta_2 u_w}{1 - \alpha_2 \beta_2}. \tag{10.25}$$

$$w = \frac{\alpha_1 + \alpha_2 \beta_1 + \alpha_3 U + \alpha_2 \beta_3 m + u_w + \alpha_2 u_p}{1 - \alpha_2 \beta_2}. \tag{10.26}$$

U may be used as an instrument for w in the price inflation equation, as before, and m can be used as an instrument for p in the wage inflation equation because it satisfies the three conditions required of an instrument. It is correlated with p, by virtue of being a determinant; it is not correlated with the disturbance term, by virtue of being assumed to be exogenous; and it is not already in the structural equation in its own right. Both structural equations are now said to be exactly identified, exact identification meaning that the number of exogenous variables available as instruments (that is, not already in the equation in their own right) is equal to the number of endogenous variables requiring instruments.

Overidentification and two-stage least squares

Next consider the model

$$p = \beta_1 + \beta_2 w + u_p. \tag{10.27}$$
$$w = \alpha_1 + \alpha_2 p + \alpha_3 U + \alpha_4 x + u_w. \tag{10.28}$$

where x is the rate of growth of productivity. The corresponding reduced form equations are

$$p = \frac{\beta_1 + \alpha_1 \beta_2 + \alpha_3 \beta_2 U + \alpha_4 \beta_2 x + u_p + \beta_2 u_w}{1 - \alpha_2 \beta_2}. \tag{10.29}$$

$$w = \frac{\alpha_1 + \alpha_2 \beta_1 + \alpha_3 U + \alpha_4 x + u_w + \alpha_2 u_p}{1 - \alpha_2 \beta_2}. \tag{10.30}$$

The wage inflation equation is underidentified because there is no exogenous variable available to act as an instrument for p. p is correlated with both U and x, but both these variables appear in the wage equation in their own right.

However, the price inflation equation is now said to be overidentified because we have two potential instruments for w. We could use U as an instrument for w, as before:

$$b_2^{IV} = \frac{\text{Cov}(U,p)}{\text{Cov}(U,w)}. \tag{10.31}$$

Alternatively, we could use x as an instrument:

$$b_2^{IV} = \frac{\text{Cov}(x,p)}{\text{Cov}(x,w)}. \tag{10.32}$$

Both are consistent estimators, so they would converge to the true value, and therefore to each other, as the sample size became large, but for finite samples they would give different estimates. Suppose that you had to choose between them (you do not, as we will see). Which would you choose? The population variance of the first is given by

$$\sigma_{b_2^{IV}}^2 = \frac{\sigma_{u_p}^2}{n\,\text{Var}(w)} \times \frac{1}{r_{wU}^2}. \tag{10.33}$$

The population variance of the second estimator is given by a similar expression with the correlation coefficient replaced by that between w and x. We want the population variance to be as small as possible, so we would choose the instrument with the higher correlation coefficient.

Two-stage least squares

In practice, rather than choose between the instruments in this situation, we would construct a linear function of them and use that instead. The main reason for this is that in general a linear function, with suitably chosen weights, will be more efficient than either instrument individually. A secondary consideration is that using a linear function eliminates the problem of conflicting estimates. Let the linear function be Z, where

$$Z = h_1 + h_2 U + h_3 x. \tag{10.34}$$

How do we choose the h coefficients? Very straightforward. Using OLS, regress w on U and x, save the fitted values, and call the saved variable Z:

$$Z = \hat{w} = h_1 + h_2 U + h_3 x. \tag{10.35}$$

The fitted values are automatically linear functions of U and x and the h coefficients will have been chosen in such a way as to maximize the correlation between the fitted values and w. As we saw in Chapter 2, provided that the model is correctly specified and that the Gauss–Markov conditions are satisfied, OLS yields estimates that are optimal according to three mutually equivalent criteria: minimizing the sum of the squares of the residuals, maximizing R^2, and (the criterion that is relevant here) maximizing the correlation between the actual and the fitted values. This is the first stage of the Two-Stage Least Squares estimator. The second stage is the calculation of the estimate of β_2 using Z as an instrument:

$$b_2^{\text{TSLS}} = \frac{\text{Cov}(Z, p)}{\text{Cov}(Z, w)} = \frac{\text{Cov}(\hat{w}, p)}{\text{Cov}(\hat{w}, w)}. \qquad (10.36)$$

The population variance of b_2^{TSLS} is given by

$$\sigma_{b_2^{\text{TSLS}}}^2 = \frac{\sigma_{u_p}^2}{n\text{Var}(w)} \times \frac{1}{r_{w\hat{w}}^2}. \qquad (10.37)$$

and in general this will be smaller than the population variances of the IV estimators using U or x because the correlation coefficient will be higher.

The order condition for identification

We have observed that in general an equation will be identified if there are enough exogenous variables not appearing in it to act as instruments for the endogenous variables that do appear in it. In a fully specified model, there will be as many equations as there are endogenous variables. Let us suppose that there are G of each. The maximum number of endogenous variables that can appear on the right side of an equation is $G-1$ (the other is the dependent variable of that equation). In such a case, we would need at least $G-1$ exogenous variables not appearing in the equation to have enough instruments.

Suppose, however, that j endogenous variables are also missing from the equation. We would then need only $G-1-j$ instruments, so only $G-1-j$ exogenous variables would have to be missing from the equation. The total number of variables missing, however, remains the same: j endogenous variables and $G-1-j$ exogenous variables make a total of $G-1$.

Thus we come to the general conclusion that an equation in a simultaneous equations model is likely to be identified if $G-1$ or more variables are missing from it. If exactly $G-1$ are missing, it is likely to be exactly identified, and if more than $G-1$ are missing, it is likely to be overidentified, calling for the use of TSLS.

This is known as the order condition for identification. It must be stressed that this is a necessary condition for identification but not a sufficient one. There are cases, which we will not discuss here, in which an equation is in fact underidentified even though the order condition is satisfied.

Unobserved heterogeneity

In the examples above, simultaneous equations bias and instrumental variables estimation were discussed in the context of fully specified multi-equation models.

BOX 10.2   Indirect least squares

Indirect least squares (ILS), an alternative procedure for obtaining consistent estimates of parameters in a simultaneous equations model, is no longer used in practice but it retains some pedagogical interest. Returning to the price inflation/wage inflation model

$$p = \beta_1 + \beta_2 w + u_p$$

$$w = \alpha_1 + \alpha_2 p + \alpha_3 U + u_w,$$

the reduced form equations for p and w were

$$p = \frac{\beta_1 + \alpha_1\beta_2 + \alpha_3\beta_2 U + u_p + \beta_2 u_w}{1 - \alpha_2\beta_2}$$

$$w = \frac{\alpha_1 + \alpha_2\beta_1 + \alpha_3 U + u_w + \alpha_2 u_p}{1 - \alpha_2\beta_2}.$$

On the assumption that U is exogenous, it is independent of u_p and u_w and so OLS will give unbiased estimates of the parameters of the equations. The parameters of these equations are of course functions of the parameters of the structural equations, but it may be possible to derive estimates of the structural parameters from them. For example, using the data for the first replication of the Monte Carlo experiment, the fitted reduced form equations are

$$\hat{p} = 2.9741 - 0.0705U$$

$$\hat{w} = 3.9871 - 0.4352U.$$

Hence, linking the numerical estimates to the theoretical coefficients, one has four equations

$$\frac{b_1 + a_1 b_2}{1 - a_2 b_2} = 2.9741 \qquad \frac{a_3 b_2}{1 - a_2 b_2} = -0.0705$$

$$\frac{a_1 + a_2 b_1}{1 - a_2 b_2} = 3.9871 \qquad \frac{a_3}{1 - a_2 b_2} = -0.4352.$$

Substituting the fourth equation into the second, one has $-0.4352b_2 = -0.0705$, and so $b_2 = 0.1620$. Further, since $\dfrac{b_1 + a_1 b_2}{1 - a_2 b_2} - b_2 \dfrac{a_1 + a_2 b_1}{1 - a_2 b_2} = b_1$, one has $b_1 = 2.9741 - 0.1620 \times 3.9871 = 2.3282$. There is no way of deriving estimates of the three remaining parameters. Indeed, since we had four equations in five unknowns, we were lucky to pin down two of the parameters. Since we have obtained (unique) estimates of the parameters of the structural price equation, that equation is said to be exactly identified, while the structural wage equation is said to be underidentified.

Next consider the model

$$p = \beta_1 + \beta_2 w + u_p$$

$$w = \alpha_1 + \alpha_2 p + \alpha_3 U + \alpha_4 x + u_w,$$

BOX 10.2   Indirect least squares (continued)

where x is the rate of growth productivity. The corresponding reduced form equations are

$$p = \frac{\beta_1 + \alpha_1\beta_2 + \alpha_3\beta_2 U + \alpha_4\beta_2 x + u_p + \beta_2 u_w}{1 - \alpha_2\beta_2}$$

$$w = \frac{\alpha_1 + \alpha_2\beta_1 + \alpha_3 U + \alpha_4 x + u_w + \alpha_2 u_p}{1 - \alpha_2\beta_2}.$$

Suppose that when these are fitted we obtain, in abstract form,

$$\hat{p} = B_1 + B_2 U + B_3 x$$

$$\hat{w} = A_1 + A_2 U + A_3 x,$$

where the B_i and the A_i are numerical regression coefficients. Linking these numerical coefficients to their theoretical counterparts, we obtain six equations in six unknowns:

$$\frac{b_1 + a_1 b_2}{1 - a_2 b_2} = B_1 \quad \frac{a_3 b_2}{1 - a_2 b_2} = B_2 \quad \frac{a_4 b_2}{1 - a_2 b_2} = B_3$$

$$\frac{a_1 + a_2 b_1}{1 - a_2 b_2} = A_1 \quad \frac{a_3}{1 - a_2 b_2} = A_2 \quad \frac{a_4}{1 - a_2 b_2} = A_3.$$

Substituting the fifth equation into the second, we have $A_2 b_2 = B_2$, and so B_2/A_2 provides an estimate of β_2. However, substituting the sixth equation into the third, we have $A_3 b_2 = B_3$, and so B_3/A_3 also provides an estimate of β_2. Thus we have more than one way of obtaining an estimate and the model is said to be overidentified. This is the counterpart of having alternative instruments in IV estimation. The estimates would both be consistent, and so in large samples they would converge to the true value, but in finite samples they would differ. One would also be able to obtain conflicting estimates of β_1. However it would not be possible to obtain estimates of the remaining parameters and the wage equation is said to be underidentified.

ILS has no advantages over IV and has the disadvantage of requiring more computation. If an equation is underidentified for IV, it is underidentified for ILS; if it exactly identified, IV and ILS yield identical estimates; if it is overidentified, ILS yields conflicting estimates, a problem that is resolved with IV by using TSLS.

However, it is common to find these issues discussed in the context of a single-equation model, where the equation is implicitly embedded in a simultaneous equations model where the other relationships are unspecified. For example, in the case of the earnings function

$$LGEARN = \beta_1 + \beta_2 S + \cdots + u, \tag{10.38}$$

it is often asserted that 'unobserved heterogeneity' will cause the OLS estimate of β_2 to be biased. In this case unobserved heterogeneity refers to unobserved

Table 10.3

	OLS	IV
Coefficient of S	0.073	0.140
Standard error	0.004	0.055

variations in the characteristics of the respondents, such as ambition and various types of intelligence and ability, that influence both educational attainment and earnings. Because they are unobserved, their influence on earnings is captured by the disturbance term, and thus S and u are positively correlated. As a consequence, the OLS estimate of β_2 will be subject to a positive bias. If this is the case, S needs to be instrumented with a suitable instrument.

However, it requires ingenuity to find a credible instrument, for most factors affecting educational attainment are also likely to affect earnings. One such example is the use of proximity to a four-year college by Card (1995), who argued that this could have a positive effect on educational attainment but was unlikely to be a determinant of earnings.

Table 10.3 presents the results of OLS and IV regressions using a sample of 3,010 males derived by Card from the National Longitudinal Survey of Young Men, a panel study that was a precursor to the NLSY. The earnings data relate to 1976. The regressions included personal, family, and regional characteristics not shown. As can be seen, using college proximity to instrument for educational attainment does make a difference—but it is in a direction opposite to that expected, for if the OLS estimate is upwards biased, the IV estimate ought to be smaller, not larger. Measurement error in S, which would cause a downwards bias in the OLS estimate, could account for part of the perverse effect, but not all of it. Card sought an explanation in terms of a higher-than-average return to education for those with relatively poorly educated parents, combined with a higher responsiveness of educational attainment to college proximity for such respondents. However, although educational attainment is positively correlated with college proximity, the correlation is weak and accordingly the standard error of the IV estimate large. It is thus possible that the apparent increase occurred as a matter of chance and that a Durbin–Wu–Hausman test would have shown that the OLS and IV estimates were not significantly different.

Durbin–Wu–Hausman test

In Chapter 9 it was shown that measurement error causes a violation of the fourth Gauss–Markov condition and that one can use the Durbin–Wu–Hausman test, which compares the OLS and IV coefficients, to test for suspected measurement error. The test can be used in the same way more broadly for suspected violations of the Gauss–Markov condition and in particular for violations caused by

Table 10.4

```
. ivreg p (w=U)

Instrumental variables (2SLS) regression

    Source |       SS       df       MS              Number of obs =      20
-----------+------------------------------           F(  1,     18) =    0.13
     Model |  5.39052472      1  5.39052472          Prob > F       =  0.7207
  Residual |  28.1781361     18   1.565452           R-squared      =  0.1606
-----------+------------------------------           Adj R-squared  =  0.1139
     Total |  33.5686608     19  1.76677162          Root MSE       =  1.2512


------------------------------------------------------------------------------
         p |     Coef.   Std. Err.      t    P>|t|     [95% Conf. Interval]
-----------+------------------------------------------------------------------
         w |  .1619431   .4459005     0.363   0.721    -.7748591    1.098745
     _cons |  2.328433   .9699764     2.401   0.027     .2905882    4.366278
------------------------------------------------------------------------------
Instrumented:  w
Instruments:   U
------------------------------------------------------------------------------

. hausman, save

. reg p w

    Source |       SS       df       MS              Number of obs =      20
-----------+------------------------------           F(  1,     18) =   26.16
     Model |  19.8854938      1  19.8854938          Prob > F       =  0.0001
  Residual |   13.683167     18  .760175945          R-squared      =  0.5924
-----------+------------------------------           Adj R-squared  =  0.5697
     Total |  33.5686608     19  1.76677162          Root MSE       =  .87188


------------------------------------------------------------------------------
         p |     Coef.   Std. Err.      t    P>|t|     [95% Conf. Interval]
-----------+------------------------------------------------------------------
         w |  1.107448   .2165271     5.115   0.000     .6525417    1.562355
     _cons |  .3590688   .4913327     0.731   0.474     -.673183    1.391321
------------------------------------------------------------------------------

. hausman, constant sigmamore

           ---- Coefficients ----
          |      (b)          (B)            (b-B)     sqrt(diag(V_b-V_B))
          |     Prior                                       o9nb          Current
Difference      S.E.
-----------+------------------------------------------------------------------
         w |  .1619431     1.107448        -.9455052        .2228577
     _cons |  2.328433     .3590688         1.969364        .4641836
-----------+------------------------------------------------------------------
```

Table 10.4 (*Continued*)

```
        b = less efficient estimates obtained previously from ivreg.
        B = more efficient estimates obtained from regress.

Test:  Ho:  difference in coefficients not systematic

            chi2(  1) = (b-B)'[(V_b-V_B)^(-1)](b-B)
                     =      18.00
            Prob>chi2 =      0.0000
```

---

simultaneous equations bias. To illustrate this, we will return to the Monte Carlo experiment described above. The regression output shows the result of performing the test for the first of the ten replications of the experiment summarized in Table 10.2.

  Under the null hypothesis that there is no simultaneous equations bias, both OLS and IV will be consistent estimators, but OLS will be more efficient. Under the alternative hypothesis, OLS will be inconsistent. As can be seen from the output, the chi-squared statistic summarizing the differences in the coefficients is 18.0. The critical value of chi-squared with one degree of freedom at the 0.1 percent level is 10.83, and hence we reject the null hypothesis. Of course, this was a foregone conclusion since the Monte Carlo experiment involved a simultaneous equations model designed to demonstrate that OLS would yield inconsistent estimates.

Exercises

10.4* The table on the next page gives consumption per capita, *cpop*, gross fixed capital formation per capita, *gfcfpop*, and gross domestic product per capita, *gdppop*, all measured in US$, for thirty-three countries in 1998. The output from an OLS regression of *cpop* on *gdppop*, and an IV regression using *gfcfpop* as an instrument for *gdppop*, are shown. Comment on the differences in the results.

10.5 The researcher in Exercise 10.3 discovers that last year's advertising budget, $A(-1)$, is also an important determinant of A, so that the model is

$$S = \beta_1 + \beta_2 A + u_S$$
$$A = \alpha_1 + \alpha_2 S + \alpha_3 A(-1) + u_A.$$

Explain how this information could be used to obtain a consistent estimator of β_2, and prove that it is consistent.

10.6 Suppose that $A(-1)$ in Exercise 10.5 also has an influence on S. How would this affect the fitting of the model?

	C	I	Y		C	I	Y
Australia	15024	4749	19461	South Korea	4596	1448	6829
Austria	19813	6787	26104	Luxembourg	26400	9767	42650
Belgium	18367	5174	24522	Malaysia	1683	873	3268
Canada	15786	4017	20085	Mexico	3359	1056	4328
China–PR	446	293	768	Netherlands	17558	4865	24086
China–HK	17067	7262	24452	New Zealand	11236	2658	13992
Denmark	25199	6947	32769	Norway	23415	9221	32933
Finland	17991	4741	24952	Pakistan	389	79	463
France	19178	4622	24587	Philippines	760	176	868
Germany	20058	5716	26219	Portugal	8579	2644	9976
Greece	9991	2460	11551	Spain	11255	3415	14052
Iceland	25294	6706	30622	Sweden	20687	4487	26866
India	291	84	385	Switzerland	27648	7815	36864
Indonesia	351	216	613	Thailand	1226	479	1997
Ireland	13045	4791	20132	UK	19743	4316	23844
Italy	16134	4075	20580	USA	26387	6540	32377
Japan	21478	7923	30124				

```
. reg cpop gdppop

    Source |       SS       df       MS              Number of obs =      33
-----------+------------------------------           F(  1,    31) = 1331.29
     Model | 2.5686e+09       1   2.5686e+09         Prob > F      =  0.0000
  Residual | 59810749.2      31   1929379.01         R-squared     =  0.9772
-----------+------------------------------           Adj R-squared =  0.9765
     Total | 2.6284e+09      32   82136829.4         Root MSE      =  1389.0


------------------------------------------------------------------------------
      cpop |     Coef.   Std. Err.      t    P>|t|     [95% Conf. Interval]
-----------+------------------------------------------------------------------
    gdppop |  .7303066   .0200156    36.487  0.000     .6894845    .7711287
     _cons |  379.4871   443.6764     0.855  0.399     -525.397    1284.371
------------------------------------------------------------------------------


. ivreg cpop (gdppop=gfcfpop)

Instrumental variables (2SLS) regression

    Source |       SS       df       MS              Number of obs =      33
-----------+------------------------------           F(  1,    31) = 1192.18
     Model | 2.5679e+09       1   2.5679e+09         Prob > F      =  0.0000
  Residual | 60494538.1      31   1951436.71         R-squared     =  0.9770
-----------+------------------------------           Adj R-squared =  0.9762
     Total | 2.6284e+09      32   82136829.4         Root MSE      =  1396.9
```

```
-----------------------------------------------------------------
   cpop |    Coef.    Std. Err.      t     P>|t|    [95% Conf. Interval]
--------+--------------------------------------------------------
 gdppop | .7183909    .0208061    34.528   0.000    .6759566    .7608252
  _cons |  600.946    456.7973     1.316   0.198   -330.6982    1532.59
-----------------------------------------------------------------
Instrumented:  gdppop
Instruments:   gfcfpop
-----------------------------------------------------------------
```

10.7 The researcher in Exercise 10.3 finds out that the average price of the product, P, and last year's sales, $S(-1)$, are important determinants of S, so that the model is

$$S = \beta_1 + \beta_2 A + \beta_3 P + \beta_4 S(-1) + u_S$$
$$A = \alpha_1 + \alpha_2 S + u_A.$$

How would this affect the fitting of the model?

10.8 In principle $ASVABC$ might be a positive function of S, in which case the educational attainment model should have two equations:

$$S = \beta_1 + \beta_2 ASVABC + \beta_3 SM + u_S$$
$$ASVABC = \alpha_1 + \alpha_2 S + u_A.$$

Using your $EAEF$ data set, fit the second equation, first using OLS, second using instrumental variables estimation with SM as an instrument. Investigate analytically the likely direction of the bias in the slope coefficient in the OLS regression, and check whether a comparison of the OLS and IV estimates confirms your analysis.

10.9 The output from a Durbin–Wu–Hausman test using the regressions in Exercise 10.4 is shown. Perform the test and state whether or not it supports your discussion in Exercise 10.4.

```
. hausman, constant sigmamore

             ---- Coefficients ----
         |     (b)          (B)           (b-B)      sqrt(diag(V_b-V_B))
         |    Prior       Current        Difference         S.E.
---------+----------------------------------------------------------------
 gdppop  |  .7183909    .7303066       -.0119157         .0052323
  _cons  |   600.946    379.4871        221.4589         97.24403
---------+----------------------------------------------------------------
         b = less efficient estimates obtained previously from ivreg.
         B = more efficient estimates obtained from regress.

Test:  Ho:  difference in coefficients not systematic

            chi2( 1) = (b-B)'[(V_b-V_B)^(-1)](b-B)
                     =     5.19
            Prob>chi2 =   0.0228
```

11 Binary choice and limited dependent models, and maximum likelihood estimation

Economists are often interested in the factors behind the decision-making of individuals or enterprises. Examples are:

- Why do some people go to college while others do not?
- Why do some women enter the labor force while others do not?
- Why do some people buy houses while others rent?
- Why do some people migrate while others stay put?

The models that have been developed are known as binary choice or qualitative response models with the outcome, which we will denote Y, being assigned a value of 1 if the event occurs and 0 otherwise. Models with more than two possible outcomes have been developed, but we will restrict our attention to binary choice. The linear probability model apart, binary choice models are fitted using maximum likelihood estimation. The chapter ends with an introduction to this topic.

11.1 The linear probability model

The simplest binary choice model is the linear probability model where, as the name implies, the probability of the event occurring, p, is assumed to be a linear function of a set of explanatory variable(s):

$$p_i = p(Y_i = 1) = \beta_1 + \beta_2 X_i. \tag{11.1}$$

Graphically, the relationship is as shown in Figure 11.1, if there is just one explanatory variable. Of course p is unobservable. One has data only on the outcome, Y. In the linear probability model this is used as a dummy variable for the dependent variable.

As an illustration, we investigate the factors influencing graduating from high school. We will define a variable $GRAD$ that is equal to 1 for those individuals who graduated, and 0 for those who dropped out, and we will regress it on $ASVABC$, the composite cognitive ability test score. The regression output in

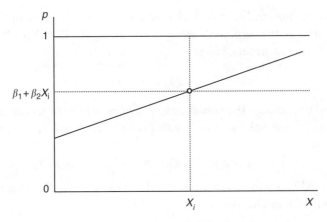

Figure 11.1 Linear probability model

Table 11.1

```
. reg GRAD ASVABC

    Source |      SS        df       MS                Number of obs =      570
-----------+------------------------------             F(  1,    568) =   112.59
     Model |  7.13422753      1   7.13422753           Prob > F       =   0.0000
  Residual |  35.9903339    568   .063363264           R-squared      =   0.1654
-----------+------------------------------             Adj R-squared  =   0.1640
     Total |  43.1245614    569    .07579009           Root MSE       =   .25172


---------------------------------------------------------------------------------
      GRAD |    Coef.   Std. Err.       t     P>|t|     [95% Conf. Interval]
-----------+---------------------------------------------------------------------
    ASVABC |  .0121518   .0011452    10.611   0.000     .0099024     .0144012
     _cons |  .3081194   .0583932     5.277   0.000     .1934264     .4228124
```

Table 11.1 shows the result of fitting this linear probability model, using *EAEF* Data Set 21.

The regression result suggests that the probability of graduating from high school increases by a proportion 0.012, that is, 1.2 percent, for every point increase in the *ASVABC* score. *ASVABC* is scaled so that it has mean 50 and standard deviation 10, so a one-standard deviation increase in the score would increase the probability of graduating by 12 percent. The intercept implies that if *ASVABC* were 0, the probability of graduating would be 31 percent. However the *ASVABC* score is scaled in such a way as to make its minimum about 20, and accordingly it is doubtful whether the interpretation should be taken at face value.

Unfortunately, the linear probability model has some serious defects. First, there are problems with the disturbance term. As usual, the value of the dependent variable Y_i in observation i has a nonstochastic component and a random component. The nonstochastic component depends on X_i and the parameters and is the expected value of Y_i given X_i, $E(Y_i|X_i)$. The random component is the disturbance term.

$$Y_i = E(Y_i|X_i) + u_i. \tag{11.2}$$

It is simple to compute the nonstochastic component in observation i because Y can take only two values. It is 1 with probability p_i and 0 with probability $(1 - p_i)$:

$$E(Y_i) = 1 \times p_i + 0 \times (1 - p_i) = p_i = \beta_1 + \beta_2 X_i. \tag{11.3}$$

The expected value in observation i is therefore $\beta_1 + \beta_2 X_i$. This means that we can rewrite the model as

$$Y_i = \beta_1 + \beta_2 X_i + u_i. \tag{11.4}$$

The probability function is thus also the nonstochastic component of the relationship between Y and X. It follows that, for the outcome variable Y_i to be equal to 1, as represented by the point A in Figure 11.2, the disturbance term must be equal to $(1 - \beta_1 - \beta_2 X_i)$. For the outcome to be 0, as represented by the point B, the disturbance term must be $(-\beta_1 - \beta_2 X_i)$. Thus the distribution of the disturbance term consists of just two specific values. It is not even continuous, never mind normal. This means that the standard errors and the usual test statistics are invalidated. For good measure, the two possible values of the disturbance term change with X, so the distribution is heteroscedastic as well. It can be shown that the population variance of u_i is $(\beta_1 + \beta_2 X_i)(1 - \beta_1 - \beta_2 X_i)$, and this varies with X_i.

The other problem is that the predicted probability may be greater than 1 or less than 0 for extreme values of X. In the example of graduating from high school, the regression equation predicts a probability greater than 1 for the 176 respondents with $ASVABC$ scores greater than 56.

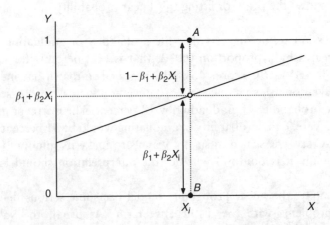

Figure 11.2 Disturbance term in the linear probability model

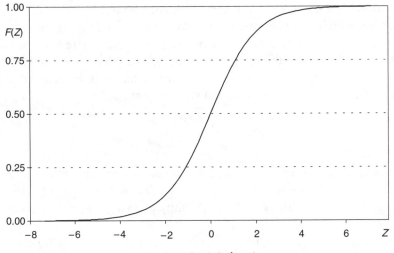

Figure 11.3 Logistic function

The first problem is dealt with by fitting the model with a technique known as maximum likelihood estimation, described in Section 11.6, instead of least squares. The second problem involves elaborating the model as follows. Define a variable Z that is a linear function of the explanatory variables. In the present case, since we have only one explanatory variable, this function is

$$Z_i = \beta_1 + \beta_2 X_i. \tag{11.5}$$

Next, suppose that p is a sigmoid (S-shaped) function of Z, for example as shown in Figure 11.3. Below a certain value of Z, there is very little chance of the individual graduating from high school. Above a certain value, the individual is almost certain to graduate. In between, the probability is sensitive to the value of Z.

This deals with the problem of nonsense probability estimates, but then there is the question of what should be the precise mathematical form of this function. There is no definitive answer to this. The two most popular forms are the logistic function, which is used in logit estimation, and the cumulative normal distribution, which is used in probit estimation. According to one of the leading authorities on the subject, Amemiya (1981), both give satisfactory results most of the time and neither has any particular advantage. We will start with the former.

11.2 Logit analysis

In logit estimation one hypothesizes that the probability of the occurrence of the event is determined by the function

$$p_i = F(Z_i) = \frac{1}{1 + e^{-Z_i}}. \tag{11.6}$$

This is the function shown in Figure 11.3. As Z tends to infinity, e^{-Z} tends to 0 and p has a limiting upper bound of 1. As Z tends to minus infinity, e^{-Z} tends to infinity and p has a limiting lower bound of 0. Hence there is no possibility of getting predictions of the probability being greater than 1 or less than 0.

The marginal effect of Z on the probability, which will be denoted $f(Z)$, is given by the derivative of this function with respect to Z:

$$f(Z) = \frac{dp}{dZ} = \frac{e^{-Z}}{(1 + e^{-Z})^2}. \tag{11.7}$$

The function is shown in Figure 11.4. You can see that the effect of changes in Z on the probability is very small for large positive or large negative values of Z, and that the sensitivity of the probability to changes in Z is greatest at the midpoint value of 0.

In the case of the example of graduating from high school, the function is

$$p_i = \frac{1}{1 + e^{-\beta_1 - \beta_2 ASVABC_i}}. \tag{11.8}$$

If we fit the model, we get the output shown in Table 11.2.

The model is fitted by maximum likelihood estimation and, as the output indicates, this uses an iterative process to estimate the parameters.

The z statistics in the Stata output are approximations to t statistics and have nothing to do with the Z variable discussed in the text. (Some regression applications describe them as t statistics.) The z statistic for $ASVABC$ is highly significant. How should one interpret the coefficients? To calculate the marginal effect of $ASVABC$ on p we need to calculate $dp/dASVABC$. You could calculate the differential directly, but the best way to do this, especially if Z is a function

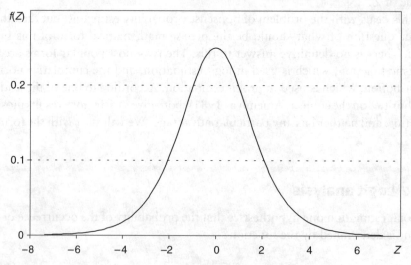

Figure 11.4 Marginal effect of Z on the probability

Table 11.2

```
. logit GRAD ASVABC

Iteration 0:  Log Likelihood =-162.29468
Iteration 1:  Log Likelihood =-132.97646
Iteration 2:  Log Likelihood =-117.99291
Iteration 3:  Log Likelihood =-117.36084
Iteration 4:  Log Likelihood =-117.35136
Iteration 5:  Log Likelihood =-117.35135

Logit Estimates                            Number of obs =     570
                                           chi2(1)       =   89.89
                                           Prob > chi2   =  0.0000
Log Likelihood = -117.35135                Pseudo R2     =  0.2769

------------------------------------------------------------------------
   GRAD |     Coef.   Std. Err.      z     P>|z|    [95% Conf. Interval]
--------+---------------------------------------------------------------
 ASVABC |   .1666022   .0211265    7.886   0.000    .1251951    .2080094
  _cons |  -5.003779   .8649213   -5.785   0.000   -6.698993   -3.308564
------------------------------------------------------------------------
```

of more than one variable, is to break it up into two stages. p is a function of Z, and Z is a function of $ASVABC$, so

$$\frac{dp}{dASVABC} = \frac{dp}{dZ}\frac{dZ}{dASVABC} = f(Z)\beta, \qquad (11.9)$$

where $f(Z)$ is as defined above. The probability of graduating from high school, and the marginal effect, are plotted as functions of $ASVABC$ in Figure 11.5.

How can you summarize the effect of the $ASVABC$ score on the probability of graduating? The usual method is to calculate the marginal effect at the mean value of the explanatory variables. In this sample the mean value of $ASVABC$ was 50.15. For this value, Z is equal to 3.3514, and e^{-Z} is equal to 0.0350. Using this, $f(Z)$ is 0.0327 and the marginal effect is 0.0054:

$$f(Z)\beta_2 = \frac{e^{-Z}}{(1+e^{-Z})^2}\beta_2 = \frac{0.0350}{(1.0350)^2} \times 0.1666 = 0.0054. \qquad (11.10)$$

In other words, at the sample mean, a one-point increase in $ASVABC$ increases the probability of graduating from high school by 0.5 percent. This is a very small amount and the reason is that, for those with the mean $ASVABC$, the estimated probability of graduating is very high:

$$p = \frac{1}{1+e^{-Z}} = \frac{1}{1+0.0350} = 0.9661. \qquad (11.11)$$

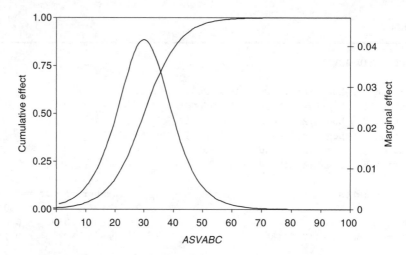

Figure 11.5 Cumulative and marginal effects of $ASVABC$

See also Figure 11.5. Of course we could calculate the marginal effect for other values of $ASVABC$ if we wished and in this particular case it may be of interest to evaluate it for low $ASVABC$, where individuals are at greater risk of not graduating. For example, when $ASVABC$ is 30, Z is -0.0058, e^{-Z} is 1.0058, $f(Z)$ is 0.2500, and the marginal effect is 0.0417, or 4.2 percent. It is much higher because an individual with such a low score has only a 50 percent chance of graduating and an increase in $ASVABC$ can make a substantial difference.

Generalization to more than one explanatory variable

Logit analysis is easily extended to the case where there is more than one explanatory variable. Suppose that we decide to relate graduating from high school to $ASVABC$, SM, the number of years of schooling of the mother, SF, the number of years of schooling of the father, and a dummy variable $MALE$ that is equal to 1 for males, 0 for females. The Z variable becomes

$$Z = \beta_1 + \beta_2 ASVABC + \beta_3 SM + \beta_4 SF + \beta_5 MALE. \tag{11.12}$$

The corresponding regression output (with iteration messages deleted) is shown is Table 11.3.

The mean values of $ASVABC$, SM, SF, and $MALE$ were as shown in Table 11.4, and hence the value of Z at the mean was 3.3380. From this one obtains 0.0355 for e^{-Z} and 0.0331 for $f(Z)$. The table shows the marginal effects, calculated by multiplying $f(Z)$ by the estimates of the coefficients of the logit regression.

According to the computations, a one-point increase in the $ASVABC$ score increases the probability of going to college by 0.5 percent, every additional year of schooling of the mother increases the probability by 0.2 percent, every

Table 11.3

```
. logit GRAD ASVABC SM SF MALE

Logit Estimates                                 Number of obs =      570
                                                chi2(4)       =    91.59
                                                Prob > chi2   =  0.0000
Log Likelihood = -116.49968                     Pseudo R2     =  0.2822
```

GRAD	Coef.	Std. Err.	z	P>|z|	[95% Conf. Interval]	
ASVABC	.1563271	.0224382	6.967	0.000	.1123491	.2003051
SM	.0645542	.0773804	0.834	0.404	-.0871086	.216217
SF	.0054552	.0616822	0.088	0.930	-.1154397	.12635
MALE	-.2790915	.3601689	-0.775	0.438	-.9850095	.4268265
_cons	-5.15931	.994783	-5.186	0.000	-7.109049	-3.209571

additional year of schooling of the father increases the probability by a negligible amount, and being male reduces the probability by 0.9 percent. From the regression output it can be seen that the effect of *ASVABC* was significant at the 0.1 percent level but the effects of the parental education variables and the male dummy were insignificant.

Goodness of fit and statistical tests

There is no measure of goodness of fit equivalent to R^2 in maximum likelihood estimation. In default, numerous measures have been proposed for comparing alternative model specifications. Denoting the actual outcome in observation i as Y_i, with $Y_i = 1$ if the event occurs and 0 if it does not, and denoting the predicted probability of the event occurring $\hat{p}_i$, the measures include the following:

- the number of outcomes correctly predicted, taking the prediction in observation i as 1 if $\hat{p}_i$ is greater than 0.5 and 0 if it is less;

Table 11.4 Logit estimation. Dependent variable: *GRAD*

Variable	Mean	b	Mean $\times b$	$f(Z)$	$bf(Z)$
ASVABC	50.151	0.1563	7.8386	0.0331	0.0052
SM	11.653	0.0646	0.7528	0.0331	0.0021
SF	11.818	0.0055	0.0650	0.0331	0.0002
MALE	0.570	-0.2791	-0.1591	0.0331	-0.0092
Constant	1.000	-5.1593	-5.1593		
Total			3.3380		

- the sum of the squared residuals $\sum_{i=1}^{n} (Y_i - \hat{p}_i)^2$;

- the correlation between the outcomes and predicted probabilities, $r_{Y\hat{p}}$.

- the pseudo-R^2 in the logit output, explained in Section 11.6.

Each of these measures has its shortcomings and Amemiya (1981) recommends considering more than one and comparing the results.

Nevertheless, the standard significance tests are similar to those for the standard regression model. The significance of an individual coefficient can be evaluated via its t statistic. However, since the standard error is valid only asymptotically (in large samples), the same goes for the t statistic, and since the t distribution converges on the normal distribution in large samples, the critical values of the latter should be used. The counterpart of the F test of the explanatory power of the model (H_0: all the slope coefficients are 0, H_1: at least one is nonzero) is a chi-squared test with the chi-squared statistic in the logit output distributed under H_0 with degrees of freedom equal to the number of explanatory variables. Details are provided in Section 11.6.

Exercises

11.1   Investigate the factors affecting going to college using your *EAEF* data set. Define a binary variable *COLLEGE* to be equal to 1 if $S > 12$ and 0 otherwise. Regress *COLLEGE* on *ASVABC*, *SM*, *SF*, and *MALE* (1) using ordinary least squares, and (2) using logit analysis. Calculate the marginal effects in the logit analysis and compare them with those obtained using OLS.

11.2*   A researcher, using a sample of 2,868 individuals from the NLSY, is investigating how the probability of a respondent obtaining a bachelor's degree from a four-year college is related to the respondent's score on *ASVABC*. 26.7 percent of the respondents earned bachelor's degrees. *ASVABC* ranged from 22 to 65, with mean value 50.2, and most scores were in the range 40 to 60. Defining a variable *BACH* to be equal to 1 if the respondent had a bachelor's degree (or higher degree) and 0 otherwise, the researcher fitted the OLS regression (standard errors in parentheses):

$$\widehat{BACH} = -0.864 + 0.023 ASVABC. \quad R^2 = 0.21$$
$$(0.042) \ (0.001)$$

She also fitted the following logit regression:

$$\hat{Z} = -11.103 + 0.189 \, ASVABC,$$
$$(0.487) \ (0.009)$$

where Z is the variable in the logit function. Using this regression, she plotted the probability and marginal effect functions shown in the diagram.

(a) Give an interpretation of the OLS regression and explain why OLS is not a satisfactory estimation method for this kind of model.

(b) With reference to the figure, discuss the variation of the marginal effect of the *ASVABC* score implicit in the logit regression.

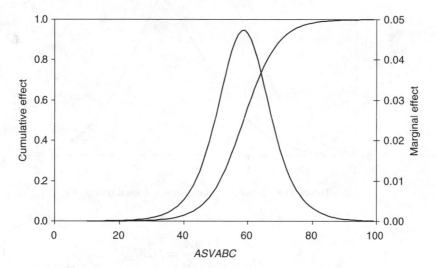

(c) Sketch the probability and marginal effect diagrams for the OLS regression and compare them with those for the logit regression. (In your discussion, make use of the information in the first paragraph of this question.)

11.3 **Probit analysis**

An alternative approach to the binary choice model is to use the cumulative standardized normal distribution to model the sigmoid relationship $F(Z)$. (A standardized normal distribution is one with mean 0 and unit variance.) As with logit analysis, you start by defining x a variable Z that is a linear function of the variables that determine the probability:

$$Z = \beta_1 + \beta_2 X_2 + \cdots + \beta_k X_k. \tag{11.13}$$

$F(Z)$, the standardized cumulative normal distribution, gives the probability of the event occurring for any value of Z:

$$p_i = F(Z_i). \tag{11.14}$$

Maximum likelihood analysis is used to obtain estimates of the parameters. The marginal effect of X_i is $\partial p / \partial X_i$ which, as in the case of logit analysis, is best

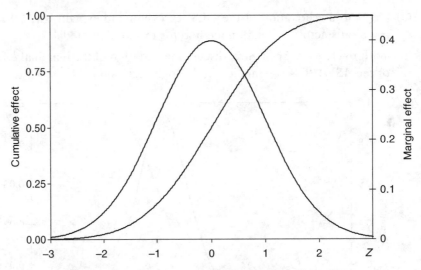

Figure 11.6 Cumulative and marginal normal effects of Z

computed as

$$\frac{\partial p}{\partial X_i} = \frac{dp}{dZ}\frac{\partial Z}{\partial X_i} = f(Z)\beta_i. \tag{11.15}$$

Now since $F(Z)$ is the cumulative standardized normal distribution, $f(Z)$, its derivative, is just the standardized normal distribution itself:

$$f(Z) = \frac{1}{\sqrt{2\pi}}e^{-\frac{1}{2}Z^2}. \tag{11.16}$$

Figure 11.6 plots $F(Z)$ and $f(Z)$ for probit analysis. As with logit analysis, the marginal effect of any variable is not constant. It depends on the value of

Table 11.5

```
. probit GRAD ASVABC SM SF MALE

Probit Estimates                              Number of obs =      570
                                              chi2(4)       =    94.12
                                              Prob > chi2   =   0.0000
Log Likelihood = -115.23672                   Pseudo R2     =   0.2900
```

GRAD	Coef.	Std. Err.	z	P>|z|	[95% Conf. Interval]	
ASVABC	.0831963	.0117006	7.110	0.000	.0602635	.106129
SM	.0353463	.0425199	0.831	0.406	-.0479913	.1186838
SF	.0057229	.032375	0.177	0.860	-.0577309	.0691766
MALE	-.1883038	.1873426	-1.005	0.315	-.5554885	.178881
_cons	-2.702067	.5335551	-5.064	0.000	-3.747816	-1.656318

Table 11.6 Probit estimation. Dependent variable: *GRAD*

Variable	Mean	b	Mean $\times$ b	$f(Z)$	$bf(Z)$
ASVABC	50.151	0.0832	4.1726	0.0732	0.0061
SM	11.653	0.0353	0.4114	0.0732	0.0026
SF	11.818	0.0057	0.0674	0.0732	0.0004
MALE	0.570	−0.1883	−0.1073	0.0732	−0.0138
Constant	1.000	−2.7021	−2.7021		
Total			1.8418		

$f(Z)$, which in turn depends on the values of each of the explanatory variables. To obtain a summary statistic for the marginal effect, the usual procedure is parallel to that used in logit analysis. You calculate Z for the mean values of the explanatory variables. Next you calculate $f(Z)$, as in (11.16). Then you calculate $f(Z)\beta_i$ to obtain the marginal effect of X_i.

This will be illustrated with the example of graduating from high school, using the same specification as in the logit regression. The regression output, with iteration messages deleted, is shown in Table 11.5.

The computation of the marginal effects at the sample means is shown in Table 11.6. Z is 1.8418 when evaluated at the mean values of the variables and $f(Z)$ is 0.0732. The estimates indicate that a one-point increase in the *ASVABC* score increases the probability of going to college by 0.6 percent, every additional year of schooling of the mother increases the probability by 0.3 percent, every additional year of schooling of the father increases the probability by a negligible amount, and being male reduces the probability by 1.4 percent. Generally logit and probit analysis yield similar marginal effects. However, the tails of the logit and probit distributions are different and they can give different results if the sample is unbalanced, with most of the outcomes similar and only a small minority different. This is the case in the present example because only 8 percent of the respondents failed to graduate, and in this case the estimates of the marginal effects are somewhat larger for the probit regression.

Exercises

11.3   Regress the variable *COLLEGE* defined in Exercise 11.1 on *ASVABC*, *MALE*, *SM*, and *SF* using probit analysis. Calculate the marginal effects and compare them with those obtained using OLS and logit analysis.

11.4*   The following probit regression, with iteration messages deleted, was fitted using 2726 observations on females in the NLSY in 1994.

WORKING is a binary variable equal to 1 if the respondent was working in 1994, 0 otherwise. CHILDL06 is a dummy variable equal to 1 if there was a child aged less than 6 in the household, 0 otherwise. CHILDL16 is a dummy variable equal to 1 if there was a child aged

```
.probit WORKING S AGE CHILDL06 CHILDL16 MARRIED ETHBLACK ETHHISP if MALE==0
```

```
Probit estimates                          Number of obs   =      2726
                                          LR chi2(7)      =    165.08
                                          Prob > chi2     =    0.0000
Log likelihood = -1403.0835               Pseudo R2       =    0.0556
```

WORKING	Coef.	Std. Err.	z	P>|z|	[95% Conf. Interval]	
S	.0892571	.0120629	7.399	0.000	.0656143	.1129
AGE	-.0438511	.012478	-3.514	0.000	-.0683076	-.0193946
CHILDL06	-.5841503	.0744923	-7.842	0.000	-.7301525	-.4381482
CHILDL16	-.1359097	.0792359	-1.715	0.086	-.2912092	.0193897
MARRIED	-.0076543	.0631618	-0.121	0.904	-.1314492	.1161407
ETHBLACK	-.2780887	.081101	-3.429	0.001	-.4370436	-.1191337
ETHHISP	-.0191608	.1055466	-0.182	0.856	-.2260284	.1877068
_cons	.673472	.2712267	2.483	0.013	.1418775	1.205066

less than 16, but no child less than 6, in the household, 0 otherwise. *MARRIED* is equal to 1 if the respondent was married with spouse present, 0 otherwise. The remaining variables are as described in *EAEF Regression Exercises*. The mean values of the variables are given in the output below:

```
.sum WORKING S AGE CHILDL06 CHILDL16 MARRIED ETHBLACK ETHHISP if MALE==0
```

Variable	Obs	Mean	Std. Dev.	Min	Max
WORKING	2726	.7652238	.4239366	0	1
S	2726	13.30998	2.444771	0	20
AGE	2726	17.64637	2.24083	14	22
CHILDL06	2726	.3991196	.4898073	0	1
CHILDL16	2726	.3180484	.4658038	0	1
MARRIED	2726	.6228907	.4847516	0	1
ETHBLACK	2726	.1305943	.3370179	0	1
ETHHISP	2726	.0722671	.2589771	0	1

Calculate the marginal effects and discuss whether they are plausible. [The data set and a description are posted on the website.]

11.4 Censored regressions: tobit analysis

Suppose that one hypothesizes the relationship

$$Y^* = \beta_1 + \beta_2 X + u, \tag{11.17}$$

with the dependent variable subject to either a lower bound Y_L or an upper bound Y_U. In the case of a lower bound, the model can be characterized as

$$Y^* = \beta_1 + \beta_2 X + u$$
$$Y = Y^* \qquad \text{for } Y^* > Y_L \qquad (11.18)$$
$$Y = Y_L \qquad \text{for } Y^* \leq Y_L$$

and similarly for a model with an upper bound. Such a model is known as a censored regression model because Y^* is unobserved for $Y^* < Y_L$ or $Y^* > Y_U$. It is effectively a hybrid between a standard regression model and a binary choice model, and OLS would yield inconsistent estimates if used to fit it. To see this, consider the relationship illustrated in Figure 11.7, a one-shot Monte Carlo experiment where the true relationship is

$$Y = -40 + 1.2X + u, \qquad (11.19)$$

the data for X are the integers from 11 to 60, and u is a normally distributed random variable with mean 0 and standard deviation 10. If Y were unconstrained, the observations would be as shown in Figure 11.7. However we will suppose that Y is constrained to be non-negative, in which case the observations will be as shown in Figure 11.8. For such a sample, it is obvious that an OLS regression that included those observations with Y constrained to be 0 would yield inconsistent estimates, with the estimator of the slope downwards biased and that of the intercept upwards biased.

The remedy, you might think, would be to use only the subsample of unconstrained observations, but even then the OLS estimators would be biased.

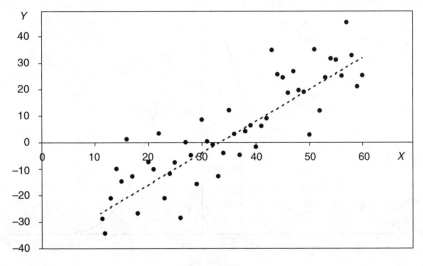

Figure 11.7

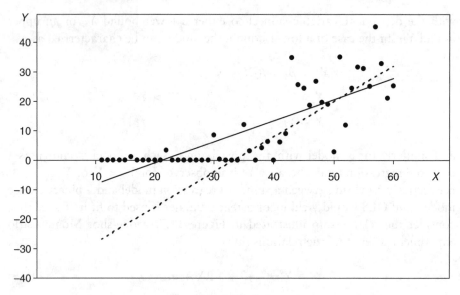

Figure 11.8

An observation i will appear in the subsample only if $Y_i > 0$, that is, if

$$-40 + 1.2X_i + u_i > 0. \qquad (11.20)$$

This requires

$$u_i > 40 - 1.2X_i \qquad (11.21)$$

and so u_i must have the truncated distribution shown in Figure 11.9. In this example, the expected value of u_i must be positive and a negative function of X_i.

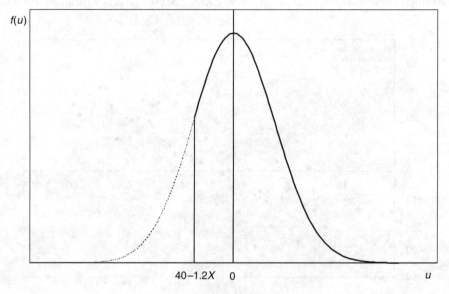

Figure 11.9

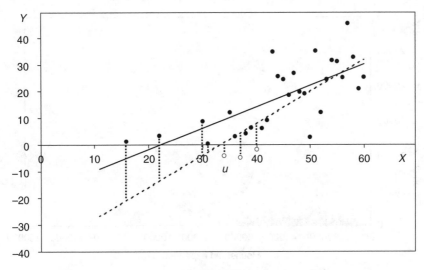

Figure 11.10

Since u_i is negatively correlated with X_i, the fourth Gauss–Markov condition is violated and OLS will yield inconsistent estimates.

Figure 11.10 displays the impact of this correlation graphically. The observations with the four lowest values of X appear in the sample only because their disturbance terms (marked) are positive and large enough to make Y positive. In addition, in the range where X is large enough to make the nonstochastic component of Y positive, observations with large negative values of the disturbance term are dropped. Three such observations, marked as circles, are shown in the figure. Both of these effects cause the intercept to tend to be overestimated, and the slope to tend to be underestimated, in an OLS regression.

If it can be assumed that the disturbance term has a normal distribution, one solution to the problem is to use tobit analysis, a maximum likelihood estimation technique that combines probit analysis with regression analysis. A mathematical treatment will not be attempted here. Instead it will be illustrated using data on expenditure on household equipment from the Consumer Expenditure Survey data set. Figure 11.11 plots this category of expenditure, *HEQ*, and total household expenditure, *EXP*. For 86 of the 869 observations, expenditure on household equipment is 0. The output from a tobit regression is shown (Table 11.7). In Stata the command is tobit and the point of left-censoring is indicated by the number in parentheses after '11'. If the data were right-censored, '11' would be replaced by 'ul'. Both may be included.

OLS regressions including and excluding the observations with 0 expenditure on household equipment yield slope coefficients of 0.0472 and 0.0468 respectively, both of them below the tobit estimate, as expected. The size of the bias tends to increase with the proportion of constrained observations. In this case only 10 percent are constrained, and hence the difference between the tobit and OLS estimates is small.

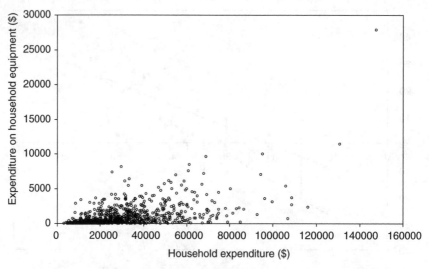

Figure 11.11 Expenditure on household equipment and total household expenditure

Tobit regression yields inconsistent estimates if the disturbance term does not have a normal distribution or if it is subject to heteroscedasticity (Amemiya, 1984). Judging by the plot in Figure 11.11, the observations in the example are subject to heteroscedasticity and it may be preferable to use expenditure on household equipment as a proportion of total expenditure as the dependent variable, in the same way that in his seminal study, which investigated expenditure on

Table 11.7

```
. tobit HEQ EXP, ll(0)

Tobit Estimates                              Number of obs =      869
                                             chi2(1)       =   315.41
                                             Prob > chi2   =   0.0000
Log Likelihood = -6911.0175                  Pseudo R2     =   0.0223

--------------------------------------------------------------------------
     HEQ |      Coef.   Std. Err.       t    P>|t|    [95% Conf. Interval]
---------+----------------------------------------------------------------
     EXP |   .0520828   .0027023   19.273   0.000    .0467789    .0573866
   _cons |  -661.8156   97.95977   -6.756   0.000   -854.0813   -469.5499
---------+----------------------------------------------------------------
     _se |   1521.896   38.6333            (Ancillary parameter)
--------------------------------------------------------------------------

Obs. summary:        86 left-censored observations at HEQ<=0
                    783 uncensored observations
--------------------------------------------------------------------------
```

consumer durables, Tobin (1958) used expenditure on durables as a proportion of disposable personal income.

Exercise

11.5   Using the CES data set, perform a tobit regression of expenditure on your commodity on total household expenditure, and compare the slope coefficient with those obtained in OLS regressions including and excluding observations with 0 expenditure on your commodity.

11.5 **Sample selection bias**

In the tobit model, whether or not an observation falls into the regression category ($Y > Y_L$ or $Y < Y_U$) or the constrained category ($Y = Y_L$ or $Y = Y_U$) depends entirely on the values of the regressors and the disturbance term. However, it may well be that participation in the regression category may depend on factors other than those in the regression model, in which case a more general model specification with an explicit two-stage process may be required. The first stage, participation in the regression category, or being constrained, depends on the net benefit of participating, B^*, a latent (unobservable) variable that depends on a set of $m - 1$ variables Q_j and a random term ε:

$$B_i^* = \delta_1 + \sum_{j=2}^{m} \delta_j Q_{ji} + \varepsilon_i. \tag{11.22}$$

The second stage, the regression model, is parallel to that for the tobit model:

$$Y_i^* = \beta_1 + \sum_{j=2}^{k} \beta_j X_{ji} + u_i$$

$$Y_i = Y_i^* \qquad \text{for } B_i^* > 0, \tag{11.23}$$

$$Y_i \text{ is not observed} \qquad \text{for } B_i^* \leq 0.$$

For an observation in the sample,

$$E(u_i | B_i^* > 0) = E\left(u_i | \varepsilon_i > -\delta_1 - \sum_{j=2}^{m} \delta_j Q_{ji} \right). \tag{11.24}$$

If ε_i and u_i are distributed independently, $E(u_i | \varepsilon_i > -\delta_1 - \sum_{j=2}^{m} \delta_j Q_{ji})$ reduces to the unconditional $E(u_i)$ and the selection process does not interfere with the regression model. However if ε_i and u_i are correlated, $E(u_i)$ will be nonzero and problems parallel to those in the tobit model arise, with the consequence that OLS estimates are inconsistent (see Box 11.1 on the Heckman two-step procedure). If

---

BOX 11.1   The Heckman two-step procedure

The problem of selection bias arises because the expected value of u is nonzero for observations in the selected category if u and ε are correlated. It can be shown that, for these observations,

$$E\left(u_i \mid \varepsilon_i > -\delta_1 - \sum_{j=2}^{m} \delta_j Q_{ji}\right) = \frac{\sigma_{u\varepsilon}}{\sigma_\varepsilon} \lambda_i,$$

where $\sigma_{u\varepsilon}$ is the population covariance of u and ε, σ_ε is the standard deviation of ε, and λ_i, described by Heckman (1976) as the inverse of Mill's ratio, is given by

$$\lambda_i = \frac{f(v_i)}{F(v_i)},$$

where

$$v_i = \frac{\varepsilon_i}{\sigma_\varepsilon} = \frac{-\delta_1 - \sum_{j=2}^{m} \delta_j Q_{ji}}{\sigma_\varepsilon}$$

and the functions f and F are as defined in the section on probit analysis: $f(v_i)$ is the density function for ε normalized by its standard deviation and $F(v_i)$ is the probability of B_i^* being positive. It follows that

$$E\left(Y_i \mid \varepsilon_i > -\delta_1 - \sum_{j=2}^{m} \delta_j Q_{ji}\right) = E\left(\beta_1 + \sum_{j=2}^{k} \beta_j X_{ji} + u_i \mid \varepsilon_i > -\delta_1 - \sum_{j=2}^{m} \delta_j Q_{ji}\right)$$

$$= \beta_1 + \sum_{j=2}^{k} \beta_j X_{ji} + \frac{\sigma_{u\varepsilon}}{\sigma_\varepsilon} \lambda_i.$$

The sample selection bias arising in a regression of Y on the X variables using only the selected observations can therefore be regarded as a form of omitted variable bias, with λ the omitted variable. However, since the components of λ depend only on the selection process, it can be estimated from the results of probit analysis of selection (the first step). If it is included as an explanatory variable in the regression of Y on the X variables, least squares will then yield consistent estimates.

As Heckman acknowledges, the procedure was first employed by Gronau (1974), but it is known as the Heckman two-step procedure in recognition of its development by Heckman into an everyday working tool, its attraction being that it is computationally far simpler than maximum likelihood estimation of the joint model. However, with the improvement in computing speeds and the development of appropriate procedures in regression applications, maximum likelihood estimation of the joint model is no more burdensome than the two-step procedure and it has the advantage of being more efficient.

---

it can be assumed that ε_i and u_i are jointly normally distributed with correlation ρ, the model may be fitted by maximum likelihood estimation, with null hypothesis of no selection bias $H_0: \rho = 0$. The Q and X variables may overlap, identification requiring in practice that at least one Q variable is not also an X variable.

The procedure will be illustrated by fitting an earnings function for females on the lines of Gronau (1974), the earliest study of this type, using the LFP94 subsample from the NLSY data set described in Exercise 11.4 (Table 11.8). *CHILDL06* is a dummy variable equal to 1 if there was a child aged less than

Table 11.8

```
. heckman LGEARN S ASVABC ETHBLACK ETHHISP if MALE==0, select(S AGE CHILDL06
> CHILDL16 MARRIED ETHBLACK ETHHISP)

Iteration 0:   log likelihood = -2683.5848  (not concave)
...
Iteration 8:   log likelihood = -2668.8105

Heckman selection model                    Number of obs   =     2661
(regression model with sample selection)   Censored obs    =      640
                                           Uncensored obs  =     2021

                                           Wald chi2(4)    =   714.73
Log likelihood =  -2668.81                 Prob > chi2     =   0.0000
```

	Coef.	Std. Err.	z	P>|z|	[95% Conf. Interval]	
LGEARN						
S	.095949	.0056438	17.001	0.000	.0848874	.1070106
ASVABC	.0110391	.0014658	7.531	0.000	.0081663	.0139119
ETHBLACK	-.066425	.0381626	-1.741	0.082	-.1412223	.0083722
ETHHISP	.0744607	.0450095	1.654	0.098	-.0137563	.1626777
_cons	4.901626	.0768254	63.802	0.000	4.751051	5.052202
select						
S	.1041415	.0119836	8.690	0.000	.0806541	.1276288
AGE	-.0357225	.011105	-3.217	0.001	-.0574879	-.0139572
CHILDL06	-.3982738	.0703418	-5.662	0.000	-.5361412	-.2604064
CHILDL16	.0254818	.0709693	0.359	0.720	-.1136155	.164579
MARRIED	.0121171	.0546561	0.222	0.825	-.0950069	.1192412
ETHBLACK	-.2941378	.0787339	-3.736	0.000	-.4484535	-.1398222
ETHHISP	-.0178776	.1034237	-0.173	0.863	-.2205843	.1848292
_cons	.1682515	.2606523	0.646	0.519	-.3426176	.6791206
/athrho	1.01804	.0932533	10.917	0.000	.8352669	1.200813
/lnsigma	-.6349788	.0247858	-25.619	0.000	-.6835582	-.5863994
rho	.769067	.0380973			.683294	.8339024
sigma	.5299467	.0131352			.5048176	.5563268
lambda	.4075645	.02867			.3513724	.4637567

```
LR test of indep. eqns. (rho = 0):  chi2(1) = 32.90  Prob > chi2 = 0.0000
```

6 in the household, 0 otherwise. *CHILDL16* is a dummy variable equal to 1 if there was a child aged less than 16, but no child less than 6, in the household, 0 otherwise. *MARRIED* is equal to 1 if the respondent was married with spouse present, 0 otherwise. The other variables have the same definitions as in the *EAEF* data sets. The Stata command for this type of regression is 'heckman' and as usual it is followed by the dependent variable and the explanatory variables and qualifier, if any (here the sample is restricted to females). The variables in parentheses after 'select' are those hypothesized to influence whether the dependent variable is observed. In this example it is observed for 2,021 females and is missing for the remaining 640 who were not working in 1994. Seven iteration reports have been deleted from the output.

First we will check whether there is evidence of selection bias, that is, that $\rho \neq 0$. For technical reasons, ρ is estimated indirectly through atanh $\rho = \frac{1}{2} \log ((1 + \rho)/(1 - \rho))$, but the null hypothesis H_0: atanh $\rho = 0$ is equivalent to H_0: $\rho = 0$. atanh ρ is denoted 'athrho' in the output and, with an asymptotic t statistic of 10.92, the null hypothesis is rejected. A second test of the same null hypothesis that can be effected by comparing likelihood ratios is described in Section 11.6.

The regression results indicate that schooling and the *ASVABC* score have highly significant effects on earnings, that schooling has a positive effect on the probability of working, and that age, having a child aged less than 6, and being black have negative effects. The probit coefficients are different from those reported in Exercise 11.4, the reason being that, in a model of this type, probit analysis in isolation yields inefficient estimates.

Table 11.9

```
. reg LGEARN S ASVABC ETHBLACK ETHHISP if MALE==0
```

Source	SS	df	MS		Number of obs =	2021
					F(4, 2016) =	168.55
Model	143.231149	4	35.8077873		Prob > F =	0.0000
Residual	428.301239	2016	.212451012		R-squared =	0.2506
					Adj R-squared =	0.2491
Total	571.532389	2020	.282936826		Root MSE =	.46092

lgearn	Coef.	Std. Err.	t	P>|t|	[95% Conf. Interval]	
S	.0807836	.005244	15.405	0.000	.0704994	.0910677
ASVABC	.0117377	.0014886	7.885	0.000	.0088184	.014657
ETHBLACK	-.0148782	.0356868	-0.417	0.677	-.0848649	.0551086
ETHHISP	.0802266	.041333	1.941	0.052	-.0008333	.1612865
_cons	5.223712	.0703534	74.250	0.000	5.085739	5.361685

It is instructive to compare the regression results with those in Table 11.9 from an OLS regression not correcting for selection bias. The results are in fact quite similar, despite the presence of selection bias. The main difference is in the coefficient of *ETHBLACK*. The probit regression indicates that black females are significantly less likely to work than whites, controlling for other characteristics. If this is the case, black females, controlling for other characteristics, may require higher wage offers to be willing to work. This would reduce the apparent earnings discrimination against them, accounting for the smaller negative coefficient in the OLS regression. The other difference in the results is that the schooling coefficient in the OLS regression is 0.081, a little lower than that in the selection bias model, indicating that selection bias leads to a modest underestimate of the effect of education on female earnings.

One of the problems with the selection bias model is that it is often difficult to find variables that belong to the selection process but not the main regression. Having a child aged less than 6 is an excellent variable because it clearly affects the willingness of a female to work but not her earning power while working, and for this reason the example discussed here is very popular in expositions of the model.

One final point, made by Heckman (1976): if a selection variable is illegitimately included in a least squares regression, it may appear to have a significant effect. In the present case, if *CHILDL06* is included in the earnings function, it has a *positive* coefficient significant at the 5 percent level. The explanation would appear to be that females with young children tend to require an especially attractive wage offer, given their education and other endowments, to be induced to work.

Exercise

11.6* Using your *EAEF* data set, investigate whether there is evidence that selection bias affects the least squares estimate of the returns to college education. Define $COLLYEAR = S - 12$ if $S > 12, 0$ otherwise, and $LGEARNCL = LGEARN$ if $COLLYEAR > 0$, missing otherwise. Use the Heckman procedure to regress *LGEARNCL* on *COLLYEAR*, *ASVABC*, *MALE*, *ETHBLACK*, and *ETHHISP*, with *ASVABC*, *SM*, *SF*, and *SIBLINGS* being used to determine whether the respondent attended college. Run the equivalent regression using least squares. Comment on your findings.

11.7* Show that the tobit model may be regarded as a special case of a selection bias model.

11.8 Investigate whether having a child aged less than 6 is likely to be an especially powerful deterrent to working if the mother is unmarried by downloading the LFP94 data set from the website and repeating the regressions in this section adding an interactive dummy variable *MARL06* defined as the product of *MARRIED* and *CHILDL06* to the selection part of the model.

11.6 **An introduction to maximum likelihood estimation**

Suppose that a random variable X has a normal distribution with unknown mean μ and standard deviation σ. For the time being we will assume that we know that σ is equal to 1. We will relax this assumption later. You have a sample of two observations, values 4 and 6, and you wish to obtain an estimate of μ. The common-sense answer is 5, and we have seen that this is scientifically respectable as well since the sample mean is the least squares estimator and as such an unbiased and efficient estimator of the population mean, provided certain assumptions are valid.

However, we have seen that in practice in econometrics the necessary assumptions, in particular the Gauss–Markov conditions, are often not satisfied and as a consequence least squares estimators lose one or more of their desirable properties. We have seen that in some circumstances they may be inconsistent and we have been concerned to develop alternative estimators that are consistent. Typically we are not able to analyze the finite-sample properties of these estimators and we just hope that the estimators are well behaved.

Once we are dealing with consistent estimators, there is no guarantee that those based on the least squares criterion of goodness of fit are optimal. Indeed it can be shown that, under certain assumptions, a different approach, maximum likelihood estimation, will yield estimators that, besides being consistent, are asymptotically efficient (efficient in large samples).

To return to the numerical example, suppose for a moment that the true value of μ is 3.5. The probability density function of the normal distribution is given by

$$f(X) = \frac{1}{\sigma\sqrt{2\pi}}e^{-\frac{1}{2}\left(\frac{X-\mu}{\sigma}\right)^2}. \tag{11.25}$$

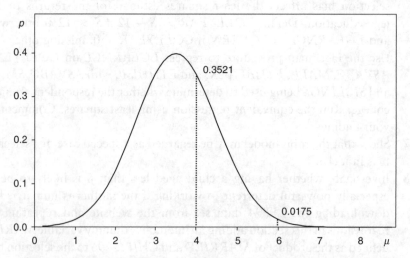

Figure 11.12 Probability densities at $X_1 = 4$ and $X_2 = 6$ conditional on $\mu = 3.5$

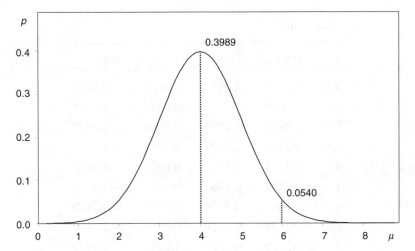

Figure 11.13 Probability densities at $X_1 = 4$ and $X_2 = 6$ conditional on $\mu = 4.0$

Figure 11.12 shows the distribution of X conditional on $\mu = 3.5$ and $\sigma = 1$. In particular, the probability density is 0.3521 when $X = 4$ and 0.0175 when $X = 6$. The joint probability density for the two observations is the product, 0.0062.

Now suppose that the true value of μ is 4. Figure 11.13 shows the distribution of X conditional on this value. The probability density is 0.3989 when $X = 4$ and 0.0540 when $X = 6$. The joint probability density for the two observations is now 0.0215. We conclude that the probability of getting values 4 and 6 for the two observations would be three times as great if μ were 4 than it would be if μ were 3.5. In that sense, $\mu = 4$ is more likely than $\mu = 3.5$. If we had to choose between these estimates, we should therefore choose 4. Of course we do not have to choose between them. According to the maximum likelihood principle, we should consider all possible values of μ and select the one that gives the observations the greatest joint probability density.

Table 11.10 computes the probabilities of $X = 4$ and $X = 6$ for values of μ from 3.5 to 6.5. The fourth column gives the joint probability density, which is known as the likelihood function. The likelihood function is plotted in Figure 11.14. You can see that it reaches a maximum for $\mu = 5$, the average value of the two observations. We will now demonstrate mathematically that this must be the case.

First, a little terminology. The likelihood function, written $L(\mu \mid X_1 = 4, X_2 = 6)$ gives the joint probability density as a function of μ, given the sample observations. We will choose μ so as to maximize this function.

In this case, given the two observations and the assumption $\sigma = 1$, the likelihood function is given by

$$L(\mu) = \left(\frac{1}{\sqrt{2\pi}} e^{-\frac{1}{2}(4-\mu)^2} \right) \left(\frac{1}{\sqrt{2\pi}} e^{-\frac{1}{2}(6-\mu)^2} \right). \qquad (11.26)$$

Table 11.10

μ	$p(4\|\mu)$	$p(6\|\mu)$	L	$\log L$
3.5	0.3521	0.0175	0.0062	−5.0879
4.0	0.3989	0.0540	0.0215	−3.8379
4.5	0.3521	0.1295	0.0456	−3.0879
4.6	0.3332	0.1497	0.0499	−2.9979
4.7	0.3123	0.1714	0.0535	−2.9279
4.8	0.2897	0.1942	0.0563	−2.8779
4.9	0.2661	0.2179	0.0580	−2.8479
5.0	0.2420	0.2420	0.0585	−2.8379
5.1	0.2179	0.2661	0.0580	−2.8479
5.2	0.1942	0.2897	0.0563	−2.8779
5.3	0.1714	0.3123	0.0535	−2.9279
5.4	0.1497	0.3332	0.0499	−2.9979
5.5	0.1295	0.3521	0.0456	−3.0879
6.0	0.0540	0.3989	0.0215	−3.8379
6.5	0.0175	0.3521	0.0062	−5.0879

We will now differentiate this with respect to μ and set the result equal to 0 to obtain the first-order condition for a maximum. We will then differentiate a second time to check the second-order condition. Well, actually we won't. Even with only two observations in the sample, this would be laborious, and when

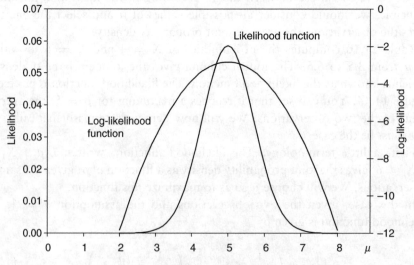

Figure 11.14 Likelihood and log-likelihood functions for μ

we generalize to n observations it would be very messy. We will use a trick to simplify the proceedings. $\log L$ is a monotonically increasing function of L. So the value of μ that maximizes L also maximizes $\log L$, and vice versa. $\log L$ is much easier to work with, since

$$
\log L = \log \left[\left(\frac{1}{\sqrt{2\pi}} e^{-\frac{1}{2}(4-\mu)^2} \right) \left(\frac{1}{\sqrt{2\pi}} e^{-\frac{1}{2}(6-\mu)^2} \right) \right]
$$

$$
= \log \left(\frac{1}{\sqrt{2\pi}} e^{-\frac{1}{2}(4-\mu)^2} \right) + \log \left(\frac{1}{\sqrt{2\pi}} e^{-\frac{1}{2}(6-\mu)^2} \right)
$$

$$
= \log \left(\frac{1}{\sqrt{2\pi}} \right) - \frac{1}{2}(4 - \mu)^2 + \log \left(\frac{1}{\sqrt{2\pi}} \right) - \frac{1}{2}(6 - \mu)^2. \qquad (11.27)
$$

The maximum likelihood estimator, which we will denote $\hat{\mu}$, is the value of μ that maximizes this function, given the data for X. It is given by the first-order condition

$$
\frac{d \log L}{d\mu} = (4 - \hat{\mu}) + (6 - \hat{\mu}) = 0. \qquad (11.28)
$$

Thus $\hat{\mu} = 5$. The second derivative is -2, so this gives a maximum value for $\log L$, and hence L. [Note that $-\frac{1}{2}(a - \mu)^2 = -\frac{1}{2}a^2 + a\mu - \frac{1}{2}\mu^2$. Hence the differential with respect to μ is $(a - \mu)$.]

Generalization to a sample of n observations

Consider a sample that consists of n observations $X_1, \ldots, X_n$. The likelihood function $L(\mu | X_1, \ldots, X_n)$ is now the product of n terms:

$$
L(\mu) = \left(\frac{1}{\sqrt{2\pi}} e^{-\frac{1}{2}(X_1 - \mu)^2} \right) \times \cdots \times \left(\frac{1}{\sqrt{2\pi}} e^{-\frac{1}{2}(X_n - \mu)^2} \right). \qquad (11.29)
$$

The log-likelihood function is now the sum of n terms:

$$
\log L = \log \left(\frac{1}{\sqrt{2\pi}} e^{-\frac{1}{2}(X_1 - \mu)^2} \right) + \cdots + \log \left(\frac{1}{\sqrt{2\pi}} e^{-\frac{1}{2}(X_n - \mu)^2} \right)
$$

$$
= \log \left(\frac{1}{\sqrt{2\pi}} \right) - \frac{1}{2}(X_1 - \mu)^2 + \cdots + \log \left(\frac{1}{\sqrt{2\pi}} \right) - \frac{1}{2}(X_n - \mu)^2.
$$

$$
(11.30)
$$

Hence the maximum likelihood estimator of μ is given by

$$
\frac{d \log L}{d\mu} = (X_1 - \hat{\mu}) + \cdots + (X_n - \hat{\mu}) = 0. \qquad (11.31)
$$

Thus

$$
\sum_{i=1}^{n} X_i - n\hat{\mu} = 0 \qquad (11.32)
$$

and the maximum likelihood estimator of μ is the sample mean. Note that the second derivative is $-n$, confirming that the log-likelihood has been maximized.

Generalization to the case where σ is unknown

We will now relax the assumption that σ is equal to 1 and accept that in practice it would be unknown, like μ. We will investigate the determination of its maximum likelihood graphically using the two-observation example and then generalize to a sample of n observations.

Figure 11.15 shows the probability distribution for X conditional on μ being equal to 5 and σ being equal to 2. The probability density at $X_1 = 4$ and $X_2 = 6$ is 0.1760 and the joint density 0.0310. Clearly we would obtain higher densities, and higher joint density, if the distribution had smaller variance. If we try σ equal to 0.5, we obtain the distribution shown in Figure 11.16. Here the individual densities are 0.1080 and the joint density 0.0117. Clearly we have made the distribution too narrow, for X_1 and X_2 are now in its tails with even lower density than before.

Figure 11.17 plots the joint density as a function of σ. We can see that it is maximized when σ is equal to 1, and this is therefore the maximum likelihood estimate, provided that we have been correct in assuming that the maximum likelihood estimate of μ is 5.

We will now derive the maximum likelihood estimators of both μ and σ simultaneously, for the general case of a sample of n observations. The likelihood function is

$$L(\mu, \sigma \,|\, X_1, \ldots, X_n) = \left(\frac{1}{\sigma\sqrt{2\pi}} e^{-\frac{1}{2}\left(\frac{X_1-\mu}{\sigma}\right)^2} \right) \times \cdots \times \left(\frac{1}{\sigma\sqrt{2\pi}} e^{-\frac{1}{2}\left(\frac{X_n-\mu}{\sigma}\right)^2} \right)$$

$$(11.33)$$

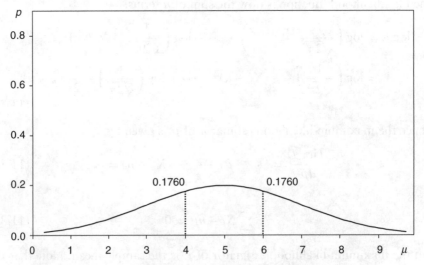

Figure 11.15 Probability densities at $X_1 = 4$ and $X_2 = 6$ conditional on $\sigma = 2$

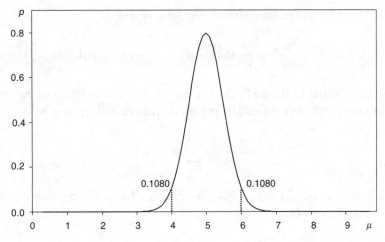

Figure 11.16 Probability densities at $X_1 = 4$ and $X_2 = 6$ conditional on $\sigma = 0.5$

and so the log-likelihood function is

$$
\log L = \log\left[\left(\frac{1}{\sigma\sqrt{2\pi}}e^{-\frac{1}{2}\left(\frac{X_1-\mu}{\sigma}\right)^2}\right)\times\cdots\times\left(\frac{1}{\sigma\sqrt{2\pi}}e^{-\frac{1}{2}\left(\frac{X_n-\mu}{\sigma}\right)^2}\right)\right]
$$

$$
=\log\left(\frac{1}{\sigma\sqrt{2\pi}}e^{-\frac{1}{2}\left(\frac{X_1-\mu}{\sigma}\right)^2}\right)+\cdots+\log\left(\frac{1}{\sigma\sqrt{2\pi}}e^{-\frac{1}{2}\left(\frac{X_n-\mu}{\sigma}\right)^2}\right)
$$

$$
=n\log\left(\frac{1}{\sigma\sqrt{2\pi}}\right)-\frac{1}{2}\left(\frac{X_1-\mu}{\sigma}\right)^2-\cdots-\frac{1}{2}\left(\frac{X_n-\mu}{\sigma}\right)^2
$$

$$
=n\log\frac{1}{\sigma}+n\log\frac{1}{\sqrt{2\pi}}+\frac{1}{\sigma^2}\left(-\frac{1}{2}(X_1-\mu)^2-\cdots-\frac{1}{2}(X_n-\mu)^2\right).
$$

$$(11.34)$$

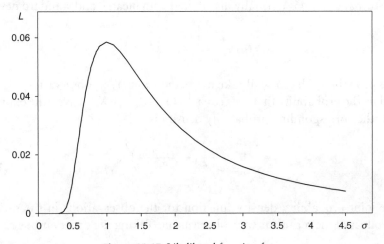

Figure 11.17 Likelihood function for σ

The partial derivative of this with respect to μ is

$$\frac{\partial \log L}{\partial \mu} = \frac{1}{\sigma^2}[(X_1 - \mu) + \cdots + (X_n - \mu)]. \tag{11.35}$$

Setting this equal to 0, one finds that the maximum likelihood estimator of μ is the sample mean, as before. The partial derivative with respect to σ is

$$-\frac{n}{\sigma} + \frac{1}{\sigma^3} \sum_{i=1}^{n} (X_i - \mu)^2. \tag{11.36}$$

Substituting its maximum likelihood estimator for μ and putting the expression equal to 0, we obtain

$$\hat{\sigma}^2 = \frac{1}{n} \sum_{i=1}^{n} (X_i - \bar{X})^2. \tag{11.37}$$

Note that this is actually biased downwards in finite samples, the unbiased estimator being given by the same expression with n replaced by $(n - 1)$. However it is asymptotically more efficient using the mean square error criterion, its smaller variance more than compensating for the bias. The bias in any case attenuates as the sample size becomes large.

Application to the simple regression model

Suppose that Y_i depends on X_i according to the simple relationship

$$Y_i = \beta_1 + \beta_2 X_i + u_i. \tag{11.38}$$

Potentially, before the observations are generated, Y_i has a distribution around $(\beta_1 + \beta_2 X_i)$, according to the value of the disturbance term. We will assume that the disturbance term is normally distributed with mean 0 and standard deviation σ, so

$$f(u) = \frac{1}{\sigma\sqrt{2\pi}} e^{-\frac{1}{2}\left(\frac{u}{\sigma}\right)^2}. \tag{11.39}$$

The probability that Y will take a specific value Y_i in observation i is determined by the probability that u_i is equal to $(Y_i - \beta_1 - \beta_2 X_i)$. Given the expression above, the corresponding probability density is

$$\frac{1}{\sigma\sqrt{2\pi}} e^{-\frac{1}{2}\left(\frac{Y_i - \beta_1 - \beta_2 X_i}{\sigma}\right)^2}. \tag{11.40}$$

The joint probability density function for the observations in the sample is the product of the terms for each observation. Taking the observations as given, and treating the unknown parameters as variables, we say that the likelihood function for β_1, β_2 and σ is given by

$$L(\beta_1, \beta_2, \sigma | Y_1, \ldots, Y_n) = \left(\frac{1}{\sigma \sqrt{2\pi}} e^{-\frac{1}{2} \left(\frac{Y_1 - \beta_1 - \beta_2 X_1}{\sigma} \right)^2} \right)$$

$$\times \cdots \times \frac{1}{\sigma \sqrt{2\pi}} e^{-\frac{1}{2} \left(\frac{Y_n - \beta_1 - \beta_2 X_n}{\sigma} \right)^2}. \tag{11.41}$$

The log-likelihood function is thus given by

$$\log L = n \log \left(\frac{1}{\sigma \sqrt{2\pi}} \right) - \frac{1}{2\sigma^2} [(Y_1 - \beta_1 - \beta_2 X_1)^2 + \cdots + (Y_n - \beta_1 - \beta_2 X_n)^2]. \tag{11.42}$$

The values of β_1 and β_2 that maximize this function are exactly the same as those obtained using the least squares principle. However, the estimate of σ is slightly different.

Goodness of fit and statistical tests

As noted in the discussion of logit analysis, there is no measure of goodness of fit equivalent to R^2 in maximum likelihood estimation. The pseudo-R^2 seen in some regression output, including that of Stata, compares its log-likelihood, $\log L$, with the log-likelihood that would have been obtained with only the intercept in the regression, $\log L_0$. A likelihood, being a joint probability, must lie between 0 and 1, and as a consequence a log-likelihood must be negative. The pseudo-R^2 is the proportion by which $\log L$ is smaller, in absolute size, than $\log L_0$:

$$\text{pseudo-}R^2 = 1 - \frac{\log L}{\log L_0}. \tag{11.43}$$

While it has a minimum value of 0, its maximum value must be less than 1 and unlike R^2 it does not have a natural interpretation. However variations in the likelihood, like variations in the residual sum of squares in a standard regression, can be used as a basis for tests. In particular the explanatory power of the model can be tested via the likelihood ratio statistic.

$$2 \log \frac{L}{L_0} = 2(\log L - \log L_0). \tag{11.44}$$

This is distributed as a chi-squared statistic with $k - 1$ degrees of freedom, where $k - 1$ is the number of explanatory variables, under the null hypothesis that the coefficients of the variables are all jointly equal to 0. Further, the validity of a restriction can be tested by comparing the constrained and unconstrained likelihoods, in the same way that it can be tested by comparing the constrained and unconstrained residual sums of squares in a least squares regression model. For example, the null hypothesis H_0: $\rho = 0$ in the selection bias model can be tested by comparing the unconstrained likelihood L_U with the likelihood L_R when the model is fitted assuming that u and ε are distributed independently. Under the null hypothesis H_0: $\rho = 0$, the test statistic $2\log L_U/L_R$ is distributed as a chi-squared statistic with one degree of freedom. In the example in Section 11.4 the test statistic, 32.90, appears in the last line of the output and the null hypothesis is rejected, the critical value of chi-squared with one degree of freedom being 10.83 at the 0.1 percent level.

As was noted in Section 11.2, the significance of an individual coefficient can be evaluated via its asymptotic t statistic, so-called because the standard error is valid only in large samples. Since the t distribution converges on the normal distribution in large samples, the critical values of the latter should be used.

Exercise

11.8*   An event is hypothesized to occur with probability p. In a sample of n observations, it occurred m times. Demonstrate that the maximum likelihood estimator of p is m/n.

11.9*   In Exercise 11.4, $\log L_0$ is -1485.62. Compute the pseudo-R^2 and confirm that it is equal to that reported in the output.

11.10* In Exercise 11.4, compute the likelihood ratio statistic $2(\log L - \log L_0)$, confirm that it is equal to that reported in the output, and perform the likelihood ratio test.

12 Models using time-series data

Hitherto the analysis has been confined to cross-section data. With samples being taken from fixed populations, it has been reasonable to assume that the classical linear regression model is the appropriate framework. Now we switch to time-series data and data generation processes. In this chapter and the next we will suppose that the classical linear regression model remains a suitable vehicle. However, in the final chapter we shall see that analysis using times-series data involves new problems and requires a different approach.

12.1 Static models

Much of the analysis will be illustrated with a core data set for fitting demand functions. It is drawn from national accounts data published by the US Bureau of the Census and consists of annual aggregate data on nineteen different categories of consumer expenditure for the period 1959–94, along with data on disposable personal income, *DPI*, and price index numbers for the nineteen categories. The Demand Functions data set, together with a manual giving more detailed information about it, can be downloaded from the website. It will be updated periodically, so the time period covered will be extended and possibly there may be changes to the categories of consumer expenditure. Two of the categories, *FOOD* and *HOUS* (consumer expenditure on food and housing services, respectively) are used as examples in the text and exercises. The other categories are intended for practical work by a small group of students, each student working with a different category, starting with a simple regression specification and gradually developing a more sophisticated one. We will start with a very simple specification for the demand equation for housing services, regressing consumer expenditure on this category, *HOUS*, on *DPI* and a price index for housing, *PRELHOUS*:

$$HOUS_t = \beta_1 + \beta_2 DPI_t + \beta_3 PRELHOUS_t + u_t. \qquad (12.1)$$

HOUS and *DPI* are measured in $ billion at 1992 constant prices. *PRELHOUS* is an index constructed by dividing the nominal price deflator for

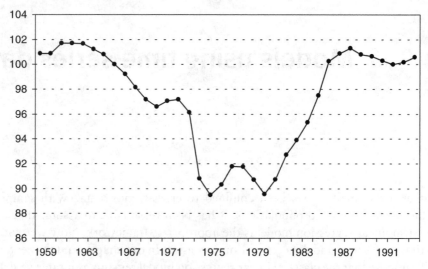

Figure 12.1 Relative price series for housing serices, 1959–94 (1992 = 100)

housing, *PHOUS*, by the price deflator for total personal expenditure, *PTPE*, and multiplying by 100. *PRELHOUS* thus is a real or relative price index that keeps track of whether housing is becoming more or less expensive relative to other types of expenditure. It is plotted in Figure 12.1, which shows that the relative price declined by about 10 percent from the early 1960s to the late 1970s and then rose again by about the same amount.

A straightforward linear regression using EViews gives the output as shown in Table 12.1.

Table 12.1

```
Dependent Variable: HOUS
Method: Least Squares
Sample: 1959 1994
Included observations: 36
```

Variable	Coefficient	Std. Error	t-Statistic	Prob.
C	2.654701	28.91571	0.091808	0.9274
DPI	0.151521	0.001243	121.9343	0.0000
PRELHOUS	-0.556949	0.290640	-1.916285	0.0640

R-squared	0.997811	Mean dependent var	429.3306
Adjusted R-squared	0.997679	S.D. dependent var	149.1037
S.E. of regression	7.183749	Akaike info criter	4.023298
Sum squared resid	1703.006	Schwarz criterion	4.155258
Log likelihood	-120.5012	F-statistic	7522.482
Durbin-Watson stat	0.809993	Prob(F-statistic)	0.000000

The equation implies that an increase of $1 billion in disposable personal income leads to an increase of $0.15 billion in expenditure on housing. In other words, out of the marginal dollar, 15 cents is spent on housing. Is this a plausible figure? It is a bit difficult to tell, but certainly housing is the largest category of consumer expenditure and one would expect a substantial coefficient. Note that we are talking about housing services, and not investment in housing. Housing services is the value of the services provided by the existing housing stock. In the case of rented housing, rents are taken as a measure of the value of the services. In the case of owner-occupied housing and housing rented at a subsidized rate, imputed rents, that is, the market rents the housing could command, are used instead. The coefficient of *PRELHOUS* implies that a one-point increase in the price index leads to a reduction of $0.56 billion in expenditure on housing. The constant term literally indicates the amount that would be spent on housing if *DPI* and *PRELHOUS* were both 0, but obviously any such interpretation is nonsense. If the observations referred to households, there might be some that had no income and yet purchased housing services and other essentials with transfer payments, but here we are talking about aggregate data for the whole of the United States and that kind of interpretation is not sensible.

It is common to hypothesize that a constant elasticity function of the type

$$HOUS = \beta_1 DPI^{\beta_2} PRELHOUS^{\beta_3} v \tag{12.2}$$

is mathematically more appropriate than a linear specification for demand functions. Linearizing it by taking logarithms, one obtains

$$LGHOUS = \beta_1' + \beta_2 LGDPI + \beta_3 LGPRHOUS + u, \tag{12.3}$$

Table 12.2

```
Dependent Variable: LGHOUS
Method: Least Squares
Sample: 1959 1994
Included observations: 36
```

Variable	Coefficient	Std. Error	t-Statistic	Prob.
C	-2.032685	0.322726	-6.298478	0.0000
LGDPI	1.132248	0.008705	130.0650	0.0000
LGPRHOUS	-0.227634	0.065841	-3.457323	0.0015

R-squared	0.998154	Mean dependent var	5.996930
Adjusted R-squared	0.998042	S.D. dependent var	0.377702
S.E. of regression	0.016714	Akaike info criter	-8.103399
Sum squared resid	0.009218	Schwarz criterion	-7.971439
Log likelihood	97.77939	F-statistic	8920.496
Durbin-Watson stat	0.846451	Prob(F-statistic)	0.000000

where *LGHOUS, LGDPI,* and *LGPRHOUS* are the (natural) logarithms of *HOUS, DPI,* and *PRELHOUS,* respectively, u is the natural logarithm of the disturbance term v, β_1' is the logarithm of β_1, and β_2 and β_3 are income and price elasticities. The regression result is shown in Table 12.2.

The coefficients of *LGDPI* and *LGPRHOUS* are direct estimates of the income and price elasticities. Is 1.13 a plausible income elasticity? Probably. It is conventional to classify consumer expenditure into normal goods and inferior goods, types of expenditure whose income elasticities are positive and negative, respectively, and to subdivide normal goods into necessities and luxuries, types of expenditure whose income elasticities are less than 1 and greater than 1. Housing is obviously a necessity, so you might expect the elasticity to be positive but less than 1. However it also has a luxury element, since people spend more on better-quality housing as their income rises. Overall the elasticity seems to work out at about 1, so the present estimate seems reasonable.

Exercises

12.1 The results of linear and logarithmic regressions of consumer expenditure on food, *FOOD*, on *DPI*, and a relative price index series for food, *PRELFOOD*, using the Demand Functions data set, are summarized below (standard errors in parentheses). Provide an economic interpretation of the coefficients and perform appropriate statistical tests.

$$\widehat{FOOD} = 232.6 + 0.089\ DPI - 0.534\ PRELFOOD. \quad R^2 = 0.989$$
$$\quad\ (31.9)\ \ (0.002) \qquad\ (0.332)$$

$$\widehat{LGFOOD} = 2.66 + 0.61\ LGDPI - 0.30\ LGPRELFOOD. \quad R^2 = 0.993$$
$$\quad\ (0.28)\ \ (0.01) \qquad\ (0.07)$$

12.2 Download the Demand Functions data set and associated manuals from the website. You should choose, or be assigned by your instructor, one category of expenditure (not *FOOD* or *HOUS*), and it may be helpful to simplify the data set by deleting the expenditure and price variables relating to the other categories. Construct a relative price index series for your category as indicated in Section 1 of the *Demand Functions Regression Exercises* manual. Plot the series and try to explain why it has changed over the time period.

12.3 Regress your category of expenditure on *DPI* and the relative price index series constructed in Exercise 12.2. Give an economic interpretation of the regression coefficients and perform appropriate statistical tests.

12.4 Regress the logarithm of expenditure on your category on *LGDPI* and the logarithm of the relative price series. Give an economic interpretation of the regression coefficients and perform appropriate statistical tests.

12.5* Perform a Box–Cox test to determine whether there is a significant difference in the fit of the linear and logarithmic regressions for your category of expenditure.

12.6 Sometimes a time trend is included in a regression as an explanatory variable, acting as a proxy for some gradual change not associated with income or price. Changing tastes might be an example. However, in the present case the addition of a time trend might give rise to a problem of multicollinearity because it will be highly correlated with the income series and perhaps also the price series. Calculate the correlations between the *TIME* variable in the data set, *LGDPI*, and the logarithm of the relative price series for your category. Regress the logarithm of expenditure on your category on *LGDPI*, the logarithm of the relative price series, and *TIME* (not the logarithm of *TIME*). Provide an interpretation of the regression coefficients, perform appropriate statistical tests, and compare the regression results with those of the same regression without *TIME*.

12.2 Dynamic models

Next, we will introduce some simple dynamics. One might suppose that some types of consumer expenditure are largely determined by current income and price, but this is not so for a category such as housing that is subject to substantial inertia. We will consider specifications in which expenditure on housing depends on lagged values of income and price. A variable X lagged one time period has values that are simply the previous values of X, and it is conventionally referred to as $X(-1)$. Generalizing, a variable lagged s time periods has the X values s periods previously, and is denoted $X(-s)$. Major regression applications adopt this convention and for these there is no need to define lagged variables separately. Table 12.3 shows the data for $LGDPI$, $LGDPI(-1)$, and $LGDPI(-2)$.

Note that obviously there is a very high correlation between $LGDPI$, $LGDPI(-1)$, and $LGDPI(-2)$, and this is going to cause problems.

The first column of Table 12.4 presents the results of a logarithmic regression using current income and price. The second and third columns show the results of regressing expenditure on housing on income and price lagged one and two time periods, respectively. It is reasonable to hypothesize that expenditure on a category of consumer expenditure might depend on both current and lagged income and price. The fourth column shows the results of a regression using current income and price and the same variables lagged one time period. The fifth column adds the same variables lagged two time periods, as well.

The first three regressions are almost identical. This is because $LGDPI$, $LGDPI(-1)$, and $LGDPI(-2)$ are very highly correlated. The last two regressions display the classic symptoms of multicollinearity. The point estimates are unstable and the standard errors become much larger when current and lagged

Table 12.3 Current and lagged values of the logarithm of disposable personal income

Year	LGDPI	LGDPI(−1)	LGDPI(−2)
1959	5.2750	—	—
1960	5.3259	5.2750	—
1961	5.3720	5.3259	5.2750
1962	5.4267	5.3720	5.3259
1963	5.4719	5.4267	5.3720
1964	5.5175	5.4719	5.4267
1965	5.5706	5.5175	5.4719
—	—	—	—
—	—	—	—
1987	6.3689	6.3377	6.3119
1988	6.3984	6.3689	6.3377
1989	6.4210	6.3984	6.3689
1990	6.4413	6.4210	6.3984
1991	6.4539	6.4413	6.4210
1992	6.4720	6.4539	6.4413
1993	6.4846	6.4720	6.4539
1994	6.5046	6.4846	6.4720

Table 12.4 Alternative dynamic specifications, expenditure on housing services

Variable	(1)	(2)	(3)	(4)	(5)
LGDPI	1.13 (0.01)	—	—	0.38 (0.15)	0.33 (0.14)
LGDPI(−1)	—	1.10 (0.01)	—	0.73 (0.15)	0.28 (0.21)
LGDPI(−2)	—	—	1.07 (0.01)	—	0.48 (0.15)
LGPRHOUS	−0.23 (0.07)	—	—	−0.19 (0.08)	−0.13 (0.19)
LGPRHOUS(−1)	—	−0.20 (0.06)	—	0.14 (0.08)	0.25 (0.33)
LGPRHOUS(−2)	—	—	−0.19 (0.06)	—	−0.33 (0.19)
R^2	0.998	0.999	0.998	0.999	0.999

values of income and price are included as regressors. For a type of expenditure like housing, where one might expect long lags, this is clearly not a constructive approach to determining the lag structure.

A common solution to the problem of multicollinearity is to hypothesize that the dynamic process has a parsimonious lag structure, that is, a lag structure that can be characterized with few parameters. One of the most popular lag structures is the Koyck distribution, which assumes that the coefficients of the explanatory variables have geometrically declining weights. We will look at two such models, the adaptive expectations model and the partial adjustment model.

Exercises

12.7 Give an economic interpretation of the coefficients of $LGDPI$, $LGDPI(-1)$, and $LGDPI(-2)$, in column 5 of Table 12.4.

12.8 To allow for the possibility that expenditure on your category is partly subject to a one-period lag, regress the logarithm of expenditure on your category on $LGDPI$, the logarithm of your relative price series, and those two variables lagged one period. Repeat the experiment adding $LGDPI(-2)$ and the logarithm of the price series lagged two periods. Compare the regression results, paying attention to the changes in the regression coefficients and their standard errors.

12.3 **The adaptive expectations model**

The modeling of expectations is frequently an important and difficult task of the applied economist using time-series data. This is especially true in macroeconomics, in that investment, saving, and the demand for assets are all sensitive to expectations about the future. Unfortunately, there is no satisfactory way of measuring expectations directly for macroeconomic purposes. Consequently, macroeconomic models tend not to give particularly accurate forecasts, and this makes economic management difficult.

As a makeshift solution, some models use an indirect technique known as the adaptive expectations process. This involves a simple learning process in which, in each time period, the actual value of the variable is compared with the value that had been expected. If the actual value is greater, the expected value is adjusted upwards for the next period. If it is lower, the expected value is adjusted downwards. The size of the adjustment is hypothesized to be proportional to the discrepancy between the actual and expected value.

If X is the variable in question, and X_t^e is the value expected in time period t given the information available at time period $t - 1$,

$$X_{t+1}^e - X_t^e = \lambda(X_t - X_t^e). \quad (0 \le \lambda \le 1) \tag{12.4}$$

This can be rewritten

$$X_{t+1}^e = \lambda X_t + (1 - \lambda)X_t^e, \quad (0 \le \lambda \le 1) \qquad (12.5)$$

which states that the expected value of X in the next time period is a weighted average of the actual value of X in the current time period and the value that had been expected. The larger the value of λ, the quicker the expected value adjusts to previous actual outcomes.

For example, suppose that you hypothesize that a dependent variable, Y_t, is related to the expected value of the explanatory variable, X, in year $t + 1$, X_{t+1}^e:

$$Y_t = \beta_1 + \beta_2 X_{t+1}^e + u_t. \qquad (12.6)$$

(12.6) expresses Y_t in terms of X_{t+1}^e, which is unobservable and must somehow be replaced by observable variables, that is, by actual current and lagged values of X, and perhaps lagged values of Y. We start by substituting for X_{t+1}^e using (12.5):

$$
\begin{aligned}
Y_t &= \beta_1 + \beta_2 \left(\lambda X_t + (1 - \lambda)X_t^e \right) + u_t \\
&= \beta_1 + \beta_2 \lambda X_t + \beta_2(1 - \lambda)X_t^e + u_t.
\end{aligned} \qquad (12.7)
$$

Of course we still have the unobservable variable X_t^e as an explanatory variable, but if (12.5) is true for time period t, it is also true for time period $t - 1$:

$$X_t^e = \lambda X_{t-1} + (1 - \lambda)X_{t-1}^e. \qquad (12.8)$$

Substituting for X_t^e in (12.7), we now have

$$Y_t = \beta_1 + \beta_2 \lambda X_t + \beta_2 \lambda(1 - \lambda)X_{t-1} + \beta_2(1 - \lambda)^2 X_{t-1}^e + u_t. \qquad (12.9)$$

After lagging and substituting s times, the expression becomes

$$
\begin{aligned}
Y_t &= \beta_1 + \beta_2 \lambda X_t + \beta_2 \lambda(1 - \lambda)X_{t-1} + \beta_2 \lambda(1 - \lambda)^2 X_{t-2} + \cdots \\
&\quad + \beta_2 \lambda(1 - \lambda)^{s-1} X_{t-s+1} + \beta_2(1 - \lambda)^s X_{t-s+1}^e + u_t.
\end{aligned} \qquad (12.10)
$$

Now it is reasonable to suppose that λ lies between 0 and 1, in which case $(1 - \lambda)$ will also lie between 0 and 1. Thus $(1 - \lambda)^s$ becomes progressively smaller as s increases. Eventually there will be a point where the term $\beta_2(1 - \lambda)^s X_{t-s+1}^e$ is so small that it can be neglected and we have a model in which all the variables are observable.

A lag structure with geometrically declining weights, such as this one, is described as having a Koyck distribution. As can be seen from (12.10), it is highly parsimonious in terms of its parameterization, requiring only one parameter more than the static version. Since it is nonlinear in the parameters, OLS should not be used to fit it, for two reasons. First, multicollinearity would almost certainly make the estimates of the coefficients so erratic that they would be worthless—it is precisely this problem that caused us to search for another way of specifying a lag structure. Second, the point estimates of the coefficients would yield conflicting estimates of the parameters. For example, suppose that the fitted relationship began

$$\hat{Y}_t = 101 + 0.60X_t + 0.45X_{t-1} + 0.20X_{t-2} + \cdots \qquad (12.11)$$

Relating the theoretical coefficients of the current and lagged values of X in (12.10) to the estimates in (12.11), one has $b_2 l = 0.60$, $b_2 l(1 - l) = 0.45$, and $b_2 l(1 - l)^2 = 0.20$. From the first two you could infer that b_2 was equal to 2.40 and l was equal to 0.25—but these values would conflict with the third equation and indeed with the equations for all the remaining coefficients in the regression.

Instead, a nonlinear estimation technique should be used. Most major regression applications have facilities for performing nonlinear regressions built into them. If your application does not, you could fit the model using a grid search. It is worth describing this technique, despite the fact that it is obsolete, because it makes it clear that the problem of multicollinearity has been solved. We rewrite (12.10) as two equations:

$$Y_t = \beta_1 + \beta_2 Z_t + u_t. \qquad (12.12)$$

$$Z_t = \lambda X_t + \lambda(1 - \lambda)X_{t-1} + \lambda(1 - \lambda)^2 X_{t-2} + \lambda(1 - \lambda)^3 X_{t-3} \cdots \qquad (12.13)$$

The values of Z_t depend of course on the value of λ. You construct ten versions of the Z_t variable using the following values for λ: $0.1, 0.2, 0.3, \ldots, 1.0$ and fit (12.12) with each of them. The version with the lowest residual sum of squares is by definition the least squares solution. Note that the regressions involve a regression of Y on the different versions of Z in a simple regression equation and so the problem of multicollinearity has been completely eliminated.

Table 12.5 shows the parameter estimates and residual sums of squares for a grid search where the dependent variable was the logarithm of housing services and the explanatory variables were the logarithms of DPI and the relative price series for housing. Eight lagged values were used. You can see that the optimal value of λ is between 0.4 and 0.5, and that the income elasticity is about 1.13 and the price elasticity about -0.32. If we had wanted a more precise estimate of λ, we could have continued the grid search with steps of 0.01 over the range from 0.4 to 0.5. Note that the implicit income coefficient for X_{t-8}, $\beta_2 \lambda (1 - \lambda)^8$, was about $1.13 \times 0.5^9 = 0.0022$. The corresponding price coefficient was even smaller. Hence in this case eight lags were more than sufficient.

Dynamics in the adaptive expectations model

As you can see from (12.10), X_t, the current value of X, has coefficient $\beta_2 \lambda$ in the equation for Y_t. This is the short-run or impact effect of X on Y. At time t, the terms involving lagged values of X are already determined and hence effectively

Table 12.5 Logarithmic regression of expenditure on housing services on disposable personal income and a relative price index, assuming an adaptive expectations model, fitted using a grid search

λ	(b_2)	s.e.(b_2)	b_3	s.e.(b_3)	RSS
0.1	1.67	0.01	−0.35	0.07	0.001636
0.2	1.22	0.01	−0.28	0.04	0.001245
0.3	1.13	0.01	−0.28	0.03	0.000918
0.4	1.12	0.01	−0.30	0.03	0.000710
0.5	1.13	0.01	−0.32	0.03	0.000666
0.6	1.15	0.01	−0.34	0.03	0.000803
0.7	1.16	0.01	−0.36	0.03	0.001109
0.8	1.17	0.01	−0.38	0.04	0.001561
0.9	1.17	0.01	−0.39	0.04	0.002137
1.0	1.18	0.01	−0.40	0.05	0.002823

form part of the intercept in the short-run relationship. However, we can also derive a long-run relationship between Y and X by seeing how the equilibrium value of Y would be related to the equilibrium value of X if equilibrium were ever achieved. Denoting equilibrium Y and X by $\bar{Y}$ and $\bar{X}$, respectively, in equilibrium $Y_t = \bar{Y}$ and $X_t = X_{t-1} = X_{t-2} = \cdots = \bar{X}$. Substituting into (12.10), one has

$$\bar{Y} = \beta_1 + \beta_2 \lambda \bar{X} + \beta_2 \lambda (1 - \lambda) \bar{X} + \beta_2 \lambda (1 - \lambda)^2 \bar{X} + \cdots$$

$$= \beta_1 + \beta_2 \bar{X}[\lambda + \lambda(1 - \lambda) + \lambda(1 - \lambda)^2 + \cdots]$$

$$= \beta_1 + \beta_2 \bar{X}. \tag{12.14}$$

To see the last step, write

$$S = \lambda + \lambda(1 - \lambda) + \lambda(1 - \lambda)^2 \cdots \tag{12.15}$$

Then

$$(1 - \lambda)S = \lambda(1 - \lambda) + \lambda(1 - \lambda)^2 + \lambda(1 - \lambda)^3 \cdots \tag{12.16}$$

Subtracting (12.16) from (12.15),

$$S - (1 - \lambda)S = \lambda \tag{12.17}$$

and hence S is equal to 1. Thus the long-run effect of X on Y is given by β_2.

An alternative way of exploring the dynamics of an adaptive expectations model is to perform what is known as a Koyck transformation. This allows us to express the dependent variable in terms of a finite number of observable variables: the current values of the explanatory variables and the dependent variable itself, lagged one time period. We start again with the original equations and combine them to obtain (12.20):

$$Y_t = \beta_1 + \beta_2 X_{t+1}^e + u_t. \tag{12.18}$$

$$X_{t+1}^e = \lambda X_t + (1 - \lambda)X_t^e. \tag{12.19}$$

$$Y_t = \beta_1 + \beta_2 \left(\lambda X_t + (1 - \lambda)X_t^e\right) + u_t$$
$$= \beta_1 + \beta_2 \lambda X_t + \beta_2(1 - \lambda)X_t^e + u_t. \tag{12.20}$$

Now if (12.18) is true for time t, it is also true for time $t - 1$:

$$Y_{t-1} = \beta_1 + \beta_2 X_t^e + u_{t-1}. \tag{12.21}$$

Hence

$$\beta_2 X_t^e = Y_{t-1} - \beta_1 - u_{t-1}. \tag{12.22}$$

Substituting this into (12.20), we now have

$$Y_t = \beta_1 + \beta_2 \lambda X_t + (1 - \lambda)(Y_{t-1} - \beta_1 - u_{t-1}) + u_t$$
$$= \beta_1 \lambda + (1 - \lambda)Y_{t-1} + \beta_2 \lambda X_t + u_t - (1 - \lambda)u_{t-1}. \tag{12.23}$$

As before the short-run coefficient of X is $\beta_2 \lambda$, the effective intercept for the relationship being $\beta_1 \lambda + (1 - \lambda)Y_{t-1}$ at time t. In equilibrium, the relationship implies

$$\bar{Y} = \beta_1 \lambda + (1 - \lambda)\bar{Y} + \beta_2 \lambda \bar{X} \tag{12.24}$$

and so

$$\bar{Y} = \beta_1 + \beta_2 \bar{X}. \tag{12.25}$$

Hence again we obtain the result that β_2 gives the long-run effect of X on Y.

We will investigate the relationship between the short-run and long-run dynamics graphically. We will suppose, for convenience, that β_2 is positive and that X increases with time, and we will neglect the effect of the disturbance term. At time t, Y_t is given by (12.23). Y_{t-1} has already been determined, so the term $(1 - \lambda)Y_{t-1}$ is fixed. The equation thus gives the short-run relationship between Y_t and X_t. $[\beta_1 \lambda + (1 - \lambda)Y_{t-1}]$ is effectively the intercept and $\beta_2 \lambda$ is the slope coefficient. When we come to time $t + 1$, Y_{t+1} is given by

$$Y_{t+1} = \beta_1 \lambda + \beta_2 \lambda X_{t+1} + (1 - \lambda)Y_t \tag{12.26}$$

and the effective intercept is now $[\beta_1 \lambda + (1 - \lambda)Y_t]$. Since X is increasing, Y is increasing, so the intercept is larger than that for Y_t and the short-run relationship has shifted upwards. The slope is the same as before, $\beta_2 \lambda$. Thus two factors are responsible for the growth of Y: the direct effect of the increase in X, and the gradual upward shift of the short-run relationship. Figure 12.2 shows the outcomes for time t as far as time $t + 4$. You can see that the long-run relationship is steeper than the short-run one.

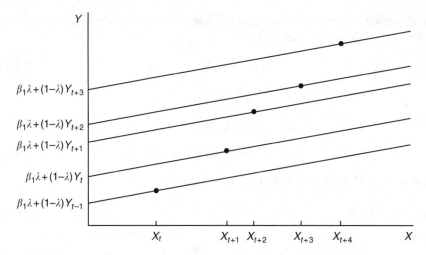

Figure 12.2 Short-run and long-run dynamics in the adaptive expectations model

Example: Friedman's permanent income hypothesis

Without doubt the most celebrated application of the adaptive expectations model is Friedman's use of it when fitting an aggregate consumption function using time-series data. In the early years after World War II, econometricians working with macroeconomic data were puzzled by the fact that the long-run average propensity to consume seemed to be roughly constant, despite the marginal propensity to consume being much lower. A model in which current consumption was a function of current income could not explain this phenomenon and was therefore clearly too simplistic. Several more sophisticated models that could explain this apparent contradiction were developed, notably Friedman's Permanent Income Hypothesis, Brown's Habit Persistence Model (discussed in the next section), Duesenberry's Relative Income Hypothesis, and the Modigliani–Ando–Brumberg Life Cycle Model.

Under the Permanent Income Hypothesis, permanent consumption, C_t^P, is proportional to permanent income, Y_t^P:

$$C_t^P = \beta_2 Y_t^P. \tag{12.27}$$

Actual consumption, C_t, and actual income, Y_t, also contain transitory components, C_t^T and Y_t^T respectively:

$$C_t = C_t^P + C_t^T. \tag{12.28}$$

$$Y_t = Y_t^P + Y_t^T. \tag{12.29}$$

It is assumed, at least as a first approximation, that the transitory components of consumption and income have expected value 0 and are distributed independently of their permanent counterparts and of each other. Substituting for C_t^P in (12.27) using (12.28) one has

$$C_t = \beta_2 Y_t^P + C_t^T. \qquad (12.30)$$

We thus obtain a relationship between actual consumption and permanent income in which C_t^T plays the role of a disturbance term, previously lacking in the model.

Earlier, when we discussed the permanent income hypothesis in the context of cross-section data, the observations related to households. When Friedman fitted the model, he actually used aggregate time-series data. To solve the problem that permanent income is unobservable, he hypothesized that it was subject to an adaptive expectations process in which the notion of permanent income was updated by a proportion of the difference between actual income and the previous period's permanent income:

$$Y_t^P - Y_{t-1}^P = \lambda(Y_t - Y_{t-1}^P). \qquad (12.31)$$

Hence permanent income at time t is a weighted average of actual income at time t and permanent income at time $t - 1$:

$$Y_t^P = \lambda Y_t + (1 - \lambda)Y_{t-1}^P. \qquad (12.32)$$

Friedman used (12.32) to relate permanent income to current and lagged values of income. Of course it cannot be used directly to measure permanent income in year t because we do not know λ and we have no way of measuring Y_{t-1}^P. We can solve the second difficulty by noting that if (12.32) holds for time t, it also holds for time $t - 1$:

$$Y_{t-1}^P = \lambda Y_{t-1} + (1 - \lambda)Y_{t-2}^P. \qquad (12.33)$$

Substituting this into (12.32), we obtain

$$Y_t^P = \lambda Y_t + \lambda(1 - \lambda)Y_{t-1} + (1 - \lambda)^2 Y_{t-2}^P. \qquad (12.34)$$

This includes the unmeasurable term Y_{t-2}^P, but we can deal with it by lagging (12.32) two periods and substituting, thus obtaining Y_t^P in terms of Y_t, Y_{t-1}, Y_{t-2}, and Y_{t-3}^P. Continuing this process indefinitely, we can write Y_t^P as a weighted sum of current and past measured income:

$$Y_t^P = \lambda Y_t + \lambda(1 - \lambda)Y_{t-1} + \lambda(1 - \lambda)^2 Y_{t-2} + \lambda(1 - \lambda)^3 Y_{t-3} + \cdots \qquad (12.35)$$

Provided that λ lies between 0 and 1, a reasonable assumption, $(1 - \lambda)^s$ is a decreasing function of s and eventually the weights attached to the lagged values of Y become so small that they can be neglected.

This still leaves us with the problem of estimating λ. Friedman's solution was to use a grid search, calculating the permanent income time series for a range of values of λ between 0 and 1, and regressing consumption on each permanent income series. He then chose that value of λ that produced the series for Y^P that gave him the best fit. Effectively, of course, he was fitting the nonlinear model

$$C_t = \beta_2\lambda Y_t + \beta_2\lambda(1-\lambda)Y_{t-1} + \beta_2\lambda(1-\lambda)^2 Y_{t-2} + \cdots + C_t^T. \quad (12.36)$$

The dynamic properties of the model are as illustrated in Figure 12.2. Mathematically they are best analyzed by performing the Koyck transformation on the model. This could be done on the lines of equations (12.21)–(12.23) above, or by lagging (12.36) one period and multiplying through by $(1-\lambda)$:

$$(1-\lambda)C_{t-1} = \beta_2\lambda(1-\lambda)Y_{t-1} + \beta_2\lambda(1-\lambda)^2 Y_{t-2} + \beta_2\lambda(1-\lambda)^3 Y_{t-3} + \cdots$$
$$+ (1-\lambda)C_{t-1}^T. \quad (12.37)$$

Subtracting (12.37) from (12.36), one has

$$C_t - (1-\lambda)C_{t-1} = \beta_2\lambda Y_t + C_t^T - (1-\lambda)C_{t-1}^T \quad (12.38)$$

and so

$$C_t = \beta_2\lambda Y_t + (1-\lambda)C_{t-1} + C_t^T - (1-\lambda)C_{t-1}^T. \quad (12.39)$$

The short-run marginal propensity to consume is $\beta_2\lambda$ and the long-run propensity is β_2. Since λ is less than 1, the model is able to reconcile a low short-run marginal propensity to consume with a higher long-run average propensity.

Exercise

12.9* The output below shows the result of fitting the model

$$LGFOOD = \beta_1 + \beta_2\lambda LGDPI + \beta_2\lambda(1-\lambda)LGDPI(-1)$$
$$+ \beta_2\lambda(1-\lambda)^2 LGDPI(-2) + \beta_3 LGPRFOOD + u$$

using the data on expenditure on food in the Demand Functions data set. *LGFOOD* and *LGPRFOOD* are the logarithms of expenditure on food and the relative price index series for food. C(1), C(2), C(3), and C(4) are estimates of β_1, β_2, λ, and β_3, respectively. Explain how the regression equation could be interpreted as an adaptive expectations model and discuss the dynamics implicit in it, both short-run and long-run. Should the specification have included further lagged values of *LGDPI*?

```
================================================================
Dependent Variable: LGFOOD
Method: Least Squares
Sample(adjusted): 1961 1994
Included observations: 34 after adjusting endpoints
Convergence achieved after 848 iterations
LGFOOD=C(1)+C(2)*C(3)*LGDPI+C(2)*C(3)*(1-C(3))*LGDPI(-1)+C(2)
       *C(3)*(1-C(3))*(1-C(3))*LGDPI(-2)+C(4)*LGPRFOOD
================================================================
                  CoefficientStd. Errort-Statistic  Prob.
================================================================
       C(1)        2.666180   0.316754   8.417199   0.0000
       C(2)        0.607542   0.013005   46.71599   0.0000
       C(3)        0.863231   0.346065   2.494419   0.0184
       C(4)       -0.303995   0.072186  -4.211252   0.0002
----------------------------------------------------------------
R-squared           0.991081   Mean dependent var  6.132194
Adjusted R-squared  0.990190   S.D. dependent var  0.179564
S.E. of regression  0.017785   Akaike info criter-5.110752
Sum squared resid   0.009490   Schwarz criterion  -4.931180
Log likelihood      90.88279   F-statistic         1111.264
Durbin-Watson stat  0.604156   Prob(F-statistic)   0.000000
================================================================
```

12.4 The partial adjustment model

In the partial adjustment model it is assumed that the behavioral equation determines the *desired* (or 'target') value, Y_t^*, of the dependent variable, rather than the actual value, Y_t:

$$Y_t^* = \beta_1 + \beta_2 X_t + u_t. \tag{12.40}$$

It is then assumed that the actual increase in the dependent variable, $Y_t - Y_{t-1}$, is proportional to the discrepancy between the desired value and the previous value, $Y_t^* - Y_{t-1}$:

$$Y_t - Y_{t-1} = \lambda(Y_t^* - Y_{t-1}). \quad (0 \le \lambda \le 1) \tag{12.41}$$

This may be rewritten

$$Y_t = \lambda Y_t^* + (1 - \lambda)Y_{t-1} \tag{12.42}$$

so it can be seen that Y_t is a weighted average of the current desired value and the previous actual value. The higher is the value of λ, the more rapid is the adjustment process. If λ is equal to 1, Y_t is equal to Y_t^* and there is full adjustment in one period. At the other extreme, if λ is equal to 0, Y_t does not adjust at all.

Substituting for Y_t^* from the target relationship, one obtains

$$Y_t = \lambda(\beta_1 + \beta_2 X_t + u_t) + (1 - \lambda)Y_{t-1}$$
$$= \beta_1\lambda + \beta_2\lambda X_t + (1 - \lambda)Y_{t-1} + \lambda u_t. \qquad (12.43)$$

Thus the parameters β_1, β_2, and λ of the behavioral model can be estimated by regressing Y_t on X_t and Y_{t-1}. The model relates Y to the current value of X and the lagged value of itself, and so has the same structure as the Koyck-transformed version of the adaptive expectations model. It follows that its dynamics are exactly the same. The coefficient of Y_{t-1} yields an estimate of $(1 - \lambda)$ and hence of λ, the speed of adjustment. The coefficient of X_t gives the short-run effect of X on Y and also, when divided by the estimate of λ, the long-run effect.

Example: Brown's habit-persistence model of aggregate consumption

The first attempts by econometricians to fit an aggregate consumption function naturally used the simple static model

$$C_t = \beta_1 + \beta_2 Y_t + u_t. \qquad (12.44)$$

With estimates of β_2 well below 1, this model implied that the average propensity to consume should fall. Nevertheless long-run data showed no tendency for this to happen. Consequently macroeconomists started looking for more elaborate models that could reconcile these apparently contradictory facts. Friedman's Permanent Income Hypothesis was one such model. Another was Brown's Habit-Persistence Model (Brown, 1952). In this model, desired consumption C_t^* was related to wage income, W_t, and nonwage income, NW_t:

$$C_t^* = \beta_1 + \beta_2 W_t + \beta_3 NW_t + \delta A + u_t. \qquad (12.45)$$

Brown used aggregate data for Canada for the years 1926–49, omitting the war years 1942–5, A being a dummy variable equal to 0 for the pre-war period and 1 for the post-war period. The division of income into wage income and nonwage income follows the observation of Michael Kalecki that the marginal propensity to consume out of wage income was likely to be much higher than that out of nonwage income, for two reasons. First, nonwage income tends to be received by relatively rich households with higher savings rates than poorer ones. Second, in a market economy, much nonwage income originates as company profits, and companies normally pass on only part of their profits as dividends to shareholders, retaining the remainder for investment in the business.

Because households are slow to adapt their spending patterns in response to changes in income, Brown hypothesized a partial adjustment process for actual consumption:

$$C_t - C_{t-1} = \lambda(C_t^* - C_{t-1}). \tag{12.46}$$

From this one obtains current consumption as the weighted average of desired consumption and consumption in the previous time period:

$$C_t = \lambda C_t^* + (1 - \lambda)C_{t-1}. \tag{12.47}$$

Substituting for C_t^* from (12.45), one then has an equation in observable variables:

$$\begin{aligned} C_t &= \lambda(\beta_1 + \beta_2 W_t + \beta_3 NW_t + \delta A + u_t) + (1 - \lambda)C_{t-1} \\ &= \beta_1\lambda + \beta_2\lambda W_t + \beta_3\lambda NW_t + (1 - \lambda)C_{t-1} + \lambda\delta A + \lambda u_t. \end{aligned} \tag{12.48}$$

Fitting the model with a simultaneous equations technique, Brown obtained (t statistics in parentheses):

$$\hat{C}_t = 0.90 + 0.61 W_t + 0.28 NW_t + 0.22 C_{t-1} + 0.69 A. \tag{12.49}$$
$$\quad\ (4.8)\quad (7.4)\qquad (4.2)\qquad\quad (2.8)\qquad\quad (4.8)$$

The variables were all measured in Canadian \$ billion at constant prices of the 1935–9 period. From the regression one obtains short-run marginal propensities to consume of 0.61 and 0.28 for wage income and nonwage income, respectively. The coefficient of C_{t-1} indicates that 0.78 of the discrepancy between desired and actual income is eliminated in one year. Dividing the short-run marginal propensities by the speed of adjustment, one obtains long-run propensities to consume of 0.78 and 0.36 for wage income and nonwage income, respectively.

Comparison of the Friedman and Brown models

Despite the fact that their theoretical frameworks are completely different, one concerned with the future and expectations, the other concerned with the past and inertia, the Friedman model, in its Koyck-transformed form (12.39), and the habit-persistence model (12.48) are virtually identical. They both incorporate short-run and long-run propensities to consume and a speed of adjustment. The only difference in the variable specification is that the Brown model divides income into wage income and nonwage income. This is a useful refinement that should be applied to Friedman model as well. Indeed it is now a standard feature of empirical models. The Friedman model does not have an intercept, but that is a minor empirical detail. The disturbance term in the Friedman model is different from that in the Brown model, and its structure may cause problems, but as will be seen in the next chapter, that is likewise not an important difference. This is an example of the problem of observationally equivalent theories, where two or more theories can be used to fit the same data set in the same way and there is no possibility of discriminating between them.

328 Introduction to econometrics

Exercises

12.10 Expenditure on housing services, *HOUS*, was regressed on *DPI*, the relative price index for housing, *PRELHOUS*, and the lagged value of *HOUS*, *HOUS*(−1), for the period 1959–94 for the United States using the Demand Functions data set. The regression was repeated in logarithmic form, *LGHOUS* being regressed on *LGDPI*, *LGPRHOUS*, and *LGHOUS*(−1), with the results summarized below. Give an interpretation of the regression coefficients, paying attention to the dynamics implicit in the model.

$$\widehat{HOUS} = 19.24 + 0.05DPI - 0.28\,PRELHOUS + 0.69HOUS(-1).$$
$$(10.14)\ (0.01)\qquad (0.10)\qquad\qquad (0.04)$$

$$R^2 = 0.9998$$

$$\widehat{LGHOUS} = -0.39 + 0.32\,LGDPI - 0.07\,LGPRHOUS$$
$$(0.15)\ (0.05)\qquad\quad (0.02)$$

$$+\ 0.70\,LGHOUS(-1).\quad R^2 = 0.9998$$
$$(0.05)$$

12.11 Perform regressions parallel to those reported in Exercise 12.10 for your category of expenditure in the Demand Functions data set. Give an interpretation of the regression coefficients, paying attention to the dynamics implicit in the model.

12.12* How would you test Kalecki's assertion concerning the coefficients of wage and nonwage income if you had access to Brown's data set?

12.13* In his classic study *Distributed Lags and Investment Analysis* (1954), Koyck investigated the relationship between investment in railcars and the volume of freight carried on the US railroads using data for the period 1884–1939. Assuming that the desired stock of railcars in year *t* depended on the volume of freight in year *t* − 1 and year *t* − 2 and a time trend, and assuming that investment in railcars was subject to a partial adjustment process, he fitted the following regression equation using OLS (standard errors and constant term not reported):

$$\hat{I}_t = 0.077\,F_{t-1} + 0.017\,F_{t-2} - 0.0033t - 0.110K_{t-1}.\quad R^2 = 0.85$$

Provide an interpretation of the equation and describe the dynamic process implied by it. (*Note*: It is best to substitute $K_t - K_{t-1}$ for I_t in the regression and treat it as a dynamic relationship determining K_t.)

12.5 **Prediction**

Suppose that you have fitted a model

$$Y_t = \beta_1 + \beta_2 X_t + u_t \tag{12.50}$$

to a sample of T time series observations $(t = 1, \ldots, T)$:

$$\hat{Y}_t = b_1 + b_2 X_t. \tag{12.51}$$

Given any post-sample period value of X, say X_{T+p}, you are now in a position to predict the corresponding value of Y:

$$\hat{Y}_{T+p} = b_1 + b_2 X_{T+p}. \tag{12.52}$$

There are two reasons why such predictions may be important to you. First, you may be one of those econometricians whose business it is to peer into the economic future. Some econometricians are concerned with teasing out economic relationships with the aim of improving our understanding of how the economy works, but for others this is only a means to the more practical objective of trying to anticipate what will happen. In most countries macroeconomic forecasting has a particularly high profile, teams of econometricians being employed by the Ministry of Finance or other branches of government, private financial institutions, universities, and research institutes, and their predictions are actively used for framing public policy, for commenting on it, or for business purposes. When they are published in the press, they typically attract far more attention than most other forms of economic analysis, both on account of their subject matter and because, unlike most other forms of economic analysis, they are easily understood by the ordinary citizen. Even the most innumerate and non-technically minded person can have a good understanding of what is meant by estimates of the future levels of unemployment, inflation, etc.

There is, however, a second use of econometric prediction, one that has made it of concern to econometricians, irrespective of whether they are involved in forecasting. It provides a method of evaluating the robustness of a regression model that is more searching than the diagnostic statistics that have been used so far.

Before we go any further, we will have to clarify what we mean by *prediction*. Unfortunately, in the econometric literature this term can have several slightly different meanings, according to the status of X_{T+p} in (12.52). We will differentiate between ex-post predictions and forecasts. This classification corresponds to what seems to be the most common usage, but the terminology is not standard.

Ex-post predictions

We will describe $\hat{Y}_{T+p}$ as an ex-post prediction if X_{T+p} is known. How can this be the case? In general, econometricians make use of all available data, to maximize the sample size and hence minimize the population variances of their estimators, so X_T will simply be the most recent recorded value of X available at the time of running the regression. Nevertheless, there are two circumstances when X_{T+p} will be known as well: when you have waited p or more periods after running the regression, and when you have deliberately terminated the sample period early so that you have a few of the most recent observations left over. The reason for doing this, as we shall see in the next section, is to enable you to evaluate the predictive accuracy of the model without having to wait.

For example, referring again to the price inflation/wage inflation model of equation (3.39), suppose that we had fitted the equation

$$\hat{p} = 1.0 + 0.80w \tag{12.53}$$

during the sample period, where p and w are the percentage annual rates of price inflation and wage inflation, respectively, and suppose that we know that the rate of wage inflation was 6 percent in some prediction period year. Then we can say that the ex-post prediction of the rate of price inflation is 5.8 percent. We should, of course, be able to compare it immediately with the actual rate of price inflation for that year, and hence we can evaluate the prediction error, which is just the difference between actual outcome and the predicted value. In general, if Y_{T+p} is the actual outcome, and $\hat{Y}_{T+p}$ the predicted value, the prediction error is defined as f_{T+p} where

$$f_{T+p} = Y_{T+p} - \hat{Y}_{T+p}. \tag{12.54}$$

Why is there a prediction error? For two reasons. First, $\hat{Y}_{T+p}$ has been calculated using the parameter estimates, b_1 and b_2, instead of the true values. And second, $\hat{Y}_{T+p}$ cannot take account of the disturbance term u_{T+p}, which is a component of Y_{T+p}. In the discussion that follows, we shall assume that the data include $T + P$ observations on the variables, the first T (the sample period) being used to fit the regression and the last P (the prediction period or prediction interval) being used to check predictive accuracy.

Example

Suppose that when we fitted the demand function for housing using the Demand Functions data set, we had only used the first thirty-two observations in the sample, that is, the observations for 1959–90, reserving the last four observations for checking predictions. The fitted equation for 1959–90 is (standard errors in parentheses):

$$\widehat{LGHOUS} = -1.96 + 1.13LGDPI - 0.24LGPRHOUS. \quad R^2 = 0.998$$
$$(0.39) \ (0.01) \qquad\quad (0.08) \tag{12.55}$$

The predicted values of $LGHOUS$ for the period 1991–4, using the equation and the actual values of disposable personal income and the relative price of

Table 12.6 Predicted and actual expenditure on housing services, 1991–4

Year	Logarithms			Absolute equivalent		
	LGHOUS	LG$\widehat{HOUS}$	Error	HOUS	$\widehat{HOUS}$	Error
1991	6.4539	6.4374	0.0166	635.2	624.8	10.4
1992	6.4720	6.4697	0.0023	646.8	645.3	1.5
1993	6.4846	6.4820	0.0026	655.0	653.3	1.7
1994	6.5046	6.5073	−0.0027	668.2	670.0	−1.8

housing services for those years, are shown in Table 12.6, together with the actual outcomes and the prediction errors. The predictions, like the basic data, are in logarithmic form. For convenience, Table 12.6 also shows the absolute values, derived from the logarithmic values, expressed in $ billion at 1992 prices.

We can see that in this case the predicted value of expenditure on housing services is roughly 2 percent below the actual outcome in 1991, and very close in the remaining three years. Is this predictive performance satisfactory? We shall see in the next section.

Forecasts

If you are willing to predict a particular value of Y_{T+p}, without knowing the actual value of X_{T+p}, you are said to be making a forecast, at least in the terminology of this text. The macroeconomic divinations published in the press are usually forecasts in this sense. Policymakers, and indeed the general public, are not much interested in two-handed economists (ones who say 'on the one hand this … but if … then on the other hand that …'). They want the best possible single-point estimates, perhaps with some indication of the likely margin of error, often not even that. Forecasts are less accurate than predictions because they are subject to an additional source of error, the error in the prediction of X_{T+p}. Obviously, those making forecasts normally attempt to minimize the additional error by modeling the behavior of X as carefully as possible, in some instances constructing a separate model for it, in others bringing the equation determining Y and the equation determining X together, usually with other relationships as well, in a simultaneous equations model of the type discussed in Chapter 10.

Properties of least squares predictors

In the discussion that follows, we will be concerned with predictions rather than forecasts, the reason being that we are in a position to make statements about the properties of the regression coefficients and the disturbance term, but not about X if its values are not known. First, there is some good news. If Y_{T+p} is generated by the same process as the sample period values of Y (that is, according to equation (12.50) with u_{T+p} conforming to the Gauss–Markov conditions), and if we make our prediction $\hat{Y}_{T+p}$ using equation (12.52), the prediction error f_{T+p} will have mean 0 and minimum variance.

The first property is easily demonstrated:

$$
\begin{aligned}
E(f_{T+p}) &= E(Y_{T+p}) - E(\hat{Y}_{T+p}) \\
&= E(\beta_1 + \beta_2 X_{T+p} + u_{T+p}) - E(b_1 + b_2 X_{T+p}) \\
&= \beta_1 + \beta_2 X_{T+p} + E(u_{T+p}) - E(b_1) - X_{T+p} E(b_2) \\
&= \beta_1 + \beta_2 X_{T+p} - \beta_1 - \beta_2 X_{T+p} = 0
\end{aligned}
\tag{12.56}
$$

since $E(b_1) = \beta_1$, $E(b_2) = \beta_2$, and $E(u_{T+p}) = 0$. We will not attempt to prove the minimum variance property (for a proof, see Johnston and Dinardo, 1997). Both of these properties carry over to the general case of multiple regression analysis.

In the simple regression case, the population variance of f_{T+p} is given by

$$
\sigma^2_{f_{T+p}} = \left\{ 1 + \frac{1}{T} + \frac{(X_{T+p} - \bar{X})^2}{T \operatorname{Var}(X)} \right\} \sigma^2_u,
\tag{12.57}
$$

where $\bar{X}$ and $\operatorname{Var}(X)$ are the sample period mean and variance of X. Unsurprisingly, this implies that, the further is the value of X from its sample mean, the larger will be the population variance of the prediction error. It also implies, again unsurprisingly, that the larger is the sample, the smaller will be the population variance of the prediction error, with a lower limit of σ^2_u. As the sample becomes large, b_1 and b_2 will tend to their true values (provided that the Gauss–Markov conditions hold), so the only source of error in the prediction will be u_{T+p}, and by definition this has population variance σ^2_u.

Confidence intervals for predictions

We can obtain the standard error of the prediction error by replacing σ^2_u in (12.57) by s^2_u and taking the square root. Then $(Y_{T+p} - \hat{Y}_{T+p})$/standard error follows a t distribution with the number of degrees of freedom when fitting the equation in the sample period, $T - k$. Hence we can derive a confidence interval for the actual outcome, Y_{T+p}:

$$
\hat{Y}_{T+p} - t_{\text{crit}} \times \text{s.e.} < Y_{T+p} < \hat{Y}_{T+p} + t_{\text{crit}} \times \text{s.e.},
\tag{12.58}
$$

where t_{crit} is the critical level of t, given the significance level selected and the number of degrees of freedom, and s.e. is the standard error of the prediction. Figure 12.3 depicts in general terms the relationship between the confidence interval for prediction and the value of the explanatory variable.

In multiple regressions, the counterpart to (12.57) is much more complicated and is best handled with matrix algebra. Fortunately, there is a simple trick that you can use to get the computer to calculate the standard errors for you. Let the

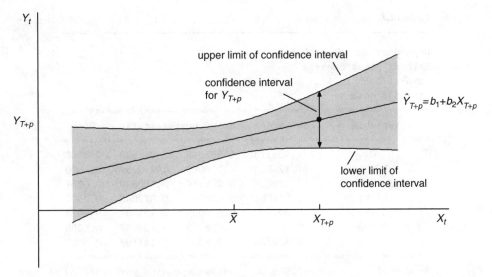

Figure 12.3 Confidence interval for a projection

sample period be denoted $1, \ldots, T$ and the prediction period $T + 1, \ldots, T + P$. You run the regression for the sample and prediction periods combined, adding a (different) dummy variable to each of the prediction period observations. This means adding to the model a set of dummy variables $D_{T+1}, \ldots, D_{T+P}$, where D_{T+p} is defined to be 0 for every observation except observation $T + p$, for which it is 1. It can be shown (Salkever, 1976; Dufour, 1980) that the estimates of the nondummy coefficients and their standard errors will be exactly the same as in the regression confined to the sample period only. The computer uses the dummy variables to obtain a perfect fit in each observation in the prediction period, and it does this by setting the coefficient of the dummy variable equal to the prediction error as defined above. The standard error of this coefficient is equal to the standard error of the prediction error.

Example

The output in Table 12.7 shows the result of a logarithmic regression of housing services on income and relative price with dummy variables for the years 1991–94. The coefficients of the dummy variables give the prediction errors presented in Table 12.6. The predicted logarithm of expenditure on housing services in 1991 in Table 12.6 was 6.4374. From the output we see that the standard error of the prediction error for that year was 0.0190. With 29 degrees of freedom, the critical value of t at the 5 percent significance level is 2.045, so we obtain the following 95 percent confidence interval for the prediction for that year:

$$6.4374 - 2.045 \times 0.0190 < Y < 6.4374 + 2.045 \times 0.0190 \qquad (12.59)$$

that is,

$$6.3985 < Y < 6.4763. \qquad (12.60)$$

Table 12.7

```
Dependent Variable: LGHOUS
Method: Least Squares
Sample: 1959 1994
Included observations: 36
==============================================================
     Variable    CoefficientStd. Errort-Statistic   Prob.
==============================================================
           C     -1.959273   0.388319  -5.045522   0.0000
       LGDPI      1.129984   0.010942   103.2737   0.0000
    LGPRHOUS     -0.239828   0.075874  -3.160890   0.0037
       D1991      0.016561   0.018991   0.872042   0.3903
       D1992      0.002325   0.019033   0.122150   0.9036
       D1993      0.002604   0.019109   0.136289   0.8925
       D1994     -0.002732   0.019268  -0.141796   0.8882
==============================================================
R-squared           0.998206   Mean dependent var 5.996930
Adjusted R-squared  0.997835   S.D. dependent var 0.377702
S.E. of regression  0.017576   Akaike info criter-5.071925
Sum squared resid   0.008958   Schwarz criterion  -4.764019
Log likelihood      98.29465   F-statistic         2689.096
Durbin-Watson stat  0.838021   Prob(F-statistic)  0.000000
```

The confidence interval does include the actual outcome, 6.4539, and thus, for that year at least, the prediction was satisfactory. The same is true for the other years in the prediction period.

Exercise

12.14 Use the Salkever indirect method to compute forecasts and their standard errors for the logarithmic demand function for your category of expenditure. Add dummy variables to the last four observations and hence obtain the prediction errors for these years, given a regression based on the first thirty-two observations. Subtract these from the actual outcomes to obtain the forecasts. Derive a confidence interval for the forecast for 1994.

12.6 Stability tests

Stability tests of a regression model are tests designed to evaluate whether the performance of a model in a prediction period is compatible with its performance in the sample period used to fit it. There are two principles on which stability tests can be constructed. One approach is to focus on the predictive performance of the model; the other is to evaluate whether there is any evidence of shifts in the parameters in the prediction period.

The Chow test of predictive failure

In the previous section we saw that we could compute the prediction errors by adding a set of dummy variables to the prediction period observations. It is natural to test whether the prediction errors are significantly different from 0, and we can do this with an F test of the joint explanatory power of the dummy variables. Combining the sample and prediction period observations, we run the regression first without the dummy variables and then with them included. Let the residual sum of squares be denoted RSS_{T+P} and RSS_{T+P}^{D}, the subscript indicating the number of observations in the regression and the superscript D indicating the inclusion of the dummy variables. We then see whether the improvement in the fit on adding the dummy variables is significant, using the F test presented in Section 4.5. The improvement is $(RSS_{T+P} - RSS_{T+P}^{D})$; the number of dummy variables is P; the residual sum of squares after adding the dummy variables is RSS_{T+P}^{D}; and the number of degrees of freedom remaining is the number of observations in the combined sample, $T + P$, less the number of parameters estimated, $k + P$. The test statistic is therefore

$$F(P, T - k) = \frac{(RSS_{T+P} - RSS_{T+P}^{D})/P}{RSS_{T+P}^{D}/(T - k)}. \tag{12.61}$$

In practice, you do not even have to run the regression with the dummy variables to perform the test, because RSS_{T+P}^{D} is identical to RSS_T, the sum of the squares of the residuals in the regression limited to the sample period. The fit for this regression is exactly the same as the fit for the first T observations in the dummy variable regression, which means that the residuals are the same. And there are no residuals in the last P observations of the dummy variable regression because the inclusion of an observation-specific dummy in each observation guarantees a perfect fit in those observations. Hence RSS_{T+P}^{D} is exactly the same as RSS_T, and the F statistic can be written

$$F(P, T - k) = \frac{(RSS_{T+P} - RSS_T)/P}{RSS_T/(T - k)}. \tag{12.62}$$

The test is usually known as the Chow test, after its originator, but the interpretation given here is later (Pesaran, Smith, and Yeo, 1985).

Example

The housing services expenditure function was fitted first for the period 1959–90, giving $RSS_T = 0.008958$, and then for the period 1959–94, giving $RSS_{T+P} = 0.009218$. The F statistic is therefore

$$F(4, 29) = \frac{(0.009218 - 0.008958)/4}{0.008958/29} = 0.21. \tag{12.63}$$

The null hypothesis is that the coefficients of the dummy variables are all equal to 0. Since the F statistic is less than 1, we do not reject it at any significance level. There is no significant difference between the sample period and prediction period fits and so we conclude that the model is stable.

F test of coefficient stability

If there are sufficient observations in the prediction period, you can perform a Chow test on the lines of that discussed in Chapter 6 to evaluate whether the coefficients in the sample period and prediction period appear to be significantly different. To perform the test, you run the regression for the sample and prediction periods separately, and then for the two periods combined, and see whether sample period/prediction period division results in a significant improvement in fit compared with that obtained with the combined regression. If it does, this is evidence that the coefficients are unstable.

Example

In the case of the housing services expenditure function, with the observations for 1959–90 being used as the sample period and those for 1991–4 as the prediction period, the sums of the squares of the residuals for the sample period, prediction period, and combination were 0.008958, 0.000002, and 0.009218, respectively. Running separate regressions for the two subperiods costs 3 degrees of freedom, and the number of degrees of freedom remaining after estimating six parameters (constant twice, coefficient of *LGDPI* twice, and coefficient of *LGPRHOUS* twice) is 30. Hence we obtain the following F statistic, which is distributed with 3 and 30 degrees of freedom:

$$F(3, 30) = \frac{(0.009218 - [0.008958 + 0.000002])/3}{(0.008958 + 0.000002)/30} = 0.29. \qquad (12.64)$$

Thus we conclude that there is no evidence of coefficient instability.

Exercises

12.15 Fit the logarithmic form of your demand function for your category of expenditure for the periods 1959–90 and 1959–94 and perform the Chow test of predictive failure.

12.16 Fit your demand function to the data for 1959–94, 1959–90, and 1991–4 and perform the F test of coefficient stability.

13 Autocorrelation

13.1 Definition of autocorrelation

To this point it has been assumed that the third Gauss–Markov condition, that the value taken by the disturbance term in any observation be determined independently of its values in all the other observations, is satisfied, and hence that the population covariance of u_i and u_j is 0, for $i \neq j$. When the condition is not satisfied, the disturbance term is said to be subject to autocorrelation, often called serial correlation (the terms are interchangeable).

The consequences of autocorrelation for OLS are somewhat similar to those of heteroscedasticity. In general, the regression coefficients remain unbiased, but OLS is inefficient because one can find an alternative unbiased estimator with smaller variance. The other main consequence, which should not be mixed up with the first, is that the standard errors are estimated wrongly, probably being biased downwards. Finally, although in general autocorrelation does not cause OLS estimates to be biased, there is an important special case where it does.

Possible causes of autocorrelation

Autocorrelation normally occurs only in regression analysis using time-series data. The disturbance term in a regression equation picks up the influence of those variables affecting the dependent variable that have not been included in the regression equation. If the value of u in any observation is to be independent of its value in the previous one, the value of any variable hidden in u must be uncorrelated with its value at the time of the previous observation.

Persistence of the effects of excluded variables is probably the most frequent cause of positive autocorrelation, the usual type in economic analysis. In Figure 13.1, Y depends on X and a number of minor variables not included explicitly in the specification. The disturbance term in the model is generated by the combined effects of these excluded variables. In the first observation, the excluded variables have a net positive effect and the disturbance term is positive. If the excluded variables change slowly, their positive effect will persist and the disturbance term will remain positive. Eventually the balance will change and the net effect of the excluded variables becomes negative. Now the persistence

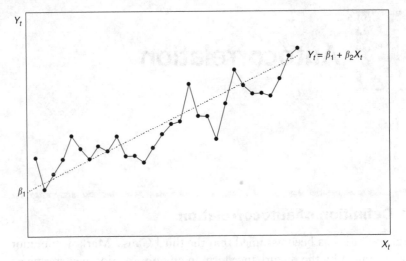

$Y_t = \beta_1 + \beta_2 X_t$

β_1

Figure 13.1 Positive autocorrelation

effect works the other way and the disturbance term remains negative for a few observations. The duration and amplitude of each positive and negative sequence are essentially random, but overall there will be a tendency for positive values of the disturbance term to be followed by positive ones and for negative values to be followed by negative ones.

One important point to note is that autocorrelation is on the whole more likely to be a problem, the shorter the interval between observations. Obviously, the longer the interval, the less likely are the effects of the excluded variables to persist from one observation to the next.

In principle autocorrelation may also be negative. This means that the correlation between successive values of the disturbance term is negative. A positive value in one observation is more likely to be followed by a negative value than a positive value in the next, and vice versa, the scatter diagram looking like Figure 13.2. A line joining successive observations to one another would cross the line relating Y to X with greater frequency than one would expect if the values of the disturbance term were independent of each other. Economic examples of negative autocorrelation are relatively uncommon, but sometimes it is induced by manipulations used to transform the original specification of a model into a form suitable for regression analysis.

13.2 Detection of first-order autocorrelation: the Durbin–Watson test

We will mostly be concerned with first-order autoregressive autocorrelation, often denoted AR(1), where the disturbance term u in the model

$$Y_t = \beta_1 + \beta_2 X_t + u_t \qquad (13.1)$$

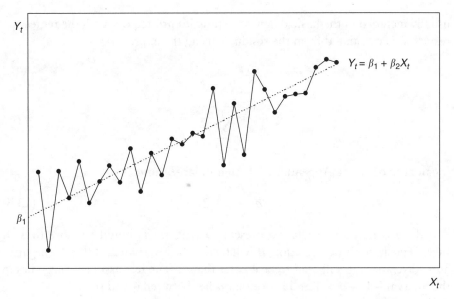

Figure 13.2 Negative autocorrelation

is generated by the process

$$u_t = \rho u_{t-1} + \varepsilon_t, \tag{13.2}$$

where ε_t is a random variable whose value in any observation is independent of its value in all the other observations. This type of autocorrelation is described as autoregressive because u_t is being determined by lagged values of itself plus the fresh element of randomness ε_t, sometimes described as an innovation. It is described as first-order because u_t depends only on u_{t-1} and the innovation. A process of the type

$$u_t = \rho_1 u_{t-1} + \rho_2 u_{t-2} + \rho_3 u_{t-3} + \rho_4 u_{t-4} + \rho_5 u_{t-5} + \varepsilon_t \tag{13.3}$$

would be described as fifth-order autoregressive autocorrelation, denoted AR(5). The main alternative to autoregressive autocorrelation is moving average (MA) autocorrelation, where u_t is determined as a weighted sum of current and previous values of ε_t. For example, the process

$$u_t = \lambda_0 \varepsilon_t + \lambda_1 \varepsilon_{t-1} + \lambda_2 \varepsilon_{t-2} + \lambda_3 \varepsilon_{t-3} \tag{13.4}$$

would be described as MA(3).

We will focus on AR(1) autocorrelation because it appears to be the most common type, at least as an approximation. It is described as positive or negative according to the sign of ρ in (13.2). Note that if ρ is 0, there is no autocorrelation after all.

Because AR(1) is such a common form of autocorrelation, the standard test statistic for it, the Durbin–Watson d statistic (Durbin and Watson, 1950), is usually included in the basic diagnostic statistics printed out with the regression results. It is calculated from the residuals using the expression

$$d = \frac{\sum_{t=2}^{T}(e_t - e_{t-1})^2}{\sum_{t=1}^{T} e_t^2}. \tag{13.5}$$

It can be shown (see Appendix 13.1) that in large samples

$$d \to 2 - 2\rho. \tag{13.6}$$

If there is no autocorrelation present, ρ is 0, so d should be close to 2. If there is positive autocorrelation, d will tend to be less than 2. If there is negative autocorrelation, it will tend to be greater than 2. The test assumes that ρ lies in the interval $-1 > \rho > 1$ and hence that d lies between 4 and 0.

The null hypothesis for the test is that ρ is equal to 0. Of course, even if H_0 is true, d will not be exactly equal to 2, except by freak chance. However a value of d much lower than 2 leaves you with two choices. One is to assume that H_0 is true and that the low value of d has arisen as a matter of chance. The other is that the disturbance term is subject to positive autocorrelation. As usual, the choice is made by establishing a critical value d_{crit} below which d would not sink, say, more than 5 percent of the time. If d were below d_{crit}, you would then reject H_0 at the 5 percent significance level.

The critical value of d at any significance level depends, as you might expect, on the number of explanatory variables in the regression equation and the number of observations in the sample. Unfortunately, it also depends on the particular values taken by the explanatory variables. Thus it is not possible to construct a table giving the exact critical values for all possible samples, as one can with the t test and the F test, but it is possible to calculate upper and lower *limits* for the critical value of d. Those for positive autocorrelation are usually denoted d_U and d_L.

Figure 13.3 represents the situation schematically, with the arrow indicating the critical level of d, which will be denoted d_{crit}. If you knew the exact value of d_{crit}, you could compare the d statistic for your regression with it. If $d > d_{crit}$,

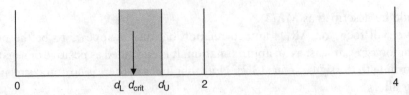

Figure 13.3 Durbin–Watson test for autocorrelation, showing the zone of indeterminacy in the case of suspected positive autocorrelation

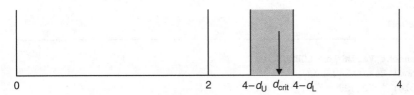

Figure 13.4 Durbin–Watson test for autocorrelation, showing the zone of indeterminacy in the case of suspected negative autocorrelation

you would fail to reject the null hypothesis of no autocorrelation. If $d < d_{crit}$, you would reject the null hypothesis and conclude that there is evidence of positive autocorrelation.

However, all you know is that d_{crit} lies somewhere between d_L and d_U. This leaves you with three possible outcomes for the test.

1. d is less than d_L. In this case, it must be lower than d_{crit}, so you would reject the null hypothesis and conclude that positive autocorrelation is present.

2. d is greater than d_U. In this case, d must be greater than d_{crit}, so you would fail to reject the null hypothesis.

3. d lies between d_L and d_U. In this case, d might be greater or less than d_{crit}. You do not know which, so you cannot tell whether you should reject or not reject the null hypothesis.

In cases (1) and (2), the Durbin–Watson test gives you a definite answer, but in case (3) you are left in a zone of indecision, and there is nothing that you can do about it.

Table A.5 at the end of this text gives d_L and d_U cross-classified by number of explanatory variables and number of observations, for the 5 percent and 1 percent significance levels, for the case of positive AR(1) autocorrelation. You can see that the zone of indecision between d_L and d_U decreases as the sample size increases. Testing for negative autocorrelation follows a similar pattern, with the zone containing the critical value symmetrically located to the right of 2. Since negative autocorrelation is relatively uncommon, you are expected to calculate the limits of the zone yourself from the figures for positive autocorrelation for the corresponding number of explanatory variables and number of observations. This is easy enough to do. As is illustrated in Figure 13.4, $4 - d_U$ gives the lower limit, below which you fail to reject the null hypothesis of no autocorrelation, and $4 - d_L$ gives the upper one, above which you conclude that there is evidence of negative autocorrelation.

It should be noted that a low d statistic does not necessarily mean that the model is subject to AR(1) autocorrelation. It will be low whenever there is a pattern of positive residuals tending to be followed by positive ones and negative ones by negative ones, and this could be caused by model misspecification. In particular, it is often caused by the omission of an important variable from the model, and it may happen if the regression is using an inappropriate mathematical function. We will discuss these cases of apparent autocorrelation below.

Table 13.1

```
Dependent Variable: LGHOUS
Method: Least Squares
Sample: 1959 1994
Included observations: 36
============================================================
    Variable      Coefficient  Std. Error  t-Statistic   Prob.
============================================================
       C           -2.032685    0.322726    -6.298478    0.0000
     LGDPI          1.132248    0.008705   130.0650      0.0000
   LGPRHOUS        -0.227634    0.065841    -3.457323    0.0015
============================================================
R-squared              0.998154   Mean dependent var    5.996930
Adjusted R-squared     0.998042   S.D. dependent var    0.377702
S.E. of regression     0.016714   Akaike info criter   -5.265522
Sum squared resid      0.009218   Schwarz criterion    -5.133562
Log likelihood        97.77939    F-statistic        8920.496
Durbin-Watson stat     0.846451   Prob(F-statistic)     0.000000
```

Example

The output shown in Table 13.1 gives the result of a logarithmic regression of housing services on disposable personal income and the relative price of housing services. The Durbin–Watson statistic is 0.85. For H_0: $\rho = 0$ and H_1: $\rho \neq 0$, d_L is 1.15 for a 1 percent significance test (2 explanatory variables, 36 observations). We would therefore reject H_0.

Exercises

13.1 Examine the Durbin–Watson statistic for the logarithmic demand function that you fitted in Exercise 12.4. Is there evidence of autocorrelation? If so, what are the implications for the statistical tests you performed?

13.2 If your regression application allows you to graph or print the residuals from a regression, do this in the case of your logarithmic demand function. Does an inspection of the residuals corroborate the presence (or absence) of autocorrelation indicated by the Durbin–Watson statistic?

13.3 What can you do about autocorrelation?

We will consider only the case of AR(1) autocorrelation. It has received the most attention in the literature because it is intuitively plausible and there is seldom sufficient evidence to make it worthwhile considering more complicated models.

If the observations are taken quarterly or monthly, however, other models may be more suitable, but we will not investigate them here.

AR(1) autocorrelation can be eliminated by a simple manipulation of the model. Suppose that the model is

$$Y_t = \beta_1 + \beta_2 X_t + u_t \tag{13.7}$$

with u_t generated by the process

$$u_t = \rho u_{t-1} + \varepsilon_t. \tag{13.8}$$

If we lag equation (13.7) by one time period and multiply by ρ, we have

$$\rho Y_{t-1} = \beta_1 \rho + \beta_2 \rho X_{t-1} + \rho u_{t-1}. \tag{13.9}$$

Now subtract (13.9) from (13.7):

$$Y_t - \rho Y_{t-1} = \beta_1(1 - \rho) + \beta_2 X_t - \beta_2 \rho X_{t-1} + u_t - \rho u_{t-1}. \tag{13.10}$$

Hence

$$Y_t = \beta_1(1 - \rho) + \rho Y_{t-1} + \beta_2 X_t - \beta_2 \rho X_{t-1} + \varepsilon_t. \tag{13.11}$$

The model is now free from autocorrelation because the disturbance term has been reduced to the innovation ε_t. In the case of the more general multiple regression model

$$Y_t = \beta_1 + \beta_2 X_{2t} + \cdots + \beta_k X_{kt} + u_t, \tag{13.12}$$

with u_t following an AR(1) process, we follow the same procedure. We lag the equation and multiply it by ρ:

$$\rho Y_{t-1} = \beta_1 \rho + \beta_2 \rho X_{2,t-1} + \cdots + \beta_k \rho X_{k,t-1} + \rho u_{t-1}. \tag{13.13}$$

Subtracting (13.13) from (13.12) and rearranging, we again derive a model free from autocorrelation:

$$Y_t = \beta_1(1 - \rho) + \rho Y_{t-1} + \beta_2 X_{2t} - \beta_2 \rho X_{2,t-1} + \cdots + \beta_k X_{kt} - \beta_k \rho X_{k,t-1} + \varepsilon_t. \tag{13.14}$$

Note that the model incorporates the nonlinear restriction that the coefficient of the lagged value of each X variable is equal to minus the product of the coefficients of its current value and Y_{t-1}. This means that you should not use OLS to fit it. If you did, there would be no guarantee that the coefficients would conform to the theoretical restrictions. Thus one has to use some nonlinear estimation procedure instead. The most common are nonlinear least squares, on the lines discussed in Chapter 5, and maximum-likelihood estimation.

Example

The output in Table 13.2 shows the result of a logarithmic regression of housing services on disposable personal income and the relative price of housing services, using the nonlinear specification represented by equation (13.14). The model is

$$LGHOUS_t = \beta_1(1-\rho) + \rho LGHOUS_{t-1} + \beta_2 LGDPI_t - \beta_2 \rho LGDPI_{t-1}$$
$$+ \beta_3 LGPRHOUS_t - \beta_3 \rho LGPRHOUS_{t-1} + \varepsilon_t. \qquad (13.15)$$

The nonlinear specification is reproduced as part of the regression output. C(1), C(2), C(3), and C(4) are estimates of β_1, ρ, β_2, and β_3, respectively. The fitted equation is therefore

$$\widehat{LGHOUS} = C(1)[1 - C(2)] + C(2)LGHOUS(-1) + C(3)LGDPI$$
$$- C(2)C(3)LGDPI(-1) + C(4)LGPRHOUS$$
$$- C(2)C(4)LGPRHOUS(-1). \qquad (13.16)$$

This equation is reproduced as part of the EViews output. You can see that the estimate of ρ is very high indeed, 0.97, suggesting that there was very severe autocorrelation in the original specification. The estimate of the income elasticity is much lower than in the OLS regression, but the estimate of the price elasticity is much the same.

We have noted that most regression applications designed for time-series analysis include the Durbin–Watson statistic as a standard component of the output. In the same way, they usually have a built-in option for fitting models where the disturbance term has an AR(1) specification, making it unnecessary to use a nonlinear equation such as (13.16) to spell out the structure of the model. In the case of EViews, adding AR(1) to the list of regressors converts the specification from OLS to that appropriate for AR(1) autocorrelation. Early regression applications tended to use the Cochrane–Orcutt iterative procedure, described in Box 13.1. It effectively enables the nonlinear AR(1) model to be fitted using linear regression analysis, a major benefit when computers were still in their infancy and nonlinear estimation was so time-consuming that it was avoided if possible. Now that nonlinear regression is a standard feature of major regression applications, the Cochrane–Orcutt iterative procedure is mainly of historical interest and most applications designed for time-series analysis offer alternative methods.

The output for the logarithmic demand function for housing is shown in Table 13.2. You can see that the regression results are identical to those for the explicit nonlinear specification. Note that the coefficient of AR(1) is the estimate of ρ, and corresponds to C(2) in the previous regression.

Exercise

13.3 Perform a logarithmic regression of expenditure on your commodity on income and relative price, first using OLS and then using the option for

Table 13.2

```
Dependent Variable: LGHOUS
Method: Least Squares
Sample(adjusted): 1960 1994
Included observations: 35 after adjusting endpoints
Convergence achieved after 6 iterations
LGHOUS=C(1)*(1-C(2))+C(2)*LGHOUS(-1)+C(3)*LGDPI-C(2)*C(3)
       *LGDPI(-1)+C(4)*LGPRHOUS-C(2)*C(4)*LGPRHOUS(-1)
==========================================================
              CoefficientStd. Errort-Statistic  Prob.
==========================================================
     C(1)       6.131576   0.727244   8.431251   0.0000
     C(2)       0.972488   0.004167   233.3567   0.0000
     C(3)       0.275879   0.078318   3.522532   0.0013
     C(4)      -0.303387   0.085802  -3.535896   0.0013
==========================================================
R-squared           0.999695   Mean dependent var 6.017555
Adjusted R-squared  0.999665   S.D. dependent var 0.362063
S.E. of regression  0.006622   Akaike info criter-7.089483
Sum squared resid   0.001360   Schwarz criterion -6.911729
Log likelihood      128.0660   F-statistic        33865.14
Durbin-Watson stat  1.423030   Prob(F-statistic)  0.000000
==========================================================


==========================================================
Dependent Variable: LGHOUS
Method: Least Squares
Sample(adjusted): 1960 1994
Included observations: 35 after adjusting endpoints
Convergence achieved after 24 iterations
==========================================================
   Variable    CoefficientStd. Errort-Statistic  Prob.
==========================================================
      C          6.131573   0.727241   8.431276   0.0000
    LGDPI        0.275879   0.078318   3.522534   0.0013
   LGPRHOUS     -0.303387   0.085802  -3.535896   0.0013
    AR(1)        0.972488   0.004167   233.3540   0.0000
==========================================================
R-squared           0.999695   Mean dependent var 6.017555
Adjusted R-squared  0.999665   S.D. dependent var 0.362063
S.E. of regression  0.006622   Akaike info criter-7.089483
Sum squared resid   0.001360   Schwarz criterion -6.911729
Log likelihood      128.0660   F-statistic        33865.14
Durbin-Watson stat  1.423031   Prob(F-statistic)  0.000000
==========================================================
Inverted AR Roots          .97
```

BOX 13.1   The Cochrane–Orcutt iterative procedure for eliminating AR(1) autocorrelation

---

The starting point for the Cochrane–Orcutt iterative procedure is equation (13.10), which may be rewritten

$$\tilde{Y}_t = \beta_1' + \beta_2 \tilde{X}_t + \varepsilon_t,$$

where $\tilde{Y}_t = Y_t - \rho Y_{t-1}, \tilde{X}_t = X_t - \rho X_{t-1}$, and $\beta_1' = \beta_1(1 - \rho)$. If you knew the value of ρ, all you would have to do would be to calculate $\tilde{Y}_t$ and $\tilde{X}_t$ from the data on Y and X, and perform a simple regression of $\tilde{Y}_t$ on $\tilde{X}_t$. The coefficient of $\tilde{X}_t$ would be a direct estimate of β_2, and the intercept could be used to derive an estimate of β_1. Of course, you do not know ρ and it has to be estimated, along with the other parameters of the model. The Cochrane–Orcutt iterative procedure does this by assuming that if the disturbance term follows an AR(1) process, the residuals will do so as well (approximately), and hence a regression of e_t on e_{t-1} will yield an estimate of ρ. The procedure involves the following steps:

1. Y is regressed on X with the original, untransformed data.
2. The residuals are calculated.
3. e_t is regressed on e_{t-1} to obtain an estimate of ρ.
4. $\tilde{Y}_t$ and $\tilde{X}_t$ are calculated using this estimate of ρ and the equation at the top of the box is fitted. The coefficient of $\tilde{X}_t$ provides a revised estimate of β_2 and the estimate of β_1' yields a revised estimate of β_1.
5. The residuals are recalculated and the process returns to step 3.

The process alternates between revising the estimates of β_1 and β_2, and revising the estimate of ρ, until convergence is obtained, that is, until the estimates at the end of the latest cycle are the same as the estimates at the end of the previous one, to a prespecified number of decimal places.

AR(1) regression. Compare the coefficients and standard errors of the two regressions and comment.

13.4 Autocorrelation with a lagged dependent variable

Suppose that you have a model in which the dependent variable, lagged one time period, is used as one of the explanatory variables (for example, a partial adjustment model). When this is the case, autocorrelation is likely to cause OLS to yield inconsistent estimates.

For example, suppose the model is of the form

$$Y_t = \beta_1 + \beta_2 X_t + \beta_3 Y_{t-1} + u_t. \tag{13.17}$$

If there were no autocorrelation, OLS would yield consistent estimates. Strictly speaking, the use of the lagged dependent variable will make OLS estimates subject to some element of bias in finite samples, but in practice this bias is not considered serious and is ignored. However, if the disturbance term is subject to autocorrelation, the situation is entirely different. We will investigate the case where u_t is subject to AR(1) autocorrelation

$$u_t = \rho u_{t-1} + \varepsilon_t. \tag{13.18}$$

Then the model may be rewritten

$$Y_t = \beta_1 + \beta_2 X_t + \beta_3 Y_{t-1} + \rho u_{t-1} + \varepsilon_t. \tag{13.19}$$

Lagging (13.17) one period, we see that

$$Y_{t-1} = \beta_1 + \beta_2 X_{t-1} + \beta_3 Y_{t-2} + u_{t-1}. \tag{13.20}$$

Hence in (13.19) we have a violation of the fourth Gauss–Markov condition. One of the explanatory variables, Y_{t-1}, is partly determined by u_{t-1}, which is also a component of the disturbance term. As a consequence, OLS will yield inconsistent estimates. It is not hard to obtain an analytical expression for the large-sample bias, but it is laborious and it will not be attempted here.

Detection of autocorrelation with a lagged dependent variable

As Durbin and Watson noted in their original article, the Durbin–Watson d statistic is invalid when the regression equation includes a lagged dependent variable. It tends to be biased towards 2, increasing the risk of a Type II error. In this case one may use the Durbin h statistic (Durbin, 1970), which is also computed from the residuals. It is defined as

$$h = \hat{\rho} \sqrt{\frac{n}{1 - ns^2_{b_{Y(-1)}}}}, \tag{13.21}$$

where $\hat{\rho}$ is an estimate of ρ in the AR(1) process, $s^2_{b_{Y(-1)}}$ is an estimate of the variance of the coefficient of the lagged dependent variable Y_{t-1}, and n is the number of observations in the regression. Note that n will usually be one less than the number of observations in the sample because the first observation is lost when the equation is fitted. There are various ways in which one might estimate ρ but, since this test is valid only for large samples, it does not matter which you use. The most convenient is to take advantage of the large-sample relationship between d and ρ:

$$d \rightarrow 2 - 2\rho. \tag{13.22}$$

From this one estimates ρ as $(1 - \frac{1}{2}d)$. The estimate of the variance of the coefficient of the lagged dependent variable is obtained by squaring its standard error. Thus h can be calculated from the usual regression results. In large samples,

h is distributed as $N(0, 1)$, that is, as a normal variable with mean 0 and unit variance, under the null hypothesis of no autocorrelation. The hypothesis of no autocorrelation can therefore be rejected at the 5 percent significance level if the absolute value of h is greater than 1.96, and at the 1 percent significance level if it is greater than 2.58, using two-tailed tests and a large sample.

A common problem with this test is that the h statistic cannot be computed if $ns^2_{b_{Y(-1)}}$ is greater than 1, which can happen if the sample size is not very large. An even worse problem occurs when $ns^2_{b_{Y(-1)}}$ is near to, but less than, 1. In such a situation the h statistic could be enormous, without there being any problem of autocorrelation. For this reason it is a good idea to keep an eye on the d statistic as well, despite the fact that it is biased.

Example

The partial adjustment model leads to a specification with a lagged dependent variable. That for the logarithmic demand function for housing services was used as an exercise in the previous chapter. The output is reproduced in Table 13.3. The Durbin–Watson statistic is 1.72. $(1 - \frac{1}{2}d) = 0.14$ gives us an estimate of ρ. The standard error of the lagged dependent variable is 0.0451. Thus our estimate of the variance of its coefficient is 0.0020. There are 36 observations in the sample, but the first cannot be used and n is 35. Hence the h statistic is

$$h = 0.14 \times \sqrt{\frac{35}{1 - 35 \times 0.0020}} = 0.86. \tag{13.23}$$

Table 13.3

```
Dependent Variable: LGHOUS
Method: Least Squares
Sample(adjusted): 1960 1994
Included observations: 35 after adjusting endpoints
================================================================
     Variable      CoefficientStd. Errort-Statistic  Prob.
================================================================
           C       -0.390249   0.152989   -2.550839   0.0159
       LGDPI        0.313919   0.052510    5.978243   0.0000
     LGPRHOUS      -0.067547   0.024689   -2.735882   0.0102
     LGHOUS(-1)     0.701432   0.045082   15.55895    0.0000
================================================================
R-squared            0.999773   Mean dependent var 6.017555
Adjusted R-squared   0.999751   S.D. dependent var 0.362063
S.E. of regression   0.005718   Akaike info criter-7.383148
Sum squared resid    0.001014   Schwarz criterion -7.205394
Log likelihood       133.2051   F-statistic        45427.98
Durbin-Watson stat   1.718168   Prob(F-statistic)  0.000000
```

BOX 13.2   Autocorrelation in the partial adjustment and adaptive expectations models

---

The partial adjustment model

$$Y_t^* = \beta_1 + \beta_2 X_t + u_t$$

$$Y_t - Y_{t-1} = \lambda(Y_t^* - Y_{t-1}) \quad (0 \leq \lambda \leq 1)$$

leads to the regression specification

$$Y_t = \beta_1\lambda + \beta_2\lambda X_t + (1 - \lambda)Y_{t-1} + \lambda u_t.$$

Hence the disturbance term in the fitted equation is a fixed multiple of that in the first equation and combining the first two equations to eliminate the unobservable Y_t^* will not have introduced any new complication. In particular, it will not have caused the disturbance term to be autocorrelated, if it is not autocorrelated in the first equation. By contrast, in the case of the adaptive expectations model,

$$Y_t = \beta_1 + \beta_2 X_{t+1}^e + u_t$$

$$X_{t+1}^e - X_t^e = \lambda(X_t - X_t^e)$$

the Koyck transformation would cause a problem. The fitted equation is then

$$Y_t = \beta_1\lambda + (1 - \lambda)Y_{t-1} + \beta_2\lambda X_t + u_t - (1 - \lambda)u_{t-1}$$

and the disturbance term is subject to moving average autocorrelation. We noted that we could not discriminate between the two models on the basis of the variable specification because they employ exactly the same variables. Could we instead use the properties of the disturbance term to discriminate between them? Could we regress Y_t on X_t and Y_{t-1}, test for autocorrelation, and conclude that the dynamics are attributable to a partial adjustment process if we do not find autocorrelation, and to an adaptive expectations process if we do?

Unfortunately, this does not work. If we do find autocorrelation, it could be that the true model is a partial adjustment process, and that the original disturbance term was autocorrelated. Similarly, the absence of autocorrelation does not rule out an adaptive expectations process. Suppose that the disturbance term u_t is subject to AR(1) autocorrelation:

$$u_t = \rho u_{t-1} + \varepsilon_t.$$

Then

$$u_t - (1 - \lambda)u_{t-1} = \rho u_{t-1} + \varepsilon_t - (1 - \lambda)u_{t-1} = \varepsilon_t - (1 - \lambda - \rho)u_{t-1}.$$

Now it is reasonable to suppose that both λ and ρ will lie between 0 and 1, and hence it is possible that their sum might be close to 1. If this is the case, the disturbance term in the fitted model will be approximately equal to ε_t, and the AR(1) autocorrelation will have been neutralized by the Koyck transformation.

This is below 1.96 and so, at the 5 percent significance level, we do not reject the null hypothesis of no autocorrelation (reminding ourselves of course, that this is a large-sample test and we have only 35 observations).

13.5 **The common factor test**

We now return to the ordinary AR(1) model to investigate it a little further. The nonlinear equation

$$Y_t = \beta_1(1 - \rho) + \rho Y_{t-1} + \beta_2 X_t - \beta_2 \rho X_{t-1} + \varepsilon_t, \qquad (13.24)$$

fitted on the hypothesis that the disturbance term is subject to AR(1) autocorrelation, is a restricted version of the more general ADL(1,1) model (autoregressive distributed lag, the first argument referring to the maximum lag in the Y variable and the second to the maximum lag in the X variable(s))

$$Y_t = \lambda_1 + \lambda_2 Y_{t-1} + \lambda_3 X_t + \lambda_4 X_{t-1} + \varepsilon_t, \qquad (13.25)$$

with the restriction

$$\lambda_4 = -\lambda_2 \lambda_3. \qquad (13.26)$$

The presence of this implicit restriction provides us with an opportunity to test the validity of the model specification. This will help us to discriminate between cases where the d statistic is low because the disturbance term is genuinely subject to an AR(1) process and cases where it is low for other reasons. The theory behind the test procedure will not be presented here (for a summary, see Hendry and Mizon, 1978), but you should note that the usual F test of a restriction is not appropriate because the restriction is nonlinear. Instead we calculate the statistic

$$n \log (RSS_R / RSS_U), \qquad (13.27)$$

where n is the number of observations in the regression, RSS_R and RSS_U are the residual sums of squares from the restricted model (13.24) and the unrestricted model (13.25), and the logarithm is to base e. Remember that n will usually be one less than the number of observations in the sample because the first observation is lost when (13.24) and (13.25) are fitted. Strictly speaking, this is a large sample test. If the original model has only one explanatory variable, as in this case, the test statistic has a chi-squared distribution with one degree of freedom under the null hypothesis that the restriction is valid. As we saw in the previous section, if we had started with the more general model

$$Y_t = \beta_1 + \beta_2 X_{2t} + \cdots + \beta_k X_{kt} + u_t, \tag{13.28}$$

the restricted model would have been

$$Y_t = \beta_1(1 - \rho) + \rho Y_{t-1} + \beta_2 X_{2t} - \beta_2 \rho X_{2,t-1} + \cdots + \beta_k X_{kt} - \beta_k \rho X_{k,t-1} + \varepsilon_t. \tag{13.29}$$

There are now $k - 1$ restrictions because the model imposes the restriction that the coefficient of the lagged value of each explanatory variable is equal to minus the coefficient of its current value multiplied by the coefficient of the lagged dependent variable Y_{t-1}. Under the null hypothesis that the restrictions are valid, the test statistic has a chi-squared distribution with $k - 1$ degrees of freedom.

If the null hypothesis is not rejected, we conclude that the AR(1) model is an adequate specification of the data. If it is rejected, we have to work with the unrestricted ADL(1,1) model

$$Y_t = \lambda_1 + \lambda_2 Y_{t-1} + \lambda_3 X_{2t} + \lambda_4 X_{2,t-1} + \cdots + \lambda_{2k-1} X_{kt} + \lambda_{2k} X_{k,t-1} + \varepsilon_t, \tag{13.30}$$

including the lagged value of Y and the lagged values of all the explanatory variables as regressors. The problem of multicollinearity will often be encountered when fitting the unrestricted model, especially if there are several explanatory variables. Sometimes it can be alleviated by dropping those variables that do not have significant coefficients, but precisely because multicollinearity causes t statistics to be low, there is a risk that you will end up dropping variables that do genuinely belong in the model.

Two further points. First, if the null hypothesis is not rejected, the coefficient of Y_{t-1} may be interpreted as an estimate of ρ. If it is rejected, the whole of the AR(1) story is abandoned and the coefficient of Y_{t-1} in the unrestricted version does not have any special interpretation. Second, when fitting the restricted version using the specification appropriate for AR(1) autocorrelation, the coefficients of the lagged explanatory variables are not reported. If for some reason you need them, you could calculate them easily yourself, as minus the product of the coefficient of Y_{t-1} and the coefficients of the corresponding current explanatory variables. The fact that the lagged variables, other than Y_{t-1}, do not appear explicitly in the regression output does not mean that they have not been included. They have.

Example

The output for the AR(1) regression for housing services has been shown above. The residual sum of squares was 0.001360. The unrestricted version of the model yields the result shown in Table 13.4.

Table 13.4

```
Dependent Variable: LGHOUS
Method: Least Squares
Sample(adjusted): 1960 1994
Included observations: 35 after adjusting endpoints
================================================================
      Variable    CoefficientStd. Errort-Statistic  Prob.
================================================================
           C     -0.386286   0.177312  -2.178563   0.0376
       LGDPI      0.301400   0.066582   4.526717   0.0001
     LGPRHOUS    -0.192404   0.078085  -2.464038   0.0199
    LGHOUS(-1)    0.726714   0.064719  11.22884    0.0000
     LGDPI(-1)   -0.014868   0.092493  -0.160748   0.8734
   LGPRHOUS(-1)   0.138894   0.084324   1.647143   0.1103
================================================================
R-squared           0.999797    Mean dependent var 6.017555
Adjusted R-squared  0.999762    S.D. dependent var 0.362063
S.E. of regression  0.005589    Akaike info criter-7.381273
Sum squared resid   0.000906    Schwarz criterion -7.114642
Log likelihood      135.1723    F-statistic        28532.58
Durbin-Watson stat  1.517562    Prob(F-statistic)  0.000000
```

Before we perform the common factor test, we should check that the unrestricted model is free from autocorrelation. Otherwise neither it nor the AR(1) model would be satisfactory specifications. The h statistic is given by

$$h = 0.24 \times \left(\frac{35}{1 - 35 \times 0.0042} \right) = 1.54. \qquad (13.31)$$

This is below 1.96 and so we do not reject the null hypothesis of no autocorrelation.

Next we will check whether the coefficients appear to satisfy the restrictions implicit in the AR(1) model. Minus the product of the lagged dependent variable and the income elasticity is $-0.7267 \times 0.3014 = -0.22$. The coefficient of lagged income is numerically much lower than this. Minus the product of the lagged dependent variable and the price elasticity is $-0.7267 \times -0.1924 = 0.14$, which is identical to the coefficient of lagged price, to two decimal places. Hence the restriction for the price side of the model appears to be satisfied, but that for the income side does not.

The common factor test confirms this preliminary observation. The residual sum of squares has fallen to 0.000906. The test statistic is $35 \log(0.001360/0.000906) = 14.22$. The critical value of chi-squared at the 0.1 percent level with two degrees of freedom is 13.82, so we reject the restrictions implicit in the AR(1) model and conclude that we should use the unrestricted ADL(1,1) model instead.

We note that the lagged income and price variables in the unrestricted model do not have significant coefficients, so we consider dropping them and arrive at the partial adjustment model specification already considered above. As we saw, the h statistic is 0.86, and we conclude that this is a satisfactory specification.

Exercises

13.4 A researcher has annual data on the rate of growth of aggregate consumer expenditure on financial services, f_t, the rate of growth of aggregate disposable personal income, x_t, and the rate of growth of the relative price index for consumer expenditure on financial services, p_t, for the United States for the period 1959–94 and fits the regressions in the table (standard errors in parentheses; method of estimation as indicated):

	1: OLS	2: AR(1)	3: OLS	4: OLS
x	1.20 (0.06)	1.31 (0.11)	1.37 (0.17)	0.32 (0.10)
p	−0.10 (0.03)	−0.21 (0.06)	−0.25 (0.08)	−0.11 (0.07)
$f(-1)$	—	—	0.61 (0.17)	0.75 (0.15)
$x(-1)$	—	—	−0.90 (0.35)	—
$p(-1)$	—	—	−0.11 (0.09)	—
constant	0.01 (0.05)	−0.04 (0.09)	−0.05 (0.10)	0.03 (0.08)
$\hat{\rho}$	—	0.55	—	—
R^2	0.80	0.82	0.84	0.81
RSS	40.1	35.2	32.1	37.1
d	0.74	1.78	1.75	1.26

Explain the relationship between the second and third specifications, perform a common factor test, and discuss the adequacy of each specification.

13.5 Perform a logarithmic regression of expenditure on your category of consumer expenditure on income and price using an AR(1) estimation technique. Perform a second regression with the same variables but adding the lagged variables as regressors and using OLS. With an h test, check that the second specification is not subject to autocorrelation.

Explain why the first regression is a restricted version of the second, stating the restrictions, and check whether the restrictions appear to be satisfied by the estimates of the coefficients of the second regression. Perform a common factor test. If the AR(1) model is rejected, and there are terms with insignificant coefficients in the second regression, investigate the consequences of dropping them.

13.6*

Year	Y	K	L	Year	Y	K	L
1899	100	100	100	1911	153	216	145
1900	101	107	105	1912	177	226	152
1901	112	114	110	1913	184	236	154
1902	122	122	118	1914	169	244	149
1903	124	131	123	1915	189	266	154
1904	122	138	116	1916	225	298	182
1905	143	149	125	1917	227	335	196
1906	152	163	133	1918	223	366	200
1907	151	176	138	1919	218	387	193
1908	126	185	121	1920	231	407	193
1909	155	198	140	1921	179	417	147
1910	159	208	144	1922	240	431	161

Source: Cobb and Douglas (1928)

The table gives the data used by Cobb and Douglas (1928) to fit the original Cobb–Douglas production function:

$$Y_t = \beta_1 K_t^{\beta_2} L_t^{\beta_3} v_t,$$

Y_t, K_t, and L_t, being index number series for real output, real capital input, and real labor input, respectively, for the manufacturing sector of the United States for the period 1899–1922 (1899 = 100). The model was linearized by taking logarithms of both sides and the regressions in the table were run (standard errors in parentheses; method of estimation as indicated):

	1: OLS	2: AR(1)	3: OLS
$\log K$	0.23	0.22	0.18
	(0.06)	(0.07)	(0.56)
$\log L$	0.81	0.86	1.03
	(0.15)	(0.16)	(0.15)
$\log Y(-1)$	—	—	0.40
			(0.21)
$\log K(-1)$	—	—	0.17
			(0.51)
$\log L(-1)$	—	—	−1.01
			(0.25)
constant	−0.18	−0.35	1.04
	(0.43)	(0.51)	(0.41)
$\hat{\rho}$	—	0.19	—
		(0.25)	
R^2	0.96	0.96	0.98
RSS	0.0710	0.0697	0.0259
d	1.52	1.54	1.46

Evaluate the three regression specifications.

13.6 Apparent autocorrelation

As has been seen above, a positive correlation among the residuals from a regression, and a correspondingly low Durbin–Watson statistic, may be attributable to the omission of one or more lagged variables from the model specification, rather than to an autocorrelated disturbance term. We will describe this as *apparent* autocorrelation. Although the examples above relate to the omission of lagged variables, it could arise from the omission of any important variable from the regression specification.

Apparent autocorrelation can also arise from functional misspecification. For example, we saw in Section 5.1 that, if the true model is of the form

$$Y = \beta_1 + \frac{\beta_2}{X} + u \qquad (13.32)$$

and we execute a linear regression, we obtain the fit illustrated in Figure 5.1 and summarized in Table 5.2: a negative residual in the first observation, positive residuals in the next six, and negative residuals in the last three. In other words, there appears to be very strong positive autocorrelation. However, when the regression is of the form

$$\hat{Y} = b_1 + b_2 X', \tag{13.33}$$

where X' is defined as $1/X$, not only does one obtain a much better fit but the autocorrelation disappears.

The most straightforward way of detecting autocorrelation caused by functional misspecification is to look at the residuals directly. This may give you some idea of the correct specification. The Durbin–Watson d statistic may also provide a signal, although of course a test based on it would be invalid since the disturbance term is not AR(1) and the use of an AR(1) specification would be inappropriate. In the case of the example just described, the Durbin–Watson statistic was 0.86, indicating that something was wrong with the specification.

Exercises

13.7* Using the fifty observations on two variables Y and X shown in the figure, an investigator runs the five regressions in the table (standard errors in parentheses; estimation method as indicated; all variables as logarithms in the logarithmic regressions):

	1	2	3	4	5
	Linear		Logarithmic		
	OLS	AR(1)	OLS	AR(1)	OLS
X	0.178	0.223	2.468	2.471	1.280
	(0.008)	(0.027)	(0.029)	(0.033)	(0.800)
$Y(-1)$	—	—	—	—	0.092
					(0.145)
$X(-1)$	—	—	—	—	0.966
					(0.865)
	—	0.87	—	0.08	—
		(0.06)		(0.14)	
constant	−24.4	−39.7	−11.3	−11.4	−10.3
	(2.9)	(12.1)	(0.2)	(0.2)	(1.7)
R^2	0.903	0.970	0.993	0.993	0.993
RSS	6286	1932	1.084	1.070	1.020
d	0.35	3.03	1.82	2.04	2.08

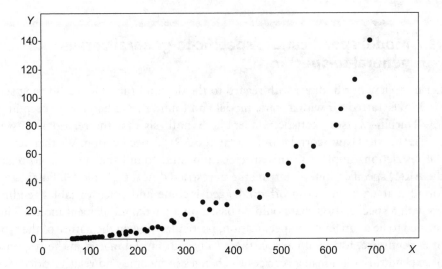

Discuss each of the five regressions, stating, with reasons, which is your preferred specification.

13.8* Using the data on food in the Demand Functions data set, the following regressions were run, each with the logarithm of food as the dependent variable: (1) an OLS regression on a time trend T defined to be 1 in 1959, 2 in 1960, etc.; (2) an AR(1) regression using the same specification; and (3) an OLS regression on T and the logarithm of food lagged one time period, with the results shown in the table (standard errors in parentheses):

	1: OLS	2: AR(1)	3: OLS
T	0.0181	0.0166	0.0024
	(0.0005)	(0.0021)	(0.0016)
LGFOOD(−1)	—	—	0.8551
			(0.0886)
Constant	5.7768	5.8163	0.8571
	(0.0106)	(0.0586)	(0.5101)
$\hat{\rho}$	—	0.8551	—
		(0.0886)	
R^2	0.9750	0.9931	0.9931
RSS	0.0327	0.0081	0.0081
d	0.2752	1.3328	1.3328
h	—	—	2.32

Discuss why each regression specification appears to be unsatisfactory. Explain why it was not possible to perform a common factor test.

13.7 Model specification: specific-to-general versus general-to-specific

Let us review our findings with regard to the demand function for housing services. We started off with a static model and found that it had an unacceptably low Durbin–Watson statistic. Under the hypothesis that the relationship was subject to AR(1) autocorrelation, we ran the AR(1) specification. We then tested the restrictions implicit in this specification, and found that we had to reject the AR(1) specification, preferring the unrestricted ADL(1,1) model. Finally, we found that we could drop off the lagged income and price variables, ending up with a specification that could be based on a partial adjustment model. This seemed to be a satisfactory specification, particularly given the nature of the type of expenditure, for we do expect there to be substantial inertia in the response of expenditure on housing services to changes in income and relative price. We conclude that the reason for the low Durbin–Watson statistic in the original static model was not AR(1) autocorrelation but the omission of an important regressor (the lagged dependent variable).

The research strategy that has implicitly been adopted can be summarized as follows:

1. On the basis of economic theory, experience, and intuition, formulate a provisional model.

2. Locate suitable data and fit the model.

3. Perform diagnostic checks.

4. If any of the checks reveal inadequacies, revise the specification of the model with the aim of eliminating them.

5. When the specification appears satisfactory, congratulate oneself on having completed the task and quit.

The danger with this strategy is that the reason that the final version of the model appears satisfactory may be that you have skilfully massaged its specification to fit your particular data set, not that it really corresponds to the true model. The econometric literature is full of two types of indirect evidence that this happens frequently, particularly with models employing time-series data, and particularly with those modeling macroeconomic relationships. It often happens that researchers investigating the same phenomenon with access to the same sources of data construct internally consistent but mutually incompatible models, and it often happens that models that survive sample period diagnostic checks exhibit miserable predictive performance. The literature on the modeling of aggregate investment behavior is especially notorious in both respects. Further evidence, if any were needed, has been provided by experiments showing that it is not hard to set up nonsense models that survive the conventional checks (Peach and Webb, 1983). As a consequence, there is growing recognition of the fact that the tests eliminate only those models with the grossest misspecifications, and the survival of a model is no guarantee of its validity.

This is true even of the tests of predictive performance described in the previous chapter, where the models are subjected to an evaluation of their ability to fit fresh data. There are two problems with these tests. First, their power may be rather low. It is quite possible that a misspecified model will fit the prediction period observations well enough for the null hypothesis of model stability not to be rejected, especially if the prediction period is short. Lengthening the prediction period by shortening the sample period might help, but again there is a problem, particularly if the sample is not large. By shortening the sample period, you will increase the population variances of the estimates of the coefficients, so it will be more difficult to determine whether the prediction period relationship is significantly different from the sample period relationship.

The other problem with tests of predictive stability is the question of what the investigator does if the test is failed. Understandably, it is unusual for an investigator to quit at that point, acknowledging defeat. The natural course of action is to continue tinkering with the model until this test too is passed, but of course the test then has no more integrity than the sample period diagnostic checks.

This unsatisfactory state of affairs has generated interest in two interrelated topics: the possibility of eliminating some of the competing models by confronting them with each other, and the possibility of establishing a more systematic research strategy that might eliminate bad model building in the first place.

Comparison of alternative models

The comparison of alternative models can involve much technical complexity and the present discussion will be limited to a very brief and partial outline of some of the issues involved. We will begin by making a distinction between nested and non-nested models. A model is said to be nested inside another if it can be obtained from it by imposing a number of restrictions. Two models are said to be non-nested if neither can be represented as a restricted version of the other. The restrictions may relate to any aspect of the specification of the model, but the present discussion will be limited to restrictions on the parameters of the explanatory variables in a single equation model. It will be illustrated with reference to the demand function for housing services, with the logarithm of expenditure written Y and the logarithms of the income and relative price variables written X_2 and X_3.

Three alternative dynamic specifications have been considered: the ADL(1,1) model including current and lagged values of all the variables and no parameter restrictions, which will be denoted model A; the model that hypothesized that the disturbance term was subject to an AR(1) process (model B); and the model with only one lagged variable, the lagged dependent variable (model C). For good measure we will add the original static model (model D).

(A) $Y_t = \lambda_1 + \lambda_2 Y_{t-1} + \lambda_3 X_{2t} + \lambda_4 X_{2,t-1} + \lambda_5 X_{3t} + \lambda_6 X_{3,t-1} + \varepsilon_t.$ (13.34)

(B) $Y_t = \lambda_1(1 - \lambda_2) + \lambda_2 Y_{t-1} + \lambda_3 X_{2t} - \lambda_2\lambda_3 X_{2,t-1} + \lambda_5 X_{3t} - \lambda_2\lambda_5 X_{3,t-1} + \varepsilon_t.$

(13.35)

(C) $Y_t = \lambda_1 + \lambda_2 Y_{t-1} + \lambda_3 X_{2t} + \lambda_5 X_{3t} + \varepsilon_t.$ (13.36)

(D) $Y_t = \lambda_1 + \lambda_3 X_{2t} + \lambda_5 X_{3t} + \varepsilon_t.$ (13.37)

The ADL(1,1) model is the most general model and the others are nested within it. For model B to be a legitimate simplification, the common factor test should not lead to a rejection of the restrictions. For model C to be a legitimate simplification, $H_0: \lambda_4 = \lambda_6 = 0$ should not be rejected. For model D to be a legitimate simplification, $H_0: \lambda_2 = \lambda_4 = \lambda_6 = 0$ should not be rejected. The nesting structure is represented by Figure 13.5.

In the case of the demand function for housing, if we compare model B with model A, we find that the common factor restrictions implicit in model B are rejected and so it is struck off our list of acceptable specifications. If we compare model C with model A, we find that it is a valid alternative because the estimated coefficients of the lagged income and price variables are not significantly different from 0, or so we asserted rather loosely at the end of Section 13.5. Actually, rather than performing t tests on their individual coefficients, we should be performing an F test on their joint explanatory power, and this we will hasten to do. The residual sums of squares were 0.000906 for model A and 0.001014 for model C. The relevant F statistic, distributed with 2 and 29 degrees of freedom, is therefore 1.73. This is not significant even at the 5 percent level, so model C does indeed survive. Finally, model D must be rejected because the restriction that the coefficient of Y_{t-1} is 0 is rejected by a simple t test. (In the whole of this discussion, we have assumed that the test procedures are not substantially

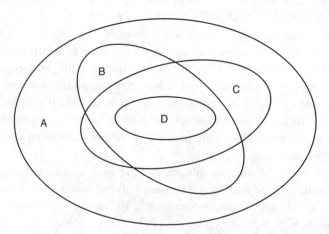

Figure 13.5 Nesting structure for models A, B, C, and D

affected by the use of a lagged dependent variable as an explanatory variable. This is strictly true only if the sample is large.)

The example illustrates the potential both for success and for failure within a nested structure: success in that two of the four models are eliminated and failure in that some indeterminacy remains. Is there any reason for preferring A to C or vice versa? Some would argue that C should be preferred because it is more parsimonious in terms of parameters, requiring only four instead of six. It also has the advantage of lending itself to the intuitively appealing interpretation involving short-run and long-run dynamics discussed in the previous chapter. However, the efficiency/potential bias trade-off between including and excluding variables with insignificant coefficients discussed in Chapter 7 makes the answer unclear.

What should you do if the rival models are not nested? One possible procedure is to create a union model embracing the two models as restricted versions and to see if any progress can be made by testing each rival against the union. For example, suppose that the rival models are

(E) $Y = \lambda_1 + \lambda_2 X_2 + \lambda_3 X_3 + \varepsilon_t.$ (13.38)

(F) $Y = \lambda_1 + \lambda_2 X_2 + \lambda_4 X_4 + \varepsilon_t.$ (13.39)

Then the union model would be

(G) $Y = \lambda_1 + \lambda_2 X_2 + \lambda_3 X_3 + \lambda_4 X_4 + \varepsilon_t.$ (13.40)

We would then fit model G, with the following possible outcomes: the estimate of λ_3 is significant, but that of λ_4 is not, so we would choose model E; the estimate of λ_3 is not significant, but that of λ_4 is significant, so we would choose model F; the estimates of both λ_3 and λ_4 are significant (a surprise outcome), in which case we would choose model G; neither estimate is significant, in which case we could test G against the simple model

(H) $Y = \lambda_1 + \lambda_2 X_2 + \varepsilon_t,$ (13.41)

and we might prefer the latter if an F test does not lead to the rejection of the null hypothesis $H_0: \lambda_3 = \lambda_4 = 0$. Otherwise we would be unable to discriminate between the three models.

There are various potential problems with this approach. First, the tests use model G as the basis for the null hypotheses, and it may not be intuitively appealing. If models E and F are constructed on different principles, their union may be so implausible that it could be eliminated on the basis of economic theory. The framework for the tests is then undermined. Second, the last possibility, indeterminacy, is likely to be the outcome if X_3 and X_4 are highly correlated. For a more extended discussion of the issues, and further references, see Kmenta (1986: 595–8).

The general-to-specific approach to model specification

We have seen that, if we start with a simple model and elaborate it in response to diagnostic checks, there is a risk that we will end up with a false model that satisfies us because, by successive adjustments, we have made it appear to fit the sample period data, 'appear to fit' because the diagnostic tests are likely to be invalid if the model specification is incorrect. Would it not be better, as some writers urge, to adopt the opposite approach. Instead of attempting to develop a specific initial model into a more general one, should we not instead start with a fully general model and reduce it to a more focused one by successively imposing restrictions (after testing their validity)?

Of course the general-to-specific approach is preferable, at least in principle. The problem is that, in its pure form, it is often impracticable. If the sample size is limited, and the initial specification contains a large number of potential explanatory variables, multicollinearity may cause most or even all of them to have insignificant coefficients. This is especially likely to be a problem in time-series models. In an extreme case, the number of variables may exceed the number of observations, and the model could not be fitted at all. Where the model may be fitted, the lack of significance of many of the coefficients may appear to give the investigator considerable freedom to choose which variables to drop. However, the final version of the model may be highly sensitive to this initial arbitrary decision. A variable that has an insignificant coefficient initially and is dropped might have had a significant coefficient in a cut-down version of the model, had it been retained. The conscientious application of the general-to-specific principle, if applied systematically, might require the exploration of an unmanageable number of possible model-reduction paths. Even if the number were small enough to be explored, the investigator may well be left with a large number of rival models, none of which is dominated by the others.

Therefore, some degree of compromise is normally essential, and of course there are no rules for this, any more than there are for the initial conception of a model in the first place. A weaker but more operational version of the approach is to guard against formulating an initial specification that imposes restrictions that a priori have some chance of being rejected. However, it is probably fair to say that the ability to do this is one measure of the experience of an investigator, in which case the approach amounts to little more than an exhortation to be experienced. For a nontechnical discussion of the approach, replete with entertainingly caustic remarks about the shortcomings of specific-to-general model-building and an illustrative example by a leading advocate of the general-to-specific approach, see Hendry (1979).

Exercises

13.9 A researcher is considering the following alternative regression models:

$$Y_t = \beta_1 + \beta_2 Y_{t-1} + \beta_3 X_t + \beta_4 X_{t-1} + u_t \tag{1}$$

$$\Delta Y_t = \gamma_1 + \gamma_2 \Delta X_t + v_t \tag{2}$$

$$Y_t = \delta_1 + \delta_2 X_t + w_t, \tag{3}$$

where $\Delta Y_t = Y_t - Y_{t-1}$, $\Delta X_t = X_t - X_{t-1}$, and u_t, v_t, and w_t are disturbance terms:

(a) Show that models (2) and (3) are restricted versions of model (1), stating the restrictions.

(b) Explain the implications for the disturbance terms in (1) and (2) if (3) is the correct specification and w_t satisfies the Gauss–Markov conditions. What problems, if any, would be encountered if ordinary least squares were used to fit (1) and (2)?

13.10 Explain how your answer to Exercise 13.9 illustrates some of the methodological issues discussed in this section.

Appendix 13.1

Demonstration that the Durbin–Watson Statistic Approximates $2 - 2\rho$ in Large Samples

$$d = \frac{\sum\limits_{t=2}^{T} (e_t - e_{t-1})^2}{\sum\limits_{t=1}^{T} e_t^2} = \frac{\sum\limits_{t=2}^{T} (e_t^2 - 2e_t e_{t-1} + e_{t-1}^2)}{\sum\limits_{t=1}^{T} e_t^2}$$

$$= \frac{\sum\limits_{t=2}^{T} e_t^2}{\sum\limits_{t=1}^{T} e_t^2} + \frac{\sum\limits_{t=2}^{T} e_{t-1}^2}{\sum\limits_{t=1}^{T} e_t^2} - 2\frac{\sum\limits_{t=2}^{T} e_t e_{t-1}}{\sum\limits_{t=1}^{T} e_t^2} \rightarrow 2 - 2\frac{\sum\limits_{t=2}^{T} e_t e_{t-1}}{\sum\limits_{t=1}^{T} e_t^2}$$

as the sample size becomes large because both $\sum\limits_{t=2}^{T} e_t^2 / \sum\limits_{t=1}^{T} e_t^2$ and $\sum\limits_{t=2}^{T} e_{t-1}^2 / \sum\limits_{t=1}^{T} e_t^2$ tend to 1. Since $\sum\limits_{t=2}^{T} e_t e_{t-1} / \sum\limits_{t=1}^{T} e_t^2$ is an estimator ρ, d tends to $2 - 2\rho$.

14 Introduction to nonstationary time series

The purpose of this final chapter is to provide a brief overview of the problems associated with the application of regression analysis to nonstationary time series. The chapter begins with an explanation of the concepts of stationarity and nonstationarity and a discussion of the consequences of nonstationarity for regression analysis. It continues with a description of methods of discriminating between stationary and nonstationary time series, and concludes with an outline of appropriate regression procedures. It should be stressed that the intention is to present these topics at a level appropriate to an introductory econometrics course and to demonstrate that more advanced study is required by those planning to work with time-series data.

14.1 Stationarity and nonstationarity

Univariate time series

Much recent work on forecasting has focused on the fitting of univariate (single-variable) processes of the type

$$X_t = \beta_1 + \beta_2 X_{t-1} + \cdots + \beta_{p+1} X_{t-p} + \varepsilon_t + \alpha_2 \varepsilon_{t-1} + \cdots + \alpha_{q+1} \varepsilon_{t-q}, \quad (14.1)$$

where the variable is written as a linear function of previous values of itself and the error term. In this case the model is said to be an ARMA(p, q) time series because it is autoregressive of order p and the error term follows a moving average process of order q. From the point of view of a conventional econometrician, a time-series model of this type appears primitive because it does not include any explanatory variables, other than lagged values of X itself. On the other hand, precisely because it is so simple, it lends itself well to the modeling of the dynamics of the process, and the time-series approach became established when it was shown that forecasts made with it were generally superior to those based on conventional econometric models (Box and Jenkins, 1970). We are not concerned with forecasting here, but time-series analysis is useful for understanding the limitations of the classical regression model.

Stationary time series

We will begin by defining stationarity and nonstationarity. A time series X_t is said to be weakly stationary (the only type of stationarity to be considered here) if its expected value and population variance are independent of time and if the population covariance between its values at time t and $t + s$ depends on s but not on time. An example of a stationary time series is an AR(1) process

$$X_t = \beta_2 X_{t-1} + \varepsilon_t \tag{14.2}$$

with $-1 < \beta_2 < 1$, where ε_t is white noise (an innovation with mean 0 and constant variance, not subject to autocorrelation). The stationarity of the series can easily be demonstrated. If equation (14.2) is valid for time period t, it is also valid for time period $t - 1$:

$$X_{t-1} = \beta_2 X_{t-2} + \varepsilon_{t-1}. \tag{14.3}$$

Substituting for X_{t-1} in equation (14.2), one has

$$X_t = \beta_2^2 X_{t-2} + \beta_2 \varepsilon_{t-1} + \varepsilon_t. \tag{14.4}$$

Continuing this process of lagging and substituting, one has

$$X_t = \beta_2^t X_0 + \beta_2^{t-1} \varepsilon_1 + \cdots + \beta_2 \varepsilon_{t-1} + \varepsilon_t. \tag{14.5}$$

The expected value of X_t is then given by

$$E(X_t) = \beta_2^t X_0 + \beta_2^{t-1} E(\varepsilon_1) + \cdots + \beta_2 E(\varepsilon_{t-1}) + E(\varepsilon_t). \tag{14.6}$$

For t large enough, $\beta_2^t X_0$ tends to 0. Each of the expectations is 0, so the expected value of X_t is 0 and thus independent of t. (Strictly speaking, the term $\beta_2^t X_0$ causes the series to be only asymptotically stationary because it is a function of t. See Exercise 14.2 for a variation that is stationary for finite samples.)

The population variance of X_t is given by the population variance of $\beta_2^{t-1} \varepsilon_1 + \cdots + \beta_2 \varepsilon_{t-1} + \varepsilon_t$ since it is unaffected by the additive constant $\beta_2^t X_0$ (Variance Rule 4). Since ε_t is not autocorrelated, the population covariance between ε_t and $\varepsilon_s (t \neq s)$ is 0 and the population variance of X_t is given by

$$\sigma_{X_t}^2 = \beta_2^{2t-2} \sigma_\varepsilon^2 + \cdots + \beta_2^2 \sigma_\varepsilon^2 + \sigma_\varepsilon^2$$

$$= \frac{1 - \beta_2^{2t}}{1 - \beta_2^2} \sigma_\varepsilon^2. \tag{14.7}$$

Since the term β_2^{2t} tends to 0 as t becomes large, the variance is asymptotically independent of t, and so the second condition for stationarity is asymptotically satisfied. (Again, see Exercise 14.2 for a variation that is stationary in finite samples.)

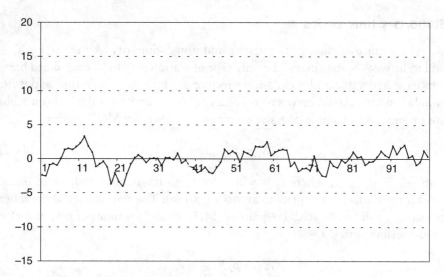

Figure 14.1 A stationary process

Similarly it can be shown that the population covariance of X_t and X_s, $t > s$, is equal to $\beta_2^{t-s}\sigma_\varepsilon^2/(1-\beta_2^2)$. This depends on the difference between t and s but is independent of t itself. Figure 14.1 provides an example of this type of stationary process with $\beta_2 = 0.7$.

A slightly more general version of the autoregressive process is

$$X_t = \beta_1 + \beta_2 X_{t-1} + \varepsilon_t, \tag{14.8}$$

where β_1 is a constant. By lagging and substituting as before, one obtains

$$X_t = \beta_2^t X_0 + (\beta_2^{t-1} + \cdots + \beta_2^2 + \beta_2)\beta_1 + \beta_2^{t-1}\varepsilon_1 + \cdots + \beta_2\varepsilon_{t-1} + \varepsilon_t. \tag{14.9}$$

Provided that β_2 is less than 1, the series remains (asymptotically) stationary, with expected value $\beta_1/(1 - \beta_2)$. The population variance of X_t and the population covariance of X_t and X_s are unaffected by the inclusion of β_1.

Nonstationary time series

In the previous examples, the condition $-1 < \beta_2 < 1$ was crucial for stationarity. If β_2 is equal to 1, the original series becomes

$$X_t = X_{t-1} + \varepsilon_t. \tag{14.10}$$

This is an example of a nonstationary process known as a random walk. If it starts at X_0 at time 0, its value at time t is given by

$$X_t = X_0 + \varepsilon_1 + \cdots + \varepsilon_t. \tag{14.11}$$

The key difference between this process and the corresponding AR(1) process (14.5) is that the contribution of each innovation, or shock, as it is often described in this context, is permanently built into the time series. Because the series incorporates the sum of the shocks, it is said to be integrated. By contrast, when $\beta_2 < 1$, as in (14.5), the contribution of each shock to the series is exponentially attenuated and eventually becomes negligible.

In the case of a random walk, the expected value and population variance of X_t do not have unconditional meanings. If the expectations are taken at time 0, the expected value at any future time t is independent of t (it is always equal to X_0); but its variance is given by

$$\sigma_{X_t}^2 = \sigma_\varepsilon^2 + \cdots + \sigma_\varepsilon^2$$
$$= t\sigma_\varepsilon^2 \tag{14.12}$$

and so increases with time. Figure 14.2 provides an example of a random walk.

In the more general version of the autoregressive process with the constant β_1, the process becomes what is known as a random walk with drift, if β_2 equals 1:

$$X_t = \beta_1 + X_{t-1} + \varepsilon_t. \tag{14.13}$$

If the series starts at X_0 at time 0, X_t is given by

$$X_t = X_0 + \beta_1 t + \varepsilon_1 + \cdots + \varepsilon_t. \tag{14.14}$$

Now the expectation of X_t at time 0, $(X_0 + \beta_1 t)$, is also a function of t. Figure 14.3 provides an example of a random walk with drift.

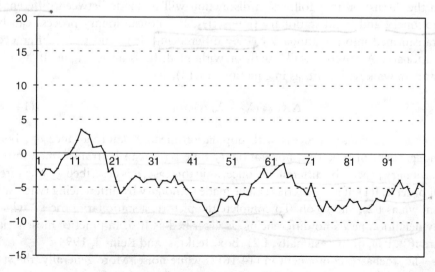

Figure 14.2 A random walk

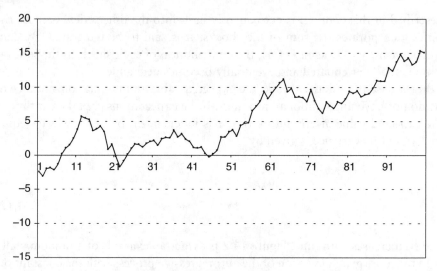

Figure 14.3 A random walk with drift

Random walks are not the only type of nonstationary process. Another common example of a nonstationary time series is one possessing a time trend:

$$X_t = \beta_1 + \beta_2 t + \varepsilon_t. \tag{14.15}$$

Its expected value at time t, $(\beta_1 + \beta_2 t)$, is not independent of t and its population variance is not defined.

Difference-stationarity and trend-stationarity

In the discussion that follows, a distinction will be made between difference-stationary and trend-stationary time series. If a nonstationary process can be transformed into a stationary one by differencing, it is said to be difference-stationary. A random walk, with or without drift, is an example. If X_t is a random walk with drift, as in equation (14.13),

$$\Delta X_t = (X_t - X_{t-1}) = \beta_1 + \varepsilon_t. \tag{14.16}$$

This is a stationary process with population mean β_1 and variance σ_ε^2, both independent of time. If a nonstationary time series can be transformed into a stationary process by differencing once, as in this case, it is described as integrated of order 1, I(1). If a time series can be made stationary by differencing twice, it is known as I(2), and so on. To complete the picture, a stationary process, which by definition needs no differencing, is described as I(0). In practice most series are I(0), I(1), or, occasionally, I(2) (Box, Jenkins, and Reinsel, 1994).

The stochastic component in (14.16) is white noise. More generally, the stationary process reached after differencing may be ARMA(p, q), in which case the original series is characterized as ARIMA(p, d, q), where d is the number of times it has to be differenced to render it stationary.

A nonstationary time series is described as being trend-stationary if it can be transformed into a stationary process by extracting a time trend. For example, the very simple model given by equation (14.15) can be detrended by fitting the equation

$$\hat{X}_t = b_1 + b_2 t \qquad (14.17)$$

and defining a new variable

$$\tilde{X}_t = X_t - \hat{X}_t = X_t - b_1 - b_2 t. \qquad (14.18)$$

The new, detrended, variable is of course just the residuals from the regression of X on t.

The distinction between difference-stationarity and trend-stationarity is important for the analysis of time series. At one time it was conventional to assume that time series could be decomposed into trend and cyclical components, the former being determined by real factors, such as the growth of GDP, and the latter being determined by transitory factors, such as monetary policy. Typically the cyclical component was analyzed using detrended versions of the variables in the model. However, as Nelson and Plosser (1982) point out, this approach is inappropriate if the process is difference-stationary, for although detrending may remove any drift, it does not affect the increasing variance of the series, and so the detrended component remains nonstationary. Further, because it ignores the contribution of real shocks to economic fluctuations, the approach causes the role of transitory factors in the cycle to be overestimated.

Exercises

14.1* Demonstrate that the MA(1) process

$$X_t = \varepsilon_t + \alpha_2 \varepsilon_{t-1}$$

is stationary. Does the result generalize to higher-order MA processes?

14.2* Demonstrate that the AR(1) process (14.2), with $\beta_2 < 1$, is stationary for finite samples if X_0 is generated as a random variable with appropriate mean and variance.

14.2 **Consequences of nonstationarity**

The consistency of least squares estimators of the regression coefficients in the classical linear regression model is assured if the sample variances and covariances of the explanatory variables tend to their population counterparts in the limit. This condition is automatically satisfied in regression models using cross-section data, and will in general be satisfied in models using time-series data if the time-series are stationary. However, if the time series are nonstationary, with the exception of a special case to be discussed in the next section, least squares estimators will be inconsistent and diagnostic statistics, such as t and F statistics, will not have their standard limiting distributions. As a consequence, with nonstationary time series, the regression coefficient of an explanatory variable may apparently be significantly different from 0 when in fact it is not a determinant of the dependent variable.

In the case of a model where the time series are nonstationary because they are subject to deterministic time trends, the risk of obtaining spurious results is evident. Suppose that a variable Y_t is regressed on a variable X_t, both of them possessing time trends but not being directly related. If the time trends give rise to a high sample correlation between the two variables, R^2 will be high because it is equal to the square of the correlation. Hence the F statistic and the t statistic for the coefficient of X_t will also be high, despite the fact that X_t is not a determinant of Y_t. A simple solution is to detrend the variables before performing the regression or, equivalently in view of the Frisch–Waugh theorem, to include a time trend in the regression model.

As Granger and Newbold (1974) demonstrated with a celebrated Monte Carlo experiment, spurious regressions can also arise in regressions using integrated time series and even regressions using stationary time series if evidence of autocorrelation in the disturbance term is ignored. They fitted the model

$$Y_t = \beta_1 + \beta_2 X_t + u_t, \tag{14.19}$$

where Y_t and X_t were independently-generated random walks. Obviously, a regression of one random walk on another ought not to yield significant results except as a matter of Type I error. Granger and Newbold replicated the regression 100 times with fresh pairs of random walks and so, using a 5 percent significance test, one would anticipate that the slope coefficient would appear to be significantly different from 0 about 5 times as a matter of Type I error. However they found that the slope coefficient had an apparently significant t statistic on 77 occasions. Using a more cautious 1 percent test made very little difference. The null hypothesis of no relationship was rejected on 70 occasions.

The reason for this finding was not the nonstationarity of the time series, for similar results are obtained if one uses highly autocorrelated stationary series (see Exercise 14.4), but the suppression of evidence of autocorrelation in the disturbance term provided by low values of the Durbin–Watson statistic. To see why autocorrelation should be anticipated in spurious regressions, suppose that Y_t and X_t are generated as

$$Y_t = \alpha_2 Y_{t-1} + \zeta_t \tag{14.20}$$

$$X_t = \gamma_2 X_{t-1} + v_t, \tag{14.21}$$

where ζ_t and v_t are unrelated white noise processes. If (14.19) is fitted, the model becomes

$$Y_t = u_t \tag{14.22}$$

under the null hypothesis $\beta_1 = \beta_2 = 0$. This means that, under the null hypothesis, u_t is a random walk if $\alpha_2 = 1$, as in the Granger–Newbold experiment, and an AR(1) process if $\alpha_2 < 1$. Either way, a low Durbin–Watson statistic will reveal that u_t is not white noise and consequently that the apparently significant results are meaningless. If the model is fitted using the AR(1) specification

$$Y_t = \beta_1(1 - \rho) + \rho Y_{t-1} + \beta_2 X_t - \beta_2 \rho X_{t-1} + \varepsilon_t \tag{14.23}$$

under the assumption $u_t = \rho u_{t-1} + \varepsilon_t$, in large samples the estimator of ρ tends to α_2 and the estimator of β_2 tends to 0. This is so even if the series are integrated and α_2 is equal to 1, in which case the model becomes asymptotically equivalent to

$$\Delta Y_t = \beta_2 \Delta X_t + \varepsilon_t \tag{14.24}$$

(Davidson and MacKinnon, 1993).

The point of the Monte Carlo experiment was to demonstrate the danger of accepting a misspecified model if evidence of autocorrelation is ignored, which Granger and Newbold asserted was common at the time, unbelievable though that may seem now. They used random walks in the experiment, not because there is anything special about nonstationary processes in this context, but because random walks demonstrated the problem most dramatically, the number of apparent Type I errors being an increasing function of α_2.

Despite the fact that a low Durbin–Watson statistic reveals that a regression using (14.19) is clearly misspecified, a number of authors have gone on to investigate the asymptotic properties of least squares estimators of the coefficients. If $\alpha_2 < 1$, least squares estimators are consistent and the coefficients tend to 0 as the sample size becomes large. However, if $\alpha_2 = 1$ and the series are random walks, least squares estimators are inconsistent. Remember that the two requirements of a consistent estimator are that its distribution should collapse to a spike as the sample size becomes large, and that this spike should be located at the true value. In all previous encounters with inconsistent estimators in this text, the reason for inconsistency has been the presence of large-sample bias, and thus a failure of the second condition. In the present case, it is the first condition, rather than the second, that is violated. Phillips (1986) shows that the distribution of β_2 converges to a nondegenerate limiting distribution, not a spike, with the probability of an apparent Type I error increasing with the sample size. He also showed that these findings extend to stationary series with ρ close to 1 (Phillips, 1987). These findings contributed to the already rapidly growing interest in the identification of nonstationary processes and the development of appropriate regression models.

Exercises

14.3 (A repeat of Granger and Newbold's experiment, with 100 observations instead of 50). Construct two independent 100–observation random walks and regress one on the other. Does the t statistic on the slope coefficient appear to be significant using a 5 percent test? Run the regression a second time using an AR(1) specification, and compare the results. Repeat the experiment several times (at least 10 times; 20 would be better) and note the frequency of Type I errors in the OLS and AR(1) specifications.

14.4 Construct two independent 100–observation AR(1) processes with $\rho = 0.95$, and regress one on the other. Does the t statistic on the slope coefficient appear to be significant using a 5 percent test? Run the regression a second time using an AR(1) specification, and compare the results. Repeat the experiment several times (at least 10 times; 20 would be better) and note the frequency of Type I errors in the OLS and AR(1) specifications. Compare the results with those in Exercise 14.3.

14.5 Repeat Exercise 14.3 with a series of 10,000 observations, and compare the results with those of Exercise 14.3.

14.6 Repeat Exercise 14.4 with a series of 10,000 observations, and compare the results with those of Exercise 14.4.

14.7* Suppose that a series is generated as

$$X_t = \beta_2 X_{t-1} + \varepsilon_t$$

with β_2 equal to $1 - \delta$, where δ is small. Demonstrate that if δ is small enough that terms involving δ^2 may be neglected, the variance may be approximated as

$$\sigma^2_{X_t} = (1 - [2t - 2]\delta) + \cdots + (1 - 2\delta) + 1)\sigma^2_\varepsilon$$
$$= (1 - [t - 1]\delta)t\sigma^2_\varepsilon$$

and draw your conclusions concerning the properties of the time series.

14.3 Detection of nonstationarity

Unfortunately for econometricians working with time-series data, many economic time series appear to be of the I(1) type. It is therefore important to assess whether a time series is nonstationary before attempting to use it in a regression model. Often it is evident from the inspection of a plot that a time series is subject to a secular upward or downward trend and is therefore nonstationary. In the case of a series such as the logarithm of *DPI*, shown in Figure 14.4, the only questions are whether the series is difference-stationary or trend-stationary, and if difference-stationary, the order of integration. Similarly, with strong upward

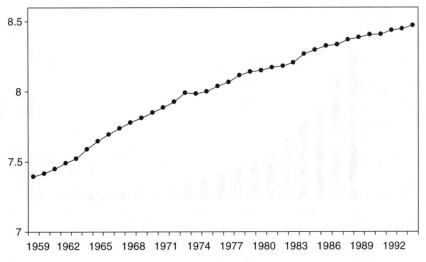

Figure 14.4 Logarithm of *DPI*

trends attributable to rising per capita income and a growing population, all of the time series of the categories of consumer expenditure in the Demand Functions data set are clearly nonstationary. Among the price series, there are some where there is a clear victor in the race between rising labor costs and falling production costs due to increasing efficiency, and these also possess time trends that indicate nonstationarity.

Correlograms

The correlogram is a tool used by time-series analysts in the identification of the orders p, d, and q of a time series assumed to be ARIMA(p, d, q). The autocorrelation function of a series X_t gives the theoretical correlation between the value of a series at time t and its value at time $t + k$, for values of k from 1 to (typically) about 20, being defined as the series

$$\rho_k = \frac{E(X_t - \mu_X)(X_{t+k} - \mu_X)}{\sqrt{E(X_t - \mu_X)^2 E(X_{t+k} - \mu_X)^2}} \quad \text{for } k = 1, \dots \qquad (14.25)$$

and the correlogram is its graphical representation. For example, the autocorrelation function for an AR(1) process $x_t = \beta_2 x_{t-1} + \varepsilon_t$ is

$$\rho_k = \beta_2^k, \qquad (14.26)$$

the coefficients decreasing exponentially with the lag provided that $\beta_2 < 1$ and the process is stationary. The corresponding correlogram is shown in Figure 14.5 for β_2 equal to 0.8.

Higher-order stationary AR(p) processes may exhibit a more complex mixture of damped sine waves and damped exponentials, but they retain the feature that the weights eventually decline to 0.

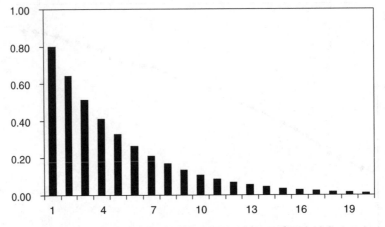

Figure 14.5 Correlogram of an AR(1) process with $\beta_2 = 0.8$

By contrast an MA(q) process has nonzero weights for only the first q lags and zero weights thereafter. In particular, the first autocorrelation coefficient for the MA(1) process

$$X_t = \varepsilon_1 + \alpha_2 \varepsilon_{t-1} \tag{14.27}$$

is given by

$$\rho_1 = \frac{\alpha_2}{1 + \alpha_2^2} \tag{14.28}$$

and all subsequent autocorrelation coefficients are 0.

In the case of nonstationary processes, the theoretical autocorrelation coefficients are not defined but one may be able to obtain an expression for $E(r_k)$, the expected value of the sample autocorrelation coefficients, and for long

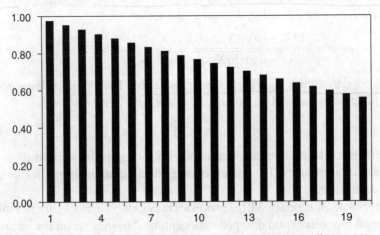

Figure 14.6 Correlogram (expected values of r_k) for a random walk, $n = 200$

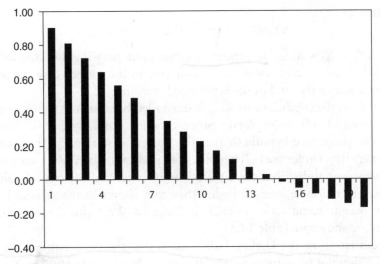

Figure 14.7 Correlogram (expected values of r_k) of a random walk, $n = 50$

time-series, these coefficients decline slowly. For example, in the case of a random walk, the correlogram for a series with 200 observations is as shown in Figure 14.6 (Wichern, 1973).

Time-series analysts exploit this fact in a two-stage procedure for identifying the orders of a series believed to be of the ARIMA(p, d, q) type. In the first stage, if the correlogram exhibits slowly declining coefficients, the series is differenced d times until the series exhibits a stationary pattern. Usually one differencing is sufficient, and at most two. The second stage is to inspect the correlogram of the differenced series and its partial correlogram, a related tool, to determine the orders p and q, a task whose complexity is limited by the fact that in practice most series are adequately represented by a process with the sum of p and q no greater than 2 (Box, Jenkins, and Reisel, 1994).

There are, however, two problems with using correlograms to identify nonstationarity. One is that a correlogram such as that in Figure 14.6 could result from a stationary AR(1) process with a high value of β_2. The other is that the coefficients of a nonstationary process may decline quite rapidly if the series is not long. This is illustrated in Figure 14.7, which shows the expected values of r_k for a random walk when the series has only 50 observations.

Unit root tests

A more formal method of detecting nonstationarity is often described as testing for unit roots, for reasons that need not concern us here. The standard test, pioneered by Dickey and Fuller (1979), is based on the model

$$X_t = \beta_1 + \beta_2 X_{t-1} + \gamma t + \varepsilon_t. \tag{14.29}$$

Rewritten as

$$\Delta X_t = \beta_1 + (\beta_2 - 1)X_{t-1} + \gamma t + \varepsilon_t, \qquad (14.30)$$

where $\Delta X_t = X_t - X_{t-1}$, the series will be nonstationary if either the coefficient of X_{t-1} is 0 or the coefficient of t is nonzero. In the former case the series is difference-stationary, and in the latter trend-stationary.

The test on the coefficient of X_{t-1} is one-tailed because a value of β_2 greater than 1 would imply an explosive process, which normally can be ruled out. Under the alternative hypothesis that the process is stationary, the coefficient will be negative. Under the null hypothesis of nonstationarity, the t statistic does not have its usual distribution, even asymptotically, and the critical value, for any given significance level, is higher than that shown in the standard tables. For this reason, some authors denote it τ instead of t. Critical values for large samples are shown in Table 14.1.

A requirement of the Dickey–Fuller test is that the disturbance term in the model should not be autocorrelated. If it is, further lagged values of X_t should be included on the right side of equation (14.29). For example, if the disturbance term in (14.29) followed an AR(1) process, an appropriate specification would be

$$X_t = \beta_1 + \beta_2 X_{t-1} + \beta_3 X_{t-2} + \gamma t + \varepsilon_t, \qquad (14.31)$$

where ε_t is white noise (see Exercise 14.8). It can be shown that in this case the process will be nonstationary if $\beta_2 + \beta_3 = 1$ or if γ is nonzero. Again, to test the first hypothesis, it is convenient to rewrite the equation as

$$\Delta X_t = \beta_1 + (\beta_2 + \beta_3 - 1)X_{t-1} - \beta_3 \Delta X_{t-1} + \gamma t + \varepsilon_t \qquad (14.32)$$

and test the null hypothesis that the coefficient of X_{t-1} is equal to 0. When one or more lagged differences in X_t are included on the right side of the model, the test is known as the augmented Dickey–Fuller (ADF) test.

It should be noted that in practice the test tends to have low power and a failure to reject the null hypothesis does not automatically mean that the series is nonstationary. In particular, as with the approach using correlograms, it is often impossible to distinguish between a nonstationary process and a highly autocorrelated stationary AR process.

Table 14.1 Asympotic critical values of the ADF statistic

	5 per cent	1 per cent
No constant, no trend	−1.94	−2.56
Constant, no trend	−2.86	−3.43
Constant and trend	−3.41	−3.96

Source: Davidson and Mackinnon (1993)

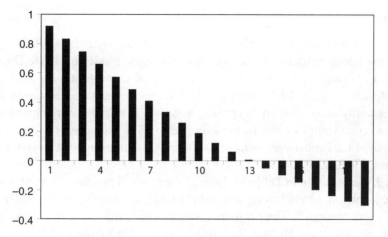

Figure 14.8 Sample correlogram for the logarithm of *DPI*

Table 14.2

```
        Augmented Dickey-Fuller Unit Root Test on LGDPI
===============================================================
ADF Test Statistic -1.108351      1%   Critical Value*-4.2505
                                  5%   Critical Value -3.5468
                                  10% Critical Value  -3.2056
===============================================================
```
*MacKinnon critical values for rejection of hypothesis of a
unit root.

```
Augmented Dickey-Fuller Test Equation
Dependent Variable: D(LGDPI)
Method: Least Squares
Sample(adjusted): 1961 1994
Included observations: 34 after adjusting endpoints
```

Variable	Coefficient	Std. Error	t-Statistic	Prob.
LGDPI(-1)	-0.067291	0.060713	-1.108351	0.2765
D(LGDPI(-1))	0.022552	0.178288	0.126489	0.9002
C	0.547372	0.449768	1.217012	0.2331
@TREND(1959)	0.001208	0.001953	0.618571	0.5409

R-squared	0.293987	Mean dependent var	0.030995
Adjusted R-squared	0.223386	S.D. dependent var	0.017597
S.E. of regression	0.015507	Akaike info criter	-5.384864
Sum squared resid	0.007214	Schwarz criterion	-5.205292
Log likelihood	95.54268	F-statistic	4.164051
Durbin-Watson stat	2.105872	Prob(F-statistic)	0.014031

Example

Figure 14.8 presents the sample correlogram for the logarithm of *DPI*. At first sight, the falling autocorrelation coefficients suggest a stationary AR(1) process with a high value of β_2. Although the theoretical correlogram for such a process, shown in Figure 14.5, looks a little different in that the coefficients decline exponentially to 0 without becoming negative, a sample correlogram would have negative values similar to those in Figure 14.8. However, the correlogram in Figure 14.8 is also very similar to that for the finite nonstationary process shown in Figure 14.7.

The EViews output in Table 14.2 shows the result of performing a unit root test on the logarithm of *DPI* using equation (14.32). The coefficient of $LGDPI_{t-1}$ is -0.07, very close to 0. The t statistic, reproduced at the top of the output where it is designated the ADF test statistic, is -1.11. Under the null hypothesis of nonstationarity, the critical value of t at the 5 percent level, also given at the top of the output, is -3.55, and hence the null hypothesis of nonstationarity is not rejected. Notice that the critical value is much larger than 1.69, the conventional critical value for a one-tailed test at the 5 percent level for a sample of this size.

Figure 14.9 shows the differenced series, which appears to be stationary around a mean annual growth rate of between 2 and 3 percent. Possibly there might be a downward trend, and equally possibly there might be a discontinuity in the series at 1972, with a step down in the mean growth rate after the first oil shock, but these hypotheses will not be investigated here. Figure 14.10 shows the corresponding correlogram, whose low, erratic autocorrelation coefficients provide support for the hypothesis that the differenced series is stationary.

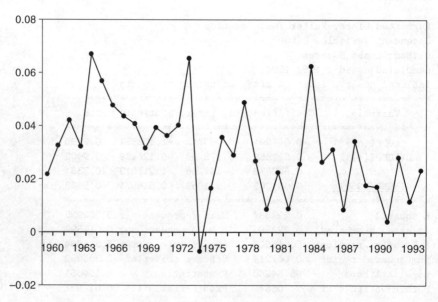

Figure 14.9 Differenced logarithm of *DPI*

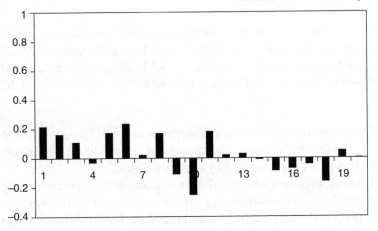

Figure 14.10 Correlogram of the differenced logarithm of *DPI*

Table 14.3

```
    Augmented Dickey-Fuller Unit Root Test on D(LGDPI)
=================================================================
ADF Test Statistic -4.512438      1%   Critical Value*-4.2605
                                  5%   Critical Value -3.5514
                                  10% Critical Value  -3.2081
=================================================================
```
*MacKinnon critical values for rejection of hypothesis of a
 unit root.

Augmented Dickey-Fuller Test Equation
Dependent Variable: D(LGDPI,2)
Method: Least Squares
Sample(adjusted): 1962 1994
Included observations: 33 after adjusting endpoints

Variable	Coefficient	Std. Error	t-Statistic	Prob.
D(LGDPI(-1))	-1.157492	0.256512	-4.512438	0.0001
D(LGDPI(-1),2)	0.081675	0.176383	0.463054	0.6468
C	0.057205	0.013740	4.163475	0.0003
@TREND(1959)	-0.001122	0.000365	-3.070723	0.0046

R-squared	0.545496	Mean dependent var	-0.000283	
Adjusted R-squared	0.498478	S.D. dependent var	0.022274	
S.E. of regression	0.015774	Akaike info criter	-5.347691	
Sum squared resid	0.007216	Schwarz criterion	-5.166297	
Log likelihood	92.23691	F-statistic	11.60194	
Durbin-Watson stat	2.046889	Prob(F-statistic)	0.000036	

The EViews output for a unit root test on the differenced series provides further support for this hypothesis (Table 14.3). The coefficient of $\Delta LGDPI_{t-1}$ is -1.16, well below 0, and the t statistic is -4.51, allowing the null hypothesis of nonstationarity to be rejected at the 1 percent level (critical value -4.26).

Exercises

14.8* Demonstrate that if the disturbance term in (14.31) is u_t, where u_t is generated by an AR(1) process, the appropriate specification for the augmented Dickey–Fuller test is given by equation (14.32).

14.9 Perform augmented Dickey–Fuller tests for difference-stationarity on the logarithms of expenditure on your commodity and the relative price series. Calculate the first differences and test these for difference-stationarity.

14.4 **Cointegration**

In general, a linear combination of two or more time series will be nonstationary if one or more of them is nonstationary, and the degree of integration of the combination will be equal to that of the most highly integrated individual series. Hence, for example, a linear combination of an I(1) series and an I(0) series will be I(1), that of two I(1) series will also be I(1), and that of an I(1) series and an I(2) series will be I(2).

However, if there is a long-run relationship between the time series, the outcome may be different. Consider, for example, Friedman's Permanent Income Hypothesis and the consumption function

$$C_t^P = \beta_2 Y_t^P v_t, \tag{14.33}$$

where C_t^P and Y_t^P are permanent consumption and income, respectively, and v_t is a multiplicative disturbance term. In logarithms, the relationship becomes

$$\log C_t^P = \log \beta_2 + \log Y_t^P + u_t, \tag{14.34}$$

where u_t is the logarithm of v_t. If the theory is correct, in the long run, ignoring short-run dynamics and the differences between the permanent and actual measures of the variables, consumption and income will grow at the same rate and the mean of the difference between their logarithms will be $\log \beta_2$. Figure 14.11 shows plots of the logarithms of aggregate personal consumer expenditure and disposable personal income for the United States for the period 1959–94, and it can be seen that the gap between the two, although affected by short-run dynamics, is more or less constant. Thus, although the two series are nonstationary, they appear to be wandering together. For this to be possible, u_t must be a stationary process, for if it were not, the two series could drift apart indefinitely, violating the theoretical relationship.

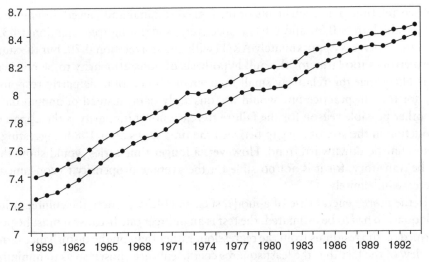

Figure 14.11 Logarithms of *PCE* and *DPI*

When two or more nonstationary time series are linked in such a way, they are said to be cointegrated. In this example, the slope coefficient of log Y^P in (14.34) is theoretically equal to 1, making it possible to inspect the divergence graphically in Figure 14.11. More generally, if there exists a relationship

$$Y_t = \beta_1 + \beta_2 X_{2t} + \cdots + \beta_k X_{kt} + u_t \qquad (14.35)$$

between a set of variables $Y_t, X_{2t}, \ldots, X_{kt}$, the disturbance term u_t can be thought of as measuring the deviation between the components of the model:

$$u_t = Y_t - \beta_1 - \beta_2 X_{2t} - \cdots - \beta_k X_{kt}. \qquad (14.36)$$

In the short run the divergence between the components will fluctuate, but if the model is genuinely correct there will be a limit to the divergence. Hence, although the time series are nonstationary, u_t will be stationary.

If there are more than two variables in the model, it is possible that there may be multiple cointegrating relationships, the maximum number in theory being equal to $k - 1$.

To test for cointegration, it is necessary to evaluate whether the disturbance term is a stationary process. In the case of the example of consumer expenditure and income, it is sufficient to perform a standard ADF unit root test on the difference between the two series. The test statistic is -1.90, which is less than -1.95, the critical value at the 5 percent level under the null hypothesis of nonstationarity. This is a surprising result, for other studies have found the logarithms of consumer expenditure and income to be cointegrated (for example, Engle and Granger, 1987). Part of the problem is the low power of the test against an alternative hypothesis of u_t being a stationary process with high autocorrelation. The coefficients of the lagged residual and lagged difference in the residual are −0.30 and 0.01, respectively, suggesting (see equation 14.32) that the process is approximately AR(1) with autocorrelation 0.70, but the standard error is too large for the null hypothesis of nonstationarity to be rejected. It is likely that the relatively small number of observations is partly responsible for this. In practice one would use quarterly data, instead of annual data. Another possible reason for the failure to reject nonstationarity is the apparent reduction in the size of the gap between the time series after 1984, suggesting a deterministic downward trend. However, a longer time series would show this to be transitory, for it is not possible for the average propensity to consume to increase indefinitely.

In the more general case of a model such as (14.35), where the cointegrating relationship has to be estimated, the test is an indirect one because it must be performed on the residuals from the regression, rather than on the disturbance term. In view of the fact that the least squares coefficients are chosen so as to minimize the sum of the squares of the residuals, the time series for the residuals will tend to appear more stationary than the underlying series for the disturbance term. To allow for this, the critical values for the test statistic are even higher than those for the standard test for nonstationarity of a time series. Asymptotic critical values for the case where the cointegrating relationship involves two variables are shown in Table 14.4. The test assumes that a constant has been included in the cointegrating relationship, and the critical values depend on whether a trend has been included as well.

In the case of a cointegrating relationship, least squares estimators can be shown to be superconsistent, in the sense that the parameter estimates approach their true values faster than they would in a regression involving cross-section or stationary time-series data (Stock, 1987). In the latter case, the population variances of the estimators are of the order of $1/n$, where n is the number of observations in the sample or series, while in the case of a cointegrating relationship, the variances are of the order of $1/n^2$. An important consequence of this is that OLS may be used to fit a cointegrating relationship, even if it belongs to a system of simultaneous relationships, for any simultaneous equations bias tends to 0 asymptotically.

Table 14.4 Asymptotic critical values of the Dickey–Fuller statistic for a cointegrating relationship with two variables

	5 percent	1 percent
Constant, no trend	−3.34	−3.90
Constant and trend	−3.78	−4.32

Source: Davidson and MacKinnon (1993)

Example

A logarithmic regression of expenditure on food on *DPI* and the relative price of food was performed using the Demand Functions data set, the fitted equation being

$$\widehat{LGFOOD} = \underset{(0.28)}{2.66} + \underset{(0.01)}{0.61} LGDPI - \underset{(0.07)}{0.30} LGPRFOOD . \quad R^2 = 0.993$$

$$(14.37)$$

The residuals are shown in Figure 14.12. They appear to be stationary and the relationship therefore cointegrated. However the test statistic is only -2.47, and so the null hypothesis of nonstationarity is not rejected, which suggests that the variables are not cointegrated. Nevertheless, the coefficient of the lagged residuals was -0.31, suggesting an AR(1) process with ρ equal to 0.69. Thus, once again, the result of the test may merely reflect its low power against the alternative hypothesis that the disturbance term is a highly autocorrelated stationary process, and consequently it is possible that the variables are in fact cointegrated.

Exercises

14.10   Generate a random walk and a stationary AR(1) series. Generate Y_t as one arbitrary linear combination and X_t as another. Test Y_t and X_t for a cointegrating relationship.

14.11   Run logarithmic regressions of expenditure on your commodity on disposable personal income and relative price, plot the residuals, and test for cointegration.

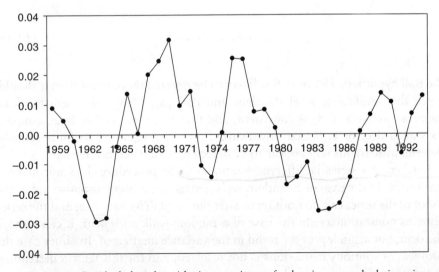

Figure 14.12 Residuals from logarithmic regression on food on income and relative price

14.5 **Fitting models with nonstationary time series**

Much to the embarrassment of those constructing them, early macroeconomic models tended to produce poor forecasts, despite having excellent sample-period fits. Often, indeed, the forecasts were no more accurate than those made by extrapolating simple linear trends (Nelson, 1973). There were two main reactions to this disappointing state of affairs. One was a resurgence of interest in the use of univariate time series for forecasting purposes, led by Box and Jenkins (1970). The other, of greater appeal to economists who did not wish to give up multivariate analysis, was to search for ways of constructing models that avoided the fitting of spurious relationships. We will briefly consider three of them: detrending the variables in a relationship, differencing them, and the construction of error-correction models.

Detrending

As noted in Section 14.2, for models where the variables possess deterministic trends, the fitting of spurious relationships can be avoided by detrending the variables before use, or, equivalently, by including a time trend as a regressor in the model.

However, if the variables are difference-stationary rather than trend-stationary—and Nelson and Plosser (1982) have shown that for many macroeconomic variables there is evidence that this is the case—the detrending procedure is inappropriate and likely to give rise to misleading results. In particular, if a random walk X_t is regressed on a time trend as in

$$X_t = \beta_1 + \beta_2 t + \varepsilon_t, \tag{14.38}$$

the null hypothesis $H_0: \beta_2 = 0$ is likely to be rejected more often than it should, given the significance level (Durlauf and Phillips, 1988). Although the least squares estimator of β_2 is consistent, and thus will tend to 0 in large samples, its standard error is biased downwards. As a consequence, in finite samples deterministic trends will appear to be detected, even when not present.

Further, if a series is difference-stationary, the procedure does not make it stationary. In the case of a random walk, extracting a non-existent trend in the mean of the series can do nothing to alter the trend in its variance, and the series remains nonstationary. In the case of a random walk with drift, it can remove the drift, but again leaves the trend in the variance unaffected. In either case the problem of spurious regressions is not resolved, and for this reason detrending is not usually considered to be an appropriate procedure.

Differencing

In early time-series studies, if the disturbance term in a model

$$Y_t = \beta_1 + \beta_2 X_t + u_t \qquad (14.39)$$

was believed to be subject to severe positive AR(1) autocorrelation $u_t = \rho u_{t-1} + \varepsilon_t$, a common rough-and-ready remedy was to regress the model in differences rather than levels:

$$\begin{aligned}
\Delta Y_t &= \beta_2 \Delta X_t + \Delta u_t \\
&= \beta_2 \Delta X_t + (\rho - 1)u_{t-1} + \varepsilon_t.
\end{aligned} \qquad (14.40)$$

Of course differencing overcompensated for the autocorrelation, but if ρ was near 1, the resulting weak negative autocorrelation was held to be relatively innocuous. Unknown to practitioners of the time, the procedure is an effective antidote to spurious regressions, and was advocated as such by Granger and Newbold (1974). If both Y_t and X_t are unrelated I(1) processes, they are stationary in the differenced model and the absence of any relationship will be revealed.

A major shortcoming of differencing is that it precludes the investigation of a long-run relationship. In equilibrium $\Delta Y = \Delta X = 0$, and if one substitutes these values into (14.40) one obtains, not an equilibrium relationship, but an equation in which both sides are 0.

Error-correction models

We have seen that a long-run relationship between two or more variables is given by a cointegrating relationship, if it exists. On its own, a cointegrating relationship sheds no light on short-run dynamics, but its very existence indicates that there must be some short-term forces that are responsible for keeping the relationship intact, and thus that it should be possible to construct a more comprehensive model that combines short-run and long-run dynamics.

For example, suppose that the relationship between two I(1) variables Y_t and X_t is characterized by the ADL(1,1) model considered in Section 13.7:

$$Y_t = \beta_1 + \beta_2 Y_{t-1} + \beta_3 X_t + \beta_4 X_{t-1} + \varepsilon_t. \qquad (14.41)$$

In equilibrium,

$$\bar{Y} = \beta_1 + \beta_2 \bar{Y} + \beta_3 \bar{X} + \beta_4 \bar{X}. \qquad (14.42)$$

Hence

$$\bar{Y} = \frac{\beta_1}{1 - \beta_2} + \frac{\beta_3 + \beta_4}{1 - \beta_2}\bar{X} \qquad (14.43)$$

and

$$Y_t = \frac{\beta_1}{1 - \beta_2} + \frac{\beta_3 + \beta_4}{1 - \beta_2} X_t \tag{14.44}$$

is the cointegrating relationship.

The ADL(1,1) relationship (14.41) may be rewritten to incorporate this relationship by subtracting Y_{t-1} from both sides, adding $\beta_3 X_{t-1}$ to the right side and subtracting it again, and rearranging:

$$
\begin{aligned}
Y_t - Y_{t-1} &= \beta_1 + (\beta_2 - 1)Y_{t-1} + \beta_3 X_t + \beta_4 X_{t-1} + \varepsilon_t \\
&= \beta_1 + (\beta_2 - 1)Y_{t-1} + \beta_3 X_t - \beta_3 X_{t-1} + \beta_3 X_{t-1} + \beta_4 X_{t-1} + \varepsilon_t \\
&= (\beta_2 - 1)\left(Y_{t-1} - \frac{\beta_1}{1 - \beta_2} - \frac{\beta_3 + \beta_4}{1 - \beta_2} X_{t-1}\right) + \beta_3(X_t - X_{t-1}) + \varepsilon_t.
\end{aligned}
\tag{14.45}
$$

Hence

$$\Delta Y_t = (\beta_2 - 1)\left(Y_{t-1} - \frac{\beta_1}{1 - \beta_2} - \frac{\beta_3 + \beta_4}{1 - \beta_2} X_{t-1}\right) + \beta_3 \Delta X_t + \varepsilon_t \tag{14.46}$$

and the model states that the change in Y in any period will be governed by the change in X and the discrepancy between Y_{t-1} and the value predicted by the cointegrating relationship. The latter term is denoted the error-correction mechanism, the effect of the term being to reduce the discrepancy between Y_t and its cointegrating level and its size being proportional to the discrepancy.

The point of this rearrangement is that, although Y_t and X_t are both I(1), all of the terms ΔY_t, ΔX_t, and $(Y_{t-1} - \frac{\beta_1}{1 - \beta_2} - \frac{\beta_3 + \beta_4}{1 - \beta_2} X_{t-1})$ in (14.46) are I(0), the latter by virtue of being just the disturbance term in the cointegrating relationship, and hence the model may be fitted using least squares in the standard way.

Of course, the β parameters are not known and the cointegrating term is unobservable. One way of overcoming this problem, known as the Engle–Granger two-step procedure, is to use the values of the parameters estimated in the cointegrating regression to compute the cointegrating term. Engle and Granger (1987) demonstrate that asymptotically the estimators of the coefficients of (14.46) will have the same properties as if the true values had been used.

Example

The EViews output in Table 14.5 shows the results of fitting an error-correction model for the demand function for food using the Engle–Granger two-step procedure, on the assumption that (14.37) is a cointegrating relationship. The coefficient of the cointegrating term, FOODCOIN, indicates that about 30 percent of the disequilibrium divergence tends to be eliminated in one year.

Table 14.5

Dependent Variable: DLGFOOD
Method: Least Squares
Sample(adjusted): 1960 1994
Included observations: 35 after adjusting endpoints

Variable	Coefficient	Std. Error	t-Statistic	Prob.
C	0.002691	0.004477	0.601116	0.5521
DLGDPI	0.520791	0.129260	4.029022	0.0003
DLGPRFD	-0.358742	0.123584	-2.902816	0.0068
FOODCOIN	-0.298173	0.129722	-2.298555	0.0284

R-squared	0.456691	Mean dependent var	0.018454
Adjusted R-squared	0.404113	S.D. dependent var	0.016271
S.E. of regression	0.012560	Akaike info criter	-5.809320
Sum squared resid	0.004891	Schwarz criterion	-5.631565
Log likelihood	105.6631	F-statistic	8.685928
Durbin-Watson stat	1.528971	Prob(F-statistic)	0.000249

Exercise

14.12 Fit an error-correction model for your commodity, assuming that a cointegrating relationship has been found in Exercise 14.11.

14.6 Conclusion

This chapter has attempted to provide a brief and limited exposition of some of the concepts and issues that arise when regression analysis is applied to non-stationary time series. The treatment has been guided by the need to avoid complexity that would be inappropriate in an introductory econometrics course. For this reason there is no mention of some important mathematical tools, such as lag operators, or some major econometric topics, such as vector autoregression, and the discussion barely scratches at the surface of those topics that are included, sidestepping problems encountered in practice, such as the extent to which asymptotic analysis is relevant to analysis of finite samples. The chapter therefore can make no pretence to provide a perspective or overview. Rather than attempting to provide tools for immediate use, the overriding objective has been to convince a reader intending to work with time-series data that there is a need for further study at a higher level, and that further study would be worthwhile. For precisely because many of the problems have been recognized only relatively recently, much remains to be explored and the econometric analysis of time series is at the present time an especially exciting and challenging field.

Appendix A:
Statistical tables

Table A.1 Cumulative standardized normal distribution

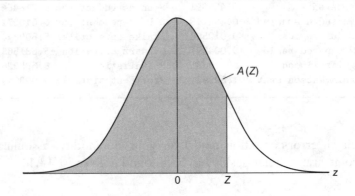

$A(Z)$ is the integral of the standardized normal distribution from $-\infty$ to Z (in other words, the area under the curve to the left of Z). It gives the probability of a normal random variable not being more than Z standard deviations above its mean.

Values of Z of particular importance in the text:

Z	$A(Z)$	
1.645	0.950	Lower limit of the right 5% tail
1.960	0.975	Lower limit of the right 2.5% tail
2.326	0.990	Lower limit of the right 1% tail
2.576	0.995	Lower limit of the right 0.5% tail

Table A.1 (*Continued*)

Z	0.00	0.01	0.02	0.03	$A(Z)$ 0.04	0.05	0.06	0.07	0.08	0.09
0.0	0.5000	0.5040	0.5080	0.5120	0.5160	0.5199	0.5239	0.5279	0.5319	0.5359
0.1	0.5398	0.5438	0.5478	0.5517	0.5557	0.5596	0.5636	0.5675	0.5714	0.5753
0.2	0.5793	0.5832	0.5871	0.5910	0.5948	0.5987	0.6026	0.6064	0.6103	0.6141
0.3	0.6179	0.6217	0.6255	0.6293	0.6331	0.6368	0.6406	0.6443	0.6480	0.6517
0.4	0.6554	0.6591	0.6628	0.6664	0.6700	0.6736	0.6772	0.6808	0.6844	0.6879
0.5	0.6915	0.6950	0.6985	0.7019	0.7054	0.7088	0.7123	0.7157	0.7190	0.7224
0.6	0.7257	0.7291	0.7324	0.7357	0.7389	0.7422	0.7454	0.7486	0.7517	0.7549
0.7	0.7580	0.7611	0.7642	0.7673	0.7704	0.7734	0.7764	0.7794	0.7823	0.7852
0.8	0.7881	0.7910	0.7939	0.7967	0.7995	0.8023	0.8051	0.8078	0.8106	0.8133
0.9	0.8159	0.8186	0.8212	0.8238	0.8264	0.8289	0.8315	0.8340	0.8365	0.8389
1.0	0.8413	0.8438	0.8461	0.8485	0.8508	0.8531	0.8554	0.8577	0.8599	0.8621
1.1	0.8643	0.8665	0.8686	0.8708	0.8729	0.8749	0.8770	0.8790	0.8810	**0.8830**
1.2	0.8849	0.8869	0.8888	0.8907	0.8925	0.8944	0.8962	0.8980	0.8997	0.9015
1.3	0.9032	0.9049	0.9066	0.9082	0.9099	0.9115	0.9131	0.9147	0.9162	0.9177
1.4	0.9192	0.9207	0.9222	0.9236	0.9251	0.9265	0.9279	0.9292	0.9306	0.9319
1.5	0.9332	0.9345	0.9357	0.9370	0.9382	0.9394	0.9406	0.9418	0.9429	0.9441
1.6	0.9452	0.9463	0.9474	0.9484	0.9495	0.9505	0.9515	0.9525	0.9535	0.9545
1.7	0.9554	0.9564	0.9573	0.9582	0.9591	0.9599	0.9608	0.9616	0.9625	0.9633
1.8	0.9641	0.9649	0.9656	0.9664	0.9671	0.9678	0.9686	0.9693	0.9700	0.9706
1.9	0.9713	0.9719	0.9726	0.9732	0.9738	0.9744	0.9750	0.9756	0.9761	0.9767
2.0	0.9772	0.9778	0.9783	0.9788	0.9793	0.9798	0.9803	0.9808	0.9812	0.9817
2.1	0.9821	0.9826	0.9830	0.9834	0.9838	0.9842	0.9846	0.9850	0.9854	0.9857
2.2	0.9861	0.9864	0.9868	0.9871	0.9875	0.9878	0.9881	0.9884	0.9887	0.9890
2.3	0.9893	0.9896	0.9898	0.9901	0.9904	0.9906	0.9909	0.9911	0.9913	0.9916
2.4	0.9918	0.9920	0.9922	0.9925	0.9927	0.9929	0.9931	0.9932	0.9934	0.9936
2.5	0.9938	0.9940	0.9941	0.9943	0.9945	0.9946	0.9948	0.9949	**0.9951**	0.9952
2.6	0.9953	0.9955	0.9956	0.9957	0.9959	0.9960	0.9961	0.9962	0.9963	0.9964
2.7	0.9965	0.9966	0.9967	0.9968	0.9969	0.9970	0.9971	0.9972	0.9973	0.9974
2.8	0.9974	0.9975	0.9976	0.9977	0.9977	0.9978	0.9979	0.9979	0.9980	0.9981
2.9	0.9981	0.9982	0.9982	0.9983	0.9984	0.9984	0.9985	0.9985	0.9986	0.9986
3.0	0.9987									

[handwritten annotation: 5% significance level 97.5]

Table A.2 t Distribution: critical values of t

Degrees of freedom		Significance level					
	Two-tailed test:	10%	5%	2%	1%	0.2%	0.1%
	One-tailed test:	5%	2.5%	1%	0.5%	0.1%	0.05%
1		6.314	12.706	31.821	63.657	318.31	636.62
2		2.920	4.303	6.965	9.925	22.327	31.598
3		2.353	3.182	4.541	5.841	10.214	12.924
4		2.132	2.776	3.747	4.604	7.173	8.610
5		2.015	2.571	3.365	4.032	5.893	6.869
6		1.943	2.447	3.143	3.707	5.208	5.959
7		1.895	2.365	2.998	3.499	4.785	5.408
8		1.860	2.306	2.896	3.355	4.501	5.041
9		1.833	2.262	2.821	3.250	4.297	4.781
10		1.812	2.228	2.764	3.169	4.144	4.587
11		1.796	2.201	2.718	3.106	4.025	4.437
12		1.782	2.179	2.681	3.055	3.930	4.318
13		1.771	2.160	2.650	3.012	3.852	4.221
14		1.761	2.145	2.624	2.977	3.787	4.140
15		1.753	2.131	2.602	2.947	3.733	4.073
16		1.746	2.120	2.583	2.921	3.686	4.015
17		1.740	2.110	2.567	2.898	3.646	3.965
18		1.734	2.101	2.552	2.878	3.610	3.922
19		1.729	2.093	2.539	2.861	3.579	3.883
20		1.725	2.086	2.528	2.845	3.552	3.850
21		1.721	2.080	2.518	2.831	3.527	3.819
22		1.717	2.074	2.508	2.819	3.505	3.792
23		1.714	2.069	2.500	2.807	3.485	3.767
24		1.711	2.064	2.492	2.797	3.467	3.745
25		1.708	2.060	2.485	2.787	3.450	3.725
26		1.706	2.056	2.479	2.779	3.435	3.707
27		1.703	2.052	2.473	2.771	3.421	3.690
28		1.701	2.048	2.467	2.763	3.408	3.674
29		1.699	2.045	2.462	2.756	3.396	3.659
30		1.697	2.042	2.457	2.750	3.385	3.646
40		1.684	2.021	2.423	2.704	3.307	3.551
60		1.671	2.000	2.390	2.660	3.232	3.460
120		1.658	1.980	2.358	2.617	3.160	3.373
∞		1.645	1.960	2.326	2.576	3.090	3.291

Example: With 25 degrees of freedom, the probability of t being greater than -2.060 is 0.025, and the probability of it being lower than -2.060 is 0.025. Hence if both tails are being used as a rejection zones, as in a two-tailed test, the significance level is 0.05 (5%). If only one tail is being used as a rejection zone, as in a one-tailed test, the significance level is 0.025 (2.5%). See Chapter 3 for further explanation.

Table A.3 *F* Distribution: critical values of *F* with ν_1 and ν_2 degrees of freedom, 5% significance level

ν_2 \ ν_1	1	2	3	4	5	6	7	8	9	10	12	15	20	24	30	40	60	120	∞
1	161.4	199.5	215.7	224.6	230.2	234.0	236.8	238.9	240.5	241.9	243.9	245.9	248.0	249.1	250.1	251.1	252.2	253.3	254.3
2	18.51	19.00	19.16	19.25	19.30	19.33	19.35	19.37	19.38	19.40	19.41	19.43	19.45	19.45	19.46	19.47	19.48	19.49	19.50
3	10.13	9.55	9.28	9.12	9.01	8.94	8.89	8.85	8.81	8.79	8.74	8.70	8.66	8.64	8.62	8.59	8.57	8.55	8.53
4	7.71	6.94	6.59	6.39	6.26	6.16	6.09	6.04	6.00	5.96	5.91	5.86	5.80	5.77	5.75	5.72	5.69	5.66	5.63
5	6.61	5.79	5.41	5.19	5.05	4.95	4.88	4.82	4.77	4.74	4.68	4.62	4.56	4.53	4.50	4.46	4.43	4.40	4.36
6	5.99	5.14	4.76	4.53	4.39	4.28	4.21	4.15	4.10	4.06	4.00	3.94	3.87	3.84	3.81	3.77	3.74	3.70	3.67
7	5.59	4.74	4.35	4.12	3.97	3.87	3.79	3.73	3.68	3.64	3.57	3.51	3.44	3.41	3.38	3.34	3.30	3.27	3.23
8	5.32	4.46	4.07	3.84	3.69	3.58	3.50	3.44	3.39	3.35	3.28	3.22	3.15	3.12	3.08	3.04	3.01	2.97	2.93
9	5.12	4.26	3.86	3.63	3.48	3.37	3.29	3.23	3.18	3.14	3.07	3.01	2.94	2.90	2.86	2.83	2.79	2.75	2.71
10	4.96	4.10	3.71	3.48	3.33	3.22	3.14	3.07	3.02	2.98	2.91	2.85	2.77	2.74	2.70	2.66	2.62	2.58	2.54
11	4.84	3.98	3.59	3.36	3.20	3.09	3.01	2.95	2.90	2.85	2.79	2.72	2.65	2.61	2.57	2.53	2.49	2.45	2.40
12	4.75	3.89	3.49	3.26	3.11	3.00	2.91	2.85	2.80	2.75	2.69	2.62	2.54	2.51	2.47	2.43	2.38	2.34	2.30
13	4.67	3.81	3.41	3.18	3.03	2.92	2.83	2.77	2.71	2.67	2.60	2.53	2.46	2.42	2.38	2.34	2.30	2.25	2.21
14	4.60	3.74	3.34	3.11	2.96	2.85	2.76	2.70	2.65	2.60	2.53	2.46	2.39	2.35	2.31	2.27	2.22	2.18	2.13
15	4.54	3.68	3.29	3.06	2.90	2.79	2.71	2.64	2.59	2.54	2.48	2.40	2.33	2.29	2.25	2.20	2.16	2.11	2.07
16	4.49	3.63	3.24	3.01	2.85	2.74	2.66	2.59	2.54	2.49	2.42	2.35	2.28	2.24	2.19	2.15	2.11	2.06	2.01
17	4.45	3.59	3.20	2.96	2.81	2.70	2.61	2.55	2.49	2.45	2.38	2.31	2.23	2.19	2.15	2.10	2.06	2.01	1.96
18	4.41	3.55	3.16	2.93	2.77	2.66	2.58	2.51	2.46	2.41	2.34	2.27	2.19	2.15	2.11	2.06	2.02	1.97	1.92
19	4.38	3.52	3.13	2.90	2.74	2.63	2.54	2.48	2.42	2.38	2.31	2.23	2.16	2.11	2.07	2.03	1.98	1.93	1.88
20	4.35	3.49	3.10	2.87	2.71	2.60	2.51	2.45	2.39	2.35	2.28	2.20	2.12	2.08	2.04	1.99	1.95	1.90	1.84
21	4.32	3.47	3.07	2.84	2.68	2.57	2.49	2.42	2.37	2.32	2.25	2.18	2.10	2.05	2.01	1.96	1.92	1.87	1.81
22	4.30	3.44	3.05	2.82	2.66	2.55	2.46	2.40	2.34	2.30	2.23	2.15	2.07	2.03	1.98	1.94	1.89	1.84	1.78
23	4.28	3.42	3.03	2.80	2.64	2.53	2.44	2.37	2.32	2.27	2.20	2.13	2.05	2.01	1.96	1.91	1.86	1.81	1.76
24	4.26	3.40	3.01	2.78	2.62	2.51	2.42	2.36	2.30	2.25	2.18	2.11	2.03	1.98	1.94	1.89	1.84	1.79	1.73
25	4.24	3.39	2.99	2.76	2.60	2.49	2.40	2.34	2.28	2.24	2.16	2.09	2.01	1.96	1.92	1.87	1.82	1.77	1.71
26	4.23	3.37	2.98	2.74	2.59	2.47	2.39	2.32	2.27	2.22	2.15	2.07	1.99	1.95	1.90	1.85	1.80	1.75	1.69
27	4.21	3.35	2.96	2.73	2.57	2.46	2.37	2.31	2.25	2.20	2.13	2.06	1.97	1.93	1.88	1.84	1.79	1.73	1.67
28	4.20	3.34	2.95	2.71	2.56	2.45	2.36	2.29	2.24	2.19	2.12	2.04	1.96	1.91	1.87	1.82	1.77	1.71	1.65
29	4.18	3.33	2.93	2.70	2.55	2.43	2.35	2.28	2.22	2.18	2.10	2.03	1.94	1.90	1.85	1.81	1.75	1.70	1.64
30	4.17	3.32	2.92	2.69	2.53	2.42	2.33	2.27	2.21	2.16	2.09	2.01	1.93	1.89	1.84	1.79	1.74	1.68	1.62
40	4.08	3.23	2.84	2.61	2.45	2.34	2.25	2.18	2.12	2.08	2.00	1.92	1.84	1.79	1.74	1.69	1.64	1.58	1.51
60	4.00	3.15	2.76	2.53	2.37	2.25	2.17	2.10	2.04	1.99	1.92	1.84	1.75	1.70	1.65	1.59	1.53	1.47	1.39
120	3.92	3.07	2.68	2.45	2.29	2.17	2.09	2.02	1.96	1.91	1.83	1.75	1.66	1.61	1.55	1.50	1.43	1.35	1.25
∞	3.84	3.00	2.60	2.37	2.21	2.10	2.01	1.94	1.88	1.83	1.75	1.67	1.57	1.52	1.46	1.39	1.32	1.22	1.00

Table A.3 F Distribution: critical values of F with v_1 and v_2 degrees of freedom, 1% significance level

v_2 \ v_1	1	2	3	4	5	6	7	8	9	10	12	15	20	24	30	40	60	120	∞
1	4052	4999.5	5403	5625	5764	5859	5928	5981	6022	6056	6106	6157	6209	6235	6261	6287	6313	6339	6366
2	98.50	99.00	99.17	99.25	99.30	99.33	99.36	99.37	99.39	99.40	99.42	99.43	99.45	99.46	99.47	99.47	99.48	99.49	99.50
3	34.12	30.82	29.46	28.71	28.24	27.91	27.67	27.49	27.35	27.23	27.05	26.87	26.69	26.60	26.50	26.41	26.32	26.22	26.13
4	21.20	18.00	16.69	15.98	15.52	15.21	14.98	14.80	14.66	14.55	14.37	14.20	14.02	13.93	13.84	13.75	13.65	13.56	13.46
5	16.26	13.27	12.06	11.39	10.97	10.67	10.46	10.29	10.16	10.05	9.89	9.72	9.55	9.47	9.38	9.29	9.20	9.11	9.02
6	13.75	10.92	9.78	9.15	8.75	8.47	8.26	8.10	7.98	7.87	7.72	7.56	7.40	7.31	7.23	7.14	7.06	6.97	6.88
7	12.25	9.55	8.45	7.85	7.46	7.19	6.99	6.84	6.72	6.62	6.47	6.31	6.16	6.07	5.99	5.91	5.82	5.74	5.65
8	11.26	8.65	7.59	7.01	6.63	6.37	6.18	6.03	5.91	5.81	5.67	5.52	5.36	5.28	5.20	5.12	5.03	4.95	4.86
9	10.56	8.02	6.99	6.42	6.06	5.80	5.61	5.47	5.35	5.26	5.11	4.96	4.81	4.73	4.65	4.57	4.48	4.40	4.31
10	10.04	7.56	6.55	5.99	5.64	5.39	5.20	5.06	4.94	4.85	4.71	4.56	4.41	4.33	4.25	4.17	4.08	4.00	3.91
11	9.65	7.21	6.22	5.67	5.32	5.07	4.89	4.74	4.63	4.54	4.40	4.25	4.10	4.02	3.94	3.86	3.78	3.69	3.60
12	9.33	6.93	5.95	5.41	5.06	4.82	4.64	4.50	4.39	4.30	4.16	4.01	3.86	3.78	3.70	3.62	3.54	3.45	3.36
13	9.07	6.70	5.74	5.21	4.86	4.62	4.44	4.30	4.19	4.10	3.96	3.82	3.66	3.59	3.51	3.43	3.34	3.25	3.17
14	8.86	6.51	5.56	5.04	4.69	4.46	4.28	4.14	4.03	3.94	3.80	3.66	3.51	3.43	3.35	3.27	3.18	3.09	3.00
15	8.68	6.36	5.42	4.89	4.56	4.32	4.14	4.00	3.89	3.80	3.67	3.52	3.37	3.29	3.21	3.13	3.05	2.96	2.87
16	8.53	6.23	5.29	4.77	4.44	4.20	4.03	3.89	3.78	3.69	3.55	3.41	3.26	3.18	3.10	3.02	2.93	2.84	2.75
17	8.40	6.11	5.18	4.67	4.34	4.10	3.93	3.79	3.68	3.59	3.46	3.31	3.16	3.08	3.00	2.92	2.83	2.75	2.65
18	8.29	6.01	5.09	4.58	4.25	4.01	3.84	3.71	3.60	3.51	3.37	3.23	3.08	3.00	2.92	2.84	2.75	2.66	2.57
19	8.18	5.93	5.01	4.50	4.17	3.94	3.77	3.63	3.52	3.43	3.30	3.15	3.00	2.92	2.84	2.76	2.67	2.58	2.49
20	8.10	5.85	4.94	4.43	4.10	3.87	3.70	3.56	3.46	3.37	3.23	3.09	2.94	2.86	2.78	2.69	2.61	2.52	2.42
21	8.02	5.78	4.87	4.37	4.04	3.81	3.64	3.51	3.40	3.31	3.17	3.03	2.88	2.80	2.72	2.64	2.55	2.46	2.36
22	7.95	5.72	4.82	4.31	3.99	3.76	3.59	3.45	3.35	3.26	3.12	2.98	2.83	2.75	2.67	2.58	2.50	2.40	2.31
23	7.88	5.66	4.76	4.26	3.94	3.71	3.54	3.41	3.30	3.21	3.07	2.93	2.78	2.70	2.62	2.54	2.45	2.35	2.26
24	7.82	5.61	4.72	4.22	3.90	3.67	3.50	3.36	3.26	3.17	3.03	2.89	2.74	2.66	2.58	2.49	2.40	2.31	2.21
25	7.77	5.57	4.68	4.18	3.85	3.63	3.46	3.32	3.22	3.13	2.99	2.85	2.70	2.62	2.54	2.45	2.36	2.27	2.17
26	7.72	5.53	4.64	4.14	3.82	3.59	3.42	3.29	3.18	3.09	2.96	2.81	2.66	2.58	2.50	2.42	2.33	2.23	2.13
27	7.68	5.49	4.60	4.11	3.78	3.56	3.39	3.26	3.15	3.06	2.93	2.78	2.63	2.55	2.47	2.38	2.29	2.20	2.10
28	7.64	5.45	4.57	4.07	3.75	3.53	3.36	3.23	3.12	3.03	2.90	2.75	2.60	2.52	2.44	2.35	2.26	2.17	2.06
29	7.60	5.42	4.54	4.04	3.73	3.50	3.33	3.20	3.09	3.00	2.87	2.73	2.57	2.49	2.41	2.33	2.23	2.14	2.03
30	7.56	5.39	4.51	4.02	3.70	3.47	3.30	3.17	3.07	2.98	2.84	2.70	2.55	2.47	2.39	2.30	2.21	2.11	2.01
40	7.31	5.18	4.31	3.83	3.51	3.29	3.12	2.99	2.89	2.80	2.66	2.52	2.37	2.29	2.20	2.11	2.02	1.92	1.80
60	7.08	4.98	4.13	3.65	3.34	3.12	2.95	2.82	2.72	2.63	2.50	2.35	2.20	2.12	2.03	1.94	1.84	1.73	1.60
120	6.85	4.79	3.95	3.48	3.17	2.96	2.79	2.66	2.56	2.47	2.34	2.19	2.03	1.95	1.86	1.76	1.66	1.53	1.38
∞	6.63	4.61	3.78	3.32	3.02	2.80	2.64	2.51	2.41	2.32	2.18	2.04	1.88	1.79	1.70	1.59	1.47	1.32	1.00

Reprinted from E. S. Pearson and H. O. Hartley (editors), *Biometrika Tables for Statisticians*, Cambridge, Cambridge University Press, 1970, with kind permission of the Biometrika Trustees.

Table A.4 χ^2 Distribution: critical values of χ^2 at 5%, 1%, and 0.1% significance levels

Degrees of freedom	5%	1%	0.1%
1	3.8415	6.6349	10.828
2	5.9915	9.2103	13.816
3	7.8147	11.3449	16.266
4	9.4877	13.2767	18.467
5	11.0705	15.0863	20.515
6	12.5916	16.8119	22.458
7	14.0671	18.4753	24.322
8	15.5073	20.0902	26.125
9	16.9190	21.6660	27.877
10	18.3070	23.2093	29.588
11	19.6751	24.7250	31.264
12	21.0261	26.2170	32.909
13	22.3620	27.6882	34.528
14	23.6848	29.1412	36.123
15	24.9958	30.5779	37.697
16	26.2962	31.9999	39.252
17	27.5871	33.4087	40.790
18	28.8693	34.8053	42.312
19	30.1435	36.1909	43.820
20	31.4104	37.5662	45.315
21	32.6706	38.9322	46.797
22	33.9244	40.2894	48.268
23	35.1725	41.6384	49.728
24	36.4150	42.9798	51.179
25	37.6525	44.3141	52.618
26	38.8851	45.6417	54.052
27	40.1133	46.9629	55.476
28	41.3371	48.2782	56.892
29	42.5570	49.5879	58.301
30	43.7730	50.8922	59.703
40	55.7585	63.6907	73.402
50	67.5048	76.1539	86.661
60	79.0819	88.3794	99.607
70	90.5312	100.425	112.317
80	101.879	112.329	124.839
90	113.145	124.116	137.208
100	124.342	135.807	149.449

Table A.5 Durbin–Watson d statistic: d_L and d_U, 5% significance level

n	$k=1$		$k=2$		$k=3$		$k=4$		$k=5$	
	d_L	d_U	d_L	d_U	d_L	d_U	d_L	d_U	d_L	d_U
15	1.08	1.36	0.95	1.54	0.82	1.75	0.69	1.97	0.56	2.21
16	1.10	1.37	0.98	1.54	0.86	1.73	0.74	1.93	0.62	2.15
17	1.13	1.38	1.02	1.54	0.90	1.71	0.78	1.90	0.67	2.10
18	1.16	1.39	1.05	1.53	0.93	1.69	0.82	1.87	0.71	2.06
19	1.18	1.40	1.08	1.53	0.97	1.68	0.86	1.85	0.75	2.02
20	1.20	1.41	1.10	1.54	1.00	1.68	0.90	1.83	0.79	1.99
21	1.22	1.42	1.13	1.54	1.03	1.67	0.93	1.81	0.83	1.96
22	1.24	1.43	1.15	1.54	1.05	1.66	0.96	1.80	0.86	1.94
23	1.26	1.44	1.17	1.54	1.08	1.66	0.99	1.79	0.90	1.92
24	1.27	1.45	1.19	1.55	1.10	1.66	1.01	1.78	0.93	1.90
25	1.29	1.45	1.21	1.55	1.12	1.66	1.04	1.77	0.95	1.89
26	1.30	1.46	1.22	1.55	1.14	1.65	1.06	1.76	0.98	1.88
27	1.32	1.47	1.24	1.56	1.16	1.65	1.08	1.76	1.01	1.86
28	1.33	1.48	1.26	1.56	1.18	1.65	1.10	1.75	1.03	1.85
29	1.34	1.48	1.27	1.56	1.20	1.65	1.12	1.74	1.05	1.84
30	1.35	1.49	1.28	1.57	1.21	1.65	1.14	1.74	1.07	1.83
31	1.36	1.50	1.30	1.57	1.23	1.65	1.16	1.74	1.09	1.83
32	1.37	1.50	1.31	1.57	1.24	1.65	1.18	1.73	1.11	1.82
33	1.38	1.51	1.32	1.58	1.26	1.65	1.19	1.73	1.13	1.81
34	1.39	1.51	1.33	1.58	1.27	1.65	1.21	1.73	1.15	1.81
35	1.40	1.52	1.34	1.58	1.28	1.65	1.22	1.73	1.16	1.80
36	1.41	1.52	1.35	1.59	1.29	1.65	1.24	1.73	1.18	1.80
37	1.42	1.53	1.36	1.59	1.31	1.66	1.25	1.72	1.19	1.80
38	1.43	1.54	1.37	1.59	1.32	1.66	1.26	1.72	1.21	1.79
39	1.43	1.54	1.38	1.60	1.33	1.66	1.27	1.72	1.22	1.79
40	1.44	1.54	1.39	1.60	1.34	1.66	1.29	1.72	1.23	1.79
45	1.48	1.57	1.43	1.62	1.38	1.67	1.34	1.72	1.29	1.78
50	1.50	1.59	1.46	1.63	1.42	1.67	1.38	1.72	1.34	1.77
55	1.53	1.60	1.49	1.64	1.45	1.68	1.41	1.72	1.38	1.77
60	1.55	1.62	1.51	1.65	1.48	1.69	1.44	1.73	1.41	1.77
65	1.57	1.63	1.54	1.66	1.50	1.70	1.47	1.73	1.44	1.77
70	1.58	1.64	1.55	1.67	1.52	1.70	1.49	1.74	1.46	1.77
75	1.60	1.65	1.57	1.68	1.54	1.71	1.51	1.74	1.49	1.77
80	1.61	1.66	1.59	1.69	1.56	1.72	1.53	1.74	1.51	1.77
85	1.62	1.67	1.60	1.70	1.57	1.72	1.55	1.75	1.52	1.77
90	1.63	1.68	1.61	1.70	1.59	1.73	1.57	1.75	1.54	1.78
95	1.64	1.69	1.62	1.71	1.60	1.73	1.58	1.75	1.56	1.78
100	1.65	1.69	1.63	1.72	1.61	1.74	1.59	1.76	1.57	1.78

Table A.5 Durbin–Watson d statistic: d_L and d_U, 1% significance level

n	$k = 1$		$k = 2$		$k = 3$		$k = 4$		$k = 5$	
	d_L	d_U	d_L	d_U	d_L	d_U	d_L	d_U	d_L	d_U
15	0.81	1.07	0.70	1.25	0.59	1.46	0.49	1.70	0.39	1.96
16	0.84	1.09	0.74	1.25	0.63	1.44	0.53	1.66	0.44	1.90
17	0.87	1.10	0.77	1.25	0.67	1.43	0.57	1.63	0.48	1.85
18	0.90	1.12	0.80	1.26	0.71	1.42	0.61	1.60	0.52	1.80
19	0.93	1.13	0.83	1.26	0.74	1.41	0.65	1.58	0.56	1.77
20	0.95	1.15	0.86	1.27	0.77	1.41	0.68	1.57	0.60	1.74
21	0.97	1.16	0.89	1.27	0.80	1.41	0.72	1.55	0.63	1.71
22	1.00	1.17	0.91	1.28	0.83	1.40	0.75	1.54	0.66	1.69
23	1.02	1.19	0.94	1.29	0.86	1.40	0.77	1.53	0.70	1.67
24	1.04	1.20	0.96	1.30	0.88	1.41	0.80	1.53	0.72	1.66
25	1.05	1.21	0.98	1.30	0.90	1.41	0.83	1.52	0.75	1.65
26	1.07	1.22	1.00	1.31	0.93	1.41	0.85	1.52	0.78	1.64
27	1.09	1.23	1.02	1.32	0.95	1.41	0.88	1.51	0.81	1.63
28	1.10	1.24	1.04	1.32	0.97	1.41	0.90	1.51	0.83	1.62
29	1.12	1.25	1.05	1.33	0.99	1.42	0.92	1.51	0.85	1.61
30	1.13	1.26	1.07	1.34	1.01	1.42	0.94	1.51	0.88	1.61
31	1.15	1.27	1.08	1.34	1.02	1.42	0.96	1.51	0.90	1.60
32	1.16	1.28	1.10	1.35	1.04	1.43	0.98	1.51	0.92	1.60
33	1.17	1.29	1.11	1.36	1.05	1.43	1.00	1.51	0.94	1.59
34	1.18	1.30	1.13	1.36	1.07	1.43	1.01	1.51	0.95	1.59
35	1.19	1.31	1.14	1.37	1.08	1.44	1.03	1.51	0.97	1.59
36	1.21	1.32	1.15	1.38	1.10	1.44	1.04	1.51	0.99	1.59
37	1.22	1.32	1.16	1.38	1.11	1.45	1.06	1.51	1.00	1.59
38	1.23	1.33	1.18	1.39	1.12	1.45	1.07	1.52	1.02	1.58
39	1.24	1.34	1.19	1.39	1.14	1.45	1.09	1.52	1.03	1.58
40	1.25	1.34	1.20	1.40	1.15	1.46	1.10	1.52	1.05	1.58
45	1.29	1.38	1.24	1.42	1.20	1.48	1.16	1.53	1.11	1.58
50	1.32	1.40	1.28	1.45	1.24	1.49	1.20	1.54	1.16	1.59
55	1.36	1.43	1.32	1.47	1.28	1.51	1.25	1.55	1.21	1.59
60	1.38	1.45	1.35	1.48	1.32	1.52	1.28	1.56	1.25	1.60
65	1.41	1.47	1.38	1.50	1.35	1.53	1.31	1.57	1.28	1.61
70	1.43	1.49	1.40	1.52	1.37	1.55	1.34	1.58	1.31	1.61
75	1.45	1.50	1.42	1.53	1.39	1.56	1.37	1.59	1.34	1.62
80	1.47	1.52	1.44	1.54	1.42	1.57	1.39	1.60	1.36	1.62
85	1.48	1.53	1.46	1.55	1.43	1.58	1.41	1.60	1.39	1.63
90	1.50	1.54	1.47	1.56	1.45	1.59	1.43	1.61	1.41	1.64
95	1.51	1.55	1.49	1.57	1.47	1.60	1.45	1.62	1.42	1.64
100	1.52	1.56	1.50	1.58	1.48	1.60	1.46	1.63	1.44	1.65

n = number of observations; k = number of explanatory variables (excluding the constant).
Reprinted from Durbin and Watson (1951) with kind permission of the Biometrika Trustees.

Appendix B: Data sets

Three major data sets and four minor ones, downloadable from the website (http://econ.lse.ac.uk/ie/), are intended to provide an opportunity for practical work. Along with their manuals, they will be updated periodically. All the data sets are provided in Stata, EViews and ASCII formats. Each major set and one minor set is accompanied by a manual proposing exercises, and each application-specific variant of the data set is accompanied by a specialized manual giving instructions for doing the exercises assuming no prior knowledge of the application.

Major data sets

The major data sets are for used with a long series of exercises that are intended to provide continuity in the practical work.

Educational Attainment and Earnings Functions (EAEF). This cross-section data set actually is in the form of 20 parallel subsets, each containing 570 observations drawn randomly from the US National Longitudinal Survey of Youth. Each subset contains the same variables and they provide an opportunity for a small group to work through a suite of 40 exercises together with some variation in the results. As the name suggests, most of the exercises involve the fitting of educational attainment functions and earnings functions, starting with simple regression analysis and developing more complex models as new topics are encountered in the cross-section part of the text, Chapters 2–11.

Demand Functions (DF). This time-series data set consists of annual observations on nineteen categories of consumer expenditure, their price series, disposable personal income, and population for the US for 1959–1994. They are intended to provide an opportunity for a small group to work in parallel, each member being assigned a different category of expenditure, the suite of exercises again starting with simple regression analysis and becoming more complex. They are primarily intended to provide practice for the time-series part of the text, Chapters 12–14.

Consumer Expenditure Survey (CES). This cross-section data set contains annual household expenditure on twenty-one categories of expenditure for 869 households in 1995, the course being the US Consumer Expenditure Survey. The suite of exercises is similar to that for *EAEF*, the data set being intended for extra practice for students out-of-class. Answers to all the exercises are provided in the on-line *Student Guide* at

http://www.oup.com/uk/best.textbooks/economics/dougherty2e

Minor data sets

The minor data sets consist of one data set each are thus not suitable for group work. They are intended to provide suitable data for specialized topics.

Labor Force Participation (LFP). This cross-section data set consists of data on labor force participation and background characteristics for 2,726 individuals in the US National Longitudinal Survey of Youth data set for 1994. The five exercises in its manual involve probit analysis, tobit analysis, and the fitting of sample selection bias models.

OECD employment and GDP growth rates (OECD). This data set contains the average annual growth rate of employment and GDP for 1988/97 for 25 OECD countries. It is provided for Exercise 5.5, an investigation into alternative nonlinear functional forms. An answer is provided in the on-line *Student Guide*.

School Cost (SC). This cross-section data set provides data on annual recurrent expenditure, numbers of students, type of curriculum, and other charateristics for 74 schools in Shanghai. The intention is to provide an opportunity for using dummy variables, investigating how type of curriculum affects the cost function.

Educational Expenditure (EDUC). This data set contains cross-section data on aggregate expenditure on education, GDP, and population for a sample of 38 countries in 1997. It is provided for Exercises 8.4 and 8.7, an investigation into heteroscedasticity and measures to alleviate it. Answers are provided in the on-line *Student Guide*.

Bibliography

Amemiya, Takeshi (1981) Qualitative response models: a survey. *Journal of Economic Literature* 19(4): 1483–1536

Amemiya, Takeshi (1984) Tobit models: a survey. *Journal of Econometrics* 24(1): 3–61

Box, George E.P., and David R. Cox (1964) An analysis of transformations. *Journal of the Royal Statistical Society Series B* 26(2): 211–243

Box, George E.P., and Gwilym M. Jenkins (1970) *Time Series Analysis: Forecasting and Control*. San Francisco: Holden Day

Box, George E.P., Gwilym M. Jenkins, and Gregory C. Reinsel (1994) *Time Series Analysis: Forecasting and Control* (third edition). Englewood Cliffs, NJ: Prentice–Hall

Brown, T.M. (1952) Habit persistence and lags in consumer behaviour. *Econometrica* 20(3): 355–371

Card, David (1995) Using geographic variation in college proximity to estimate the return to schooling. In Louis N. Christofides, E. Kenneth Grant and Robert Swidinsky (editors), *Aspects of Labour Market Behaviour: Essays in Honour of John Vanderkamp*. Toronto: University of Toronto Press

Chow, Gregory C. (1960) Tests of equality between sets of coefficients in two linear regressions. *Econometrica* 28(3): 591–605

Cobb, Charles W., and Paul H. Douglas (1928) A theory of production. *American Economic Review* 18(1, Supplement): 139–165

Cramer, Jan S. (1986) *Econometric Applications of Maximum Likelihood Methods*. Cambridge: Cambridge University Press

Davidson, Russell, and James G. MacKinnon (1993) *Estimation and Inference in Econometrics*. New York: Oxford University Press

Dickey, David A., and Wayne A. Fuller (1979) Distribution of the estimators for autoregressive time series with a unit root. *Journal of the American Statistical Association* 74(366): 427–431

Dufour, Jean-Marie (1980) Dummy variables and predictive tests for structural change. *Economics Letters* 6(3): 241–247

Durbin, James (1954) Errors in variables. *Review of the International Statistical Institute* 22(1): 23–32

Durbin, James (1970) Testing for serial correlation in least-squares regression when some of the regressors are lagged dependent variables. *Econometrica* 38(3): 410–421

Durbin, James, and G.S. Watson (1950) Testing for serial correlation in least-squares regression I. *Biometrika* 37(3–4): 409–428

Durlauf, Steven N., and Peter C.B. Phillips (1988) Trends versus random walks in time series analysis. *Econometrica* 56(6): 1333–1354

Eisner, Robert (1967) A permanent income theory for investment: some empirical explorations. *American Economic Review* 57(3): 363–390

Engle, Robert F., and Clive W.J. Granger (1987) Co-integration and error correction: representation, estimation, and testing. *Econometrica* 50(2): 251–276

Engle, Robert F., and Clive W.J. Granger (1991) *Long-Run Economic Relationships: Readings in Cointegration* (editors). Oxford: Oxford University Press

Fowler, Floyd J. (1993) *Survey Research Methods* (second edition). Newbury Park: Sage Publications

Friedman, Milton (1957) *A Theory of the Consumption Function*. Princeton: Princeton University Press

Friedman, Milton (1959) The demand for money: some theoretical and empirical results. *Journal of Political Economy* 67(4): 327–351

Frisch, Ragnar, and Frederick V. Waugh (1933) Partial time regressions as compared with individual trends. *Econometrica* 1(4): 387–401

Goldfeld, Stephen M., and Richard E. Quandt (1965) Some tests for homoscedasticity. *Journal of the American Statistical Association* 60(310): 539–547

Granger, Clive W.J., and Paul Newbold (1974) Spurious regressions in econometrics. *Journal of Econometrics* 2(2): 111–120

Gronau, Reuben (1974) Wage comparisons – a selectivity bias. *Journal of Political Economy* 82(6): 1119–1155

Hausman, J.A. (1978) Specification tests in econometrics. *Econometrica* 46(6): 1251–1271

Heckman, James (1976) The common structure of statistical models of truncation, sample selection, and limited dependent variables and a simple estimator for such models. *Annals of Economic and Social Measurement* 5(4): 475–492

Hendry, David F. (1979) Predictive failure and econometric modelling in macroeconomics: the transactions demand for money. In Paul Ormerod (editor), *Modelling the Economy*. London: Heinemann

Hendry, David F., and Grayham E. Mizon (1978) Serial correlation as a convenient simplification, not a nuisance. *Economic Journal* 88(351): 549–563

Johnston, Jack, and John Dinardo (1997) *Econometric Methods* (fourth edition). New York: McGraw-Hill

Kaldor, Nicholas (1966) *Causes of the Slow Rate of Economic Growth of the United Kingdom*. Cambridge: Cambridge University Press

Kmenta, Jan (1986) *Elements of Econometrics* (second edition). New York: Macmillan

Koyck, Leendert M. (1954) *Distributed Lags and Investment Analysis*. Amsterdam: North-Holland

Kuh, Edwin, and John R. Meyer (1957) How extraneous are extraneous estimates? *Review of Economics and Statistics* 39(4): 380–393

Liviatan, Nissan (1963) Tests of the Permanent-Income Hypothesis based on a reinterview savings survey. In Carl Christ (editor), *Measurement in Economics*. Stanford: Stanford University Press

MacKinnon, James G., and Halbert White (1985) Some heteroskedasticity-consistent covariance matrix estimators with improved finite sample properties. *Journal of Econometrics* 29(3): 305–325

Moser, Claus, and Graham Kalton (1985) *Survey Methods in Social Investigation* (second edition). Aldershot: Gower

Nelson, Charles R. (1973) *Applied Time Series Analysis*. San Francisco: Holden Day

Nelson, Charles R., and Charles I. Plosser (1982) Trends and random walks in macroeconomic time series: some evidence and implications. *Journal of Monetary Economics* 10(2): 139–162

Nerlove, Marc (1963) Returns to scale in electricity supply. In Carl Christ (editor), *Measurement in Economics*. Stanford: Stanford University Press

Peach, James T., and James L. Webb (1983) Randomly specified macroeconomic models: some implications for model selection. *Journal of Economic Issues* 17(3): 697–720

Pesaran, M. Hashem, R.P. Smith, and J. Stephen Yeo (1985) Testing for structural stability and predictive failure: a review. *Manchester School* 53(3): 280–295

Phillips, Peter C.B. (1986) Understanding spurious regressions in econometrics. *Journal of Econometrics* 33(3): 311–340

Phillips, Peter C.B. (1987) Towards a unified asymptotic theory for autoregression. *Biometrika* 74(3): 535–547

Salkever, David S. (1976) The use of dummy variables to compute predictions, prediction errors and confidence intervals. *Journal of Econometrics* 4(4): 393–397

Spitzer, John J. (1982) A primer on Box–Cox estimation. *Review of Economics and Statistics* 64(2): 307–313

Stock, James H. (1987) Asymptotic properties of least squares estimators of cointegrating vectors. *Econometrica* 55(5): 1035–1056

Thomas, J. James (1983) *An Introduction to Statistical Analysis for Economists* (second edition). London: Weidenfeld and Nicholson

Tobin, James (1958) Estimation of relationships for limited dependent variables. *Econometrica* 26(1): 24–36

Wichern, Dean W. (1973) The behaviour of the sample autocorrelation function for an integrated moving average process. *Biometrika* 60(2): 235–239

White, Halbert (1980) A heteroskedasticity-consistent covariance matrix estimator and a direct test for heteroskedasticity. *Econometrica* 48(4): 817–838

Wonnacott, Thomas H., and Ronald J. Wonnacott (1990) *Introductory Statistics for Business and Economics* (fourth edition). New York: John Wiley

Wu, De-Min (1973) Alternative tests of independence between stochastic regressors and disturbances. *Econometrica* 41(4): 733–750

Zarembka, Paul (1968) Functional form in the demand for money. *Journal of the American Statistical Association* 63(322): 502–511

Author index

Subject index

C

D

Neshab

01482 - 803 112